DIPLOMATIC PRIVILEGES
AND IMMUNITIES

DIPLOMATIC PRIVILEGES
AND IMMUNITIES

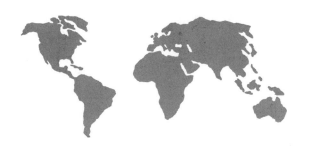

CLIFTON E. WILSON

THE UNIVERSITY OF ARIZONA PRESS
TUCSON, ARIZONA

CLIFTON E. WILSON is Associate Professor of Government and Research Specialist in the Institute of Government Research at the University of Arizona. He has been an instructor in Political Science at the Universities of Minnesota and Montana. He also has served as Research Fellow and Assistant Director of the Center for International Relations and Area Studies and as Assistant Director of the World Affairs Program at the University of Minnesota. He is in charge of the United Nations program at Arizona and is a specialist in international law and organization. He is the author of *Cold War Diplomacy* and of articles on international law. He received his Ph.D. degree from the University of Minnesota.

THE UNIVERSITY OF ARIZONA PRESS

TO MY MOTHER

Preface

THE INTERNATIONAL RULES of diplomatic privileges and immunities, which are among the oldest examples of international law, are firmly entrenched in practice, treaties and municipal legislation. Over the centuries these rules have slowly evolved along traditional lines and have always been subject to the vicissitudes of rapidly changing international political events. However, the legal order of the world community has never faced a greater challenge than that posed by the explosive military, political and ideological changes since World War II.

What has been the impact of this turbulent period of history upon the traditional rules of diplomatic privileges and immunities? This writer has sought the answer by exploring the legal developments, as they are reflected in judicial decisions, observations of publicists, foreign office decisions, etc., and the political developments, as reported from critical areas of international conflict by diplomats, journalists, and others.

The study centers on the interlocking legal and political developments since 1945 as they have affected the privileged status of (a) diplomatic agents, including subordinate personnel, families of diplomats, and local nationals employed by diplomatic missions and (b) non-diplomatic personnel such as military, information, economic and similar agents and members of special missions. It excludes immunities extended to consular officers, persons associated with international organizations, and diplomatic premises. The post-World War II era is emphasized, but consideration is given to earlier periods and to general historical trends to provide a foundation for comparative analysis.

Since this book stresses the impact of the so-called Cold War upon diplomatic privileges and immunities, the basic post-World War II research was largely restricted to the 1945-60 period. United States-Soviet Union tensions have been greatly reduced since that time. However, some reports of pertinent incidents and developments during the early 1960's were added when the manuscript was prepared for publication in 1965.

The basic "cold war" thesis of this study that violations of traditional diplomatic privileges and immunities are a byproduct of international political conflict is re-enforced by events in China in early 1967. Foreign diplomats, and especially those from the Soviet Union, were badly mistreated by the Chinese in much the same way as foreign envoys were harassed during the East-West Cold War.

Footnote and bibliographic references are not abbreviated on first usage in this book except for five commonly cited sources. These are *AJIL* (*American Journal of International Law*), *BYIL* (*British Year Book of International Law*), *DSB* (*United States Department of State Bulletin*), *AD* (*Annual Digest*), and *ILR* (*International Law Reports*). Abbreviations are used for all court reports in keeping with accepted practice. Except for judicial decisions in the United States and Great Britain, which are easily identified by the citations themselves, the country where the legal opinions were given is used in all cases.

It should be pointed out that while some writers distinguish between privileges (as positive courtesies or rights granted diplomats) and immunities (as restrictive rules curbing the exercise of jurisdiction by host states), this study makes no attempt to distinguish precisely between the two terms and follows the more widely accepted usage of privileges and immunities as fused in meaning and "consecrated by usage."

Portions of the materials used for this work appeared in a different form in the *Journalism Quarterly* under the title of "The Information Agent Abroad: New Dimensions in International Law." The chapter on the retinue and families of diplomatic agents was first published by the *International and Comparative Law Quarterly*. Other aspects of developing rules of privileges and immunities were analyzed in a companion study, *Cold War Diplomacy* (1966), which deals with restrictions on diplomatic travel and communications.

A special debt of gratitude is extended to Professor Charles H. McLaughlin of the University of Minnesota, who originally aroused my interest in international law and diplomacy. He also gave generously of his time and talent in assisting me in designing the framework for this work and in suggesting improvements in the first draft.

Further, an extensive survey of retired American diplomats was financed under a grant from the University of Minnesota Graduate School and the Tozer Foundation. More than two hundred of these ex-foreign service officers and staff members provided information which would otherwise have been unavailable. Miss Gertrude Kuehl was a patient and highly competent collaborator in the survey project.

The Institute of Government Research at the University of Arizona provided funds which permitted me to devote time to undertake part of the research and writing. For this I extend thanks to Professor Currin V. Shields and the Institute Committee. The manuscript was typed with great skill and care by Mrs. Shelly Poore of the Institute and Department of Government Staff. I also appreciate the assistance of the University of Arizona Press staff.

Finally, my wife not only has shared in my frustrations and satisfactions, but offered encouragement and understanding as well as constructive criticism of content and form.

C. E. W.

Contents

CHAPTER 1

Diplomatic
Privileges and Immunities
In Theory

FROM HIS PRIMITIVE BEGINNINGS, man has extended certain rights to representatives of other political units, in peace and in war, in order to facilitate intercourse with them. The reasons why such conditions existed are less certain, and at least a dozen juristic theories have been advanced to justify the extension of diplomatic privileges and immunities.[1] However, writers have consistently turned to one of three traditional theories to explain this practice. These are the theories of *personal representation, exterritoriality,* and *functional necessity*.[2]

While these theories may have gained historical ascendancy in the above order,[3] it is doubtful whether the chronological pattern was actually so well formed. The modern development of each of the three theories dates back to about the sixteenth century although, at least for personal representation and functionalism, evidence of their acceptance is found in earlier historical periods. An analysis of the three provides a theoretical framework for the review of post-1945 practice in granting diplomatic privileges and immunities.

The Theory of Personal Representation

Under the theory of personal representation, the diplomatic agent is the personification of his ruler or of a sovereign state whose independence must be respected.[4] This idea predates the Renaissance emergence of the various theories and is found among the so-called civilized ancients, such as those in India who developed the concept that the ambassador enjoyed personal inviolability because he was the "mouthpiece" of his

---

[1] Harvard Law School, "Research in International Law: I. Diplomatic Privileges and Immunities," *AJIL,* XXVI (April, 1932), Supp., 26. Cited hereafter as Harvard Draft.

[2] For a detailed and excellent discussion of the development and status of these three theories, see Montell Ogdon, *Juridical Bases of Diplomatic Immunity* (Washington: John Byrne & Co., 1936), pp. 63–194.

[3] For a discussion of this suggestion, see Sir Cecil Hurst, "Diplomatic Immunities — Modern Developments," *BYIL,* X (1929), 1–13.

[4] Four distinct versions of this theory are given by Ogdon, pp. 105–114.

sovereign.[5] The Greek city-states also viewed diplomatic persons as the personification of the sovereignty of the sending state.[6] The theory gained widespread acceptance during the Renaissance when diplomacy was dynastically oriented.[7] Sovereigns of the period were extremely sensitive to the affronts or insults accorded their diplomatic representatives.[8] In part, the famed Act of Anne by the British Parliament in 1708, which protected the diplomat from legal action, was enacted in order to pacify the Russian Czar whose envoy had been grossly insulted.[9]

Support for the theory of representation is found in the writings of theorists such as Grotius[10] and Wheaton[11] and in judicial decisions. Ogdon maintains that Chief Justice Campbell's dictum to the effect that "the diplomat's privilege equals that of his sovereign" is the best known of all judicial enunciations of the theory.[12] However, the observations of Chief

---

[5] Frank M. Russell, *Theories of International Relations* (New York: Appleton-Century-Crofts, Inc., 1936), p. 42, who refers to the *Mahabharata,* the great Indian epic narrative of ancient times. A similar point is made by Ogdon, p. 14, who cites S. V. Viswantha, *International Law in Ancient India* (Bombay, 1925), pp. 29–30, 64–89.

[6] Ragnar Numelin, *The Beginnings of Diplomacy* (New York: Philosophical Library, 1950), p. 299.

[7] Garrett Mattingly, *Renaissance Diplomacy* (Boston: Houghton Mifflin Co., 1955), Chapter 16.

[8] Ogdon, p. 105. Some of the widely quoted sixteenth- and seventeenth-century cases included those of the Bishop of Ross (see David Jayne Hill, *A History of Diplomacy in the International Development of Europe,* Vol. II: *The Establishment of Territorial Sovereignty* [New York: Longmans, Green and Co., 1905], pp. 515–516); Mendoza (see Arthur Nussbaum, *A Concise History of the Law of Nations* [Rev. ed.: New York: The Macmillan Co., 1954], p. 68); and L'Aubespine (see E. R. Adair, *The Exterritoriality of Ambassadors in the Sixteenth and Seventeenth Centuries* [London: Longmans, Green & Co., 1929], p. 50).

[9] Great Britain, Act of Parliament for Preserving the Privileges of Ambassadors and Other Publick Ministers of Foreign Princes and States, 7 Anne Ch. 12, 1708, I *British and Foreign State Papers* 903. Admittedly, the act was required to close a gap in British law and permit the government to take action against those persons who brought "writs and processes" against diplomatic persons and to protect the diplomat from civil jurisdiction. However, the British were extremely sensitive to the insult indirectly accorded the Czar, See *The Mattueof Case* (1710), 10 Mod. 4; 88 Eng. Reprint 598.

[10] Diplomats "as if by a kind of fiction are considered to represent those who sent them." Hugo Grotius, *De Jure Belli ac Pacis Libri Tres,* 1646 edition, trans. Francis W. Kelsey and Others (Classics of International Law, ed. James Brown Scott; New York: Oxford University Press, 1925), II, 442.

[11] "Envoys are endowed with what is called the *representative* character, being . . . entitled to the same honors to which their constituent [sovereign] would be entitled, were he personally present." Henry Wheaton, *Elements of International Law,* 8th Dana edition of 1866, ed. George Grafton Wilson (Classics of International Law, ed. James Brown Scott; New York: Oxford University Press, 1936), p. 246.

[12] *The Magdalena Steam Navigation Co. v. Martin* (1859), 2 E. & E. 94, 111. "He is to be left at liberty to devote himself body and soul to the business of his embassy. He does not owe even a temporary allegiance to the Sovereign to whom he is accredited, and he has at least as great privileges from suit as the Sovereign he represents." Ogdon, p. 127.

Justice McKean appear to be the most far reaching since he believed that an offense against a diplomat not only affronts his sovereign but the "whole world as well."[13] Jurists also accept the theoretical distinctions that, under the representational theory, the diplomat is the "alter ego" of his ruler,[14] and enjoys in the host state rights and privileges identical to those which would be accorded his master;[15] or the envoy is the personification, not merely of the sovereign, but of the state itself, which because of its equal, independent status is entitled to immunity of its representatives.[16]

In addition, people are perhaps even more sensitive to insults to national honor during the present period of patriotic intensity and nationalistic fervor than they were in the past. There is little question but that to deny rights to or to wound the dignity of a diplomatic representative would be taken by many as an affront to the state which he represents. Respect and courtesy are extended the sending state through the privileged treatment of its official representatives. Further, diplomats assigned by states with charismatic or strong leaders — such as France, the United Arab Republic, or Cuba — might to a degree be considered the personal representatives of De Gaulle, Nasser, or Castro. The same might have been said for India before the death of Nehru or for Indonesia and Ghana before the downfall of Sukarno and Nkrumah. Nonetheless, the existence

----

[13] *Respublica v. de Longchamps,* 1 Dallas 111, 116 (1784). "The person of a public minister is sacred and inviolable. Whoever offers any violence to him, not only affronts the sovereign he represents, but also hurts the common safety and well-being of nations; he is guilty of a crime against the whole world." See also Chief Justice Marshall's *dicta* in *Schooner Exchange v. McFaddon,* 7 Cranch 116 (1812).

[14] *Bergman v. de Sièyes,* 71 F. Supp. 334 (1946); 170 F. 2d 360 (1948), in which the court observes *inter alia* that "a foreign minister is immune from the jurisdiction, both criminal and civil, of the courts in the country to which he is accredited, on the grounds that he is the representative, the *alter ego,* of his sovereign who is, of course, entitled to such immunity." The court also notes that such subjection would interfere with the minister's performance of duty. Cf. *Hannes v. Kingdom of Roumania,* 20 N.Y.S. 2d. 825, 832 (1940).

[15] *Holbrook v. Henderson,* 4 Sanford 619, 628 (1839): "The respect rendered the minister is not personal, merely, but is in truth, the respect due from one sovereign to another. . . ." *Taylor v. Best* (1854), 14 C.B. 487, 494; 139 Eng. Reprint 201, 203. The court quotes Blackstone: "They [diplomats] represent the persons of their respective masters, who owe no subjection to any laws but those of their own country. . . ." Cf. *Schooner Exchange v. McFaddon,* 7 Cranch 116 (1812).

[16] For example, a French writer, De Sinner, has stated the theory in this way: "Le ministre public est . . . en quelque sorte la personification de l'État représenté, par suite il faut le traiter comme l'on traiterait l'État qui l'a delégué. . . ." Quoted by Lawrence Preuss, "Capacity for Legation and the Theoretical Basis for Diplomatic Immunity," *New York University Law Quarterly Review,* X (December, 1932), 179. See also *Ghossein v. Vila Alquila* (S.de L.R.) (Argentina, 1955), *ILR* (1955), 539: "As is well known, ambassadors, ministers plenipotentiary, etc., have *diplomatic immunity,* which in our opinion may not be founded in the fiction of extraterritoriality but rather in the attributes of sovereignty of the State and not of the persons. . . ."

of this type of leader-diplomat relationship helps but little in determining the precise extent of privileges and immunities.

In essence, then, even though some credence might be accorded the idea of personal representation, this theoretical approach is not fully accepted in modern diplomatic practice for three reasons.

First, it is impossible to reconcile the personal "representative character" of the diplomatic agent with the supremacy of the receiving sovereign. As Professor Reiff observes, in the sense that personal representation places a sovereign and his agents above the law of the host state the "theory is altogether too wide and too fallacious for the business of conducting international business."[17]

Second, the theory has lost much of its validity with the rise of the modern nation-state system following the American and French revolutions. The concept was somewhat more difficult to accept, even theoretically, after sovereign authority was transferred to the people, especially in presidential systems where rule-making is shared by the executive, legislative, and judicial branches.[18] It might now be asked: the ambassador is the personification of whom?[19]

Third, as reasoned by Professor Preuss, the scope of the theory of personal representation is too narrow in that while it may furnish a sound basis in extending immunities for official acts, it offers no theoretical basis for exemptions enjoyed by diplomats for private acts.[20] Since the theory of personal representation fails to extend a foundation for immunity to private acts, it must be rejected as the sole juridical foundation of diplomatic privileges and immunities.[21]

Nonetheless, according to Professor Preuss, the theory of personal representation cannot be discarded since immunities for all acts, both pri-

---

[17] Henry Reiff, *Diplomatic and Consular Privileges, Immunities, and Practice* (Cairo: Ettemad Press, 1954), p. 26.

[18] Although the United States Constitution authorizes the sending of ambassadors (Article II, Section 2, Paragraph 2), this country did not adopt the practice until the latter part of the nineteenth century since "there was the feeling that ambassadors, personal representatives of monarchs, ill-befitted the simple social democracy of America." Ogdon, p. 144.

[19] The Havana Convention in its preamble notes that "diplomatic officers do not in any case represent the person of the Chief of State but only their governments. . . ." Convention on Diplomatic Officers, Adopted at Havana, February 20, 1928, reprinted in *AJIL*, XXVI (April, 1932), Supp., 175, from English text in *Sixth International Conference of American States: Final Act* (Habana, 1928), pp. 142–150. Cited hereafter as the Havana Convention.

[20] Preuss, *N.Y.U.L.Q. Rev.*, X, 179–181.

[21] *Ibid.*, p. 180. Courts also have found that the theory fails to explain private acts. See *Harrie Lurie v. Steinmann* (Italy, 1927), *AD* (1927-1928), Case No. 246 Cf. *Società Arethusa Film v. Reist* (Italy, 1953), *ILR* (1955), 547–548, and *Cimino Bosco v. Luijano Escheverri* (Italy, 1930), *AD* (1929–1930), 304.

vate and public, can be explained by combining the theories of personal representation and functional necessity.[22] In fact, the International Law Commission of the United Nations accepted this fusion of theories in its codification efforts in the 1950's. The Commission said that it "was guided by" the theory of functional necessity "in solving problems on which practice gave no clear pointers, while also bearing in mind the representative character of the head of mission and of the mission itself."[23]

The Theory of Exterritoriality

The theory of exterritoriality[24] apparently dates from the sixteenth-century emergence of the nation-state system when jurists still were influenced by the idea of feudal overlordship and its attendant aspects of personal and territorial obedience.[25] However, the juristic theory of exterritoriality was logically consistent only because of the practice, which began in the fifteenth-century, of countries' maintaining permanent missions in foreign states. It was not until sovereigns actually established these outposts of "foreign territory" on a continuing basis that privileges of exterritoriality could be claimed.[26]

This theory refers either to the concept of residence — that is, the diplomat is not subject to local law because he does not reside in the host country — or to the concept of territory — that is, the local authorities consider the diplomatic premises to be the same as foreign territory. The

---

[22] Professor Preuss observed: "The two theories — of representation and of *ne impediatur legatio* — together form the theoretical basis of the special position of the envoy in the territory of the receiving state.

"The above theory, combining the theory of representation with that of the interest of function, is capable of comprising and of explaining all of the immunities of diplomatic agents as established by international law." Preuss, *N.Y.U.L.Q. Rev.,* X, 181.

[23] United Nations, International Law Commission, "Report to the General Assembly Covering the Work of Its Tenth Session, 28 April-4 July, 1958" (A/3859), *Yearbook: 1958,* Vol. II (A/CN.4/SER. A/1958/Add.1), p. 95.

[24] The terms "exterritoriality" and "extraterritoriality" have traditionally been used interchangeably when referring to this theory of diplomatic immunity. However, the more cumbersome of the two terms, "extraterritoriality," is becoming obsolete, and the modern trend is toward use of the shorter version, or "exterritoriality."

[25] Ogdon, pp. 62–63.

[26] According to many writers, the first resident embassy in the modern sense was that accredited in 1450 to Cosimo dei Medici by the Duke of Milan. The ambassador selected was Nicodemus dei Pontremoli, known to his contemporaries as "Sweet Nicodemus." Mattingly, p. 69. The permanent missions spread during the sixteenth century and became a common practice following the Peace of Westphalia in 1648. United Nations, Secretariat, "Memorandum on Diplomatic Intercourse and Immunities," International Law Commission, *Yearbook: 1956,* Vol. II (A/CN/4/98), p. 132.

statement of the concept of residence, found often in the writings of international law,[27] also permeated the thinking of jurists. A representative view is that of Justice O'Gorman who noted in *George Wilson v. Fuzman Blanco*[28] that this rule of international law

> derives support from the legal fiction that an ambassador is not an inhabitant of the country to which he is accredited, but of the country of his origin and whose sovereign he represents, and within whose territory, in contemplation of law, he always resides.

Similar observations on the theory are found in *The King v. Guerchy,*[29] *United States v. Benner,*[30] *Taylor v. Best,*[31] *The Magdalena Steam Navigation Co. v. Martin,*[32] and *Attorney General v. Kent.*[33] The second concept, that of territory, finds its theoretical formulation in the work of publicists such as Vattel who stated that "an ambassador's house is, at least in all common cases of life, like his person, considered as out of the country,"[34] and in draft codes such as that of Johann Kasper Bluntschli.[35]

In general, then, exterritoriality means that the ambassador must be

---

[27] For example, Lorimer observed that "an English ambassador, with his family and his suite, whilst abroad in the public service, is domiciled in England." James Lorimer, *The Institutes of the Law of Nations* (Edinburgh: William Blackwood and Sons, 1883), I, 248.

[28] 56 N.Y. Sup. Ct. 582 (1889).

[29] (1765), 96 Eng. Reprint 315. The court held that the ambassador owes no subjection to the courts of the country to which he is sent but is supposed by a fiction of law to still be a resident of his own country.

[30] Fed. Cas. 14568 (1830). The court observed that the minister "is considered as not resident of the country to which he is sent, but near to it, and is not amenable to the laws, or jurisdiction of its courts."

[31] (1854), 14 C.B. 487, 517; 139 Eng. Reprint 201, 213. Jervis, D.J.: "The foundation of the privilege [exemption from the jurisdiction of English courts] is that the ambassador is supposed to be in the country of his master." See Ogdon, p. 77, and John Bassett Moore, *A Digest of International Law* (Washington: Government Printing Office, 1906), IV, 657–658.

[32] (1859), 2 E. & E. 94; 121 Eng. Reprint 36, 43. Lord Campbell, C.J.; "He [the ambassador] is not supposed to even live within the territory of the Sovereign to whom he is accredited, and, if he has done nothing to forfeit or to waive his privilege, he is for all judicial purposes supposed still to be in his own country."

[33] (1862), 158 Eng. Reprint 782, 786. The defense, citing Grotius, *On the Law of War and Peace* (Book II, Chapter XVIII, Section IV, Paragraph 5) and Story's *Conflict of Law* (Section 48), concludes that diplomatic immunity is based on the principle that an ambassador is "deemed to be resident in the country by which he is accredited."

[34] Emmerich de Vattel, *The Law of Nations or the Principles of Natural Law,* 1st edition of 1758, trans. Charles G. Fenwick (Classics of International Law, ed. James Brown Scott; New York: Oxford University Press, 1916), p. 394.

[35] Dans le but de sauvegarder l'indépendance des souverains étrangers et en général des personnes qui représentent un état en pays étranger, on admet la fiction qu'ils sont hors du territoire étranger et dans la même position que s'ils avaient pu emporter leur patrie avec eux." Bluntschli's Draft Code of 1868, *AJIL,* XXVI (1932), Supp., 144.

treated as if he still is living in the territory of the sending state. This "fiction" is not without its supporters and its usage still is not uncommon. For example, Lauterpacht-Oppenheim finds the word of value since "it demonstrates clearly the fact that envoys must, in most respects, be treated as though they were not within the territory of the receiving States."[36] One of the most eloquent defenses of the term has been made by E. R. Adair, who finds it helpful, but within limitations.[37] Adair's view of the concept in terms of personal jurisdiction means that an ambassador is free from the juridical jurisdiction of the host nation — and no more. Reference to the theory of exterritoriality as a "dangerous fiction," Adair contends, might apply to modern times but it ignores the historical evolution of this aspect of international law.[38] He claims that the replacement of "exterritoriality," which has definite legal implications, by a broader term such as "inviolability," places the ambassador's immunity at the mercy of the government to which he is accredited. This tendency to exclude exterritoriality from the lexicon of international law, Adair argues further, leads to a casting into "complete oblivion of the honorable part it played in the international life of the sixteenth and seventeenth centuries."[39]

Many jurists have followed lines of reasoning which would tend to dispel Adair's fears. Even in modern times, judges have utilized the discredited concept of exterritoriality as a basis for extending privileges and immunities. For example, *In re Zoltán Sz.,*[40] the accused took part in inducing authorities at the Hungarian Legation in Vienna to issue a passport as the result of false information and a false photograph. The question arose as to where the offense was committed. The Supreme Court of Hungary held that

> the offense was committed not abroad but on the territory of the Hungarian State. The premises of the Royal Hungarian Legation which enjoyed the privileges of extraterritoriality must be regarded as Hungarian territory. Accordingly, all acts committed therein must be judged according to the rules of Hungarian criminal law.[41]

---

[36] L. Oppenheim, *International Law,* Vol. I: *Peace,* ed. H. Lauterpacht (8th ed.; London: Longmans, Green and Co., 1955), p. 793.

[37] Adair, pp. 260–264.

[38] *Ibid.,* p. 261.

[39] *Ibid.* p. 264.

[40] (Hungary, 1928), *AD* (1927–1928), Case No. 252.

[41] *Ibid.,* p. 373. Cf. *In re Ledoux* (Uruguay, 1941), *AD* (1943–1945), Case No. 75, in which the court said that "diplomatic agents are protected by the regime of exterritoriality, which means exemption of their persons and their property from the jurisdiction of the [host] country. . . ." For a criticism of the decision, see A. B. Lyons, "Immunities Other Than Jurisdictional of the Property of Diplomatic Envoys," *BYIL,* XXX (1953), 125.

A similar conclusion was reached by an Italian court in Milan in 1951. An injunction against Yugoslavia was denied on the ground that Italian law does not provide for injunctions against persons resident abroad. The presence of the Yugoslav ambassador was not enough to justify jurisdiction since he had exterritoriality and could not "be regarded as the manager of the country's interests. The juridical person called Yugoslavia resides entirely and exclusively abroad."[42]

Some courts accept what appears to be this literal application of the theory of exterritoriality but with modifications. In these cases, the theory is restricted in its application either to types of persons or to certain situations. Examples of modern practice illustrate this point. One is that exterritoriality applies to diplomatic premises, but only if the property is occupied by "extra-territorial persons."[43] Another is that the "fiction of exterritoriality" is intended for diplomatic agents and its benefits cannot be extended to private persons such as commercial traders.[44]

Further, German courts have held that the principle applies to transactions on diplomatic premises except to those which have a legal impact within Germany. In 1922, a German court ruled that while a legation is foreign territory for certain purposes, the fiction of "extraterritoriality" has no relevance to a turnover tax, the purpose of which is to protect the home producer from an influx of foreign goods.[45] In 1931, another German court ruled that while the premises of the Soviet Commercial Representation in Germany "must be deemed extraterritorial and therefore Russian soil, German law must be applied to the acts done on those premises and having legal effect in Germany."[46]

A final example of this type of inconsistency is that some credence must be given to the theory of exterritoriality since "the diplomatic archives

---

[42] *Case of Castiglioni* (Italy, 1951), *AJIL,* XLIX (1955), 100. Other courts have based their decisions on exterritoriality but were somewhat more circumspect in their use of the theory. See for example [*Russian Trade Delegation in Germany Case*] (Germany, 1931), *AD* (1931-1932), 333–334, and *Roumanian State v. Arricastre* (France, 1937), *AD* (1935–1937), Case No. 91.

[43] *Republic of Latvia Case* (West Germany, 1953), *ILR* (1953), 181–182. Cf. *Petrococchino v. Swedish State* (France, 1929), *AD* (1929–1930), 307, in which the court held that in order to be invested with the "privilege of exterritoriality," the property must be "completely appropriated to the service of the embassy."

[44] *In re Société Anonyme des Grands Garages Parisiens* (France, 1930), *AD* (1929–1930), Case No. 192. The court held that the sale of motor cars to various diplomatic agents could not be considered as exports out of France.

[45] *Legation Buildings (Turnover Tax) Case* (Germany, 1922), *AD* (1919–1922), Case No. 207.

[46] [*Russian Trade Delegation in Germany Case*] (Germany, 1931), *AD* (1931–1932), 333. The court's observation emphasizes the weakness of the exterritoriality principle in that German law is applied to acts committed on "Russian soil."

deposited in the mission have been accorded a greater degree of inviolability than those anywhere else."[47] Use of the term also has been endorsed
because it serves as a convenient label for diplomatic privileges and
immunities.[48] Still others would not abandon it merely because it is "a
form of expression which experience has shown to be objectionable."[49]

Despite this widespread use and abuse of the term, the modern tendency has definitely been toward a repudiation of the "fiction" even as a
description, as well as a reason for diplomatic immunity. For example,
Montell Ogdon in his definitive work on diplomatic immunity states that
the "recent and current trend is conclusively in favor of repudiating the
extraterritorial concept in every form";[50] Hyde refers to a "complete
abandonment" of the theory;[51] Stowell calls it a "wornout fiction";[52]
Eagleton declares that the "idea of the exterritoriality of the legation as a
basis for the claim of inviolability has been abandoned";[53] and J. C. Gregory claims the theory is "outmoded and, logically, no longer applicable."[54] A similar conclusion was reached in 1932 by the legal experts
brought together by the Harvard Law School[55] and by other groups in this

---

[47] Meredith B. Colket, Jr., "The Inviolability of Diplomatic Archives," *American Archivist,* VIII (January, 1945), 34.

[48] One writer refers to the use of exterritoriality as a "convenient fiction." Patrick Stirling, "The Immunities of Diplomatic Agents," *Law Journal,* CVIII (April 18, 1958), 243. A jurist calls it a "convenient word to denote any group of privileges." Lord Hobhouse in *Secretary of State v. Charlesworth* (A.C. 373, 383) as cited by Joseph O. Janousek, "Some Aspects of the Law of Diplomatic Immunity," *Journal of the Bar Association of the District of Columbia,* VIII (May, 1941), 183.

[49] Chief Justice Duff in *In the Matter of a Reference as to the Powers of the Corporation of the City of Ottawa and the Corporation of the Village of Rockcliffe Park to Levy Rates on Foreign Legations and High Commissioners' Residences,* [1943] Canada Law Reports, S.C.R. 208; *AD* (1941–1942), Case No. 106. Duff, in citing Lord Atkin in *Chung Chi Cheung v. the King* [1939] A.C. 160, admits that the theory of exterritoriality does not provide a theoretical framework for immunities and that if carried to a logical extreme would deny local jurisdiction. However, he claims that it reflects the principles laid down by leading jurists and publicists and thus should be retained.

[50] Ogdon, p. 94.

[51] Charles Cheney Hyde, *International Law: Chiefly as Interpreted and Applied by the United States* (2d rev. ed.; Boston: Little, Brown and Company, 1947), II, 1266.

[52] Ellery C. Stowell, "Diplomatic Privileges and Immunities," *AJIL,* XX (October, 1926), 737.

[53] Clyde Eagleton, "The Responsibility of the State for the Protection of Foreign Officials," *AJIL,* XIX (April, 1925), 298.

[54] J. C. Gregory, "Privileges, Immunities and Disabilities," *Chicago-Kent Law Review,* XXV (September, 1947), 333.

[55] "The theory of exterritoriality has not been used in formulating the present draft convention." Harvard Draft, p. 26. A careful perusal of the text of the convention revealed not one instance of the employment of the concept of exterritoriality in any way. Ogdon, p. 98.

century which have attempted to codify rules of diplomatic privileges and immunities.[56]

Not only have the publicists and codifiers of international law rejected the theory, but some courts also have refused to accept its one literal, precise meaning: to wit, that diplomatic premises are foreign soil. In a wide range of civil cases, many since 1945, courts consistently rejected claims that premises occupied by a foreign legation become, under the principle of exterritoriality, the territory of the sending state. For example, an Italian court in 1938, while admitting the use of the word "exterritoriality" to cover certain immunities, held that the concept did not cover exemption from jurisdiction. In its dicta, the court added that

> the traditional doctrine leads to the conclusion that the residences of diplomatic agents are outside the territory in which they are situated and exempt from the jurisdiction of the local State, a result which is undoubtedly excessive and which is disregarded by international practice and by the courts of all States.[57]

The literature of international law abounds with cases in which similar conclusions have been reached on this interpretation of exterritoriality. An Italian court in 1955 ruled that the fact that a contract was signed in the Greek Embassy did not alter the fact that it was concluded in Italy.[58] Courts also have held that diplomatic premises cannot be considered foreign territory to validate nationality of offspring in marriage cases.[59] Also,

---

[56] Groups which have abandoned the term include the League of Nations, drafters of the Havana Convention, and The Institute of International Law (Ogdon, pp. 94-98). The concept also was rejected by the International Law Commission of the United Nations in its codification efforts. United Nations, International Law Commission, "Report to the General Assembly Covering the Work of Its Tenth Session, 28 April-4 July, 1958" (A/3859), *Yearbook: 1958,* Vol. II (A/CN.4/SER.A/1958/Add.1), pp. 94–95.

[57] *Trenta v. Ragonesi* (Italy, 1938), *AD* (1938-1940), 439.

[58] *La Mercantile v. Kingdom of Greece* (Italy, 1955), *ILR* (1955), 242. The court observed: "A series of immunities and limitations of the normal powers of the [receiving] State are a part of the privileges which the foreign diplomat enjoys. However, we cannot believe that these immunities extend to the place in which the diplomatic official performs his mission, so that that place is regarded as being outside the territory of the [receiving] State. . . . This is in keeping with the most modern opinion which, for the very purpose of eliminating any doubt on this point, has rejected the fiction of exterritoriality to which earlier authorities referred in order to explain the basis of the immunities." Also see Ogdon, pp. 89–90, for a series of contract cases between 1880 and 1921 in which German, French, and Italian courts refused to accept the validity of exterritoriality.

[59] See *Marriage in Bulgarian Legation Case* (Austria, 1952), *ILR* (1952), 393, in which the Supreme Court declared that "the court of Appeal has rightly held that the concept of exterritoriality is — generally speaking — limited to the personal immunity of the ambassador and the personnel of the embassy, and that a marriage celebrated in the legation building of a foreign State is a marriage which has, in fact, been celebrated in Austria, and not in a foreign country." Cf. decisions by French courts in 1872 and 1873 (Ogdon, pp. 90–91).

the absolute concept of exterritoriality has not been accepted when courts have dealt with the legal domicile of diplomatic personnel.[60]

Similar rejections of claims based on exterritoriality are found in cases involving a plea for tax exemption,[61] a dispute over adoption proceedings,[62] and a claim arising from purchases consummated on diplomatic premises.[63] The decisions have not always involved host states' rulings about premises of foreign diplomatic establishments. In 1954, a Belgian court held that its embassy in Germany was not to be considered "Belgian territory," a decision which precluded the filing of war reparation claims.[64] In addition, the rejection of the fiction that diplomatic premises are deemed to be exterritorial is also supported by numerous decisions in criminal cases.[65]

There are three basic reasons why serious consideration should be given suggestions that the label of exterritoriality be dropped from the language of international law. One reason arises from inconsistencies in present and past usage of the term; the other two are concerned with the weakness of exterritoriality as a theory.

---

[60] *Baron Arnold de Cartier de Marchienne v. L. A. de Cartier* (Belgium, 1948), *AD* (1948), Case No. 101. While the court agreed that a diplomatic representative remains domiciled on the territory of the sending state, it rejected the contention that an ambassador domiciled at the Belgian Embassy in London was actually domiciled on Belgian territory by virtue of the rule of exterritoriality. "It is quite wrong to suggest that exterritoriality can transform the Embassy building in Eaton Square [London] into Belgian territory." *Ibid.,* p. 311.

Status of Legation Buildings Case (Germany, 1930), *AD* (1929–1930), Case No. 197. The plaintiff, employed by the German ambassador in London as a steward, filed for unemployment benefits under a law which stipulated a period of prior German residence. He claimed that as a member of the German diplomatic establishment abroad he had been in effect residing on German soil. The court, in holding that he was not entitled to the benefits, noted that "the principle of exterritoriality does not include the fiction that the house of the official representation is to be regarded as territory of the sending state." *Ibid.,* p. 306.

Attorney General v. Kent (1862), 158 Eng. Reprint 782. The court ruled that the domicile of a Portuguese, which had been established in Great Britain, was not revived in his native land as the result of his appointment as attaché to serve on the "exterritorial" premises of the Portuguese Embassy.

[61] *In re Succession of Doña Carmen de Goyeneche* (Peru, 1921), *AD* (1919–1922), Case No. 209.

[62] *Consul Barat v. Ministère Public* (France, 1948) *AD* (1948), Case No. 102.

[63] *Gnome and Rhone Motors v. Gatteano* (Italy, 1930), *AD* (1929–1930), Case No. 199.

[64] *Belgian State (Minister of Public Works and Reconstruction) v. Maréchal* (Belgium, 1954), *ILR* (1954), 249–250. The court observed that "the parts of foreign territory in which international custom or treaty gives Belgium rights of exterritoriality do not, by virtue of that fact, become Belgian territory." *Ibid.,* p. 250.

[65] See *The Nikitschenkoff Case* (France, 1865), *Journal du Palais* (1866), 51, as cited by Herbert W. Briggs, *The Law of Nations* (2d ed.; New York: Appleton-Century-Crofts, Inc., 1952), pp. 787–788. A Russian subject had assaulted the first secretary of the Russian Embassy in the embassy at Paris. The court rejected a Russian claim that French courts lacked jurisdiction over acts within Russia's "exterritorial" premises. See *Ibid.,* pp. 790–791, for supporting cases.

In the first place, the term is subject to such a wide variety of definitions that it has become meaningless in practice as a theory to explain the granting of diplomatic privileges and immunities. The word itself has several distinct meanings;[66] sometimes different definitions are attached to the words "exterritoriality" and "extraterritoriality";[67] and the words "exterritoriality" and "inviolability" are used interchangeably or imprecisely.[68] In essence, the word "exterritoriality" thus becomes meaningless and artificial and its use in theorizing or explaining leads not only to erroneous conclusions[69] but a "confusion of ideas."[70]

A good deal of the confusion also arises from the fact that the term is persistently used not to describe the diplomatic mission as foreign territory, but to encompass "the sum total of the immunities and privileges" which are enjoyed by diplomatic personnel.[71] Thus, in many cases the words "exterritoriality" and "extraterritoriality" are used as convenient labels which are little more than synonyms for diplomatic privileges and

---

[66] For example, Thornely lists four: literal — physically outside a certain territory; primary — outside the jurisdiction of the sovereign in whose territory a diplomat finds himself; popular — applying the term to almost anyone receiving a special privilege; and specialized — control of persons by a sovereign by means of "extraterritorial laws" when those persons are physically outside of the state. P. W. Thornely, "Extraterritoriality," *BYIL*, VII (1926), 121, fn. For various other meanings and applications of the word "exterritoriality," see Ogdon, pp. 77–84.

[67] For example, Janousek *(J. Bar Assn. D.C.,* VIII, 183, fn.) notes that some writers have attempted to draw a distinction between "extra" and "ex," the former referring to the privileges and immunities extended to the ambassador and his suite, and the latter referring to the act by which a state extends its jurisdiction beyond boundaries into the territory of another state. Different meanings are given the two terms by Sir Francis Piggott in his work on *Extraterritoriality* (as noted by Thornely, *BYIL*, VII, 121, fn.). Sir Francis distinguishes between extraterritoriality as being the governing of privileged persons by their own authorities from home, and exterritoriality as being a condition of the persons taken out of the ordinary jurisdiction of the sovereign in whose territory they are living.

[68] John Bassett Moore, "Asylum in Legations and Consulates and in Vessels," *Political Science Quarterly,* VII (September, 1892), 397. In one sense, inviolability might be considered the basis for extending diplomatic privileges and immunities, and exterritoriality a privilege which flows from this principle. However, this distinction is really not helpful. See Stirling, *Law J.,* CVIII, 243, for a discussion of this problem.

[69] Justice Holmes observes that "as long as the matter to be considered is debated in artificial terms there is danger of being led by a technical definition to apply a certain name, and then to deduce consequences which have no relation to the grounds on which the name was applied." *Guy v. Donald,* 203 U.S. 399, 406 (1906).

[70] Moore, *Pol. Sci. Q.,* VII, 397. "The exemption of diplomatic officers from the local jurisdiction is often described as 'extraterritoriality.' The word, however, is in this relation peculiarly metaphorical and misleading." Moore, *Digest,* IV, 630.

[71] *Baron Arnold de Cartier de Marchienne v. L. A. de Cartier* (Belgium, 1948), *AD* (1948), 311, which illustrates this vague and theoretically void usage.

immunities.[72] In other cases, the definition by courts of the term is in essence a definition of the theory of functional necessity.[73]

Thus, it obviously is impossible to interpret exterritoriality strictly according to its literal meaning. It also is impossible to agree upon one of the other meanings which have become part of the vocabulary of international law. The term is a metaphor — some have said a "picturesque metaphor"[74] — and not a legal fact, and should be discarded when determining the immunities of the different diplomatic classes.[75] The term would be useful if it were defined and applied consistently, but it is not because of its long association with a discredited fiction. As Professor Preuss contends:

> In the interest of accuracy of thought and expression, it is desirable that the word "exterritoriality" be dropped from the language of international law. A term which is susceptible of so many diverse

---

[72]See, for example, *Claim Against Foreign Embassy Case* (Yugoslavia, 1956), *ILR* (1956), 431–432; *Chinese Embassy (Immunities) Case* (Germany, 1925), *AD* (1925–1926), Case No. 243; *Kopytoff v. The Commercial Representation of the U.S.S.R.* (Norway, 1932), *AD* (1931–1932), 333; *In re Khan* (Austria, 1932), *AD* (1931–1932), Case No. 182; *Deposit (Land in Czechoslovakia) Case* (Czechoslovakia, 1936), *AD* (1938–1940), 429, fn.; and *Diplomatic Envoys, Exemption from Taxation (Germany) Case, AD* (1927–1928), Case No. 248.

The *New York Times* (September 9, 1947, p. 7) referred to Yugoslav soldiers who "violated the extraterritorial rights of the United States embassy" when they entered the grounds to arrest a gardener. See also "Diplomatic Immunity from Court Process: Resident Foreign Legations," *New Zealand Law Journal,* XXII (May 21, 1946), 113.

[73]The "privilege of exterritoriality" which is "generally accepted by the law of nations is based on the independence required by diplomatic agents for the fulfillment of their duties and to maintain the dignity of their person." *M. C. v. Société Foncière du Nouveau Parc* (Belgium, 1934), *AD* (1933–1934), 380–381.

"The so-called extraterritorial persons are only exempt, in general, from the jurisdiction of German courts; this is so in order to facilitate the undisturbed fulfillment of the official functions of missions accredited to the German Reich." *Afghan Embassy Case* (Germany, 1934), *AD* (1933–1934), 386.

"The purpose of exterritoriality is merely to prevent such jurisdiction as may hinder the ambassador in the fulfillment of his mission." *Immunities (Foreign State in Private Contracts) Case* (Austria, 1920), *AD* (1919–1922), 119.

See also *Warsaw Mission of International Red Cross Committee v. City of Warsaw* (Poland, 1925), *AD* (1925–1926), Case No. 248, and *Diplomatic Immunities (Germany Foreign Office) Case* (Germany, 1926), *AD* (1925–1926), Case No. 244.

[74]"This picturesque metaphor must be regarded as a fiction of vivid description rather than a legal rule." "Notes: Immunity of Diplomatic Agents," *Harvard Law Review,* XII (February 25, 1899), 495. Exterritoriality is a "picturesque metaphor transformed into a legal doctrine or fact." Janousek, *J. Bar Assn. D.C.,* VIII, 186.

[75]Sir Ernest Satow, *A Guide to Diplomatic Practice* (2d ed.; London: Longmans, Green and Co., 1922), I, 249–250.

connotations cannot serve the purpose of precise juristic terminology.[76]

Even if the word is not completely abandoned it should not be used to explain the extension of diplomatic rights or privileges or as a synonym for functional necessity. It would be of greater utility to use the latter phrase itself. The word "exterritoriality" possibly could be used with some justification in two ways — both unrelated to theory: one, historically in its original context as a description of diplomatic status during the modern formative period; and two, symbolically or metaphorically as a collective term to describe the group of immunities which the diplomat enjoys. To avoid confusion, if used at all, it should be used only in its historical sense.

The second reason for abandoning exterritoriality is that it fails to fulfill the basic function of a theory. The idea that the envoy should be treated juridically as though he is not present in the host state is little more than a fiction and does not provide a legal or theoretical basis for the extension of diplomatic privileges and immunities.[77] The "fiction" has been held to be inadmissible as a juridical construction because it fails to accommodate all rules dealing with exterritoriality and to conform to positive law.[78] Some observers go even further in their criticism of this theory. For example, a British writer notes that the right of expulsion means that an envoy or other visiting dignitary ultimately is subject to the jurisdiction of the host nation and thus essentially has no exterritorial rights.[79]

Finally, the acceptance of exterritoriality (if the fiction is carried to a logical extreme) could result in dangerous consequences in that it presupposes a theory of unlimited privileges and immunities which would go beyond those actually extended to diplomats.[80] Because exterritoriality is a fiction and not true in fact, it could lead to "absurd results if pressed to a

---

[76] Preuss, *N.Y.U.L.Q. Rev.,* X, 187.

[77] Lyons refers to exterritoriality as "a palpable fiction, which hardly provides a basis upon which to build a body of legal rules." Lyons, *BYIL,* XXX, 148. Ogdon concurs, noting that it would be difficult to discover "any rational process by which 'extraterritoriality,' in theory or fact may be made to become the reason for diplomatic immunity." Ogdon, p. 98.

[78] Preuss, *N.Y.U.L.Q. Rev.,* X, 184. See *Ibid.,* pp. 182–187, for an excellent discussion of the practical as well as theoretical reasons for abandoning the fiction of exterritoriality.

[79] Thornely, *BYIL,* VII, 126–127.

[80] *Ibid.;* Ogdon, p. 101. For example, Thornely, asks if a British ambassador's house is British soil as some [e.g., Lorimer] maintain, then how was the *eminent domain* transferred? If it were transferred, then the British ambassador could defend the property in the same manner Britain defends its own home soil against outside attack. Thornely, *BYIL,* VII, 128.

logical conclusion."[81] History provides ample warning that the literal application of exterritoriality has, in fact, led to some "absurd results." The extreme application of the theory was based on the so-called *franchise du quartier,* which some writers look upon as the basis for extension of immunities.[82] This extreme form of exterritoriality was used to justify the inviolability of the entire quarter of the city in which the diplomatic premises were located. The quarters of ambassadors became havens for thieves and other persons of ill repute. Stuart claims that the practice was renounced in Madrid in 1684 and by 1686 the Pope had succeeded in convincing all important European sovereigns except the king of France to reject the practice because of these abuses.[83] This concept of *franchise du quartier,* "one of the most exaggerated claims made in the name of diplomatic immunity,"[84] is today an anachronism.[85] One respected work in international law notes that it had "totally disappeared" by the eighteenth century,[86] leaving only the right of asylum which appears to be most widespread in Latin American states.[87] The United States does not recognize the right of asylum, and the granting of refuge to Josef Cardinal Mindszenty by the United States Legation in Hungary in 1956 was an exception to this country's usual practice.

Two other notions also flowed from the exaggerated interpretation of exterritoriality. One involved treaty arrangements (capitulations) which permitted consular officers from Western nations to exercise full

---

[81] D. C. Holland, "Diplomatic Immunity in English Law," *Current Legal Problems,* IV (1951), 92.

[82] "Diplomatic immunity, as it was regarded in the sixteenth century, is most compendiously summed up in three general phrases: *droit de chapelle, droit du quartier,* and *droit de l'hotel.* The principles upon which these ideas rest can furnish with little alteration a guide to diplomats in the exercise of their functions under modern conditions." Sir Geoffrey Butler and Simon Maccoby, *The Development of International Law* (London: Longmans, Green and Co., Ltd., 1928), p. 88.

"Historically immunity is, no doubt, grounded on franchise du quartier." J. Mervyn Jones, "Immunities of Servants of Diplomatic Agents and the Statute of Anne 7, c. 12," *Journal of Comparative Legislation and International Law,* XXII (February, 1940), 29.

[83] Graham H. Stuart, *American Diplomatic and Consular Practice* (2d ed.; New York: Appleton-Century-Crofts, Inc., 1952), p. 123.

[84] Ogdon, p. 82.

[85] Jones, *J. Comp. Leg. & Int. L.,* XX, 29.

[86] Oppenheim, I, 794; Adair, p. 142.

[87] Under this "right," foreign legations offer asylum to political refugees from other countries. For a concise discussion of diplomatic asylum see C. Neale Ronning, *Law and Politics in Inter-American Diplomacy* (New York: John Wiley & Sons, Inc., 1963), pp. 89–105. For a consideration of the problem before the International Court of Justice, see *Colombian-Peruvian Asylum Case,* Judgment of November 20, 1950, *I.C.J. Reports 1950,* and *Haya de la Torre Case,* Judgment of June 13, 1951, *I.C.J. Reports 1951.*

civil and criminal jurisdiction and a protective authority over their nationals in such states as Turkey, China, Persia, and Japan. This extreme utilization of the territorial principle was abolished following World War I.[88] Under the second exaggerated practice, prevalent in the sixteenth and seventeenth centuries, chiefs of mission were granted the right to exercise civil and criminal jurisdiction over their staffs. It is unthinkable today that an ambassador could serve in such a judicial capacity.[89]

As has been suggested, while the word "exterritoriality" might be retained for historical descriptive purposes, the theory itself should be abandoned in considering the rights, privileges and immunities to be enjoyed and the responsibilities to be accepted by diplomats. First, it rests upon an untenable theory of the general nature of international law, that is, unrestricted territorial sovereignty. The theory not only leads to false conclusions concerning diplomatic immunity, but it is superfluous. The fiction of exterritoriality becomes authoritative only by the consent of states or by the necessity of diplomatic intercourse. Thus, exterritoriality is not the cause of immunity, but these forces become the cause and lead logically into the theory of necessity or functional immunity.[90]

Second, since the term is imprecise, is used "loosely and figuratively"[91] and is subject to varied meanings, and since it does not provide the actual reasons for determining rights and duties, it is of little value as a guideline in the determination of the scope and limits of diplomatic privileges and immunities. Whether viewed as a fiction or used literally, it simply does not, as League of Nations experts found, supply "a satisfactory basis for practical conclusions."[92] Such a restrictive concept is of little value today in moulding international law and practice to fit new social, economic, and political needs. It implies a static condition which impedes legal growth since it starts from the major premises of the absolute sovereignty and independence of states. It is necessary to go outside the framework of territoriality to develop a theory of diplomatic privileges and immunities.

---

[88] Oppenheim, I, 50. See G. B. Ravndal, *The Origins of the Capitulations and the Consular Institution,* 67 Cong., 1st Sess., Senate Document No. 34, 1921.

[89] "No civilized State would nowadays allow an envoy himself to try a member of his retinue." Oppenheim, I, 805, who cites the famed Duc de Sully case of 1603 in which a Frenchman was tried by a jury comprised of members of a special French diplomatic mission in London. This illustrates the now abandoned practice.

[90] See Preuss, *N.Y.U.L.Q. Rev.,* X, 183, for an analysis of the "superfluous" nature of the theory of exterritoriality upon which the comments in this paragraph are based.

[91] According to John Bassett Moore, *Digest,* II, 775.

[92] League of Nations, Committee of Experts for the Progressive Codification of International Law, "Diplomatic Privileges and Immunities," reprinted in *AJIL,* XX (1926), Spec. Supp., 149.

The Theory of Functional Necessity

Under the theory of functional necessity, or functionalism, the diplomatic agent must have freedom of movement and freedom of communication, as well as immunity from local jurisdiction, in order that nations may carry on international intercourse. In contrast with personal representation and exterritoriality, it seeks a dynamic explanation of diplomatic privileges and immunities. The theory is based on the idea of interdependence of states, and their need for mutual freedom and noninterference in their relations.

Evidence of the theory is found in the eras which preceded the rise of the modern nation-state system. The primitive peoples recognized, in their relations, "certain complexes of mutual interests,"[93] and their messengers, heralds, envoys, and couriers were "almost always" inviolable.[94] And while immunities extended by the civilizations of early Greece and Rome were based not on law but on religion,[95] the "sacrosanct" position, it might be presumed, stemmed at least in part from the necessities of relations by the Greek city states and by Rome in its far flung activities.

In its modern form, functionalism emerged in the sixteenth and seventeenth centuries when theorists and jurists stressed the importance of functions performed by the ambassador.[96] Its theoretical enunciation goes back at least to the widely quoted dictum by Grotius, *omnis coactio abesse a legato debet,* "an ambassador ought to be free from all compulsion."[97] A practical application of the theory is found in all modern efforts to codify the rules of diplomatic intercourse. The fact that immunities stem from the traditional need to protect the dignity of the diplomat and to assure him of "free and unhampered exercise" of his functions was fully accepted by international law experts of the Harvard Law School,[98] the

---

[93] Numelin, p. 124.

[94] *Ibid.,* p. 147.

[95] Oppenheim, I, 769; Coleman Phillipson, *The International Law and Custom of Ancient Greece and Rome* (London: Macmillan and Co., Limited, 1911), I, 328; and Ogdon, p. 15.

[96] Ogdon, pp. 166–170.

[97] Grotius, p. 448. The Grotian statement was echoed in the following century by Vattel who maintained that an ambassador should be free from local jurisdiction "in order that he may be free from molestation in the exercise of his function." Vattel, p. 389.

[98] The Harvard Drafters described their work as "frankly pragmatic" and predicated on a three-point framework: one, the "necessity of permitting free and unhampered exercise of the diplomatic function"; two, "maintaining the dignity of the diplomatic representative and the State which he represents"; and three, "the respect properly due time-honored traditions." Harvard Draft, p. 26.

League of Nations,[99] and the United Nations. The Vienna Convention on Diplomatic Privileges and Immunities, the first such successful international effort since 1815, is in this tradition. The preamble states that the purpose of diplomatic privileges and immunities is "to ensure the efficient performance of the functions of diplomatic missions as representing States."[100]

Modern publicists, who disagree on scope and categories when discussing diplomatic privileges and immunities, tend to agree on the reason why the diplomatic rights are recognized. Perhaps the type of reasoning most often found is best summarized by Sir Cecil Hurst in a lecture delivered at the Academy of International Law in 1926:

> The writers of textbooks have dealt at great length with the question why immunities are given to diplomatic representatives, and the nature of the obligation upon States to recognize such immunities. In reality the matter is very simple. The privileges and immunities are founded on the necessities of the case. They are essential to the maintenance of international relations. On no other basis than that of exemption from subjection to the local jurisdiction would sovereign States have been willing in times past or today to send their representatives to the headquarters of another State. On no other terms would it have been possible for foreign diplomatic representatives to fulfill the tasks allotted to them.[101]

Other writers agree that the ambassador must have the necessary independence, based on reciprocity, to perform his governmental functions on foreign soil.[102]

---

[99] The Committee of Experts for the Progressive Codification of International Law concluded that the "one solid basis for dealing with the subject is the necessity of permitting free and unhampered exercise of the diplomatic function and of maintaining the dignity of the diplomatic representative and the state which he represents. . . ." League of Nations, Committee of Experts, *AJIL,* XX, Spec. Supp., 149.

[100] United Nations, Conference on Diplomatic Intercourse and Immunities, 2 March - 14 April, 1961, *Official Records,* Vol. II: *Vienna Convention on Diplomatic Relations* (A/CONF.20/14/Add.1) (New York, 1962), pp. 82–88 for text; also in *AJIL,* LV (October, 1961), 1064-1077.

[101] Sir Cecil Hurst, *International Law: Collected Papers* (London: Stevens & Sons Limited, 1950), p. 174. Also see *Engelke v. Musmann,* [1928] A.C. 433, in which Sir Cecil restates his views. Also, one of the leading current British writers on diplomatic immunities observed: "If the functional theory is to prevail, as would appear from the authorities at present, then its logical implications must be explored and analysed." K. R. Simmonds, "The 'Rationale' of Diplomatic Immunity," *International and Comparative Law Quarterly,* XII (October, 1962), 1210.

[102] This doctrine is found in two of the leading British books on the subject:
Lauterpacht-Oppenheim: "The exterritoriality which must be granted to diplomatic envoys . . . is . . . based on . . . the necessity that envoys must, for the purpose of fulfilling their duties, be independent of the jurisdiction, control and the like, of the receiving states." Oppenheim, I, 793.
Satow: "These immunities are founded on common usage and tacit consent; they are essential to the conduct of the relations between independent sovereign states; they are given on the understanding that they will be reciprocally accorded. . . ." Sir Ernest Satow, *A Guide to Diplomatic Practice,* ed. Sir Neville Bland (4th ed.; London: Longmans, Green and Co., 1957), p. 175.

Statesmen have accepted this theory of functional representation in their dealings with foreign diplomats. For example, in 1906 Secretary of State Elihu Root commented that "governments may not be hampered in their foreign relations by the arrest or forcible prevention of the exercise of a duty" by such agents.[103] And in 1935, Secretary of State Cordell Hull declared that the immunities extended to diplomatic officers were for a "practical purpose," specifically "to allow governments to transact official business free from interruption which might flow from molestation of or interference with their representatives."[104]

Jurists also have professed adherence to the theory in cases dating at least back to the early eighteenth century when the Lord Chancellor, in *Barbuit's Case,* held that the privileges of the public minister arise from "the necessity of the thing, that nations may have intercourse with one another . . . ."[105] Whether the courts emphasize this reciprocal interest of states[106] of the necessity "to safeguard the free exercise of the diplomatic mission (*ne impediatur legatio*),"[107] the endorsement of the theory of

---

[103] Cited in Green Haywood Hackworth, *Digest of International Law* (Washington: Government Printing Office, 1942), IV, 513.

[104] In a letter to Senator Key Pittman as cited by Lawrence Preuss, "Protection of Foreign Diplomatic and Consular Premises Against Picketing," *AJIL,* XXXI (October, 1937), 708.

[105] (1737), 25 Eng. Reprint 777.

[106] The following cases illustrate this viewpoint:
In re Chayet (Chile, 1932), *AD* (1931–1932), 330: "The immunities from jurisdiction are founded upon the reciprocal interests of States, which demand that their diplomatic representatives be in a position to carry out with the fullest liberty the missions entrusted to them. . . ."
In re Nazare Agha (France, 1921), *AD* (1919–1922), 287: Diplomatic immunity "is founded on the necessity for the mutual independence of States."
Salm v. Frazier (France, 1933) *AD* (1933–1934), Case No. 161: "The principle of immunity from jurisdiction . . . is founded on the interest that States . . . have in reciprocally guaranteeing the respect and independence of their representatives."

[107] As stated *In re DiSorbello (Marchese)* (Italy, 1941), *AD* (1941-1942), 361. Other examples of this philosophy include:
Parkinson v. Potter (1885), 16 Q.B.D. 152: Justice Wills observed that an exemption from jurisdiction of the courts was essential to the duties which the ambassador must perform.
Bergman v. de Sièyes, 71 F. Supp. 334 (1946); 170 F. 2d 360 (1948): The court held that immunity, in part, was based on the need to avoid interference with diplomatic duties.
Consular Premises (Greece) Case (Greece, 1931), *AD* (1931–1932), 338: Full immunities are necessary to guarantee "unhampered exercise of diplomatic duties."
Cholam Samsani v. Società Urbe (Italy, 1940), *AD* (1941–1942), 370: "The privilege of immunity . . . has its origin and its reason in the need . . . to place foreign diplomatic representatives . . . in a position where they can freely fulfill their high mission, safe from every danger of disturbance."
De Meeus v. Forzano (Italy, 1940), *AD* (1938–1940), 424: "To subject a foreign representative to . . . jurisdiction would entail a diminution of that freedom of action which he was to be granted as a prerequisite for the protection of the interests of his own country."
Angelini v. The French Government (Italy, 1921), *AD* (1919–1922), 289: Diplomatic privilege "is justified on the grounds of the necessity of guaranteeing the absolute independence of the diplomatic function."

functional necessity is overwhelming, emphatic, and clear. It has thus come to be accepted both in theory and practice that the basing of privileges and immunities "upon the interest of function, the necessity of insuring free communication among states" is in line with the modern trend.[108] In practice, the Grotian *omnis coactio abesse a legato debet* and *ne impediatur legatio* conveniently express "the rational foundation" of immunities as they now appear.[109]

The theory of functional necessity differs from rival concepts such as the "concession theory"[110] or, as it is sometimes called, the "doctrine of tacit consent,"[111] and the "doctrine of the interplay of applicable competences,"[112] both of which border on the functional approach but neither of which appears to explain adequately the granting of diplomatic privileges and immunities. The concession theory presumes that certain exemptions automatically flow from the act of receiving a diplomat.[113] This fiction rationalizes the privileged position of a diplomat but does not help in assessing the extent of these privileges.[114] The "applicable consequences" approach has the same failing in that it pits the territorial competence, which presumably is superior, against the secondary competence of diplomatic service. It offers little more than a doctrine of modified exterritoriality which only compounds the confusion.[115]

There are a number of obvious reasons why the functional theory has grown in importance during the period since 1945. The most signifi-

---

[108] Briggs, p. 763. For extensive analyses, see Ogdon, pp. 166–224, and Preuss, *N.Y.U.L.Q. Rev.,* X, 181–187. Also see Virginia Mueller, "Notes and Comments," *Cornell Law Quarterly,* XXXI (June, 1946), 509.

[109] Preuss, *N.Y.U.L.Q. Rev.,* X, 182. Another writer summarizes this approach thus: "The most logically sound, and therefore the most widely accepted theory, adopts the principle of *ne impediatur legatio* whereby the free and unhindered fulfillment of the purposes of the ambassador's mission is of utmost importance not only to the nations immediately concerned but also to the entire family of nations in their endeavor to maintain peaceful relations with one another." Gregory, *Chi.-Kent Rev.,* XXV, 333.

[110] Gregory, *Chi.-Kent Rev.,* XXV, 333.

[111] By Preuss, *N.Y.U.L.Q. Rev.,* X, 177.

[112] Steven Glichitch, "Some Legal Aspects of the Petrov Affair," *Australian Quarterly,* XXVI (June 1954), 22.

[113] The statement of the doctrine is found in Vattel: "It is impossible to believe that it is the intention of the prince who sends an ambassador, or any other minister, to subject him to the authority of a foreign power. . . . If it can not be reasonably presumed that the sovereign of the minister would consent to subject him to the sovereign to whom he is sent, the latter, in receiving the minister, consents to receive him upon that footing of independence; and this constitutes between the two princes a tacit convention which gives a new force to the natural obligation." Vattel, p. 376.

[114] See Preuss, *N.Y.U.L.Q. Rev.,* X, 176–178.

[115] For a different viewpoint, see the careful discussion by Glichitch, *Aus. Q.,* XXVI, 20–26. Glichitch bases his discussion on the legal method of Professor J. Basedevant and cites the latter's "Règles générales du droit de la paix" (*Hague Recueil,* LVIII [1956], 475–691) and his *Droit des gens* (1946).

cant, possibly, is the expansion in the absolute size of national missions, such as the United States Foreign Service, which more than quintupled in the period from 1924 to the mid-sixties.[116] The trend has been worldwide, of course, and is reflected in the burgeoning official lists in most nations.[117]

Secondly, the phenomenal increase of so-called "non-diplomatic" personnel suggests the need for emphasizing the functional theory. The increase is found not only in special *ad hoc* missions and commissions of various types, but in specialized representation, such as military, economic, and informational, whose links with the diplomatic missions are not uniformly construed. The consolidation of diplomatic and consular corps, a development since World War I, also has shifted large numbers of persons into the privileged category.[118]

Finally, the rapid increase in the number of international organizations, especially since the end of World War II, has required the granting of immunities to additional thousands of persons. Since such organizations are without territory or representational status, only the theory of functional necessity adequately explains this development. One writer contends that a "new concept has developed in international law and organization," namely the granting of diplomatic privileges and immunities to international organizations and their personnel on the basis of "functional utility."[119]

---

[116] The number of civilian employees, American and alien in foreign countries. totaled 3,447 in 1924; 4,236 in 1939; 4,477 in 1941; 10,936 in 1945; 15,812 in 1950 (U.S., Senate, Committee on Government Operations, Subcommittee on National Security Staffing and Operations, *Study, the Ambassador and the Problem of Coordination*, 88th Cong., 1st Sess., 1963, p. 80); and 16,800 in 1962 (U.S., Senate, Committee on Government Operations, Subcommittee on National Security Staffing and Operations, *Hearings, Administration of National Security*, 88th Cong., 1st Sess., 1963, Part 2, Exhibit III).

[117] In Great Britain, for example, the number of staff personnel entitled to diplomatic privileges and immunities was 543 in 1913; 1,084 in 1938; and 2,532 in 1955. Figures given by Earl Jowett in support of a resolution introduced in the House of Lords that the number of persons entitled to immunity should be diminished. *The Times* (London), November 17, 1955, p. 5. The 1955 figure topped 4,000 when the 1,517 on the staffs of seven high commissions and the embassy of the Irish Republic were added. *Ibid.*

[118] For further information about the growth of non-diplomatic representation and the methods devised to provide for at least limited privileges and immunities, see Chapter 10.

[119] Edwin H. Fedder, "Functional Basis of International Privileges and Immunities: A New Concept in International Law and Organization," *American University Law Review*, IX (January, 1960), 60.

Personnel of and representatives to international organizations (except for commissions and similar groups) are not covered in this study. For helpful discussions on this subject, see Martin Hill, *Immunities and Privileges of International Officials* (Washington: Carnegie Endowment for International Peace, 1947); John Kerry King, *The Privileges and Immunities of the Personnel of International Organizations* (Denmark: Strandberg Bogtryk-Odense, 1949); and Wilfred C. Jenks, *International Immunities* (New York: Oceana Publications, 1961).

One negative development — the split between the Communist and non-Communist nations following World War II — has necessitated recourse to the functional theory in determining rights of personnel. Exterritoriality and personal representation are of little value when privileges and immunities are re-evaluated in the face of ideological conflicts, nuclear age security requirements, and the international political struggle.

Diplomatic relations are essential for the existence and functioning of the nation-state system. In order to conduct these relations, nations must dispatch agents to foreign states and will do so only if such persons are exempt from local jurisdiction and are extended basic privileges and immunities. Thus, on the basis of reciprocity, diplomatic privileges and immunities assure the normal operation of the international system through free and unhampered diplomatic communication and functions, through maintenance of the dignity of the sending state, and through ensuring efficient performance of the diplomatic missions. The great increase in both diplomatic and non-diplomatic personnel, and the proliferation of functions which are part of — or which are on the periphery of — the diplomatic establishment require a theoretical framework which can accommodate a dynamic and expanding international political system. Functional immunity also helps to explain the immunities extended to diplomats in third states and persons attached to international organizations who have no representational or territorial status, to non-diplomatic and lower ranking personnel who have no representational status, to informational, military and other mission members scattered throughout a nation, and to *ad hoc* missions, commissions or temporary agents, who have no territorial status. As a result, the theory of functional necessity has been universally accepted as the guideline for extension of diplomatic privileges and immunities in the postwar period.

Although it seems clear that functional necessity, more so than exterritoriality or personal representation, facilitates replies to questions of diplomatic privileges and immunities raised in practice, it too could be considered by some as being disturbingly vague. The rule might be that "immunities are justified only so far as they can be shown to assist the performance of functions essential to the accepted practice of diplomacy."[120] But how far is "so far"? And what is "the accepted practice of diplomacy"? Ogdon would utilize the "adequate protection" test. If a question arises as to whether or not a jurisdictional act by a host state violates diplomatic immunities as guaranteed by international law, it must be asked "whether the particular act in question violates the security which

---

[120] Lyons, *BYIL,* XXX, 118–119.

is necessary for the diplomat's official function."[121] In other words, "adequate protection of the diplomatic function" is "the essence of the law and the test of what the law commands."[122] Lyons puts it in another way. He contends that international law requires that all states grant at least a certain minimum of privileges and immunities. That minimum should be at a level which would permit exercise of the diplomatic function "without hindrance of avoidable difficulty" since "nothing less will ensure compliance with the maxim *ne impediatur legatio*."[123]

However, this traditional basis for diplomatic privileges and immunities — a need to safeguard the unhampered operation of the diplomatic mission — does not fully explain why identical immunities are extended to all diplomatic agents.[124] It might be presumed that the ambassador from a major power, because of his heavy schedule, requires continuous immunities while the envoy from a small nation, with time on his hands, could respond to a civil summons without adversely affecting his diplomatic function. Perhaps it could be said that all envoys are potentially busy or, like local firemen, are always ready to respond to a call for action.

In reality, most diplomats, even though from Upper Volta or Trinidad-Tobago, probably maintain a reasonably full schedule. Even if they have time to engage in civil and criminal court actions, the myth of the sovereign-equal state, incorporated into the United Nations Charter and underlying much of traditional international law, would justify equal treatment for all foreign representatives. Also, as noted earlier, nations appear to be more sensitive to affronts to their national honor than in the past. To the extent that nations desire to avoid these affronts, it might be said that the representation theory still applies even though the basic reason for extending immunities remains *ne impediatur legatio*.

This qualification of the theory of functional necessity applies to the status of the diplomat who is the recipient of privileges and immunities. However, the security and the welfare of the receiving state also are factors to be considered in determining limits, if any, to be placed on the foreign diplomat. Certainly, the diplomat cannot invoke immunity to engage freely in unregulated commercial activities, or to circumvent cavalierly local laws, or to engage in flagrant espionage activities. Because of greatly increased international tensions, nations tend to rely upon the functional necessity of protecting national security when a need arises to

---

[121] Ogdon, p. 175.

[122] *Ibid.*

[123] Lyons, *BYIL,* XXX, 148.

[124] The continued applicability of the theory of representation as discussed in this paragraph was suggested to the writer by Professor C. H. McLaughlin.

justify the placing of unusual curbs on diplomatic personnel. The Communist nations serve as the best examples since security considerations have been given as reasons for restricting and harassing diplomatic personnel.

However, possibly the best judicial example of state security taking precedence over diplomatic immunity when the two are in conflict is the Canadian case of *Rose v. The King*.[125] The court, in authorizing the submission of documents stolen from the Russian Embassy, which might otherwise have been held privileged, followed the discretion of the executive branch in protecting national security. In a similar case, another Canadian judge speculated that it might be necessary to consider "whether even a foreign Ambassador is entitled to the privilege of diplomatic immunity" in cases where the acts under question "are contrary to the safety and welfare of Canada."[126]

Thus diplomatic immunities rest upon what two British publicists call the "shifting consideration of conveniences,"[127] to which might be added, "as dictated by the security and welfare of the receiving nation."[128]

Functional necessity provides the logical, theoretical guidelines (as discovered by both The League of Nations and United Nations codification experts), and the meaningful rules emerge only through a study of the determination by international agencies and by national bodies, executive, legislative, and judicial, of the functional limits of diplomatic privileges and immunities.[129] Perhaps it would be more appropriate to term the theory one of reciprocal functionalism. The traditional theory emphasizes primarily the need to guarantee the unfettered function of the diplomatic agent. The new element would be, as mentioned, the need to assure protection of state security.

Thus *reciprocal* is not used in its traditional sense.[130] Rather, a theory

---

125 [1947] 3 D.L.R. 618. See discussion in Chapter 4.

126 *Rex v. Lunan,* [1947] 3. D.L.R. 710; *AD* (1947), 150.

127 Butler and Maccoby, p. 94.

128 The "true rationale" of diplomatic immunities, observed an American writer, is "found in the practical considerations of statesmanship and not in the subtleties of political theory." Patrick F. McCartan, "Recent Decisions — Diplomatic Immunity," *Notre Dame Law Review,* XXXII (May 1957), 532.

129 The theory of personal representation would be an influential factor if it is viewed as assuring rights to diplomats because they are representatives of "sovereign, independent" states. However, reliance must be placed on functional necessity when states are faced with the specific determination of particular privileges and immunities.

130 Recipocity between states is a universally accepted practice. It was succinctly described by the Harvard drafters who summarized their "pragmatic approach" as follows: "Diplomatic intercourse is a normal function of states in the international community. On the basis of reciprocity, diplomatic privileges and immunities are the accepted means by which such normal functioning is assured." Harvard Draft, p. 26.

of reciprocal functionalism emphasizes the need for diplomatic personnel, including intelligence agents in the guise of diplomats, to reciprocate for the receiving of personal immunities by avoiding actions which would impinge upon state security. In some ways, the security needs in the post-1945 period have had a restrictive effect upon immunities. The suggestion of a theory of reciprocal functionalism is not an endorsement of policies which curb diplomatic activity. Rather it is a recognition of the political realities of the mid-twentieth century. This study thus centers on analyzing political and legal practice in an attempt to ascertain if existing rules guiding states in their treatment of diplomatic personnel have been modified. Any alterations in traditional practice are theoretically rationalized only by dependence upon functional necessity or reciprocal functionalism.

CHAPTER 2

Diplomatic
Privileges and Immunities
In Practice

IT IS A WELL ESTABLISHED AND WIDELY ACCEPTED RULE of international law — based on custom, augmented by laws and municipal regulations, and constantly reinforced by practice — that the diplomatic agent enjoys both widespread privileges and, in the absence of a waiver, substantial immunities from the jurisdiction of the receiving state.[1] These rules, resting securely on the theoretical framework of functional necessity, are found in international custom, bilateral and multilateral agreements, and in national legislation and practice.

In general, nations faithfully adhere to the law of immunities, primarily because of the rule of reciprocity, or, restated less diplomatically, primarily because of the fear of retaliation. However, the proper national posture is not always easy to determine, or to maintain, because of a lack of consensus on some of the basic general rules. This situation is further complicated by the problem of determining the categories of diplomats, quasi-diplomats, and non-diplomats — all claiming at least a degree of rights and immunities — who have been dispatched in great numbers throughout the international community.

Jurisdictional Immunity

It is not always easy to ascertain the basic guidelines which determine the treatment of diplomatic agents. For one reason, the so-called

---

[1]For an early, but still extremely useful discussion, see Francis Deák, "Classification, Immunities and Privileges of Diplomatic Agents," *Southern California Law Review* I (March, May, 1928), 209–252, 332–354. Also refer to basic works cited in the Selected Bibilography.

"right of legation," like state sovereignty, is a legal fiction;[2] for another, it is sometimes uncertain whether a given immunity arises from a matter of law or from an act of courtesy;[3] for still another reason, state practice, as will be illustrated throughout this study, often varies. On the other hand, while modern rules of diplomatic privileges and immunities are "based largely" on sometimes ill-defined customary rules of international law,[4] a much greater degree of certainty has been given the law by local legislation and by international agreement.

Although domestic legislation is not required to give effect to rules of international law covering jurisdictional immunity,[5] many countries, including the United States, have enacted laws "which are generally declaratory of international law and are designed to give it a specific local application."[6] This legislative restatement of jurisdictional immunity found an early expression in the famed British Diplomatic Act of 1708.[7] Whether or not diplomatic immunity existed in common law prior to the act remains uncertain.[8] However, the courts consistently have regarded the act as a declaration of international law and not an exhaustive definition or the

---

[2] States neither have a "right" to send diplomats nor an obligation to receive them from other states. This conclusion is supported by the United States policy of refusing recognition on moralistic grounds. This practice would seem to support an earlier conclusion by international law experts that "the right of legation constitutes merely a capacity or aptitude to enter into diplomatic relations, and that there exists no veritable legal right or obligation to do so." Harvard Law School, "Research in International Law: I. Diplomatic Privileges and Immunities," *AJIL*, XXVI (April, 1932), Supp., 31–32. Cited hereafter as Harvard Draft.

[3] J. L. Brierly, *The Law of Nations*, ed. Sir Humphrey Waldock (6th ed.; New York: Oxford University Press, 1963), p. 256.

[4] Herbert W. Briggs (ed.), *The Law of Nations* (2d ed.; New York: Appleton-Century-Crofts, Inc., 1952), p. 748.

[5] Courts in the United States are bound to apply international law as part of the law of the land. See U.S., Constitution, Article 1, Section 8; Charles Cheney Hyde, *International Law: Chiefly as Interpreted and Applied by the United States* (2d rev. ed.; Boston: Little, Brown and Company, 1947), I, 11–13.

[6] William Barnes, "Diplomatic Immunity from Local Jurisdiction," *DSB*, XLIII (August 1, 1960), 176. Also see United Nations, Secretariat, *United Nations Legislative Series*, Vol. VIII: *Laws and Regulations Regarding Diplomatic and Consular Privileges and Immunities* (New York, 1958), *passim*. Cited hereafter as *U.N. Laws and Regulations*.

[7] Great Britain, Act of Parliament for Preserving the Privileges of Ambassadors and Other Publick Ministers of Foreign Princes and States, 7 Anne Ch. 12, 1708, I British and Foreign State Papers 903. Cited hereafter as Act of Anne.

[8] For example, E. R. Adair (*The Exterritoriality of Ambassadors in the Sixteenth and Seventeenth Centuries* [London: Longmans, Green and Co., 1929], pp. 237–243) contends that the Act of Anne is a source of law. For a criticism of Adair's view, see A. Berriedale Keith, "The Exterritoriality of Ambassadors," *Journal of Comparative Legislation and International Law*, XII (1930), 126–128, and for Adair's response see E. R. Adair, "The Law of Nations and the Common Law of England," *Journal of Comparative Legislation and International Law*, XIII (1931), 133–137.

creation of new law.[9] It has been suggested that the act seems to be of little or no importance at present in considering the scope of diplomatic immunity and should be repealed,[10] although this viewpoint does not appear to be widely held. The Protocol Department of the British Foreign Office has, however, pointed out that the privileges of persons entitled to diplomatic immunities rest on the unwritten common law as much as on the Act of Anne.[11]

United States legislation providing for jurisdictional immunities is copied after the British model. The pertinent laws provide immunity from criminal and civil jurisdiction[12] and for exception as to suits against servants.[13] The basic United States laws[14] are derived from the Revised Statutes,[15] in turn originating from the Act of April 30, 1790,[16] which followed in almost identical language the Act of Anne.[17] The principle of jurisdictional immunity is incorporated not only into American and British laws but also into the legal codes of many other nations.[18]

---

[9] Lord Chancellor Talbot commented that the act was "only declaratory of the ancient universal *jus gentium*." *Barbuit's Case* (1737), 25 Eng. Reprint 777, 936. Also MacKinnon, L.J.: "It is plain under the authorities that the Act was not meant to define exhaustively the nature of the diplomatic privilege, but was merely conformatory of the common law," *Engelke v. Musmann,* [1928] A.C. 433, 458; Lord Campbell: "It was never intended by this statute to abridge the immunity which the law of nations gives to ambassadors," *Magdalena Steam Navigation Co. v. Martin* (1859), 28 L.J. (Q.B.) 310, 315; and Mathew, J.: "It appears from the authorities that the privilege of the embassy is recognized by the common law of England as forming a part of international law, and according to that law it is clear that all persons associated in the performance of the duties of the embassy are privileged," *Parkinson v. Potter* (1885), 16 Q.B.D. 152, 157. See also *Ghosh v. D'Rozario* [1962] 2 All E.R. 640; *In re The Amazone,* [1940] 1 All E.R. 269; *Triquet v. Bath* (1764), 3 Burrow 1478; *Heathfield v. Chilton* (1767), 4 Burrow 2016; *Viveash v. Becker* (1814), 105 E.R. 619; *Novello v. Toogood* (1823), 107 E.R. 204; *Taylor v. Best* (1854), 14 C.B. 478; 139 Eng. Reprint 201; *The Parlement Belge* (1880), 42 L.T. 273; *In re Suarez, Suarez v. Suarez,* [1917] 2 Ch. 131; and *In re Republic of Bolivia Exploration,* [1914] 1 Ch. 139. See also D. C. Holland, "Diplomatic Immunity in English Law," *Current Legal Problems,* IV (1951), 87; A. B. Lyons, "Immunities Other Than Jurisdiction of the Property of Diplomatic Envoys," *BYIL,* XXX (1953), 123; and J. Mervyn Jones, "Immunities of Servants of Diplomatic Agents and the Statute of Anne 7, c. 12," *Journal of Comparative Legislation and International Law,* XXII (February, 1940), 19.

[10] Holland, *Cur. Leg. Prob.,* IV, 81–106.

[11] Great Britain, Foreign Office, Protocol Department, *Diplomatic and Consular Immunities and Privileges* (Memorandum describing the practice of Her Majesty's Government in the United Kingdom) (September, 1957), p. 3.

[12] 22 U.S.C. 252, 253; Rev. Stat. 4063, 4064.

[13] 22 U.S.C. 254; Rev. Stat. 4065, 4066. Other U.S. legislation provides penalties for assaulting diplomatic officers, 18 U.S.C. 112, and prohibits picketing of foreign diplomatic missions, Act of Congress of February 15, 1938, 52 Stat. 30.

[14] 22 U.S.C. 252–254.

[15] Sections 4063–4066.

[16] 1 Stat. 117.

[17] *In re Baiz,* 135 U.S. 403 (1890), the court said the Act of 1790 was drawn from the Act of Anne which in turn was simply declaratory of the law of nations.

[18] See *U.N. Laws and Regulations, passim.*

Also, these immunities are firmly endorsed both by noted writers of international law and by foreign policy spokesmen and are firmly implanted in various international agreements. A widespread practice of incorporating immunities into bilateral treaties has developed since the end of World War II.[19] And while only two multilateral conventions dealing with diplomatic privileges and immunities had been signed by the mid-sixties, both were comprehensive and explicit in their sections on jurisdictional immunities. The Convention of Havana of 1928 states that diplomatic officers are exempt from "all civil or criminal jurisdiction."[20] The Vienna Convention of 1961 provides for absolute criminal immunity and modified civil immunity.[21] The same principle is contained in the various draft codes: the Cambridge Draft of the Institute of International Law, 1895; [22] Project No. 22 of the American Institute of International Law, 1925;[23] the Draft of the International Commission of American Jurists, 1927;[24] and the New York Draft of the Institute of International Law, 1929.[25]

Furthermore, "almost all" the great classic and modern publicists have accepted this principle.[26] United States Secretary of State Cordell Hull was only one of many statesmen who emphasized the need for diplomatic immunity in a forthright manner. He declared that the immunity of

---

[19] For examples of these treaties, see Chapter 10.

[20] Article 19. See Convention on Diplomatic Officers, Adopted at Havana, February 20, 1928, reprinted in *AJIL,* XXVI (April, 1932), Supp., 175–177, from English text in *Sixth International Conference of American States: Final Act* (Habana, 1928), pp. 142–150. Cited hereafter as the Havana Convention.

[21] Article 31. See United Nations, Conference on Diplomatic Intercourse and Immunities, 2 March - 14 April, 1961, *Official Records,* Vol. II: *Vienna Convention on Diplomatic Relations* (A/CONF.20/14/Add.1) (New York, 1962), pp. 82–88 for text of the Convention; also in *AJIL* LV (October, 1961), 1064–1077. Cited hereafter as the Vienna Convention.

[22] Article 12. See Resolution of the Institute of International Law, 1895, reprinted in *AJIL,* XXVI (April, 1932), Supp., 162-164, from text in J. B. Scott (ed.), *Resolutions of the Institute of International Law Dealing with the Law of Nations* (New York, 1916), pp. 119–123.

[23] Article 25. See Project of American Institute of International Law, 1925; Project No. 22 — Diplomatic Agents, reprinted in *AJIL,* XXVI (April, 1932), pp. 168–171, from text submitted by the American Institute of International Law to the Governing Board of the Pan American Union, March 2, 1925 (Washington: Pan American Union, 1925).

[24] Article 25. See Project of the International Commission of American Jurists, 1927; Project No. VII — Diplomatic Agents, reprinted in *AJIL,* XXVI (April, 1932), pp. 171–174, from text in *Comisión International de Jurisconsoltos Americanos Reunión de 1927, IV* (Rio de Janeiro, 1927).

[25] Article 6. See Resolution of the Institute of International Law; V — Immunités Diplomatiques, reprinted in *AJIL,* XXVI (April, 1932), pp. 186–187, from text in *Annuaire de l'Institut de Droit International,* Session de New York (1929), II, pp. 307 ff.

[26] According to Professor Stuart who mentions, *inter alia,* Bynkershoek, Vattel, Bluntschli, Calvo, Wheaton, Hall, Pradier-Fodéré, Satow, and Genet. Graham Stuart, *American Diplomatic and Consular Practice* (2d ed.; New York: Appleton-Century-Crofts, Inc., 1952), p. 250.

representatives and their staffs from arrest, detention, or molestation "is a practice, the necessity of which has for many centuries been universally recognized by civilized nations."[27] Earlier, Secretary of State Elihu Root had explained that these immunities were essential to guarantee the functions of diplomatic representation.[28] This basic rule, as supported by the secretaries of state, has also been incorporated into instructions issued to American diplomatic officers.[29]

On the other hand, the diplomat who occupies such a favored position while at his foreign post, is subject to the jurisdiction of his home state. This view is incorporated into the Vienna Convention[30] and appears to be self evident, generally accepted, and in keeping with traditional practice. The United States Department of State, in responding to an inquiry whether an American diplomatic agent would be immune to service of process in civil actions in the United States, said that no existing statute granted such immunity.[31] This ruling is compatible with a decision of the High Court of Cassation and Justice in Rumania to the effect that a commercial attaché of Rumania in Italy could be pursued in Rumania for *trafic d'influence* when the crime was punishable both in Rumania and Italy.[32] Later practices reveal that states have exercised jurisdiction over their own personnel in criminal cases.[33]

Courts, in considering whether the diplomat should be treated as a national living at home or as a national living abroad, appear to agree that the diplomat's *situs* is his home country. In a post-World War II case of

---

[27] U.S. Department of State, *Press Releases,* XIII, No. 323 (December 7, 1939), 497.

[28] He noted that immunities were necessary to assure that "governments may not be hampered in their foreign relations by the arrest or forcible prevention of the exercise of a duty in the person of a governmental agent or representative." Green Haywood Hackworth, *Digest of International Law* (Washington: Government Printing Office, 1942), IV, 513.

[29] The first paragraph of the section devoted to immunities states: "A diplomatic representative possesses immunity from the criminal and civil jurisdiction of the country of his sojourn and cannot be sued, arrested or punished by the laws of that country. . . . It is not to be supposed that any representative of this country would intentionally avail himself of this right to evade just obligations." U.S., *Foreign Service Regulations of the United States* (January, 1941), VII, 1, as cited by Stuart, pp. 250–251.

[30] Article 31(4): "The immunity of a diplomatic agent from the jurisdiction of the receiving state does not exempt him from the jurisdiction of the sending state."

[31] Hackworth, IV, 541.

[32] Cited by Chesney Hill, "Sanctions Constraining Diplomatic Representatives to Abide by the Local Law," *AJIL,* XXV (April, 1931), 255.

[33] For examples, see the incidents involving an American military attaché, a Haitian first secretary, and U.S. marine guards in Chapter 4.

this type, a Belgian court was called upon to decide whether a diplomatic agent would be subjected, under Belgian law, to the Court of First Instance of Brussels, as with nationals resident abroad, or to the court which would have jurisdiction were he domiciled in the country. The court, in *Baron Arnold de Cartier de Marchienne v. L.A. de Cartier*,[34] contended that, in matters of civil jurisdiction, the diplomatic representative remained domiciled on the territory of the sending state:

> Courts and writers are agreed that diplomatic representatives retain their domicile in the sending State, however long their mission, and however close their connection with the place to which they are sent.[35]

Not surprisingly, Italian courts have approached this question with customary ambivalence. The Tribunal of Milan in the *Case of Castiglioni*[36] denied an injunction against Yugoslavia on the grounds that Italian law does not provide for such orders against persons resident abroad. The court reasoned that the presence in Italy of the Yugoslav ambassador was not enough since he had exterritoriality "and cannot be regarded as the manager of his country's interests." This means, said the court, that "the juridical person called Yugoslavia resides entirely and exclusively abroad." However, an opposite conclusion apparently was reached the following year in *Castiglioni v. Federal People's Republic of Yugoslavia*.[37] The Tribunal of Rome declared that while the Yugoslav minister was not debarred from acting as an organ of the state in a private law matter, he also was not immune from being joined as defendant in such proceedings.

Presumably, under international practice, the court of jurisdiction would be decided by the sending state.[38] For example, the International Law Commission at its ninth session[39] deleted from the approved draft of the Provisional Articles[40] the provision stating that the court at the seat of

---

[34] (Belgium, 1948), *AD* (1948), Case No. 101.

[35] *AD* (1948), p. 310. Cf. *Van Der Elst v. Commissioner of Internal Revenue,* 223 F. 2d 771 (1955).

[36] (Italy, 1951), *AJIL,* XLIX (1955), 100.

[37] (Italy, 1952), *ILR* (1952), Case No. 43.

[38] See, for example, Switzerland's comments on the provisional draft in United Nations, International Law Commission, "Report to the General Assembly Covering the Work of Its Tenth Session, 28 April-4 July, 1958" (A/3859), *Yearbook: 1958,* Vol. II (A/CN.4/SER.A/1958/Add.1), p. 130.

[39] United Nations, International Law Commission, "Report to the General Assembly Covering the Work of Its Ninth Session, 23 April-28 June, 1957" (A/3623), *Yearbook: 1957,* Vol. II (A/CN.4/SER.A/1957/Add.1), p. 139.

[40] Article 24.

the diplomat's government is the competent court to hear an action against him.

Jurisdictional immunity remains as a universally recognized principle incorporated into the body of international law which civilized nations accept as binding through custom, municipal legislation, and judicial decisions, and has been consistently restated by publicists, jurists, and statesmen.[41] However, diplomats do not escape the jurisdiction of the courts of their home state. It would appear as if they remain domiciled on the territory of the sending state in matters of civil and criminal jurisdiction. Although the Italian court in the *Case of Castiglioni* emphasized domicile, the fiction of exterritoriality has been discredited[42] and nationality normally would be considered as the legal basis for jurisdiction by the sending state.

This does not mean that the host state cannot exercise jurisdiction in certain cases involving civil or criminal actions. Rather, it means that the diplomat does not escape the jurisdictional authority of the sending state if jurisdiction is not taken by courts of the host state.

The Principle of Reciprocity

In general, governments expect that other governments will reciprocate in the extension of immunities to similar categories of diplomatic and non-diplomatic personnel. This principle has been a basic guideline for state practice in the post-World War II period as attested by the consistent declaration of diplomats as *persona non grata* and the imposition of travel bans as retaliatory measures. The principle is also incorporated into municipal legislation, especially as it applies to the granting of customs courtesies. The Soviet Union, for example, stipulated that reciprocity will be the only basis for its extending privileges to diplomatic couriers and granting privileges and exemptions from duties, taxes, and baggage inspection.[43] Since the United States has historically followed the rules of international law in extending diplomatic privileges and immunities, it "has sought from other nations reciprocal treatment for its own diplomatic officers

---

[41] Its application, of course, varies among individual states as will be seen throughout this study.

[42] See discussion of this concept in Chapter 1.

[43] See *U.N. Laws and Regulations,* pp. 338, 340–341, 347.

abroad,"[44] and has incorporated the concept of reciprocity into its law.[45]

Courts also have endorsed the principle of reciprocity.[46] Possibly the greatest attention was given the problem in Great Britain where reciprocity for diplomats was the subject of public debate and a governmental investigation which culminated in legislative and executive action designed to assure that foreign countries grant to the same categories of persons employed in British embassies the diplomatic immunities which are granted in Britain.

The issue came to a head in a case not directly concerning diplomatic privileges and immunities, but which touched off a chain of events culminating in the first major amendment to the legislation of 1708.[47] The case was *Krajina v. Tass Agency*[48] in which the Court of Appeals extended the doctrine of state immunity to a Russian news-gathering agency. The misgiving was not over the doctrine of state immunity, which is traditionally accepted in international law — usually on a reciprocal basis — but rather over the doctrine that a business firm operating in Great Britain could link itself with a foreign state and leave a claimant without legal redress.[49] Although there was no question about the connection of the Tass news agency with the Soviet government, the decision did represent an extreme instance of state immunity.[50] The granting of immunity to Russian journalists in Great Britain when the Soviet government did not reciprocate in the reception of British journalists raised the analogous situation of the extension of immunities to servants in the Soviet's London Embassy when servants in Britain's Moscow Embassy were not accorded immunity from civil and criminal prosecution.

---

[44]Barnes, *DSB*, XLIII, 177.

[45]"Such privileges [duty-free entry of diplomatic baggage] are, however, based on, and subject to, strict reciprocity on the part of foreign governments and may be modified or changed if foreign governments do not accord like privileges to American representatives abroad." *U.S. Foreign Service Manual,* Vol. I, Part I, Section 251.1, as cited in *U.N. Laws and Regulations,* p. 376. Reciprocity also covers other areas of diplomatic activity. See, for example, U.S., Act of October 11, 1962 (Amending Communications Act of 1934), Public Law 87–795 (76 Stat. 903) which permits the installation of low-power radio stations by foreign missions in Washington only if reciprocal privileges have been extended to United States missions.

[46]See *De Meeus v. Forzano* (Italy, 1940), *AD* (1938–1940), Case No. 164. However, Italian practice has not been consistent. Cf. *Società Arethusa Film v. Reist* (Italy, 1953), *ILR* (1955), 549, and *Comina v. Kite* (Italy, 1922), *AD* (1919–1922), Case No. 202.

[47]Act of Anne.

[48][1949] 2 All E.R. 274.

[49]See J. C. Arnold, "State and Diplomatic Immunity," *Solicitor,* XIX (March, 1952), 68.

[50]*Ibid.*

As a result of the *Krajina* decision, the British government in 1950 appointed an Interdepartmental Committee on State Immunities under the chairmanship of Lord Justice Somervell to study the twin problems of state immunity and diplomatic immunity. On the subject of diplomatic immunities, the committee was asked to consider two questions:

1. Whether the law or practice of the United Kingdom affords to persons possessing diplomatic immunity an immunity in any respect wider than is desirable or is strictly required by the principles of international law.

2. What, if any, changes in the law of the United Kingdom the Committee recommends should be made having regard to its . . . [answer to question 1] and to the question of reciprocity.[51]

The committee report of July 13, 1951, to the Foreign Office, which presented it to Parliament in January, 1952, recommended:

(1) That the Foreign Secretary should in the future refuse to accept any local national as holding any position in a foreign embassy in this country, including the position of a "domestic servant," except on the condition that such person shall not enjoy a personal diplomatic immunity.

(2) Subject to (1), the immunities at present granted are either certainly or probably required by International Law and we recommend no change.

(3) That consideration should be given to the question whether there should be legislation empowering His Majesty's Government by appropriate procedure to reduce the immunities at present accorded to the embassy or mission of any foreign country so that they shall correspond with the immunities granted by that foreign country to our own embassies and missions.[52]

The British Parliament carried out the Somervell committee's recommendations by passing the Diplomatic Immunities Restriction Act, 1955,[53] which empowers the Queen to withdraw by Order in Council personal immunities in any category of officials employed at diplomatic missions in the United Kingdom when similar immunities are not extended to the corresponding category of British officials stationed in diplomatic missions abroad. Thus the principle of reciprocity was officially adopted as a determinant in the extension of immunities.

---

[51] Great Britain, Foreign Office, Parliamentary Papers *(Reports),* Cmd. 8460, January, 1952, "Report on Diplomatic Immunity by an Interdepartmental Committee on State Immunities," p. 2.

[52] *Ibid.,* p. 7. Also see *The Times* (London), January 29, 1952, p. 2.

[53] Eliz. 2, Ch. 21.

While the Act covers envoys, families, official staffs, and unofficial staffs, parliamentary debate made it clear that the chief problem was the legal position of servants of British envoys in certain countries and embassy officials and their families.[54] The Act itself does not curtail diplomatic immunities; it merely states the basic concept, long accepted in international practice, that extension of immunities should be based on reciprocity. Also the British lawmakers refrained from including officials of international and inter-governmental organizations, who were being stationed in Britain in growing numbers, since the "principle of reciprocity could not have been applied without doing violence to accepted rules of international law."[55] In essence, a "liberal" state utilized statutory action in an attempt to bring "restrictive" states into line with modern practice.

The action was not taken without opposition. In fact, a Member of Parliament, Hector Hughes, claimed that the measure was "provocative and unnecessary" since the minister in charge of the bill had admitted that there was "no evidence of wide-spread abuse" by foreign diplomats, and would invite retaliation.[56] The government countered that it was only carrying out "widely recognized requirements of international law"[57] in the face of ever-increasing numbers of diplomatic persons in Great Britain,[58] and in 1956 the implementing Order in Council was issued.[59] The Order, *inter alia,* withdrew immunities from suit or legal process (except for actions connected with official duties) for members of the staff below the rank of attaché in the missions of eleven nations,[60] and withdrew immunities for private acts for servants connected with missions from twenty-one countries.[61]

---

[54] F. H., "The Diplomatic Immunities Restriction Act, 1955," *Law Journal,* CVI (February 10, 1956), 86.

[55] *Ibid.*

[56] *The Times* (London), November 22, 1955, p. 9.

[57] Mr. Turton, Under Secretary of Foreign Affairs, in Commons debate. *Ibid.,* October 26, 1955, p. 5.

[58] In 1938, there were about 1,000 persons in 54 foreign missions in Great Britain; in 1955, there were some 2,500 in 72 missions. *Ibid.* It was predicted that the Act of 1955 would permit a reduction, in round figures, from 2,500 to 2,000 persons entitled to immunity. *Ibid.,* February 28, 1956, p. 4.

[59] Diplomatic Immunities Restriction Order, 1956. *Statutory Instruments, 1956,* No. 84 (effective March 31, 1956).

[60] Argentina, Brazil, Finland, France, Laos, Lebanon, Peru, Poland, Soviet Union, Switzerland, and Yugoslavia.

[61] Afghanistan, Argentina, Bolivia, Brazil, Colombia, Finland, France, Iceland, Indonesia, Japan, Korea, Laos, Lebanon, Mexico, Nicaragua, Poland, Switzerland, Soviet Union, Uruguay, Venezuela, and Yugoslavia.

The Order applied to servants employed in the service of the mission or, except for Finland and Switzerland, in the personal service of the envoy.

The British act, designed to guarantee reciprocity in the extension of diplomatic immunities, quickly achieved its objective in the major target area, the Soviet Union. Whereas under 1927 legislation, the Soviet Union granted — exclusively on a basis of reciprocity — diplomatic privileges and immunities only to those of diplomatic rank,[62] it substantially amended these regulations by a Decree of the Presidium of the Supreme Soviet of the U.S.S.R. of March 27, 1956. This extended the reciprocal privileges and immunities included in the 1927 act to clerical and auxiliary personnel of foreign missions and embassies in the U.S.S.R., with the exception of Soviet nationals.[63] Thus, under Soviet practice, "auxiliary personnel" (such as chauffeurs, couriers, lift operators, door-keepers, concierges, *et al.*) as well as clerical personnel, as a rule are extended diplomatic immunities on a reciprocal basis.[64] Otherwise, they are subject to criminal, administrative, and civil laws, and they "enjoy inviolability only in the official premises of the embassy and mission."[65]

The Soviet and British governments in 1956 concluded an agreement whereby personnel below diplomatic rank in the British Embassy in Moscow and in the Soviet Embassy in London were granted diplomatic immunity.[66] In keeping with the agreement, the British Foreign Office on June 15, 1956, extended diplomatic privileges and immunities to eighty-five members of the staff of the Soviet Embassy in London.[67] The British decision came on the heels of a similar action by the Soviet Union on June 14 when diplomatic privileges, including immunity from arrest, were granted to junior staff members and service attachés whose countries granted the same privileges to Soviet officials abroad.[68] The Soviets clarified the action further on October 29, 1956, when, in response to a specific inquiry from the U.S. Department of State, the Ministry of Foreign Affairs declared that non-diplomatic members of the United States Embassy in Moscow were entitled to diplomatic privileges and immunities.[69]

Neither the British action nor post-World War II developments have influenced the United States in the direction of statutory alteration of its

---

[62] Y. A. Korovin and Others, *International Law,* trans. Dennis Ogden (Moscow: Foreign Language Publishing House, 1961), pp. 295, 304.

[63] *Ibid.,* p. 304.

[64] *Ibid.*

[65] *Ibid.*

[66] G. Tunkin, "Some Developments in International Law Concerning Diplomatic Privileges and Immunities," *International Affairs* [n.v.] (December, 1957), p. 70.

[67] *The Times* (London), June 16, 1956, p. 7.

[68] *Ibid.*

[69] Tunkin, *International Affairs* [n.v.] (December, 1957), p. 70.

regulations covering diplomatic privileges and immunities. However, several attempts have been made in the United States Congress to enact legislation which would restrict immunities granted to diplomatic agents. The proposed methods varied but in general were of three types: (a) reduction of jurisdictional immunities, (b) automatic recall under specified conditions, and (c) transferral of the liability for personal and property damage from the diplomat to the United States government. None of these efforts, which extended from 1925 to 1956, was successful.

Two of these "anti-immunity" measures were introduced in the late 1920's. One provided that the President request the recall of diplomats operating vehicles while drunk;[70] the other provided that the President take similar action against diplomats who violated the Eighteenth Amendment.[71] In 1930, Senator Kenneth McKellar introduced a bill which would have removed the immunity of diplomats who had violated traffic laws.[72] Even stronger measures would have been taken against the diplomat by Representative Samuel A. Weiss who in 1941 introduced a bill designed to subject foreign diplomats to prosecution for offenses against federal or state laws.[73] A later attempt in this futile legislative effort was made in 1956 by Representative Joel Broyhill who offered a measure which would have avoided the obvious violation of international law inherent in the Weiss bill by shifting the responsibility in death, injury, and property damage cases from the diplomat to the United States government.[74]

The attitude of the United States is undoubtedly reflected in a statement by the editor-in-chief of the *American Bar Association Journal,* who concluded that despite cases of abuse it probably would be unwise and improper for Congress to take statutory action narrowing immunities since such a move would probably "infringe upon long-established and accepted

---

[70] S.Res. 283, 70th Cong., 2d Sess.

[71] H. J. Res. 8, 69th Cong., 1st Sess.

[72] S. 3964. "Be it enacted, etc., That in the execution of the traffic laws in Washington, D.C., no immunity shall be given to violators of the traffic laws because the offender or alleged offender is part of or connected with foreign legations." U.S., *Congressional Record,* 71st Cong., 2d Sess., 1930, LXXII, Part 6, 5827.

[73] H.Res. 3977, 77th Cong., 1st Sess. This bill and S.Res. 283 and H.J.Res. 8 mentioned above were brought to the writer's attention in a Memorandum of August 17, 1962, from Edwin B. Kennerly, Editor, *Bill Digest,* Legislative Reference Service, the Library of Congress, to Representative Morris Udall of Arizona.

[74] H.Res. 10988, 84th Cong., 2d Sess. The bill provided, in brief: "That the United States shall be liable, in the same manner and to the same extent as a private individual under like circumstances, for money damages for injury or loss of property, or personal injury or death, caused by the negligent or wrongful act or omission of any individual granted diplomatic immunity by the United States. . . ." Kennerly Memorandum. See also U.S., *Congressional Record,* 84th Cong., 2d Sess., 1956, CII, Part 6, 7478.

principles of international law" and result in "unfavorable repercussions" on the United States diplomats abroad.[75]

In essence, the British and Russians clarified through national legislation the existing practice among most nations, which is that certain privileges and immunities should be extended to those in missions below diplomatic rank. The legislation in the two nations also re-emphasized the vital importance of reciprocity as a guideline in this area of international law.

Determination of Categories

As has been indicated in the previous sections, a substantial body of diplomatic rules, based on reciprocity, is available to guide the conduct of nations in their legal and political treatment of foreign diplomatic representatives. However, two problems still remain: (1) the extent of such privileges and immunities as are enjoyed by diplomatic personnel under current international practice, and (2) the categories of persons to whom these acts of international courtesy and practice are extended.

International practice is reasonably uniform in the treatment of diplomatic personnel, extending from the ambassador and minister down through the ranks of the counsellor, secretary, and attaché. There is less concurrence among states about which privileges and immunities should be extended to the administrative and technical staffs, the service staff, the unofficial staff, and families. However, post-World War II divergencies in treatment possibly have been most pronounced in the policies adopted toward nationals of the host state serving with foreign diplomatic missions and toward that growing group of overseas agents who might broadly be grouped under the heading of non-diplomatic personnel. These latter categories are not clearly defined or mutually exclusive. Furthermore, subordinate personnel are now performing tasks once performed by those in the traditional categories and are charged at times with highly confidential and vital tasks. Another problem centers around the vast increase in the size of overseas diplomatic establishments, especially those of the larger powers and especially in economic, propaganda, and military categories which are the stepchildren of the traditional diplomatic groupings.

The problem of classification has long bedeviled both writers and statesmen. Earlier drafts and conventions dealing with this question, as well as more recent efforts, reflect the difficulty experienced by statesmen in determining the categories entitled to diplomatic privileges and immuni-

---

[75] Richard Young, "Diplomatic Immunities," *American Bar Association Journal,* XXXIX (September, 1953), 840.

ties. The 1895 Cambridge Draft of the Institute of International Law (Articles 1 and 2) granted full immunities to public ministers and to both "official" and "unofficial" personnel and limited immunities to nationals.[76] Reference is made only to "diplomatic agents" throughout the 1925 American Institute of International Law Draft.[77] The categories included in the 1927 Project of the International Commission of American Jurists (Article 19)[78] and the Convention on Diplomatic Officers adopted at Havana, February 20, 1928 (Article 14),[79] are almost identical. The Havana Convention included diplomatic officers, "official personnel," and families "under the same roof" in the immune categories. The American jurists adopted the same text except that diplomatic officers were referred to as agents and a special exclusion from full immunity was made for nationals among the official personnel.

Section V of the Harvard Draft (Personal Privileges and Immunities)[80] extends immunity to members of a mission who perform diplomatic duties and to members of diplomatic families and to administrative and service personnel, although the latter, under Article 23, would enjoy immunity only to the extent that it would not interfere with the proper functioning of the mission. A draft code prepared by Japanese jurists (Article III) makes a similar distinction placing diplomatic agents, official staff, and the families of both groups in a category enjoying traditional immunities, and assigning employees of the agents and staff to a category enjoying lesser immunities.[81]

While these approaches to the codification of diplomatic practices differed concerning categories, the extension of immunities to official diplomatic personnel and families has not been challenged and the limitation of immunities to certain categories has been accepted, although not on a uniform basis. For example, the various drafters apply these limitations, but not uniformly, to nationals and to administrative and service personnel.

Publicists also have struggled with the problem of establishing diplo-

---

[76] Resolution of the Institute of International Law, 1895.

[77] Project of American Institute of International Law, 1925: Project No. 22 — Diplomatic Agents.

[78] Project of the International Commission of American Jurists, 1927: Project No. VII — Diplomatic Agents.

[79] Havana Convention.

[80] Harvard Draft.

[81] Draft Code of International Law Adopted by the Japanese Branch of the International Law Association and the Kokusaiho Gakkwai (International Law Association of Japan) in International Law Association, *Report of the Thirty-Fourth Conference: Vienna, 1926* (London: Sweet and Maxwell, Ltd., 1927), pp. 390–392.

matic and non-diplomatic categories as guides for the extension of privileges and immunities. Perhaps the most useful categorization is that of Sir Cecil Hurst,[82] an expert on diplomatic immunities whose work has left a definite impact in the field of international law. Hurst lists three categories of persons entitled to diplomatic immunities.[83] The first category is made up of the official staff which includes the head of the mission and those directly engaged in diplomatic functions such as counsellors, secretaries, and attachés. This category also would include doctors and chaplains if they were part of the staff and if their duties were wholly or primarily concerned with the mission, and dragomans and interpreters in Eastern countries. Also grouped under the official staff is the office staff attached to the mission (archivists, stenographers, typists, porters, *et al.*). The second category includes wives and families of the officials listed in the first category. The third category is comprised of the unofficial staff, including stewards, personal private secretaries, governesses, tutors, gardeners, chauffeurs, or others employed by official members of the staff. The first and third categories are distinguished by the fact that the first group is paid by the state, the third by individual employers.

An agreement on categories which goes beyond some previous draft efforts and which is somewhat more refined than the listings by Sir Cecil was reached at the United Nations conference on diplomatic immunities held in Vienna in 1961.[84] The categorization carries considerable weight since the Vienna Convention was signed by forty-five states. Under Article 1 of the Convention, a diplomatic agent includes the head of a mission and members of the diplomatic staff, or those having diplomatic rank, all of whom are entitled to maximum immunities. Other categories include the administrative and technical staff, the service staff (employed by the mission), and private servants (employed by a member of the mission), all of whom receive limited immunities of different degrees (Article 37).

---

[82] Sir Cecil Hurst, *International Law: Collected Papers* (London: Stevens & Sons Limited, 1950), pp. 205–206.

[83] For example, Patrick Stirling, "The Immunities of Diplomatic Agents (II)," *Law Journal,* CVIII (June 13, 1958), 375, in discussing immunity entitlements, adopts the Hurst categories without change.

[84] The Vienna Convention also reflects the functional approach in that it places some limitations on immunities from civil jurisdiction extended diplomatic agents (Article 31), and extends to administrative and technical personnel immunity from civil actions only for their official acts (Article 37). The Convention "does at least formulate rules relating to status, privilege and immunity with consistent regard to what is reasonable and necessary between sovereign States." K. R. Simmonds, "The 'Rationale' of Diplomatic Immunity," *International and Comparative Law Quarterly,* XII (October, 1962), 1210.

Members of the family of the diplomatic agent are entitled to the same immunities granted to the agents (Article 37), and nationals of the receiving state have immunity only in the carrying out of their official actions (Article 38). The concept of functionalism is recognized in the Convention by the fact that the categories of agents under Article 37 are listed in this descending order of their entitlement to immunities: agents and members of their families, administrative and technical staff, service staff, and private servants.

While it is true that an actual determination of those entitled to immunity easily might be made by referring to diplomatic and mission employee lists[85] rather than by drawing categories of personnel, such a reference would answer only in part the basic questions raised about diplomatic privileges and immunities. The lists do not help in establishing rules to cover personnel not included in the official listing or in determining the scope of immunities and privileges granted to the various groups of privileged persons. These answers are found only through a perusal of state practices and judicial decisions. For that matter, while a line may be drawn between those entitled to full immunities and those entitled to limited immunities, a true analysis of the categories may be circumvented as there is nothing to prevent missions from upgrading personnel, for example, describing all clerks as third secretaries.[86]

An earlier survey by a British writer indicated that most nations follow a "scrutiny of function" test in determining categories,[87] and the wholesale expulsion of diplomatic personnel, especially military attachés, since the end of World War II by various countries — principally those in the Communist orbit — indicate that foreign offices believe that functions should be compatible with diplomatic titles, as determined by the host state. Under the functional test, a person in order to be entitled to privileges and immunities would have to show that his work actually was diplomatic. One writer has suggested that under such a test the individual must carry on his work at the "seat" of a foreign mission, be concerned with relations between nations and not with sectional or party interests, and carry out his duties so as not to interfere with the internal affairs of

---

[85] For example, two regular publications of the United States Department of State: *Diplomatic List,* a bimonthly listing of names and positions of foreign diplomatic representatives in Washington, D.C., and the *List of Employees of Diplomatic Missions,* a monthly listing of persons employed by foreign diplomatic missions in Washington, D.C., who are not included in the *Diplomatic List.*

[86] As noted in *The Times* (London), November 17, 1955, p. 5.

[87] S. H. Brookfield, "Immunity of the Subordinate Personnel of a Diplomatic Mission," *BYIL,* XIX (1938), 155–157.

the host country.[88] The Vienna Convention is more explicit. Under Article 3, the functions of a diplomatic mission consist *inter alia* of:

(a) representing the sending State in the receiving State;

(b) protecting in the receiving State the interests of the sending State and of its nationals, within the limits permitted by international law;

(c) negotiating with the Government of the receiving State;

(d) ascertaining by all lawful means conditions and developments in the receiving State, and reporting thereon to the Government of the sending State;

(e) promoting friendly relations between the sending State and the receiving State, and developing their economic, cultural and scientific relations.

The position of the United States regarding the functional test was said to be "not very clear."[89] However, in England the functional test has "become part of the common law . . . ."[90] France and Italy also appear to look into the functions of foreign government personnel, while Germany apparently has followed a contrary practice of maintaining that receiving states must accord diplomatic privileges to all persons whose names appear on the official lists.[91] This formal test is reflected in Article 10 of the Havana Convention which stipulates that "each mission shall have the personnel determined by its government." Under Article 7 of the Vienna Convention, the "sending State may freely appoint members of the staff of the mission" subject to provisions in Article 5 (accreditation to more than one state), Article 8 (nationals), Article 9 (*persona non grata*), and Article 11 (size of mission).

The basic problem was stated in the 1930's by the Harvard group which pointed out that no standard has been established under customary international law by which diplomatic missions may clearly be distinguished in all cases from non-diplomatic missions on the basis of differences in their respective functions.[92] The Harvard group noted that the

---

[88] *Ibid.*, p. 155.

[89] However, as noted *ibid.*, p. 158, such cases as *U.S. v. Liddle*, 2 Wash. C.C. 205 (1808), and *In re Baiz*, 135 U.S. 403 (1890), indicate that the Department of State certification while acceptable, as it is in Great Britain, as conclusive evidence of diplomatic status, in fact is based upon an investigation of the function of the person concerned.

[90] *Ibid.*, pp. 156–157. For example, see *Barbuit's Case* (1737), 25 Eng. Reprint 777; *Parkinson v. Potter* (1885), 16 Q.B.D. 152; *Assurantie Compagnie Excelsior v. Smith* (1923), 40 T.L.R. 105; and *In re Cloete* (1891), 7 T.L.R. 565.

[91] Brookfield, *BYIL*, XIX, 160. See also *Diplomatic Immunities (German Foreign Office) Case, AD* (1925–1926), Case No. 244.

[92] Harvard Draft, p. 43.

development of new types of government agencies operating on foreign soil tended to obscure the distinction between the two categories.

This difficulty in drawing a line between diplomatic and non-diplomatic or quasi-diplomatic personnel is even more pronounced with states' sending new categories of military, economic, and information personnel into the foreign field. In addition, the numbers entitled to immunity have been steadily rising since the end of World War II. This situation has caused concern on the part of both officials and nationals of receiving states. The United States Department of State said in 1960 that an estimated 7,000 persons, including wives and family members, were entitled to diplomatic immunity in the United States;[93] a speaker before the House of Lords in 1961 estimated the number in Great Britain at 6,000.[94]

The Harvard drafters concluded that the distinction between a diplomatic and a "non-diplomatic" mission must rest on "purely formal" grounds and that recourse to the diplomatic lists appears to be the accepted practice.[95] However, this does not imply that either the host or the sending state should fail to recognize the obligations inherent in this vital sphere of international intercourse. As stated in 1958 in a leading article of *The Times* (London), there is both an obligation on the part of the host nation "not to be too censorious in its scrutiny of the list of those privileged" and on the part of the sending nation to keep the size of their missions at "an absolute minimum."[96]

As far as strictly diplomatic personnel is concerned, nations are quite specific in designating categories entitled to privileges and immunities, and in most instances these are similar since reciprocity has long been a guiding principle among nations. The practice in the United States, the United Kingdom, and the Soviet Union is perhaps indicative of the general trend.

Two basic categories of persons are entitled to diplomatic immunity in the United States.[97] The first includes diplomatic officers, duly accredited to the government of the United States, members of their immediate families living under their roof and dependent upon them for support, and servants of such officers, regardless of nationality.[98] This immunity is

---

[93] Barnes, *DSB,* XLIII, 181.

[94] Lord Stonham as quoted in *The Times* (London), April 26, 1961, p. 18.

[95] Harvard Draft, p. 43.

[96] *The Times* (London), March 18, 1958, p. 11.

[97] It should be kept in mind that this study deals only with traditional, bilateral diplomatic practices and that in the United States, as elsewhere, immunity is extended to other groups such as members of permanent delegations to the United Nations and to regional organizations.

[98] For summary of categories, see Barnes, *DSB,* XLIII, 180–181.

extended on the basis of universally accepted principles of international law as incorporated into United States legislation.[99] In the second category are employees of diplomatic missions in Washington, regardless of nationality, but not including members of their families.[100]

The listing of categories in Great Britain, as directed under Section 6 of the Act of Anne,[101] includes the names of "persons regarded by Her Majesty's Government in the United Kingdom as entitled to claim diplomatic immunity."[102] Listed in addition to heads of missions are: (a) members of the diplomatic staffs (e.g., counsellors, secretaries, attachés); (b) any other officials employed directly under the orders of a head of mission in his diplomatic capacity (e.g., archivists, clerks, typists), and (c) servants employed by a head of mission in his personal household or in the chancery of his mission (but not servants employed by members of the staff of the mission).[103] As a matter of policy, the British government is not prepared to include nationals on the diplomatic list.[104]

In the Soviet Union, diplomatic representatives and members of the diplomatic missions (e.g., counsellors — including commercial counsellors; first, second, and third secretaries; and attachés — including commercial, financial, military and naval attachés) "shall enjoy, subject to reciprocity, all the rights and privileges attaching to their status under the rules of international law."[105] These rights and privileges also are extended to spouses and minor children of personnel entitled to the immunities.[106]

Immunities for official personnel from the top ranks down through counsellors, third secretaries, and attachés are granted on a uniform basis by all three nations. However, some differences exist in the official pronouncements with relation to lower ranking and unofficial personnel (not included in the Soviet order), to servants (all servants in the United States except for debts transacted prior to assumption of their functions; nonnational servants in the United Kingdom; and no reference to servants in the Soviet Union), and families (the Soviet Union order being restricted to minor children). However, in actual practice these distinctions are not self-contained.

---

[99] 22 U.S.C. 252–254.

[100] Act of April 30, 1790 (1 Stat. 118; 22 U.S.C. 254).

[101] Act of Anne.

[102] Great Britain, *Diplomatic and Consular Immunities and Privileges,* p. 3.

[103] *Ibid.*

[104] See Chapter 9.

[105] Section I (2) of Regulations Concerning the Diplomatic and Consular Missions of Foreign States in the Territory of the Union of Soviet Socialist Republics (Order of 14 January 1927 of the Central Executive Committee and the Council of People's Commissars of the U.S.S.R.) as cited in *U.N. Laws and Regulations,* p. 336.

[106] Note 2 of Section I (2), *ibid.,* p. 337.

The obvious point to be made from a discussion of the materials on categories taken from draft codes, writings of publicists, national legislation, the concept of functional tests, etc., is that sharp lines, other than for official diplomatic personnel, cannot be drawn. Practices among states vary, and it would be difficult to draw up any list of general rules which would not be bound by reservations. However, certain categories can be distinguished. For example, immunities for lower ranking personnel are more limited; staff members assigned to quasi-diplomatic work do not have absolute immunity; families and nationals can be distinguished for purposes of analysis, etc. Thus, for purposes of this study, personnel have been divided into four main categories, which reflect most strongly the classifications of Sir Cecil Hurst and the delegates to the Vienna conference, but which also have been shaped in part by the analysis of national policy, state practice, the draft codes, etc. The categories are:

CATEGORY I: The Official Diplomatic Staff:

A. Diplomatic agents (including secretaries and attachés).[107]

B. Administrative and technical agents (including chancellors, archivists, clerks, secretaries and stenographers, messengers, dragomans, interpreters, guards, couriers, and porters).

CATEGORY II: The Retinue and Families of the Diplomatic Staff:

A. Service and unofficial staff: domestics in the service of the mission (including maids, gardeners, chauffeurs); personnel in the service of members of the mission (including servants and personal secretaries).

B. Families (including members of the family of a diplomatic agent).

CATEGORY III: Nationals and Domiciliaries:

Persons who are nationals of or permanently resident in the receiving state.

CATEGORY IV: Non-diplomatic Personnel:

Persons whose rank tends to correspond in general with the diplomatic agent but whose duties are not clearly defined as diplomatic (including trade delegations, military, economic and information personnel, observers, commissioners, *et al.*).

---

[107] Since agents of ambassadorial and secretarial rank are uniformly entitled to the full immunities discussed in Chapters 3, 4, 5 and 6, they are not considered in the analysis in Chapter 7 of privileges and immunities extended to lower ranking persons.

CHAPTER 3

Personal Immunities
of Diplomatic Agents

PERSONAL INVIOLABILITY OF THE DIPLOMATIC AGENT historically has been viewed as the "fundamental principle from which have been derived all diplomatic privileges and immunities"[1] or as "a universally accepted rule"[2] although opinion varies as to the categories of diplomatic personnel entitled to its benefits[3] and as to whether a special right to personal inviolability is needed as a rule of international law.[4]

There seems to be little basic disagreement that Article 29 of the 1961 Vienna Convention on Diplomatic Relations which states that the "person of the diplomatic agent" is "inviolable"[5] is in general accord with "accepted principles of international law and practices."[6] The principle

---

[1] Harvard Law School, "Research in International Law: I. Diplomatic Privileges and Immunities," *AJIL*, XXVI (April, 1932), Supp., 91. Cited hereafter as Harvard Draft.

[2] Francis Deák, "Classification, Immunities and Privileges of Diplomatic Agents," *Southern California Law Review*, I (March, 1928), 231. Deák refers to a series of cases in which governments apologized for mistreatment of diplomats to support his assertion. *Ibid.*, pp. 231–233. See *Republica v. de Longchamps*, 1 Dallas III (1784).

[3] For a full discussion, see Chapter 2.

[4] For example, Professor Lyons admits the right may have existed in the past in an imperfect form but, with modernization of the state and its apparatus and settled conditions in most countries, ordinary provisions of municipal law are ample to insure diplomatic protection. A. B. Lyons, "Personal Immunities of Diplomatic Agents," *BYIL*, XXXI (1954), 299–305, 338. In contrast, the most recent edition of Satow's *Diplomatic Guide* argues at some length that inviolability implies a higher degree of protection to the diplomat than is accorded private persons. Sir Ernest Satow, *A Guide to Diplomatic Practice*, ed. Sir Neville Bland (4th ed.; London; Longmans, Green and Co., 1957), pp. 176–180.

[5] United Nations, Conference on Diplomatic Intercourse and Immunities, 2 March - 14 April, 1961, *Official Records*, Vol. II: *Vienna Convention on Diplomatic Relations* (A/CONF.20/14/ADD.1) (New York, 1962), pp. 82–88 for text; also in *AJIL*, LV (October, 1961), 1064–1077. Cited hereafter as the Vienna Convention. Article 29 reads: "The person of a diplomatic agent shall be inviolable. He shall not be liable to any form of arrest or detention. The receiving State shall treat him with due respect and shall take all appropriate steps to prevent any attack on his person, freedom or dignity."

[6] The observation of the United States delegation during discussion of Article 29. See U.S., Department of State, *United Nations Conference on Diplomatic Intercourse and Immunities: Report of the Delegation of the United States*, Department of State Publication No. 7289 (Washington: U.S. Government Printing Office, 1962), p. 16.

of personal inviolability is not subject to serious challenge.[7] Even though diplomats may not be, as a leading writer maintains, "just as sacrosanct as heads of State,"[8] they are entitled to special treatment and protection.[9] Governments must at least take "reasonable" steps to protect diplomats.[10]

This personal inviolability is based on "the necessity of permitting free and unhampered exercise of the diplomatic function," the need to maintain the dignity of both the diplomatic representative and the sending state, and "the respect properly due to . . . traditions."[11] The principle also is widely recognized by nations in their domestic legislation.[12]

The problems encountered in the application of this rule will be considered under the general headings of protection, assault and attack, arrest and detention, and violation of diplomatic dignity.

Protection

The universally recognized inviolability of the diplomatic agent may be infringed upon either (1) by the state itself, in the form of official actions, or (2) by persons operating outside the scope of governmental authority, in which case "there appears to be general agreement as to the

---

[7] For example, Article 29 was approved by nations at the 1961 conference in Vienna without change from the text (Article 27) presented by the United Nations International Law Commission. See United Nations, International Law Commission, "Report to the General Assembly Covering the Work of Its Tenth Session, 28 April - 4 July, 1958" (A/3859), *Yearbook: 1958*, Vol. II (A/CN.4/SER.A/1958/Add.1), p. 97.

[8] L. Oppenheim, *International Law,* Vol. I: *Peace,* ed. H. Lauterpacht (8th ed.; London: Longmans, Green and Co., 1955), p. 789.

[9] President Fillmore, in referring to an attack on a Spanish consular officer in New Orleans, told Congress in a December, 1851, message that both consular and diplomatic officers "are objects of special respect and protection, each according to the rights belonging to his rank and station." John Bassett Moore, *A Digest of International Law* (Washington: Government Printing Office, 1906), VI, 813.

[10] The law of nations requires every government to take all reasonable precaution to prevent acts which would intimidate, coerce, harass, or bring into public disrepute any diplomatic or similar representative of a foreign government. *Frend et al. v. U.S.,* 100 F. 2d 691 (1938).

[11] League of Nations, Committee of Experts for the Progressive Codification of International Law, "Diplomatic Privileges and Immunities," reprinted in *AJIL,* XX (1926), Spec. Supp., 149.

[12] For example, see Section I(2) of Regulations Concerning the Diplomatic and Consular Missions of Foreign States in the Territory of the Union of Soviet Socialist Republics (Order of 14 January 1927 of the Central Executive Committee and the Council of People's Commissars of the U.S.S.R.), as cited in United Nations, Secretariat, *United Nations Legislative Series,* Vol. VIII: *Laws and Regulations Regarding Diplomatic and Consular Privileges and Immunities* (New York, 1958), pp. 336–337. Cited hereafter as *U.N. Laws and Regulations,* See also Section 231.1, *U.S. Foreign Service Manual,* Vol. 1, Part I, as cited *ibid.,* pp. 274–375. Cf. 22 U.S.C. 252–254.

right of diplomatic agents . . . to have their persons and personalities respected by the authorities."[13] However, the practice varies as to the extent of special protection accorded in differing circumstances.[14] Protection normally requires prosecution for the offense as well as apology and redress. In *Respublica v. de Longchamps* (1784),[15] which involved a threat to assault the secretary of the French Legation, the court held:

> The *person* of a public minister is sacred and inviolable. Whoever offers any violence to him, not only affronts the Sovereign he represents, but also hurts the common safety and well-being of nations: — he is guilty of a crime against the whole world.[16]

Special laws have been enacted by a majority of nations to provide adequate means for punishing offenses committed by individuals against diplomatic agents.[17] During the past four centuries, states have enacted laws and regulations designed not only to give precision to these immunities but sometimes to extend them beyond the minimum requirements of international law.[18]

This type of legislation is contained in the United States statute which specifically provides:

> Whoever assaults, strikes, wounds, imprisons, or offers violence to the person of an ambassador or other public minister, in violation of the law of nations, shall be fined not more than $5,000 or imprisoned not more than three years, or both.
>
> Whoever, in the commission of any such acts uses a deadly or dangerous weapon, shall be fined not more than $10,000 or imprisoned not more than ten years, or both.[19]

While the original United States legislation (Act of Congress of April 30, 1790) was based on the British model[20] and is similar to other national

---

[13] Memorandum of the Swiss Federal Council, League of Nations (C.196.M. 70.1927.V.p.242), as cited in Harvard Draft, p. 93.

[14] *Ibid.*

[15] 1 Dallas 111.

[16] See Moore, IV, 622–626.

[17] Satow, p. 178.

[18] The earliest legislation on this subject apparently was that of the Netherlands in 1651 which forbade "offending, damaging, injuring by word, act or manner, the ambassadors, residents, agents or other ministers . . . or to do them injury or insult." Féraud-Giraud, *États et souverains* (1895), I, 333, as cited in Harvard Draft, p. 94.

[19] 18 U.S.C. 112; Rev. Stat. 4062.

[20] Great Britain, Act of Parliament for Preserving the Privileges of Ambassadors and Other Publick Ministers of Foreign Princes and States, 7 Anne Ch. 12, 1708, I British and Foreign State Papers 903. Cited hereafter as Act of Anne.

legislation,[21] it extended provisions of the British act in affording protection to the diplomat against unlawful attacks. The British have not adopted specific legislation recognizing offenses against the person, property, or reputation of a diplomat.[22] However, one publicist, Professor Lyons, contends that the normal processes of criminal law are adequate to protect the diplomat, a view not fully accepted by all writers.[23] He reasons that because the state has a general duty toward all persons within the realm — national and alien, official and private — legislation affecting only diplomats is not necessary. In addition, British courts have always been able to deal with such acts.[24]

While nations vary in their legislative approach in the normal course of events, some, in times when national emotions are inflamed — as in the case of war — take special measures such as those protecting diplomats against propaganda.[25] However, if no special law exists, the ordinary processes under the nation's penal code should apply.[26] In actual practice, it would appear that states tend to accord the protection expected under international law and municipal legislation. This conclusion is supported by observations made by retired United States Foreign Service officers and staff members.[27] Of twenty-two who commented specifically or at some length on the matter of protection of personnel, fifteen agreed that in general it had been at least adequate[28] in the posts where they had served throughout the world. A few were more generous in their ap-

---

[21]Cf. Article 108, Korean Criminal Law No. 293 of 18 September 1953; Article 118, Netherlands Penal Code; and Articles 111(1) and 112(1) of the Polish Penal Code, approved by Order of the President of the Republic, 11 July 1932, as cited in *U.N. Laws and Regulations,* pp .189, 201, 245.

[22]See Harvard Draft, p. 94.

[23]Lyons, *BYIL,* XXXI, 305. For a contrary view that the right of a diplomatic agent to protection is derived from international law, he refers to Pradier-Fodéré. *Traité de droit international public* (1885), II, 12. This view has been adopted by Sir Cecil Hurst, *International Law: Collected Papers* (London: Stevens & Sons Limited, 1950), p. 176. Hurst cites with approval Ward's *Foundation and History of the Law of Nations in Europe* (1795), II, 494, that protection accorded diplomats must be "far greater than that enjoyed by ordinary citizens."

[24]See Richard Young, "Diplomatic Immunities," *American Bar Association Journal,* XXXIX (September, 1953), 840.

[25]Hurst, pp. 185–186.

[26]Satow, p. 178.

[27]Foreign Service Survey. (A survey conducted by the writer in 1960 and 1961 of retired United States Foreign Service officers and staff members whose names were included in the annual listing of the *Foreign Service Journal.*)

[28]E. T. Mooers, who served in ten different countries, observed that in the places where police protection was required (Portugal, Italy, Haiti, and France) "such protection was adequate." *Ibid.*

praisal.[29] However, there did appear to be some agreement that the extent of protection in so-called "civilized countries"[30] was greater than in the newly emerging nations.[31] And in the latter area, the degree of protection apparently sometimes coincided with the level of political stability and the role of the political leader.[32]

The situation is quite different behind the Iron Curtain, according to Francis Deák, who served in virtually all of the Eastern European countries with the U. S. Foreign Service.[33] In this area, the violations or abuses of diplomatic rights and immunities stemmed not necessarily from public irresponsibility or malice, but rather from calculated manipulation by authorities who either permitted or instigated actions against diplomatic personnel. On the other hand, Mr. Deák found that demonstrations were rare and protection "adequate" in other countries. Similar observations were made with regard to Egypt and Latin America in general.

A minority expressed some doubts that protection has been as adequate since World War II as it had been in an earlier period.[34] However, the reasons seem to stem not so much from the laxity of governments as from the "new diplomacy" of the Communist countries, or from revolutionary activities.[35]

---

[29] John H. Madonne, who served in Poland, Syria, Lebanon, Egypt, Switzerland, Morocco, and France, noted that "as a rule the local police always gave full protection to diplomatic and consular establishments, much more so after World War I." An ex-ambassador, who served for more than thirty years in Europe and Latin America, noted that diplomatic personnel still count on "first class protection." *Ibid.*

[30] One ex-diplomat commented: "I served for nearly four decades in civilized countries, where law and order was maintained. If the host government would have dreamed of tolerating demonstrations and mob violence, my own Government would have known very well how to protect its diplomats. . . ." *Ibid.*

[31] A diplomat whose service ranged from European to Asian countries declared: "Those countries with old tradition and long experience in the exchange of diplomats and in Protocol, would generally give better protection and tend more to follow the rule of international law. In the so-called underdeveloped countries, more depends upon the personality of the leader and upon expediency in the case at hand, rather than international law." *Ibid.*

[32] Arthur C. Frost, a thirty-plus-year veteran of European, Asian, Latin American, and African consular service, found that effectiveness of protection in "backward countries" depends chiefly upon the extent of police and army control and the state of "general tranquility, efficiency and stability" of civilian authorities and in the dictatorial countries on the attitude of the ruler and the status of United States political relations with the government. *Ibid.*

[33] *Ibid.*

[34] For example, Colonel Lawrence A. Higgins found no changes in the extent of protection for the period 1926–1929, but from 1945–1960, when he lived abroad as a private citizen, he noted an increase in the intensity of demonstrations against American personnel without a corresponding increase in the effectiveness of protection. *Ibid.*

[35] One ex-diplomat declared that Russia "practices not diplomacy but something else." Another observed that the auxiliary police of the Nazi and Communist dictatorships were either under instructions of their governments or "uneducated as to the rights of foreign diplomats." *Ibid.*

The personal protection of the diplomat also extends into periods of war.[36] Although the treatment of diplomats who were taken into custody by enemy governments has fallen below minimum standards in some instances,[37] nations tend to extend acceptable protection and courtesies to the representatives of enemy nations following the outbreak of hostilities. This appeared to be true for the United States,[38] Japan,[39] and Germany[40] following the outbreak of World War II. With the conclusion of hostilities, the occupation forces in Japan continued to treat former German diplomats, although Nazi party members, "with the respect due their professional immunity."[41] One of the most unique developments in this area of diplomacy was the permission granted U. S. diplomats to serve as members of the Swedish staff after Turkey closed the U. S. missions during World War I.[42]

Assault and Attack

Historically, the concept of personal inviolability has met its most rigorous test in instances of assault and attack on the person of the diplomatic agent. Diplomacy has long been a dangerous game. A number of

---

[36] *United States v. Liddle,* 2 Wash. C.C. 205 (1808).

[37] The experiences of Hooker A. Doolittle, a former United States minister whose service spanned nearly thirty-five years, illustrates this type of undiplomatic treatment. Mr. Doolittle was arrested and threatened with shooting after the Russian Revolution and, at the start of World War II, was arrested in Tunis and held for a week with his wife before escaping to join the Anglo-American forces. Foreign Service Survey.

[38] The American government took Japanese diplomats into protective custody for internment at Hot Springs, Virginia, until a mutual exchange could be arranged. Elmer Plischke, *Conduct of American Diplomacy* (2d ed.; Princeton, N.J.: D. Van Nostrand Co., 1961), p. 336.

[39] The Japanese government ordered embassy personnel confined to the embassy compound but, according to U.S. Ambassador Joseph C. Grew, directed that "members of the Embassy and the Consulates be accorded protection and living facilities in accordance with international usages." Joseph C. Grew, *Turbulent Era,* ed. Walter Johnson (Boston: Houghton Mifflin Co., 1952), II, 1253.

[40] A retired U.S. Foreign Service officer noted that during the six months internment of diplomatic personnel in Bad Nauheim after the United States entered the war "we were treated with the utmost consideration." Foreign Service Survey.

[41] *New York Times,* July 25, 1947, p. 17. Diplomats returning to Germany were allowed to ship out four tons of personal effects and permitted to retain the value of $250 in any currencies except yen. By comparison the figures for two other groups of Germans were: "Objectionable Germans," $50 and 350 pounds; "non-objectionable," $250 and 500 pounds.

[42] An American diplomat reported that the Turks, in private, apologized for having been compelled by the Germans to break off diplomatic relations with the United States. Then, realizing the inadequacy of the Swedish staff which was in charge of American interests, they invited American subordinate personnel to continue to make governmental contacts as "representatives of the Swedish Legation." Foreign Service Survey.

heads of mission met sudden death in the first quarter of the 1900's.[43] Others suffered indignities and lesser injuries in the period before World War I.[44] The framers of the Vienna Convention no doubt had these historical facts as well as more recent developments in mind when they incorporated a protective rule of international law into the new code. Article 29 stipulates that the receiving state "shall take all reasonable steps to prevent any attack" on the "person, freedom or dignity" of the diplomatic agent.

This action appears to be quite logical in view of the hazards still faced by diplomatic agents. The public records would not seem to support the charge made in 1950 by Senator Joseph McCarthy that "dilettante diplomats" do the fighting for us "with kid gloves in perfumed drawing rooms."[45] The *New York Times,* in an editorial reference to assassination threats received by the United States Minister to Indochina, Donald R. Heath, lauded the diplomatic corps for its courage in the face of danger.[46] At least thirteen diplomatic, quasi-diplomatic, and consular personnel have been killed since 1947, including five Americans, five nationals assigned to United States establishments, one British

---

[43] Plischke, pp. 336–337. Some major cases, summarized by Plischke, included the murder of the following: Baron von Kattler, German Minister in China, by Chinese soldiers during the Boxer Rebellion in 1900; Count Wilhelm Mirbach, first German Ambassador to the Soviet Republic, by Russian revolutionaries in 1918; Mechilav Vorovsky, official Soviet observer at the Lausanne Conference in Switzerland, by White Russians in 1923; and Peter Vorkoff, Soviet Minister to Warsaw, by a Russian monarchist in 1927.

[44] These cases included: Second secretary of the American Legation in Havana, assaulted in a restaurant by a Cuban citizen in 1908; American chargé d'affaires in Cuba, assaulted by a newspaper reporter in a Havana hotel in 1912; the Salvadoran chargé d'affaires, assaulted in his Washington Legation in 1931; American minister resident, attacked by Ethiopian police and members of a crowd which was threatening to harm his chauffeur in 1932; and British subject employed as a messenger in the American Legation in Santo Domingo, shot and beaten by a member of the Dominican Army in 1935. Green Haywood Hackworth, *Digest of International Law* (Washington: Government Printing Office, 1942), IV, 508–510. See also the case of Colonel Krastitch, Yugoslav Military Attaché at Sofia. Clyde Eagleton, "The Responsibility of the State for the Protection of Foreign Officials," *AJIL,* XIX (April, 1925), 299.

[45] *New York Times,* June 18, 1950, p. 4. At the time, a marble memorial in the Department of State Building bore the names of four diplomatic and consular officers " 'who while on active duty lost their lives under heroic or tragic circumstances.' " Those named were "Thomas C. Wasson, U.S. consul, sniper, Jerusalem, 1948; Douglass MacKiernan, vice consul, murdered by Tibetan border guards while he was fleeing over Himalayan mountains from Communist China to India; J. Theodore Marriner, murdered, Beirut, 1937; Robert W. Imrie, killed in Teheran, 1924." *Ibid.,* October 18, 1954, p. 19.

[46] *Ibid.,* December 25, 1951, p. 30. The editorial said, in part: "These American diplomats are literally on the firing line; they are performing their tasks under conditions of hardship and danger; and we know of no instance yet where any of them has failed in his duty. This is not the 'cookie-pusher' diplomacy of the 'striped-pants' school that critics of the State Department are so fond of talking about."

subject, one Spaniard, and one Turk. The Americans were: Thomas C. Wasson, a consul general, who died May 23, 1948, in Jerusalem from bullet wounds inflicted by a sniper the previous day as he was returning from an attempt to arrange an Arab-Jewish truce;[47] Herbert M. Walker, a United States Navy communications expert, who died of wounds in Jerusalem the same day;[48] William Pierce Boteler, a vice consul, who was killed on June 16, 1956, by bombs tossed by terrorists into a restaurant in Nicosia, Cyprus;[49] Miss Barbara A. Robbins, who worked in the office of the special assistant to the U.S. Ambassador in Vietnam, who was killed in a 1965 terrorist bombing of the American Embassy in Saigon which left more than 150 dead or injured;[50] and Joseph W. Grainger, an American aid official, captured by the Viet Cong in 1965 who was reportedly killed while escaping.[51]

Employees killed while assigned to United States establishments were: Johannes A. Semerjibashian, a stateless Arab employed as a dragoman-interpreter by the United States Legation in Ethiopia, who was fatally shot on October 9, 1947, as he entered the driveway of his home in an official legation automobile bearing diplomatic license plates;[52] George Dyke, an Arab radio operator, killed when a bomb shattered the U.S.I.S. building in Damascus on March 28, 1952;[53] and three Vietnamese who were employed in the Saigon Embassy at the time of the 1965 bombing.[54]

The other "diplomatic fatalities" included Colonel P. L. Graham, Military Attaché and Comptroller of the Household, killed by a stray bullet when the British Embassy in Baghdad was sacked and burned on July 14, 1958; José Gallostra y Coello, diplomatic agent of the Franco government, shot on a downtown Mexican street on February 20, 1950; and Army Captain Faud Guzaltan, Turkish diplomatic courier, who died of gunshot wounds under mysterious circumstances on a train in the Soviet Union on May 30, 1949.[55]

---

[47] In a deathbed statement, Wasson said: "It was the Arabs." *Ibid.,* May 23, 1948, pp. 1, 6; May 24, p. 18; May 27, p. 48.

Two months later, a sniper put a bullet through a car driven by Wasson's successor, John J. MacDonald. *Ibid.,* July 11, 1948, p. 17.

[48] *Ibid.,* May 27, 1948, p. 48.

[49] *Ibid.,* June 17, 1956, p. 1.

[50] *Ibid.,* March 31, 1965, p. 1; April 3, p. 3.

[51] *Ibid.,* April 14, 1965, p. 1.

[52] "Murder in Addis Ababa of Alien Employed by American Legation," *DSB,* XVII (October 26, 1947), 834; *New York Times,* October 12, 1947, p. 36.

[53] *New York Times,* March 29, 1952, p.4.

[54] *Ibid.,* April 1, 1965, p. 12.

[55] *Ibid.,* July 15, 1948, p. 4; *The Times* (London), July 15, 1948, p. 8; *New York Times,* February 4, 1952, p. 6; June 3, 1949, p. 4; June 14, p. 16.

Traditionally, the receiving states are not only held "strictly account-able" for the murder or killing of diplomats but must extend personal protection to at least the official staff of a mission.[56] Pre-World War II practices also indicated that states in general adhered to the need for satisfactory redress, including apologies, punishment of offenders, assur-ances against repetition, and indemnity.[57]

These rules, at least to a degree, were followed in the more recent incidents. In a statement apparently directed both to the Greeks and British, the U.S. Department of State called the Cyprus violence a "blind and senseless course in the settlement of international problems."[58] The Greek delegation to the United Nations viewed the death with "shock and sorrow,"[59] and the Greek Cypriot underground (the National Organization for Cyprus Liberation or E.O.K.A.) assumed full blame and expressed "deep regret" for the "terrible misfortune."[60] The organi-zation pointed out that the bomb had been meant for a Briton. The Syrian government expressed sympathy and "abhorrence" over the death of Dyke.[61]

In the Turkish courier case, the Russians claimed that Guzaltan shot himself while he was alone in a train compartment and died later in a hospital. A Turkish "hero's burial" for the courier attended by nine top generals and an announcement that in the future Turkish couriers to Russia would travel in pairs indicated that Turkish officials had little faith in the Russian story.[62]

Relatively severe punishment in the Mexican case was meted out to Gabriel Salvador Fleitas Rouco, a Cuban who had fought with the Spanish Loyalists. He was sentenced to sixteen years in prison for the shooting.[63] Colonel Adeeb Shishekly, Syrian Army Chief of Staff, said he would do his utmost to arrest and punish those responsible for Dyke's death.[64] American Minister Cavendish Cannon, in filing a vigorous pro-test, pointed out that the bombing was the fourth such incident since

---

[56] Plischke, p. 336; Eagleton, *AJIL,* XIX, 299.

[57] Hackworth, IV, 508–510.

[58] *New York Times,* June 19, 1956, p. 3.

[59] *Ibid.,* June 20, 1956, p. 4.

[60] *Ibid.,* July 4, 1956, p. 6.

[61] *Ibid.,* March 30, 1952, p. 16.

[62] *Ibid.,* June 14, 1949, p. 16.

[63] *Ibid.,* February 4, 1952, p. 6. Mexico, which still recognized the Spanish Republican government, had no diplomatic relations with Franco. Gallostra, as diplomatic agent of the present Spanish government, was authorized to issue visas to travelers to Spain.

[64] *Ibid.,* April 1, 1952, p. 3.

1948 and that those responsible for the previous outrages still were not discovered.[65] In the Boteler case, police seized three Cypriot youths soon after the bombing.[66]

The only public report noted with reference to compensation revealed that Iraq paid $336,000 to Great Britain for its losses and Graham's death.[67] The Russians sought indemnity in reverse when they submitted to Turkey a medical bill for 40,000 Turkish pounds (about $16,000) to meet hospital and operation expenses for Guzaltan.[68] It might be concluded that nations tend to follow the traditional pattern but perhaps not to the same extent as a quarter century earlier, and not when a "cold war" foe is involved.

For every diplomatic agent or staff member killed during the period under study, countless others were subjected to attack, assault, insults, and other indignities. These fell into two general categories: (1) diplomatic agents who were subjected to affront by government representatives and (2) agents (a far larger group) who were victims of actions taken by nationals or other unofficial personnel in the host state. In the latter group, the diplomatic persons were harassed or physically injured as the result of (a) mob assaults, (b) internal strife, or (c) individual action (e.g., snipers, potential assassins, *et al.*).

At the official level, since World War II, Western powers have entered a long series of complaints about the treatment of diplomatic personnel in Communist nations. Typical of these was a 1947 complaint over Bulgarian currency controls. Envoys of the United States, Great Britain, France, Switzerland, Italy, and Sweden in Sofia complained about what the British called "disgraceful and discourteous" treatment of foreign representatives by Bulgarian officials and militia. The British Foreign Office said their conduct was a "serious breach of accepted standards of international courtesy."[69]

The British Foreign Office said the French minister was assaulted when he remonstrated against soldiers who attempted to drag members of the French Institute from their car.[70] The French Foreign Office claimed militiamen struck both the minister and a correspondent for the French News Agency; the Bulgarians claimed the diplomat started the fracas by swinging with his portfolio.[71] During the same year, when

---

[65] *Ibid.,* March 30, 1952, p. 16.

[66] *Ibid.,* June 17, 1956, p. 1.

[67] *Minneapolis Tribune,* April 15, 1960, p. 5.

[68] *New York Times,* August 30, 1949, p. 8.

[69] *Ibid.,* March 12, 1947, p. 9. The restrictions on Western diplomatic activity in the Soviet Union and Eastern Europe are discussed throughout this study.

[70] *Ibid.*

[71] *Ibid.,* March 15, 1947, p. 6; March 16, p. 24.

relations between the East and West were rapidly deteriorating, the Soviet Union charged that its diplomats received similar treatment in Brazil.[72] The incidents preceded a break in diplomatic relations, and the U.S.S.R. took the rather strong action of holding the Brazilian ambassador under surveillance as hostage until the safe departure of Russian diplomats from Brazil was assured.[73]

In a more serious case involving a government representative, the United States charged that Cuban Army Captain Jorge Robreno Mariegos "intentionally and in cold blood" shot and seriously wounded E. Wayne Henderson, a U.S. Embassy clerk, outside a night club in Havana on November 19, 1960, a charge the Cubans denied.[74] A number of other persons connected with diplomatic establishments were wounded by assailants, usually unidentified. While some were connected with American missions, such as a U.S.I.S. employee in Italy who was the victim of a knife attack[75] and a vice consul in Cyprus who was shot while working in his garden,[76] representatives of other nations also were wounded and hospitalized.[77]

---

[72] Moscow Radio charged that members of the Soviet staff in Rio de Janeiro were subjected to insults and attacks by "hooligans" who were encouraged by Brazilian authorities and police. The Soviets claimed that police-inspired crowds tossed bad eggs and stones at the Russian chargé d'affaires and first secretary of the embassy as they left a car. *Ibid.,* October 25, 1947, p. 9.

[73] *Ibid.*

[74] "U.S. Protests Cuban Shooting of Embassy Staff Member," *DSB,* XLIII (December 19, 1960), 924–925; *New York Times,* November 20, 1960, p. 20; November 21, p. 8; December 1, p. 4. The Americans contended that the shooting followed a dispute over currency offered for payment of a night club bill and that Robreno shot Henderson without reason, then "nonchalantly" left the scene. The State Department claimed that a policeman turned Henderson over to a bystander who was "well intentioned" but an "incompetent driver," and who was involved in an accident while taking Henderson to a hospital. The Cubans countered that the dispute stemmed from Henderson's refusal to pay in Cuban pesos, which he called "communist money." They claimed the shooting was accidental. See *New York Times,* November 21, 1960, p. 8, for details.

[75] In 1957, a young man knifed Mrs. Edvige Govoni, a Swiss-born British subject and U.S.I.S. employee in Italy, in an American reading room, then left shouting anti-American slogans. *Ibid.,* May 26, 1957, p. 5.

[76] Some mystery surrounded the wounding of John Page Wentworth who was shot three times. British security officers were unable to determine if he was ambushed or if random shots came from a passing automobile. *Ibid.,* September 19, 1958, p. 2. Taylor Belcher, United States Consul General at Nicosia, said he believed that the gunmen identified Wentworth as a British civilian and shot him by mistake. *Ibid.,* September 20, 1958, p. 4. He was the second U.S. consular officer to become a victim of the terroristic campaign on Cyprus. *Supra,* p. 53.

[77] For example, Jean Gaspard, French Vice Consul, was critically wounded while en route by auto from the airport in Beirut. *Ibid.,* August 23, 1958, p. 3; the Counsellor of the Italian Legation in Burma, André Nicolethi, was hospitalized when wounded by stray bullets which struck the home of a wealthy businessman near Rangoon. *Ibid.,* September 14, 1953, p. 8; and Lieutenant Colonel M. T. Harjone, Indonesian Military Attaché, suffered head injuries when assaulted by a group of men in The Hague. *Ibid.,* May 25, 1952, p. 10.

Some of the cases reported in the press could almost have been taken from the pages of mystery novels. For example, John Bankhead, United States Consul at Windsor, Ontario, who earlier had reported the receipt of poisoned liquor and candy, was fired on twice as he drove to his home,[78] and a Cuban diplomat saved himself and his family from possible death when he tossed a hand grenade out of his car seconds before it exploded.[79] Other cases also were far from routine,[80] especially a 1959 incident on a Japanese train in which a drunken stevedore and the Russian ambassador were cast as protagonists. A case of mistaken identity apparently prompted the stevedore, Takanori Matsushima, to accost Ambassador Nikolai T. Fedorenko. Matsushima, who attempted to force the Russian to take a drink with him, said he thought Fedorenko was an American. The response of the Japanese government was a model of adherence to rules of international courtesy. Officials apologized immediately, a normal diplomatic procedure which the Russians, for some strange reason, interpreted as meaning the incident had not been an accident. Fedorenko also said the stevedore challenged him to a fight. Matsushima was charged with violence and intimidation, causing bodily injuries, and interfering with the execution of official duties — rather stiff charges for this type of molestation.[81] For his brief indiscretion, Matsushima was sentenced to serve one and one-half years at forced labor.[82]

Other diplomats have been the victims of mob or crowd action ranging from the roughing up of an American attaché in Moscow[83] to

---

[78] *Ibid.,* March 30, 1948, p. 3. Bankhead, known for his "tight" border policy, had testified before the United States House Un-American Activities Committee which was probing illegal entry of Communists and undesirable aliens from Canada.

[79] *Ibid.,* May 3, 1959, p. 20.

[80] For example armed men attacked Colonel Luis Trujillo Reynoso, Dominican Military Attaché in Haiti, at his Port-au-Prince home (*Ibid.,* June 24, 1959, p. 13), and two Chinese attacked Anadan Andrew, an Indian messenger for the United States in New Delhi, in an attempt to wrest away the telegrams he was packing (*Ibid.,* November 29, 1959, p. 22).

[81] For details of the case see *ibid.,* January 30, 1959, p. 2; February 1, p. 1; February 8, p. 12.

[82] By the Fukuoka District Court on February 7, 1959. The Japanese government pointed out that the direct victim of Matsushima's attack was not Fedorenko but a Japanese official traveling with the ambassador whose face was slapped and Japanese railroad security officers who suffered bruises and hurts from kicks and blows. Letter and Memorandum to the writer from Kazuhiko Ishihara, Legal Attaché, Embassy of Japan, Washington, D.C., September 18, 1962.

[83] The U.S. Embassy in Moscow charged that Navy Commander Raymond D. Smith, Assistant Naval Attaché, was "physically assaulted and forcibly deprived of items of personal property by allegedly non-official Soviet citizens," before being detained for four and one-half hours by two militia officers. "U.S. Protests Soviet Violation of Attaché's Diplomatic Rights," *DSB,* XLVII (October 29, 1962), p. 654.

the disruption of a diplomatic address in Latin America.[84] A United States courier was injured in Cairo in 1951 by a crowd which mistook him for a Britisher,[85] and a group of United States Embassy personnel narrowly escaped being lynched by an angry crowd in Leopoldville in 1960 after their automobile had knocked down and killed a Congolese cyclist.[86] Diplomatic personnel also have been victims of internal conflict, as, for example, on Cyprus, in the Middle East, and elsewhere.[87]

It is difficult to determine from the scattered reports the precise adherence or the lack of adherence to rules of international law in these cases. It is obvious, however, that in many of the incidents involving Communist and non-Communist nations the traditional procedures were distorted by the conflicting claims, and charges and counter-charges replaced the accepted pattern of apology, restitution, etc. In other instances, there was no substantial evidence to indicate that nations adhere wholly to accepted diplomatic practices. At times, the Western version of diplomatic procedures was not compatible with traditions of the new nations. For example, in the African traffic case, the *New York Times* reported that Congolese officials apparently were unimpressed by the accident or the mob attacks since such scenes are standard sequels of accidents, which take a high toll in Africa. In some areas of sub-Saharan Africa, drivers are instructed to continue directly to the nearest police station and file a report rather than stop if they have killed or injured a person accidentally.[88]

The diplomatic agent's immunity apparently is not violated if he is injured as a consequence of his own unjustifiable behavior or if he willfully places himself in a dangerous position,[89] or if he provokes attack

---

[84] United States Ambassador Carl W. Strom was unable to deliver a scheduled lecture at Cochabamba, in Central Brazil, on November 12, 1950, where a crowd which he said was dominated by Communists stoned his car and threw tear gas into the auditorium. *New York Times,* November 16, 1960, p. 13; November 19, p. 2; November 22, p. 10.

[85] *Ibid.,* November 27, 1951, p. 17.

[86] *Ibid.,* November 21, 1960, pp. 1, 12. Two of the four Americans in the car, Chief Warrant Officer Clyde St. Lawrence, member of the staff of the United States military attaché and Frank Carlucci, Second Secretary, were beaten and knifed. A motorist saved St. Lawrence from the mob and Carlucci managed to get aboard a passing bus.

[87] Five other Americans, all attached to the United States Consulate in Cyprus, were injured by the bomb which killed Boteler. *Ibid.,* June 17, 1956, p. 1.

[88] *Ibid.,* June 17, 1956, p. 1.

[89] *United States v. Liddle,* 2 Wash. C.C. 205 (1808).

through behavior incompatible with the character of his office,[90] or if he first assaults another person.[91] But states do have the responsibility of taking "reasonable steps"[92] in the protection of diplomatic personnel from attack and of extending to them special treatment.[93] Nations in general have recognized this responsibility in the post-World War II period. This not only encompasses efficient police protection,[94] but courts also have granted the diplomat a preferred status in considering damage claims. Perhaps the most graphic, if not the most significant, illustration of this practice was an Italian court's award of damages to a French diplomat for a finger injury which prevented him from engaging in the diplomatic pastime of shaking hands.[95] On the other hand, the laxity

---

[90]*The State v. Acuña Araya* (Costa Rica, 1927), *AD* (1927–1928), Case No. 243. A national had been charged with assaulting the Peruvian chargé d'affaires *ad interim* and calling him a "miserable coward" and a "discredit to your country." The court ruled that diplomatic immunity had not been violated since it appeared that the Peruvian had a moment previously called the defendant a "miserable character" and a "drunkard" and made a gesture as though to strike the Costa Rican with an umbrella. The court conceded that the diplomat was entitled to immunity both under international law and the Costa Rican penal code but that such immunity did not apply if the diplomat provoked an attack. "That it is a principle of public international law that offences by word or deed perpetrated to the injury of a diplomatic agent do not constitute an attempt against the inviolability if the agent offended 'through conduct indiscreet, blameworthy or incompatible with his public character' has exposed himself to the insult or to the offence."

[91] "If a foreign minister commits the first assault he forfeits his immunity so far as to excuse the defendant for returning it." Moore, IV, 624; see also *United States v. Ortega,* 4 Wash. C.C. 531 (1825).

[92] Article 27, Vienna Convention.

[93] See *United States (Chapman Claim) v. Mexico,* United States-Mexico, General Claims Commission, 1930 (Opinions of Commissioners, 1931), 121, cited in Herbert W. Briggs (ed.), *The Law of Nations* (2d ed.; New York: Appleton-Century-Crofts, Inc., 1952), pp. 697–703.

[94] For example, United States diplomats reported amazingly efficient police action in two robbery cases. Two men were seriously wounded while trying to escape following the stealing of 70,000 pesetas ($6,400) from Lieutenant Colonel Robert B. Stimpson, United States Military Attaché in Spain. *New York Times,* June 16, 1951, p. 2. United States Ambassador Loy Henderson reported to the Iranian police that his pocket was picked while he stood in a crowd gathered to welcome home Premier Mohammed Mossadegh from a foreign tour. "Then the fur began to fly, and before I hardly knew what happened police handed my wallet to me." *Ibid.,* November 25, 1951, p. 40.

[95] Jean Meziere, a former French consul general in Genoa, was awarded damages of 4,000,000 lire (about $6,500) in 1959 from a Genoa transport concern whose truck was judged responsible for an accident three years earlier in which the diplomat suffered a fractured finger. Meziere's lawyer claimed that the injury seriously hampered the envoy's diplomatic career in that it prevented him from taking part in many social and public events. The attorney argued that shaking hands is an "important act of diplomatic life." *Ibid.,* July 27, 1959, p. 6.

and·indifference revealed by local officials in some cases have been flagrant.[96]

In a series of "threat" incidents, governments responded in a positive and emphatic manner. These occurrences involved individuals or groups who opposed either the attitudes and actions of individual diplomats or the policies of the sending states and who engaged in their own form of psychological warfare — issuing death threats, a not uncommon occurrence on the "firing line" of diplomacy.[97] This technique appears to have gained its greatest popularity in the Latin American countries, and several United States ambassadors have been numbered among potential victims. In 1950, the press carried stories of reported threats against the life of Richard C. Patterson, United States Ambassador to Guatemala and an outspoken foe of communism, for allegedly interfering in internal affairs of that country, a charge which the State Department emphatically denied.[98] In 1960, the State Department and the FBI said Castro agents had been assigned to assassinate Robert C. Hill, United States Ambassador to Mexico, who had suggested that Mexico's sugar quota to the United States be increased.[99] In 1951, the Spanish government warned United States Ambassador Stanton Griffis that "anti-Franco" elements were plotting his assassination.[100] Two assassination threats from Vietminh terrorists were received the same year by Donald R. Heath, American Minister to Indochina. [101] Of an equally serious nature was the death note signed by a "National Committee for National Freedom" and addressed to the United States (H. A. Doolittle) and Swedish consuls in Cairo. The writers said Doolittle ignored a previous demand that he fly the Egyptian flag with the United States colors.[102]

The receiving states avoided serious international repercussions by taking precautionary measures to prevent harm from befalling the threatened diplomats. For example, the Spanish government assigned four plain-clothesmen to keep constant watch over Griffis,[103] and special details

---

96 A retired United States diplomat reported that "one of our diplomatic personnel (non-American) was murdered due to the failure of the host-government to furnish adequate protection." He apparently referred to the Semerjibashian case, *supra*, p. 53.

97 See *New York Times*, December 25, 1951, p. 30.

98 *Ibid.*, March 31, 1950, p. 28; April 6, pp. 1, 8; April 7, pp. 1, 18; April 11, p. 14.

99 *Ibid.*, July 4, 1960, p. 2. Cuba had traditionally opposed any increase in the Mexican quota.

100 *Ibid.*, August 12, 1951, p. 21.

101 *Ibid.*, December 25, 1951, p. 30.

102 *Ibid.*, March 27, 1960, p. 14.

103 *Ibid.*, August 12, 1951, p. 21.

of Mexican police were assigned to protect Hill for more than a year.[104] In 1948, the Cuban government said it had taken "precautionary measures" to prevent a reported plot against the United States and Mexican ambassadors.[105] It might also be noted that diplomats were required to take special precautionary measures in their own behalf. The State Department said in 1950 that it had ordered diplomats in certain posts in Southeast Asia to carry firearms for protection,[106] and Griffis carried a pistol as part of his beach equipment while vacationing in San Sebastian.[107]

It appears obvious from these publicly reported cases that diplomacy is a rather "dangerous game."[108] A number of persons entitled to some form of diplomatic protection were killed; scores were threatened, harassed, and injured. The position of the diplomat seems less secure than it was in the earlier periods. This can be explained partly, but certainly not entirely, by the emergence of the Soviet Union, with its differing concepts of diplomacy and diplomatic privileges and immunities, and of the Asian-African nations, with less than full acceptance of a system which stems from European cultures and traditions.

In the death cases, there appeared to be a reasonable adherence to the procedures of diplomatic tradition — apologies, attempts to punish the culprits, etc. In the attack cases involving government agents, perhaps a new chapter in diplomacy is now being written. There was no question of the host state's apologizing or punishing persons involved since, almost invariably, the host state contended that it was the wronged party. In attempting to achieve ends through political manipulation rather than through military action, states may be tending to become less strict in their adherence to traditional courtesies and rights.

Most of the assault and attack cases involving nonofficial personnel were of such a nature (e.g., mobs, snipers, etc.) as to make it extremely difficult if not impossible to apprehend and punish the guilty parties. Perhaps states were not as zealous as they might have been in ferreting

---

[104] According to sources quoted by the Associated Press, *Minneapolis Tribune,* July 3, 1960, p. 2.

[105] *New York Times,* October 26, 1948, p. 7.

[106] *Ibid.,* June 18, 1950, p. 4.

[107] *Ibid.,* August 12, 1951, p. 21.

[108] It is difficult to compare the period with earlier eras since most writers in international law have confined their illustrations to the handful of well publicized cases, such as those found in Hackworth, Hyde, Lauterpacht-Oppenheim, *et al.,* and to the judicial decisions. This writer has found no studies which attempted to include a wide range of incidents below the *cause célèbre* level, or which did not reach the judicial stage, or which were not readily accessible in the conventional sources. The difficulty in finding this material is recognized, and the limitations of this present effort have already been mentioned.

out the offenders. In situations where states were at political odds, such laxity is understandable.[109] In the more traditional type of attack (e.g., as that on the Russian Fedorenko), the host state tended to fulfill its international obligations. And in cases of threats against the diplomat, there seems to be little question but that the receiving state had no desire to become involved with any diplomatic corpse.

Arrest and Detention

While the failure of states to provide adequate protection for threatened diplomats or the failure to punish offenders — especially if they held official positions — constituted a serious breach of traditional diplomatic practice, a more widespread type of infringement since the end of World War II has been the arrest and detention of diplomatic agents. An analysis of various materials indicates a high incidence of police interference with diplomatic freedom. While this development has not been confined to the Soviet Union and its Eastern European partners, a majority of the arrest and detention incidents studied have involved agents stationed in these countries. These actions do not appear to be unguided or irresponsible; rather, new rules are being devised for the treatment of diplomats in a "closed" Communist society.

The arrest and detention of diplomats, as such, is not a new development in international relations. The *cause célèbre* in this category still remains *The Mattueof Case* which prompted the British Parliament in 1708 to pass its first diplomatic immunity law.[110] On July 21, 1708, M. de Mattueof (Mathveoff, Matveev), the Russian Ambassador to England who was about to present his letters of recall, was arrested on the streets of London by officers on the basis of a warrant obtained by merchants to whom he owed money. He was treated with violence and indignity and confined for a short period. Although the Queen apologized and declared that the offenders would be rigorously prosecuted, he left without presenting his letters of recall.

Other cases of a similar nature have involved diplomats of various countries. In 1917, the American minister to Guatemala was briefly detained following his arrest by a police officer in the city of Guatemala.[111]

---

109 A parallel might be found in the pre-war United States-Mexican claims cases.

110 Act of Anne. The facts are taken from Briggs, pp. 763–765, who refers to Charles de Martens. *Causes Célèbres du Droit des Gens* (2d ed.; Leipzig, 1858), I, 73–96, for a more detailed account.

111 Hackworth, IV, 508.

In 1918, the Rumanian minister was arrested in Russia. He was released the next day after a stiff protest had been delivered by the American ambassador as dean of the diplomatic corps in Petrograd.[112]

Most arrest cases in themselves have not resulted in the rupture of diplomatic relations, although this did happen when a Maryland constable arrested the Iranian minister in a wild melee on November 27, 1935. While charges were dismissed on grounds of diplomatic immunity, a later reproof by Secretary of State Hull so angered the Iranian government that it closed its legation in Washington.[113]

Two points are clear: First, nations have on occasion arrested diplomatic agents, although the practice has been an exception to the rule of diplomatic immunity; second, it is universally accepted that diplomats are immune from arrest, detention, or imprisonment,[114] except, presumably, when they pose a threat to the security or safety of the receiving state or do not have their identity papers in their possession. For example, Iranian police claimed that the arrest of a Soviet diplomat in 1956 was legal since the Russian was without proper papers.[115] A precedent was found in an incident five years earlier involving a French attaché and the Czechoslovakian police.[116]

However, a survey of some publicly reported incidents since 1945[117] reveals a consistent pattern of arrests and detention of diplomats, ranging from petty harassment to subsequent judicial action and imprisonment, and involving ranks from minor functionaries to heads of diplomatic missions.[118]

---

[112] *Ibid.,* 508–509. See also *U.S. Foreign Relations, 1918, Russia,* I, 477.

[113] U.S., Department of State, *Press Releases,* XIII, No. 323 (December 7, 1935), 497, as cited by Briggs, p. 773. See section on Police Jurisdiction in Chapter 4 for comment on the case as an example of erroneous police action.

[114] "It seems to be universally recognized that a diplomatic minister is immune from bodily restraint, i.e., arrest or imprisonment in the country to which he is accredited." *Bergman v. de Sièyes,* 71 F. Supp. 334 (1946); *AD* (1947), Case No. 73, 151. The diplomatic agent "shall not be liable to any form of arrest or detention." Article 29, Vienna Convention.

[115] Major Anatoli Kuznetsov, Soviet Assistant Military Attaché, was arrested, while in the company of an Iranian warrant officer in an automobile which contained secret documents, and ordered expelled. Iran said the arrest of Kuznetsov was legal since he carried no identification papers and was not in an official diplomatic car and thus not immune to arrest. *New York Times,* March 2, 1956, pp. 1, 7.

[116] The Czechoslovakian police stopped Colonel J. Gastaldo, French Military Attaché, who had not yet received his credentials. A scuffle ensued. The police later apologized when Gastaldo's identity was established. However, the French attaché admitted being at fault for not having his papers in his possession. *Ibid.,* January 7, 1951, p. 6.

[117] Primarily from the *Department of State Bulletin, The Times* (London), and the *New York Times.*

[118] Most of the incidents which progressed beyond the arrest stage will be covered in other chapters.

The first category of cases involved what appeared to be little more than harassment of diplomatic personnel by detention for brief periods to several days. Many diplomats were detained only long enough for them to produce their identification and to respond to a few questions.[119] Victor Cavendish-Bentwick, the British Ambassador who had been implicated in an internal matter, was detained for an hour and released by Polish authorities.[120] In contrast, two members of a Canadian military mission were held by the Russians for twelve days.[121] However, a detention for several hours[122] or about a day[123] appeared to be a more common practice. In addition to objections expressed over undue delays in holding diplomats under custody, Americans have been especially incensed over the gunpoint searching of diplomats.[124]

A second group of cases, involving diplomats who were carrying cameras, all occurred in the Soviet Union and Eastern Europe. The pattern of arrest was similar in each of the cases, accusations of taking pictures in "forbidden zones" which extended from military installations to department store queues, followed by penalties ranging from expulsion on espionage charges to reprimands and confiscation of the film.

A typical case involved two diplomats: Paul Green, Attaché, and

---

[119] For example, the detention of a Swedish language expert in Moscow for "undiplomatic" actions *(The Times* [London], February 18, 1957, p. 7), and a Cuban attaché who had rushed to the aid of a compatriot who was being deported by police at Rio de Janeiro *(New York Times,* August 2, 1960, p. 7).

[120] *New York Times,* January 3, 1947, p. 11.

[121] The pair, J. D. M. Weld, of the External Affairs Department, and Captain A. W. Clabon of the National Defense Department, apparently became lost in East Prussia on a trip from Warsaw. *Ibid.,* November 25, 1947, p. 3.

[122] Two incidents will illustrate the point. A Yugoslav military attaché was detained for several hours by Bulgarian police in Sofia, an action which Yugoslavia interpreted as an attempt to prevent its diplomatic representatives in Sofia "from carrying on with their duties." *Ibid.,* May 10, 1952, p. 8. Two United States military attachés refused to leave their car when halted by Russian troops in Hungary and were questioned for five hours through the auto window. *Ibid.,* April 8, 1957, p. 1.

[123] For example, four United States consular employees were held by the Russians for twenty-four hours after their boat drifted from the British to the Russian side of Travemunde Bay in Germany. *Ibid.,* June 1, 1949, p. 3. Also, Colonel Joseph D. Mobutu's army regime in the Congo arrested and detained for one day a secretary of the Ghanian Embassy, Lovelace Measch. *Ibid.,* November 17, 1960, p. 1; November 19, p. 1. He was expelled a week later with other Ghanian diplomats after relations had been severed by the two nations. *Ibid.,* November 23, 1960, p. 1.

[124] In 1947, Senator William Knowland told the Senate that "a Mr. Ferguson" in a car bearing an American flag was stopped by Rumanian authorities and searched at gunpoint. (C. Vaughn Ferguson was listed by the State Department as Second Secretary and Vice Consul in Bucharest at the time.) Senator Knowland denounced the action as a "police state" method. *Ibid.,* December 9, 1947, p. 11. Ten years later, Marine Sergeant Robert James Mott, guard at the United States Embassy in Damascus, was arrested at gunpoint while he was en route home from a Halloween party in Arab dress. He was released ten hours later. *Ibid.,* November 3, 1957, p. 15.

Wayne W. Fisher, Third Secretary and Vice Consul, and two clerks, Peggy Maggard and Virginia Garr, all assigned to the United States Legation in Rumania.[125] The four were arrested September 6, 1948, at the city of Giurgiu on a charge of "taking photographs in a forbidden zone" of the city and port area.[126] They were held sixteen hours without food or water and without being able to communicate with the American Legation.[127] The State Department claimed that the group had taken only seven pictures, the subjects being a herd of water buffalo, a native well, an ox cart, and a peasant, and all more than thirty miles from the military and port facilities at Giurgiu.[128]

The Rumanian government maintained that the four Americans had used their diplomatic status to cover espionage activities and requested their recall in the "shortest possible time."[129] The United States government complied but "categorically" rejected the Rumanian statement and energetically protested "the inexcusable action of the Rumanian authorities in detaining members of the American Legation in denial of the diplomatic courtesy such officials are customarily entitled to expect."[130]

This disagreement over what actually had been filmed typified the "camera" cases. In a series of incidents in which Communist officials in Eastern Europe claimed pictures had been taken of forbidden military zones or installations, the accused diplomats countered that their camera subjects, in turn, had been "a ruined castle,"[131] a road sign,[132] and family

---

[125] "American Diplomatic Personnel Detained in Rumania," *DSB*, XIX (September 26, 1948), 403–407.

[126] *Ibid.*, p. 404.

[127] The Americans later pointed out that their identities could have been quickly verified by a check with the Rumanian Ministry of Foreign Affairs.

[128] "American Diplomatic Personnel . . . ," *DSB*, XIX, 405-406.

[129] *Ibid.*, p. 405. Acting Minister of Foreign Affairs Eduard Mezincescu charged that "this is not the first time employees of the United States Government, having an official mission and enjoying diplomatic protection accorded by the Rumanian Government in accordance with international usage, have undertaken actions or committed deeds which affect the security of the Rumanian state." He added that the group "used the status of diplomatic immunity . . . to carry out an act of espionage by obtaining photographic documents affecting the national territorial defense" of Rumania. *Ibid.*

[130] *Ibid.*, p. 403.

[131] The camera and identification papers of John M. Cabot, American Chargé d'Affaires in Yugoslavia, were seized, then later returned without apology or explanation, by local authorities in the small town of Pec on May 2, 1947. He claimed that he had taken no pictures except for a ruined castle. Following an American protest, the Foreign Ministry expressed regret over what it called a "misunderstanding," the apology being unique in this series of incidents. *New York Times,* May 14, 1947, p. 9.

[132] As claimed by three secretaries of the United States Embassy in Vienna who were detained near the Austro-Hungarian border by Russian soldiers who charged that they had photographed forbidden military installations. *Ibid.,* October 6, 1953, p. 12.

groups and landscapes.[133] Other diplomatic personnel were detained, and in some cases expelled, on similar charges of photographing restricted buildings. In a 1954 case, two Americans were detained on charges of photographing the Stalin Auto Works in Moscow.[134] The State Department said by their actions the Soviet police "violated the diplomatic immunity of the pair."[135] In a similar case in 1957, two U.S. military attachés were expelled for "espionage" after their arrest on charges of photographing a restricted building.[136] In a 1964 case two attachés were denied future travel rights.[137] Other foreign personnel found that Communist police considered a vacation photograph,[138] a May Day parade,[139] and a line of customers at a department store[140] as part of the "forbidden zones."

Communist diplomats apparently had less camera trouble while on diplomatic assignment, although an "authoritative police source" in

---

[133] Colonel James C. Todd, United States Military Attaché at Budapest, and his assistant, Captain Thomas R. Gleason, so identified their pictures after they had been halted and questioned for five hours through an auto window by Soviet military authorities on a charge by Hungarian police that they had taken pictures of a Soviet occupied barracks. *Ibid.,* April 8, 1957, p. 1.

[134] The two, Lieutenant (j.g.) Arthur R. Hasley, Assistant U.S. Naval Attaché, and Miss Joyce Marshall, a translator, denied the accusation but were detained three hours and their camera and film confiscated. They both identified themselves by showing diplomatic cards but were refused permission for one and one-half hours in calling the embassy and were subjected to the "indignity" of being photographed by police. *Ibid.,* August 7, 1954, p. 2; "Detention of Staff Members of U.S. Embassy at Moscow," *DSB,* XXXI (August 23, 1954), 274.

[135] "Detention of Staff Members . . . ," *DSB,* XXXI, 274.

[136] The two, Marine Captain Paul R. Uffelman and Navy Lieutenant William S. Lewis, U.S. Assistant Military Attachés in Moscow, were also taken to a police station, and the film was removed from their cameras. *New York Times,* February 8, 1957, pp. 1, 2.

[137] Navy Commander Stuart Savage and Navy Lieutenant Leonard Anthony Bracken were ordered, along with three other attachés accused on different charges, to do no more traveling around the Soviet Union for ninety days. Savage and Bracken had been accused of taking illegal photographs in Leningrad on February 14, 1964. *Arizona Daily Star,* April 14, 1964, p. 14.

[138] Karl Verdonck, Netherlands Economic Attaché in Belgrade, was forced to give up his camera on a charge of taking a picture while passing through Sarajevo in Yugoslavia while en route back to his post from a vacation on the Adriatic coast. *New York Times,* September 24, 1947, p. 4.

[139] Martin Bowe, United States Consul in Prague, and his wife were queried, their film held for inspection, then released, for photographing the parade. *Ibid.,* May 3, 1949, p. 3.

[140] The British Embassy in Moscow reported that two of its staff members, David C. Thomas, Third Secretary, and Michael G. F. Duncan, Second Secretary, were accosted by irate citizens after Thomas took pictures of a queue before a sales counter for scarves in an Odessa department store. The British diplomats were held for two and one-half hours in jail while they were being questioned by police and denounced by Soviet citizens for charges ranging from espionage to defaming the country. The film was developed and the men were released after police confiscated the three pictures of the queue. *Ibid.,* October 12, 1960, p. 12.

Rio de Janeiro said four members of the Russian Embassy staff were questioned about picture taking, then released after establishing their immunity.[141] This was the only incident involving photography by Communist diplomats noted in the course of research for this study.

A third category of arrests, and closely linked with and often overlapping the second, involved diplomats who were accused of transgressing in forbidden zones or involvement in some type of espionage activities. As might be expected, military attachés, who engage in a type of politically accepted espionage, were involved far more often than other types of diplomatic agents. The usual pattern of the "forbidden zones" cases was the halting of the attachés, normally traveling in pairs, detention for several hours, accusations of traveling in restricted areas, their release, and subsequent denial of all charges by the government involved. One of the more highly publicized cases, late in 1964, involved four attachés in Moscow — three American and one British — who were halted while traveling through Siberia and accused of espionage. British and American accounts of the incident indicated that Soviet officials broke into hotel rooms occupied by the attachés, restrained them while searching their luggage and confiscated some of their belongings. The Russians said they confiscated 900 photographs taken by the attachés along with twenty-six notebooks filled with incriminating evidence.[142]

Nations also are tending to be less cautious, not only in detaining diplomats, but in the manner of treatment.[143] If protests are to be taken at face value, physical mistreatment both in arrest and confinement is no longer a unique occurrence in this phase of diplomatic intercourse. For example, Communist police were accused of roughly handling a British diplomat[144] while Communist nations have hurled similar charges

---

[141] *Ibid.,* May 13, 1947, p. 13.

[142] *Ibid.,* October 6, 1964, p. 1; October 8, p. 1; October 9, p. 8; Many of the cases involved diplomatic exchanges, expulsion, etc., without arrest or detention. These arrest incidents are included at this point to illustrate a type of detention which seems to have become more common during the past decade.

[143] For example, nations rarely apologized over the "camera" and similar incidents discussed above since both of the disputing nations no doubt believed, or so stated for public consumption, that they were the wronged party. An exception involved Yugoslavian authorities who apologized for the seizure of a camera and films from American Chargé d'Affaires John M. Cabot. *Supra,* fn. 131.

[144] A British Secretary charged that he was "'battered about," his glasses broken, and his coat torn by Czech police in the process of forcing him into an automobile. *New York Times,* October 20, 1948, p. 4; *The Times* (London), October 19, 1948, p. 3. Another British diplomat, Roderick Sarell, First Secretary at the Legation in Bucharest, claimed that he was subjected to "high handed" methods following his arrest and detention for two hours on a charge of organizing a mass escape into Austria of Rumanian employees of the Legation. *New York Times,* July 28, 1949, p. 3; July 29, p. 6; August 14, p. 30; *The Times* (London), July 29, 1949, p. 5; August 15, p. 4.

at Western powers.[145] And not all cases have involved nations who are on rival sides of the international political conflict.[146]

The Chinese Communists were involved in one of the more bizarre cases of this nature, an incident in India which was described by Prime Minister Nehru as sounding "more like some piece of fiction than reality." Although the reports are conflicting, apparently a Chinese Communist defected, spent a night in American custody, then changed his mind and returned to the Chinese Consulate where he had worked as an official of the Chinese Import-Export Corporation. The Chinese, Chang Chien-yuh, left a taxi in which he had been accompanied by U.S. Marine Sgt. Robert Armstrong, security guard at the United States Consulate General. Armstrong then was forced into the Chinese Consulate and held for six hours during which time he reportedly was bound and mistreated. Armstrong filed a complaint charging the Chinese with illegal detention, but the case ended with Chang returning to China, and Nehru noted that while Armstrong had been abducted and assaulted, facts in the case were too vague for further action to be taken. Thus India was not forced into a position of settling a dispute between two powerful protagonists, neither of whom would have been pleased by an adverse decision.[147] Earlier, the Chinese Communists also had demonstrated a disregard for diplomatic procedures in the arrest and alleged mistreatment of a U.S. foreign service officer on the quixotic charge of obstructing a parade.[148]

---

[145] In 1961, the Soviet Union expelled the Dutch Ambassador in protest against what it called the mishandling of its ambassador, Panteleimon K. Ponomarenko, by Dutch police. The Netherlands Government had declared Ponomarenko *persona non grata* following a scuffle with police who were attempting to interrogate a Soviet woman whose husband had defected to the West. *Arizona Daily Star,* October 10, 1961, p. 1A. In similar incidents, the Soviet Union protested the "frisking" of one of its Secretaries by British police *(New York Times,* June 28, 1952, p. 3) and the Polish government claimed that one of its vice consuls, who was arrested on a charge of espionage, was "severely beaten" while being interrogated by French police *(The Times* [London], November 30, 1949, p. 3).

[146] For example, the United States complained to Israel that a code clerk was bound and mistreated and accused of being a British spy. "Kidnaping of American Code Clerk in Jerusalem Protested," *DSB,* XIX (September 5, 1948), 301. The United States and Brazil also protested the halting and searching of diplomatic vehicles. *Tucson Daily Citizen,* May 2, 1963, p. 19.

[147] For the United States account of the incident, see "U.S. Protests Communists' Seizing of Consular Employee in Bombay," *DSB,* XLI (December 21, 1959), 902–904. For a newspaper account, see *New York Times,* November 28, 1959, p. 1; November 29, p. 1; November 30, p. 1; December 1, p. 3; December 3, p. 21; December 18, p. 11; January 13, 1960, p. 8; January 23, p. 3; February 18, p. 3.

[148] The American, Vice Consul William M. Olive, was held for sixty-six hours in a wayside police station and, according to State Department spokesmen, was handcuffed for twenty-four hours, subsisted on bread and insufficient water for three days, and was "brutally beaten" and humiliated. The Communists claimed that Olive signed an apology for assaulting policemen and damaging police station property during an altercation, but United States Consul General John M. Cabot countered that the action was taken under "duress." For details on this case, see *New York Times,* July 8, 1949, p. 1; July 10, p. 1; July 13, p. 17.

Diplomats also have been subjected to some rather humiliating and bitter experiences in Africa.[149] For example, U.S. consular representatives were beaten and forced to "eat" the American flag by rebels in Leopoldville during the 1964 Congo uprising. And in Brazzaville, in the former French Congo, an American aid official reportedly was held incommunicado for sixty hours in a cell so crowded with criminals he was unable to lie down. The Russians also were subjected to some of this barefisted diplomacy in the Congo prior to suspension of diplomatic relations with the U.S.S.R. by the Leopoldville government. Two Soviet diplomats, later expelled, were reportedly arrested, beaten, and stripped of important documents while three other Communist diplomats were forced to stand for three hours in the rain before troops permitted them to take cover.

Although the materials are limited, the publicized documents noted in the course of this study strongly indicate that the practice of arrest and detention, while not an innovation, became an important by-product of the cold war in what might be called a modern version of the Byzantine school of diplomacy.[150] Communist officials do not consider it in their national interest to permit unlimited prowling through their territory by diplomats and staff members, perhaps justifiably so in many cases. An analysis of reports on the arrest and detention of 69 diplomatic officers and staff members in the 1946–1960 period shows that a high proportion of these incidents were in Communist countries.[151] Of the 69 persons entitled to diplomatic immunity who were arrested and detained, 52 were in Communist countries at the time; 5 each in the Middle East, South America, and Europe; and 1 each in the Far East

---

[149]See *Ibid.,* November 25, 1964, p. 16; March 13, 1965, p. 2; (Western Edition), November 21, 1963, p. 1; November 22, p. 1.

[150]See Harold Nicolson, *The Evolution of Diplomatic Method* (New York: Macmillan and Company, 1954), pp. 24–27, for comments on diplomatic methods of the Byzantine emperors. The term is also used by Charles W. Thayer, *Diplomat* (New York: Harper & Brothers, 1959), p. 203.

[151]It should be emphasized that these reports come primarily from newspapers in the United States and Great Britain and thus are only a crude sampling. A full study would require considerable resources in men and materials, and the release of official records. The material used no doubt distorts some national representation. While Western media tend to emphasize incidents which illustrate a Communist intransigeance toward traditional Westernized diplomacy, the press probably does not follow a rigid, calculated policy of censoring or deleting incidents which fail to support Western policy. A number of incidents which involved neither the United States nor Great Britain were found in the reports. Furthermore, all usable items uncovered through a check of the *New York Times* Index, country by country, and the diplomacy and diplomatic privileges and immunities sections of *The Times* (London) are included. The study thus is representative to the extent that these news reports represent a cross-section of events bearing on diplomatic immunity. Nonetheless, it would appear as if these sources are at least useful tools for investigating the modern period.

and Africa. [152] Of the 69 diplomats, 33 represented the United States (with 30 in Communist countries); 8, Great Britain; 7, the Soviet Union; 4, France; and the rest, scattered. In all but 3 of the 69 cases, a Communist country was involved either as the arresting country or in the person of the detained diplomat.

As might be expected, a majority, or 51, of those held under various charges were (as nearly as could be determined from available accounts) in the officer class. Of the 51, 25 were either ranking secretaries or attachés, chiefly military. Of the 18 staff members involved, 15 were in the secretarial-clerical categories. The remainder ranged from 2 ambassadors to an embassy electrician. The stated reasons for arrest and detention reveal even more how diplomacy reflects mid-twentieth century international politics: 43 were picked up for charges based on threats to state security;[153] 7 for interfering with internal affairs.[154] Twelve others were detained for a variety of reasons ranging from losing their way while traveling to interfering with police and blocking a parade.

States also apparently have been remiss in notifying heads of missions prior to the detention of embassy employees, although it appears as if this practice, as stated for example by the British Foreign Office in 1948,[155] is accepted under the rules of international law. In some instances, those arrested were denied the right to call their missions and were held for extended periods even after showing their diplomatic identification. The period of detention varied and, while excessive, did not appear to be extreme and apparently was designed (a) as a means of harassment[156] and (b) as a means to control foreigners in a "closed" society. In 37 of the 69 cases, the period during which the diplomatic agent was detained was stated. Of these 37 cases, 28 were detained less

---

[152]The number of arrests by countries: U.S.S.R., 18; Rumania and Czechoslovakia, 8 each; Hungary and Poland, 5 each; Brazil 4; Yugoslavia and Bulgaria, 3 each; China and Switzerland, 2 each; and the United Arab Republic, Syria (before union), Israel, Iran, Turkey, Argentina, Italy, Great Britain, France, Pakistan, and the Congo, 1 each.

[153]Espionage, 7; taking photographs in restricted zones or of restricted buildings and areas, 22; involvement with espionage rings, 5; entering restricted zones, 5; and gathering or attempting to gather classified and military materials, 4.

[154]Distributing subversive literature, helping individuals evade local authorities, and involvement in "internal affairs," 2 each; engaged in an "internal plot," 1. These are the reasons given by the arresting state; without exception the sending state denied the accusations, often in vehement language. In 7 cases, no reason was given in the reports or the reason was not clear.

[155]*The Times* (London), October 19, 1948, p. 3.

[156]The Chinese Communist newspaper, the *Emancipation Daily,* noted that the treatment received by William M. Olive *(supra,* p. 68.) was a sample of what foreigners could expect and warned "all American imperialists to abandon provocative actions or take the consequences." *New York Times,* July 11, 1949, p. 8.

than 12 hours (assuming that 4 cases in which the time was stated as "several" hours fell within this limitation), and of these, 21 were in custody for 6 hours or less. Another 5 were held for periods ranging from 12 hours to 3 days and the remaining 4 were held for 12, 17, 30, and 41 days.

The reaction by the aggrieved powers, and understandably so, has been (a) to deny categorically charges placed against their diplomats and (b) to call the arresting nations sternly to task in the name of international law. Diplomatic notes of protest from the Western powers have bristled with such terms as "inexcusable"[157] and "improper and unwarranted."[158] The Communist powers displayed similar irritation both when involved with a Western power[159] and with each other.[160]

The widespread arrest and detention of diplomatic agents in the post-World War II period has its grave implications[161] and, although many precedents for the practice are found during the previous two centuries, may be a retrogression as far as traditional diplomatic practices are concerned. While the principle of diplomatic immunity from arrest and detention remains as a rule of international law among non-Communist states, it is a qualified principle as far as relations between Communist and non-Communist states are concerned since such arrests have become rather commonplace. It is also clear that these restrictions on diplomats are considered essential in a Communist state and will continue to be an offshoot of the co-existence of the rival political systems. The Communist nations apparently find such controls necessary in order

---

[157] By the United States Department of State (*DSB*, XIX [September 26, 1948], 403) and the British Foreign Office (quoted in the *New York Times,* July 29, 1949, p. 6).

[158] State Department quoted in the *New York Times,* October 3, 1960, p. 2.

[159] Bulgaria protested to the Turkish Legation in Sofia against a "rude violation" of diplomatic privileges and immunities of Dimiter Yanakiev, Vice Consul in Edirne on the Turkish frontier, when he was arrested in that city. *Ibid.,* April 8, 1951, p. 25.

[160] Newspapers in Belgrade reported the "gross ill-treatment" of Dragomir Vucinic, Yugoslav Minister to Austria, who was said to have been detained with his wife and insulted by Soviet sentries at the interzonal border in Austria. *Ibid.,* May 17, 1953, p. 14.

[161] However, the serious business of arresting envoys is not without its lighter side. For example, Italian police followed a suspicious person and arrested what they thought was a spy when the man was given an envelope. It turned out that the recipient was Dusan Fortic, Press Counsellor of the Yugoslav Legation in Rome, and the envelope contained nothing more compromising than the Italian translation of a speech delivered by the Yugoslav Foreign Minister. *Ibid.,* May 30, 1952, p. 3. Polish security police probably were even more embarrassed when, according to a report from an Austrian businessman, in their zeal to make arrests during the Poznan riots of 1956, they nabbed the Czechoslovakian minister by mistake. *Ibid.,* July 4, 1956, p. 5.

to protect their internal security and even arrests which appear to be little more than harassment might well be part of this protective pattern. The other reasons for detaining diplomats, entry into and photographing "forbidden zones," espionage activities, etc., are obviously in this category. Also the fact that most of those detained have been military attachés or others in the officer class supports this conclusion.

However, it would be naive to conclude that the actions by Communist authorities have been completely unjustified. The link between diplomacy and espionage, while perhaps stronger and more obvious in totalitarian nations, certainly is not restricted to Communist states today nor do these states bear sole responsibility for activities which might be classified as interference in international affairs of another nation. It is not surprising that nations would take measures to curb espionage activities and to curtail other undiplomatic excesses by diplomatic personnel. Nor is it strange that nations are more security conscious today than they were in the past. On the other hand, while arrest of diplomatic agents might be explained in these terms, the Communist reasoning still would not justify undue detention or mistreatment. Apparently, the periods of detention have been relatively brief, although it could be claimed that any period longer than that needed to display credentials or to call the embassy, legation, or foreign office is excessive; however, many cases of mistreatment ranging from physical assaults and threats to the humiliation of submitting to a police photographer, discourtesies, etc., have been noted. Also pressures which transcend normal relations apparently have been applied.

No doubt arrest and detention of envoys will continue as long as traditional and Byzantine diplomacy co-exist; however, efforts toward reaching agreement on the treatment of restrained diplomats might be useful.

Violation of Diplomatic Dignity

Most of the incidents involving assault, attack, arrest and detention violate the tradition that diplomatic personnel not only are entitled to personal inviolability but also are entitled to respectful treatment in accord with the dignity of their office. The physical mistreatment of a diplomat is a gross violation of this international practice; insulting behavior on the part of local authorities or petty harassments, while of a minor nature, still violate a basic rule of international law.

Except for the excessive zeal of some local officers, the United States has tended to extend to diplomats the rights and privileges of their offices and might be ranked among the liberal nations in this respect. However, this nation now finds it difficult to guarantee full privileges to a certain sector of the diplomatic corps — those envoys and their staffs from Africa and, to a lesser degree, those from Asia. The problem stems from an internal racial problem and is compounded by the fact that more than half of the diplomatic missions which have been accredited to the United States are from Asian and African countries. Long an irritant, the situation assumed ugly proportions in the early 1960's with the sharp increase in the number of African nations sending diplomats to Washington and to the United Nations.

The discrimination encountered by African diplomats in renting or leasing property and in patronizing restaurants, department stores, and barber shops is, in the words of Angier Biddle Duke, who at the time was Chief of Protocol for the Department of State, "most discouraging."[162] Secretary of State Dean Rusk, in a letter to the United States Attorney General, pinpointed the problem:

> Diplomatic representatives have met varying difficulties and limitations in living and carrying out their functions in this country because of racially discriminatory laws and practices. Many of these difficulties are never officially drawn to the attention of the Department of State, but the hurt and resentment are nevertheless lasting. On occasion, difficulties are of such a gross character as to call for investigation and official apologies, which, however, cannot correct the wrong.[163]

The Department, of course, is hampered by the fact that the discriminatory practices usually result from enforcement by state and local officials of state and local laws and regulations. In addition, some of the affronts are not easy to pinpoint, such as the voluntary waiving of immunities by African diplomats in order to obtain housing,[164] the gross overcharges by landlords for the official residents,[165] and other indirect methods of discrimination.[166]

---

[162] Cabell Phillips, "Officials Are Desperate Over Racial Barriers," *U.S. News and World Report,* L (June 12, 1961), 86–87.

[163] "Department Supports Desegregation in Interstate Bus Facilities," *DSB,* XLIV (June 19, 1961), 975–976. See also *New York Times,* October 20, 1964, p. 10.

[164] *New York Times,* February 19, 1961, p. 24. Normally, this immunity would protect diplomats from such legal action as suits for non-payment of rent or for vacating premises before the termination of a lease.

[165] Accusations along this line were reportedly made in 1961 by the Ambassadors from the Cameroon Republic and Mali. "Color in Diplomacy," *America,* CIV (February 18, 1961), 654.

[166] One technique, reportedly used by restaurants, is to seat colored diplomats at obscure tables. One unnamed diplomat reportedly observed that "It takes a little time to discover the places where you can dine and bring guests without embarrassment." *Ibid.*

The United States, as Rusk noted, has issued apologies in the more serious cases. One of the more embarrassing incidents involved Indian Ambassador Gaganvihari Lallubhai Mehta and his secretary who were directed from the dining room to a smaller room at the Houston International Airport with the explanation that the staff had been asked to show them every courtesy. The ambassador said later that he did not realize discrimination was involved and the mayor of Houston, a few days after the incident, said the move to the smaller room was to pay the ambassador honor as a dignitary. However, the restaurant manager was quoted at the time as saying that the Indians looked like Negroes and "the law is the law."[167] Apologies were issued on a wholesale basis: Secretary of State John Foster Dulles apologized to the Indian government and to the ambassador; the Houston mayor apologized to the ambassador and invited Mehta to his home, an invitation which was politely rejected; and United States Ambassador John Sherman Cooper called at the Indian Foreign Ministry in New Delhi to apologize informally.[168]

While the Mehta case was highly publicized, it has been the African diplomat who has encountered the brunt of the discriminatory practices in his quest for housing and in the use of public facilities in Washington, D.C., and New York City. The Department of State was again called upon to issue its regrets when C. C. Uchuno, Second Secretary of the Nigerian Embassy, was refused service at a Charlottesville, Virginia, railroad station restaurant on January 5, 1961. Secretary of State Christian Herter asked the Interstate Commerce Commission to investigate and expressed his "profound regret" for the "discourteous act."[169]

The refusal by restaurants to serve Negro diplomats has become one of the touchiest questions before the federal government. The Uchuno affair was only one of a long series. The State Department issued its regrets, and President Eisenhower invited the Finance Minister of Ghana to breakfast with him at the White House after the Negro official had been ejected from a restaurant in Dover, Delaware, in 1957.[170]

The Maryland section of Highway 40 between New York City and Washington has become the focal point of this problem. Most African and Asian nations cannot afford to maintain separate staffs in Washington and at the United Nations Headquarters in New York City. Thus

---

[167] Texas law forbids Negroes and whites from eating in the same dining room. However, the city of Houston's contract with the federal government for operating the airport includes a clause banning all discrimination at airport facilities. *New York Times*, August 24, 1955, p. 4; August 25, p. 23; August 28, p. 82.

[168] *Ibid.*, August 24, 1955, p. 4; August 25, p. 23.

[169] "U.S. Expresses Regret for Incident Involving Nigerian Diplomat," *DSB*, XLIV (January 30, 1961), 156–157.

[170] Plischke, p. 337.

the route between "the capital of the United States and the capital of the world" is "crowded with black limousines shuttling between the two cities."[171] One writer reported that between February and October of 1961 nine diplomats from African nations were refused service along the Maryland section of Route 40.[172] One of these diplomats was Dr. William H. Fitzjohn, Chargé d'Affaires of the Sierra Leone Mission who, with his chauffeur, was refused service at a Howard Johnson restaurant near Hagerstown, Maryland. President Kennedy expressed personal regrets, the State Department apologized, the mayor of Hagerstown expressed dismay, the restaurant changed its policy, and Dr. Fitzjohn was feted at a community dinner in Hagerstown.[173] In July of 1961 the governor of Maryland, under State Department pressure, issued a blanket apology to diplomats from Chad, Niger, Cameroon, and Togo who had been involved in similar incidents.[174]

Additional steps to head off housing and dining rebuffs have been taken by the State Department and other groups. The Department has established a Special Protocol Service Section; the Washington Real Estate Board sent out circulars offering to help new countries find housing; the Afro-American Institute established a liaison office to help African diplomats solve various problems.[175] The State Department went on record in support of an application by the United States government to the Interstate Commerce Commission to effect desegregation of facilities related to interstate bus transportation,[176] assisted in organizing prominent Washington realtors and apartment house operators to combat diplomatic discrimination,[177] and led in formulating a state-federal plan to head off future incidents.[178]

---

[171] J. Anthony Lukas, "Trouble on Route 40," *The Reporter,* XXV (October 26, 1961), 41.

[172] *Ibid.*

[173] *Ibid.*

[174] *Ibid.,* p. 42.

[175] See *ibid.; New York Times,* October 10, 1960, p. 10; December 11, p. 19; February 5, 1961, p. 2; "The Color Line in Diplomacy: Washington Tackles a New and Delicate Problem," *U.S. News and World Report,* L (March 27, 1961), 78–79; Betty Beale, "When African Diplomats Come to Washington," *U.S. News and World Report,* L (June 12, 1961), 87–88; and Phillips, *U.S. News and World Report,* L, 86–87.

[176] "Department Supports . . . ," *DSB,* XLIV, 975–976.

[177] "Housing Committee to Help Erase Discrimination Against Diplomats," *DSB,* XLV (July 24, 1961), 154.

[178] Officials of the Departments of State and Justice and White House representatives launched a program in 1961 at a meeting with spokesmen from seventeen states to discuss ways and means to prevent racial incidents against diplomats in restaurants and other public places. The state representatives agreed to cooperate with the federal government. "Campaign Launched in U.S. to Erase Race Incidents Involving Diplomats," *DSB,* XLIV (May 15, 1961), 732–733.

The cooperation of the states was solicited to prevent insult to African diplomats as they visited other parts of the nation. To coordinate the program, a nationwide network of governors' advisory committees was created and by 1963, according to Mr. Duke, because of gubernatorial cooperation "a diplomat can now travel without fear [of racial incidents] in all but a few States."[179] It is the goal of the State Department to extend this guarantee for human dignity to all fifty states.[180] In the Department's view, as expressed by Chester Bowles, Under Secretary of State, housing discrimination is not just a matter of promoting brotherhood, or of property rights, but rather "involves the very security of the nation."[181]

With the increase in the number of new nations and in the size of the African diplomatic establishments, both in Washington and New York City,[182] as well as more widespread diplomatic travel throughout the nation, the State Department no doubt will find pressures even greater in the future. The "menace of insulting incidents" still threatens these representatives of African nations,[183] a sad commentary on American democracy.[184]

---

[179] Angier Biddle Duke, "Protocol and the Conduct of Foreign Affairs," *DSB*, XLIX (November 4, 1963), 702.

[180] As Mr. Duke observed: "The day may someday come when leaders from any part of the world can travel in safety anywhere in this country." *Ibid.*

[181] "Housing Committee to Help...," *DSB*, XLV, 154. Bowles reasoned that young African diplomats, the future policy-makers in their nations, if rebuffed on racial grounds "will carry bitter feelings to their graves." *Ibid.*

[182] The influx of new African nations into the United Nations has created a similar problem in New York City, where there are some 5,000 diplomats and members of their families. Numerous African delegates and their families, who understandably refuse to be forced into the ghettos of Harlem, have encountered prejudice in their attempts to obtain adequate housing. It has been estimated that one-third of the approximate 80 African diplomats arriving for the 1960 General Assembly experienced difficulties in their quest for homes or apartments. Agencies such as the United States Mission to the United Nations, the United Nations Housing Office, the New York City Commission on Intergroup Relations; the State Commission Against Discrimination, the Hospitality Committee for United Nations Delegations and others, are cooperating in an attempt to convince landlords not to discriminate against the visiting diplomats. Heads of the U.S. Mission to the U.N. also have used the influence of their office in the campaign on behalf of the Africans. For a review of the situation by Nan Robertson see the *New York Times,* February 19, 1961, pp. 1, 24. In September, 1964, the First Secretary of the Mauritanian delegation to the United Nations, was attacked and injured by a group of white youths in New York City. The Afro-Asian nations officially protested to Secretary General U Thant. Such cases continue to plague U.S. officials who are attempting to reach a solution which will assure delegates that the city is anxious to offer them both security and hospitality. *Ibid.,* September 20, 1964, p. 122. Also see *ibid.,* December 20, 1964, p. 52, and Jane Kreiger Rosen, "Africans in Darkest New York," *New York Times Magazine,* February 28, 1965, pp. 31, 88–89.

[183] Mr. Duke observed in 1963 that "even in our nation's Capitol today it is not safe for some diplomats to go out and look for an apartment without first requesting the assistance of my office." Duke, *DSB*, XLIX, 702.

[184] As one publication noted: "It is a sad comment on democracy in the capitol of the world's greatest democracy that such a problem should even have arisen." "Diplomats Housing," *America,* CIV (October 22, 1960), 108.

However, both from the viewpoint of meeting international standards of conduct in coping with unfortunate incidents and from the viewpoint of taking a lead in attempting to minimize this type of insulting behavior within the framework of a federal system, the Department of State would seem to be acting in the most acceptable tradition of international conduct concerning the problem of diplomatic dignity and privilege.

CHAPTER 4

Immunities
From Criminal and Police
Jurisdiction

THE CONTENTION THAT VIRTUALLY ALL CATEGORIES of diplomatic personnel — from the envoy downward through the ranks of his retinue — are
immune from criminal jurisdiction of the courts of the host country appears to be accepted by most publicists and jurists.[1] The unequivocal
United States support of the doctrine[2] reflects a nearly universal rule as
was indicated by inclusion in the 1961 Vienna Convention of an article
providing for such immunities.[3]

In addition, the diplomat is entitled to police protection while at the
same time he is obligated to adhere to police regulations if they do not
interfere with his official duties.

Criminal Jurisdiction

Perhaps the strongest case for criminal immunity has been made in
Great Britain. Although writers disagree whether that historic landmark
of diplomatic legislation, the eighteenth century Act of Anne, applies to

---

[1] See "Diplomatic Immunity and the Criminal Law," *Law Journal,* LXVIII
(October 12, 1929), 226, and Joyce A. C. Gutteridge, "Immunities of the Subordinate Diplomatic Staff," *BYIL,* XXIV (1947), 150. Westlake also declares that
members of the diplomatic service "in any rank" are "exempt from the criminal
jurisdiction of the territory." John Westlake, *International Law* (Cambridge: At the
University Press, 1910), I, 276.

[2] The attitude of the American government was expressed in 1960 by a State
Department historian: "A diplomatic representative is . . . immune from arrest,
trial, or punishment for any criminal offense he may commit in the country to
which he is accredited. . . ." William Barnes, "Diplomatic Immunity From Local
Jurisdiction," *DSB,* XLIII (August 1, 1960), 177–178.

[3] Forty-five nations signed the Vienna Convention which states (Article 31)
without qualification: "A diplomatic agent shall enjoy immunity from the criminal
jurisdiction of the receiving state." See United Nations, Conference on Diplomatic
Intercourse and Immunities, 2 March - 14 April, 1961, *Official Records,* Vol. II:
Vienna Convention on Diplomatic Relations (A/CONF.20/14/Add.1) (New York,
1962), pp. 82–88 for text of the Convention; also in *AJIL,* LV (October, 1961),
1064–1077. Cited hereafter as Vienna Convention.

criminal cases,[4] the point is often made that no court of superior jurisdiction has ever even been called upon to decide whether diplomatic status carries immunity from the criminal law.[5] Quite simply stated, the executive branch rarely, if ever, institutes criminal suits against diplomats.[6] The absence of legal activity is often cited as the best evidence that envoys occupy such a favored position.[7] The British appear to be content to await possible future developments and let the courts decide the question[8] should a case ever arise.[9]

---

[4] Great Britain, Act of Parliament for Preserving the Privileges of Ambassadors and Other Publick Ministers of Foreign Princes and States, 7 Anne Ch. 12, 1708, I British and Foreign State Papers 903. "The original Grotian concept of immunity meant freedom from civil jurisdiction of the receiving state and it was upon this theory that the act was passed." Harvard Law School, "Research in International Law: I. Diplomatic Privileges and Immunities," *AJIL,* XXVI (April, 1932), Supp., p. 99. Under Anne, the immunity of ambassadors and suites in civil matters is complete, but in criminal matters "there seems to be no warrant in law for saying that the representatives of foreign countries are exempt from the original jurisdiction of this country, that privilege only extending to the King and to foreign sovereigns." "Diplomatic Privilege," *Law Times,* CLXV (January 28, 1928), 72. For an opposing view, see Adair who states that "there is not the slightest doubt that it [Act of Anne] provides, so far as an act of Parliament can, absolute legal protection to a criminal ambassador or to his criminal servant." E. R. Adair, *The Exterritoriality of Ambassadors in the Sixteenth and Seventeenth Centuries* (London: Longmans, Green and Co., 1929), p. 56. See also *ibid.,* pp. 88–89, 237–243.

[5] See D. C. Holland, "Diplomatic Immunity in English Law," *Current Legal Problems,* IV (1951), 97; J. T. Taylor, "Diplomatic Immunity," *Criminal Law Review* [n.v.] (April, 1955), p. 230; and *Halsbury's Laws of England,* ed. Lord Simonds (3rd ed.; London: Butterworth & Co. [Publishers] Ltd., 1954), VII, 269. In *The King v. Guerchy* (1765), 96 Eng. Reprint 315, the French Ambassador in London was indicted for soliciting an individual to assassinate another. On the application of the attorney general, a *nolle prosequi* was entered. This practice still is followed. Two centuries after the *Guerchy* case, a United States federal judge yielded to a "direct request" from Attorney General Robert F. Kennedy in dismissing espionage charges against Igor Y. Melekh, a Russian United Nations employee. *New York Times,* March 2, 1961, p. 1.

[6] Recent British practice illustrates this point. The British Home Secretary reported to the House of Commons that in the twelve-month period ended September 30, 1955, officials had brought to his attention ninety-three cases arising in England and Wales in which police refrained from taking criminal proceedings against foreign persons as the result of their diplomatic immunity being established. *The Times* (London), December 20, 1955, p. 9. This total represented about three per cent of the approximate 3,000 persons accredited with diplomatic immunity to Great Britain. *Ibid.,* October 22, 1954, p. 3; June 30, 1955, p. 5.

[7] Sir Cecil Hurst, *International Law: Collected Papers* (London: Stevens & Sons Limited, 1950), p. 217.

[8] This was the conclusion reached by a British committee which studied the problems of state and diplomatic immunities. See Great Britain, Foreign Office, Parliamentary Papers *(Reports),* Cmd. 8460, January, 1952, "Report on Diplomatic Immunity by an Interdepartmental Committee on State Immunities," p. 6.

[9] One British writer conjectured: "Probably the question will never be decided by the courts owing to executive policy in not initiating prosecutions in the case of diplomats. If the question ever does come before the courts, then the consensus of opinion amongst writers on international law, the tendency of the courts to regard the rules of international law on diplomatic immunity as a part of the common law, and the provisions of the Act of 1708 seem to suggest that the courts would favor exemptions from jurisdiction." Holland, *Cur. Leg. Prob.,* IV, 98.

Publicists in Great Britain and elsewhere support this position of absolute immunity from criminal jurisdiction. Many have claimed categorically that under both the theory and practice of international law diplomatic agents cannot be tried or punished by local courts for committing an ordinary crime "in any circumstance whatever."[10] These writers assert that no instance has ever been cited in which a diplomatic agent has been subject to the criminal jurisdiction of the country to which he is accredited without his consent.[11]

Courts also have strongly stated the case for criminal immunity, primarily along the following lines: exemption of diplomats from jurisdiction in criminal cases, allowed both under municipal legislation and general rules of international law, is necessary both to maintain public order and to preserve free and unfettered relations among states.[12] Blackstone succinctly stated the doctrine when he wrote that the "security of ambassadors" takes priority over the punishment of a particular crime.[13]

It is not intended that this immunity should give the diplomat a license to violate the laws of the receiving state. Although the record is replete with reports of instances where envoys conspired against the host state and were not subjected to local jurisdiction,[14] there is general

---

[10] This unqualified reference is found in L. Oppenheim, *International Law,* Vol. I, *Peace,* ed. H. Lauterpacht (8th ed.; London: Longmans, Green and Co., 1955), p. 790. Other publicists concur. Satow notes that such immunity extends to any "ordinary crime." Sir Ernest Satow, *A Guide to Diplomatic Practice,* ed. Sir Neville Bland (4th ed.; London: Longmans, Green and Co., 1957), p. 181. Fenwick concurs that public ministers are "completely immune" from criminal jurisdiction. Charles G. Fenwick, *International Law* (3rd ed.; New York: Appleton-Century-Crofts, Inc., 1948), p. 469. Woolsey stresses the functional necessity of criminal immunity and the unanimity among writers as to its acceptance. Theodore Dwight Woolsey, *Introduction to the Study of International Law,* ed. Theodore Salisbury Woolsey (6th ed.; New York: Charles Scribner's Sons, 1898), p. 134.

[11] The claim is made by Hurst, p. 127, and has been widely quoted, for example, by Satow, p. 181, and Graham Stuart, *American Diplomatic and Consular Practice* (2d ed.; New York: Appleton-Century-Crofts, Inc., 1952), p. 251.

[12] Based on *dicta* from the *Case of Ludovico Cenzi* (Argentina, 1927), *AD* (1929–1930), 303, fn. The court observed: "The exemption constitutes a principle of public order, necessary for the maintenance of international relations, which recognizes as its cause the inviolability which ought to protect diplomatic agents and the necessity of assuring their independence and guaranteeing their security; for in the field of international relations, the utility or convenience of respecting these privileges of ambassadors is, as Grotius says, of more weight than punishing crimes." *Ibid.* The court reached a similar conclusion in a series of auto injury cases involving a Japanese naval attaché, *Case of Ito* (Argentina, 1934), *AD* (1933–1934), 383, fn.; a British commercial counsellor, *In re Irving* (Argentina, 1934), *AD* (1933–1934), 383, fn.; and a Paraguayan commercial attaché, *In re Alberto Grillon (Hijo)* (Argentina, 1929), *AD* (1929–1930), Case No. 194.

[13] Blackstone, *Commentaries,* I, 254.

[14] See examples in Oppenheim, I, 791; Satow, pp. 181–182, 279–294; and S. Prevezer, "Peacetime Espionage and the Law," *Current Legal Problems,* VI (1953), 93–94.

agreement that the diplomatic agent should adhere to local regulations and avoid disturbance of the public order.[15] Most nations assume that law-breaking foreign diplomats who escape local jurisdiction will not go scot-free. For example, the New York Police Department, which probably deals with more diplomats than any other law-enforcement agency, operates on the premise that the government involved, United States or foreign, "may be expected to deal with violations in an appropriate manner."[16] The fact that the sending state retains jurisdiction over its own diplomats serves as one safeguard.[17]

In more serious crimes, the ambassador will collect evidence and send the offender home for trial in his own country. Such an instance occurred in a murder case involving two Haitian diplomats assigned to the United States. André Toussaint, First Secretary, was charged with fatally shooting the minister counsellor in the Haitian Embassy in Washington. He was returned to Haiti by joint agreement of the two nations, accused of murder, and acquitted following a brief, two-day trial in Port-au-Prince, some two years after the shooting.[18] The United States also has tried persons attached to foreign embassies. In 1919, an assistant military attaché was tried and acquitted on charges stemming from a fatal auto accident in Switzerland.[19] In 1960, seven marine guards at the United States Embassy in London were tried for crimes allegedly committed abroad.[20]

In other cases where the sending state does not assume jurisdiction over diplomats accused of crimes, it is not unusual for immunity to be waived. For example, in *Rex v. A. B. (or Kent)*[21] a United States Embassy code clerk was convicted in Great Britain on a criminal indictment con-

---

[15] The approach of the United States government is typical. The U.S. contends that immunity from criminal jurisdiction "in no wise relieves" the diplomat "from the obligations of observing local laws and regulations." Barnes, *DSB,* XLIII, 178.

[16] New York City, Police Department, Office of the Police Commissioner. *Diplomatic Immunity* (n.d., received from Department in August, 1962), p. 2.

[17] See Chapter 2.

[18] *New York Times,* April 15, 1958, pp. 1, 36; June 27, p. 14.

[19] The Swiss government had suggested either that a waiver of immunity might be requested or that the United States might prosecute. Green Haywood Hackworth, *Digest of International Law* (Washington: Government Printing Office, 1942), IV, 519–520.

[20] The guards, court-martialed for selling cigarettes and whiskey that had not gone through customs, were fined, reduced in rank, and ordered to leave Great Britain. Earlier a London court had convicted a Netherlands national who admitted buying goods from the guards. The prosecution said diplomatic immunity from British jurisdiction had been claimed for the marines. *New York Times,* February 2, 1960, p. 3.

[21] [1941] 1 K.B. 454.

taining a number of charges, some under the Official Secret Acts of 1911 and 1920, and one on a charge of larceny. He was dismissed and his immunity waived before prosecution was started. More recently in Ireland, a diplomat suspected of smuggling was released before being charged. However, his immunity was subsequently waived by his ambassador.[22] An even more dramatic example of this policy of stripping errant diplomats of their immunity involved two former ambassadors from Latin American nations who were sentenced in separate cases in 1961 and 1964 on charges of smuggling heroin into the United States. In both instances, the accused diplomats, Salvador Pardo-Bolland, Mexican Ambassador to Bolivia, and Mauricio Rosal, Ambassador of Guatemala to Belgium and the Netherlands, were dismissed from their official posts.[23]

This type of criminal action has been used by some writers as evidence that the diplomat enjoys immunity from criminal jurisdiction, presumably on the basis that the concept of waiver means that in legal theory the diplomat does commit a crime.[24] While these cases involved prosecution of diplomatic personnel on criminal charges, because of the waivers, the courts did not have to decide any issue of criminal immunity. If the immunity is not waived, and this is sometimes the case,[25] the host government may, and often does, refuse to continue to accept the individual as a person possessing diplomatic status.

These rules of immunity from criminal jurisdiction are also modified when the envoy's conduct threatens the safety and security of the host state. Exceptions to the inviolability of the diplomat occur when

---

[22] See *The Times* (London), February 25, 1954, p. 6.

[23] For reports on their sentencing see *New York Times,* January 12, 1961, p. 1 (Rosal) and July 23, 1964, p. 24 (Pardo-Bolland). Immunity of an ex-Uruguayan diplomat also was waived in the 1964 case. See *United States v. Arizti,* 229 F. Supp. 53 (1964).

[24] A British writer cites the Kent and Irish cases along with observations by Glanville L. Williams, *The Criminal Law* (London: Stevens & Sons, Limited, 1953), as evidence that diplomatic immunity from criminal law does exist. Taylor, *Crim. L. Rev.* [n.v.] (April, 1955), p. 230. Williams argues that the "possibility of waiver shows that the diplomatic agent does in legal theory commit a crime." Williams, p. 628. As indicated, however, the above cases were inconclusive on judicial determination of the issue. The "legal theory" line of reasoning, while intriguing, has had little impact on actual practice or on the learned observations by publicists. See also Holland, *Cur. Leg. Prob.,* IV, 98, for comments on *Rex. v. A.B. (or Kent)* indicating that English law on this issue is doubtful.

[25] For example, when a Dutch Embassy car struck and killed a man in Great Britain, the Netherlands ambassador was asked to waive diplomatic immunity of the driver. After consulting his government, he declined to do so. A report of this decision before the House of Commons brought cries of "Shame." *The Times* (London), May 23, 1958, p. 13.

a violent act of the diplomat disturbs the internal order of the state or when an agent conspires against the receiving state.[26] In such situations, he may be restrained, although in due time he will normally be sent home. Usually, jurisdiction is not claimed. The United States departed in principle from this policy in the 1916 case of Wolf von Igel, an attaché of the German Embassy. Von Igel was entrusted with maintaining the office of a former military attaché at New York whose name appeared on the diplomatic list.[27] Von Igel was arrested at his office and his papers were seized. They were said to contain evidence of their owner's complicity in conspiracies against the neutrality of the United States. The Secretary of State at that time, Robert Lansing, maintained that he did not think the German government could legally claim diplomatic immunity for the envoy, in part because of the seriousness of the crime, an opinion which drew the rebuke of a leading American publicist.[28] Germany disagreed with Lansing and both states maintained their position. When diplomatic relations were severed in 1917, von Igel's bond was cancelled, and he returned to Germany on parole. The case was dismissed in 1927 since von Igel had never returned to the United States.

The doctrine of "national security," which no doubt influenced Lansing's attitude in the von Igel case, is probably as old as "modern" international law.[29] Since World War II the security concept in the area of diplomatic privileges and immunities has become more significant due to the ever-present threat of nuclear world-wide destruction. Certainly one of the most impressive statements that a state's "own security" must be given priority over "granting or recognizing a privilege to another state" is found in the "realistic" *dicta* of Canadian Justice Bissonnette in the widely publicized case of *Rose v. The King.*[30]

---

[26] Oppenheim, I, 790–791. Or, as stated another way: "Freedom from arrest means that an ambassador can commit any crime with impunity, except if the offense endangers the safety of the receiving state." John Sand, "Diplomatic Immunity," *Free Europe,* IV (October 31, 1941), 254.

[27] Hackworth, IV, 517–519.

[28] Hyde contends that Lansing "seemingly lost sight of" the fact that criminal immunity is not affected "by the enormity of the offense." Charles Cheney Hyde, *International Law: Chiefly as Interpreted and Applied by the United States* (2d rev. ed.; Boston: Little, Brown and Company, 1947), I, 1267.

[29] The "safety of the State" was the reason why Swedish Ambassador Count Gyllenborg was seized by the British in 1717 in connection with a plot to overthrow George I. As noted in "Diplomatic Immunity and the Criminal Law," *Law Journal,* LXVIII (October 12, 1929), 226–227.

[30] [1947] 3 D.L.R. 618, cited with approval by Prevezer, *Cur. Leg. Prob.,* VI, 941. The prosecution in a Syrian case also maintained that diplomatic immunity did not apply to offenses against the security of the state. *New York Times,* July 10, 1958, p. 6.

The Rose case is an eloquent expression of security taking priority.[31] It arose on a question of admitting evidence taken by police from the Soviet Embassy premises, and the court noted that it had to follow the exercise of a discretion vested in the executive branch in protecting national security. The reasoning of Justice Bissonnette is worthy of consideration, especially since the concept of state security, coupled with the fact that international politics in a nuclear age may have radically altered some aspects of diplomatic immunities, has assumed even greater significance than during the seventeenth and eighteenth centuries when monarchs were uncovering diplomatic plots. Bissonnette reasoned from the assumption that ultimately the responsibility of a state, its granting of "first privileges," is to its own citizens.[32] The Justice contended further that diplomatic immunity is relative and not absolute,[33] and that the diplomat has two groups of duties: loyalty to his own state and fidelity to and respect for the sovereignty of the host state.[34] If the diplomat violates this trust, the receiving state may take full repressive measures to guard its security since, in offending the tacitly accepted code of honor, the diplomat has in effect renounced his privilege of inviolability.[35] Any agent engaging in espionage and sabotage is denied the privilege of

---

[31] The case involved the admissibility of documents taken from the Soviet Embassy as evidence. A similar issue of state security was raised in *United States v. Coplon and Gubitchev,* 84 F. Supp. 472 (1949), 88 F. Supp. 915 (1950). Gubitchev, a Soviet engineer and architect, employed by the United Nations Headquarters and Planning Staff, was indicted with Judith Coplon, an American, on a charge of violating U.S. espionage laws. The court held, *inter alia,* that even if Article 105 of the U.N. Charter were self-executing, espionage was not within the scope of a diplomat's recognized activities, nor could the International Organization Immunities Act be invoked for the same reason. However, the U.N. Secretary General had on March 7, 1949, two months before the case appeared before the District Court, announced that Gubitchev had been suspended and his immunity waived. "The judgment, therefore, though apparently sound and logical, and in the reports, containing no mention of waiver, would not appear to be conclusive." Prevezer, *Cur. Leg. Prob.,* IV, 95, fn. Cf. *United States v. Melekh* (1960), 190 F. Supp. 67.

[32] *Rose v. The King* (1946), 2 Can. C.R., 107; [1947] 3 D.L.R. 618; cited from *AD* (1946), Case No. 76. On state security, the court stated: "A State, before according or conceding a privilege to another State, has the right to grant itself a first privilege, that of its own security. To decide otherwise would be to concede to a rule claimed to be international in authority, superior to the precise, rigid, and necessary rule that the State, having its own citizens in mind, must first and above all, independently of its external duties, make sure of its own security and repress the crimes that its own citizens may commit against the King and the safety of the country. The first duty of an envoy is to respect the safety of the State." *AD* (1946), 165.

[33] *Ibid.,* p. 162.

[34] "From this fact it must be deduced that the diplomatic agent must do or attempt nothing against the safety of the State that has consented to receive him." *Ibid.,* p. 163.

[35] Bissonnette cites as support Pradier-Fodéré, *Cours de droit diplomatique,* II, 36; *AD* (1946), 163.

immunity and should be expelled and not tried before civil courts since the state is not justified in violating immunity just because the diplomat violates the law of nations.[36]

Bissonnette's reasoning seems to be compatible with the nature of the nation-state system and with traditional international law. It might also be noted that the "state security" principle is a two-edged sword insofar as Western nations are concerned. Communist governments have used the concept to justify arrest, detention, and expulsion of diplomats, usually to the dismay of the nation whose representatives are involved.

One might well conclude then that exemption of the envoy from criminal jurisdiction does not mean "complete immunity" since an ambassador can be restrained if he threatens the safety of the state and if he is not withdrawn immediately.[37] The essential point is that the diplomat is merely restrained and/or expelled; he is not subjected to the criminal jurisdiction of the state. If he were, there would then be a departure from long-accepted rules of international law.

There also seems to be little doubt that the doctrine of state security would take precedence over diplomatic immunity in cases involving war crimes, and both French and Danish courts have ruled to this effect.

In the Danish case, *In re Best and Others*,[38] the accused Best had been appointed Reich plenipotentiary to establish diplomatic relations with Denmark following the German occupation of that country in World War II. Along with two non-diplomats, Best was charged with responsibility for killings and demolitions carried out by German forces as part of a campaign of sabotage in Denmark. The provincial court held that Best did not enjoy diplomatic immunity in a country which did not have an independent government.[39] The Supreme Court, in upholding the convictions, reasoned further that the 1946 Danish War Crimes Act, by its very nature and under rules of international law, would apply to persons whether or not they were entitled to diplomatic immunity.

The reasoning of the French court in a corresponding case, *In re Abetz*,[40] was similar. The defendant had appealed a twenty-year war crimes sentence by a military tribunal on grounds that at the time of the

---

[36] *AD* (1946), 164.

[37] See Patrick Stirling, "The Immunities of Diplomatic Agents," *Law Journal*, CVIII (April 18, 1958), 243.

[38] (Denmark, 1949, 1950), *ILR* (1950), Case No. 146.

[39] The court said: "Denmark had no government independent of Germany; such *government* is the prerequisite of representation by persons of diplomatic status." *Ibid.*

[40] *In re Abetz* (France, 1950), *ILR* (1950), Case No. 89.

commission of the crime he was the accredited ambassador of Germany to (Vichy) France, and thus was immune from criminal jurisdiction unless his home state agreed to the prosecution. The court noted in rejecting his appeal the incredibility of permitting a former enemy nation to ascertain jurisdiction in a case of this type. The court held, *inter alia,* that the Ordinance of August 28, 1944, concerning war crimes, "excludes by its very object the application of a rule of municipal or of international law, the effect of which would be to make a prosecution subject to preliminary authorization of the Government of the country to which the accused belongs."[41]

Infringement of diplomatic privileges and immunities since World War II has not been restricted to these cases involving state security and war crimes, and this encroachment perhaps constitutes even a more serious deviation from accepted legal standards. There is strong indication in more recent state practice that immunity from jurisdiction of local courts over diplomatic personnel in criminal cases is losing what it may have had of absolute character.[42] Jurisdiction was not taken by the host state in a few of the incidents reported below; however, these states appeared to believe that such a legal right existed. In other situations, actual criminal jurisdiction was exercised over diplomatic personnel, contrary to the traditional practice as discussed earlier in this chapter.

A forerunner to the postwar cases, and in many ways compatible with them, was a 1935 decision by the Argentine Supreme Court that under Article 101 of the Constitution it had original jurisdiction over the criminal prosecution against the diplomatic secretary of a foreign embassy in a traffic case.[43] The claim to jurisdiction also was made, although prosecution did not follow in a 1951 incident involving Byron Gutheil, Jr., a clerk in the United States Embassy at La Paz, Bolivia. He was arrested in connection with the fatal shooting of a Brazilian citizen who he said was trying to break into his apartment. The Bolivians brought no charges, but Gutheil was arrested nearly two months after the shooting on criminal charges filed by the victim's father. The United States insisted that Gutheil was entitled to diplomatic immunity, and the clerk was allowed to leave Bolivia after the Superior Court of Justice ruled on

---

[41] *Ibid.,* p. 279.

[42] For example, one writer maintains that the attitude of the Lauterpacht-Oppenheim work to the effect that states have no right to punish diplomats "under any circumstances" (Oppenheim, I, 790) is "too categorical." Prevezer, *Cur. Leg. Prob.,* VI, 93.

[43] *In the case of Celso Vargas* (Argentina, 1935), *AD* (1935–1937), 394, fn. The case was dismissed, not on a question of immunity, but in the absence of proof of criminal intent.

the case. However, according to the *New York Times,* the court granted Gutheil his freedom but denied that diplomatic immunity was involved, an action which would indicate that embassy personnel were not entitled to protection in cases of this type.[44]

Since World War II the traditional immunity of diplomats from criminal jurisdiction has been challenged several times in the Soviet Union. One case involved two junior officers in the British Embassy in Moscow who had engaged in a street fight with Soviet policemen. The press reported that the two were permitted to leave the country "although criminal charges had been preferred against them and they did not have diplomatic immunity."[45]

In a similar case, Soviet officials indicated that they wished to try Sergeant Joseph O'Brien, who was attached to the United States Embassy, for an alleged altercation with a Soviet citizen and Soviet police. An exit visa was delayed, but O'Brien left six months later in Ambassador W. Bedell Smith's personal plane after the Russians requested that the United States take disciplinary action against the sergeant.[46]

The Soviets were even less inclined to follow traditional procedure in another case against a British Embassy staff member. George Bundock, a clerk, was convicted in March, 1948, *in absentia,* on a charge involving a Russian woman. He denied the charge and, on the advice of the embassy, refused to appear in court, or pay 6,200 rubles (about £300 at the 1948 exchange rate) to the girl as compensation, or to surrender and serve an eighteen-month sentence. He spent the next five years within the walls of the embassy grounds. In 1953 he was released by a general Soviet amnesty and returned to Great Britain.[47]

A court in Poland in 1963 rejected a claim of immunity by Sergeant James S. Chase, a marine guard at the U.S. Embassy in Warsaw, who was finally released with a suspended sentence after being convicted of involuntary manslaughter. An Embassy car driven by Chase on a trip to a former Nazi concentration camp struck and killed a Polish laborer. Diplomatic immunity was denied even though the United States grants immunity to similar ranking Polish personnel stationed in Washington.[48]

---

[44] *New York Times,* May 11, 1951, p. 19; May 26, p. 3.

[45] *Ibid.,* October 30, 1954, p. 2. The British Foreign Office declined comment except to say that the two were junior officers no longer employed in the Foreign Service. *The Times* (London), October 30, 1954, p. 6.

[46] *New York Times,* January 13, 1948, p. 9; August 1, p. 12.

[47] *Ibid.,* May 1, 1953, p. 4; May 6, p. 2; *The Times* (London), May 1, 1953, p. 6.

[48] *New York Times,* January 2, 1963, p. 2.

In 1953 the Greeks denied diplomatic immunity in a criminal case involving a British subject, a first secretary of the British Embassy in Athens. The court held that under Article 26, Code of Civil Procedure, diplomats are immune except when charged with a misdemeanor.[49] Switzerland exercised jurisdiction over Zolvan Vitianu, Economic Counsellor of the Rumanian Legation, who was found guilty by a federal court of economic spying and financial crimes. He was sentenced to eighteen months in prison and fifteen years banishment from Switzerland.[50]

These post-war cases indicate that the concept of diplomatic immunity from criminal jurisdiction is not as absolute as claimed by some publicists and jurists. Furthermore, judges, legislators, and members of the public have expressed resentment over failure of governments to take criminal action against diplomats. A few recent incidents illustrate this point. In 1957, a British judge publicly labeled as "nonsense" the dismissal by his court, under government pressure, of moral charges against diplomats.[51] The following year, a British lawmaker strongly protested the extension of immunity to the driver of a Dutch Embassy car which struck and killed a pedestrian while it was being used to carry diplomatic mail to the London airport.[52] The public was reportedly aroused in another incident involving an unnamed American ambassador who was not prosecuted in connection with a fatal shooting.[53]

The argument here is not that immunity from criminal jurisdiction is not still a part of the rules of international law. Practice has in general

---

[49] *Greek State v. X* (Greece, 1953), *ILR* (1953), 378. "That is because according to international law the proceedings have no connection with the *public* character of the person entitled to immunity. (Spiropoulos, *Public International Law,* 1949 ed., pp. 121 seq.)" The court further noted that Article 2 of the Code of Criminal Procedure, which exempts foreign diplomats from jurisdiction of Greek courts, does not have the effect of depriving the act with which the defendant was charged of its character.

[50] *New York Times,* July 1, 1949, p. 5.

[51] *The Times* (London), September 25, 1957, p. 5. A West London court in 1957 fined a Spaniard five pounds for committing an improper act with a man who was released by the police after claiming diplomatic immunity. A few days later in the same court, an eighteen-year-old Danish girl, who was employed as a domestic servant, was charged with committing an act of indecency. The man arrested with her claimed diplomatic immunity and was released. Magistrate E. R. Guest, who was on the bench in these cases, could not exercise jurisdiction but he did tartly comment. "Not really, that is the second time this week this nonsense has happened."

[52] *Ibid.,* May 23, 1958, p. 13.

[53] Martin Abramson, "Scofflaws in Striped Pants," *Coronet,* XLVIII (August, 1960), 124–125. This writer reported the following: An unnamed American ambassador heard a noise on the roof of a shed adjoining his embassy. He grabbed a pistol, shouted an unheeded warning, and fired three shots. The son of a popular labor leader, who had been courting an embassy maid, tumbled from the roof, fatally wounded. Feeling ran high, and some demands were made that the ambassador be tried for murder. He was not.

followed theory; the modern trend has seen both a reinforcement of the concept of state security taking precedence over diplomatic immunity and the practice of extending continuance of criminal immunity to diplomatic agents. But forces unrecognized by some observers are chipping away at the traditional doctrine. One must admit the difficulty of finding judicial decisions which support this concept, although admittedly as a rule executive branches, now as in the past, are reluctant to institute such proceedings. The fact that states have exercised jurisdiction over persons who are protected by diplomatic immunities or have made claims of such competence for security or other reasons offers more compelling evidence that the traditional rules do not always provide a protective shield for the diplomatic staff member.

Police Jurisdiction

There has been considerable activity since World War II in the area of immunity from jurisdiction of local police, a right traditionally inherent in the diplomat's immunity from criminal and civil process. Unquestionably, in order to perform his functions, the foreign representative needs to be free from police jurisdiction, as he is free from jurisdiction of the local courts for criminal and civil actions.[54] On the other hand, the diplomat is expected to obey police regulations insofar as they do not interfere with his official responsibilities.[55] Diplomats clearly have been the most lax in adhering to this accepted international practice in the operation of their motor vehicles.

Host states do not as a rule consider traffic violations as falling outside a diplomat's responsibility to observe local regulations. For example, the United States policy was bluntly stated by Secretary of State Cordell Hull following the arrest of the Iranian minister on a traffic charge in 1933. He pointed out that this government impressed upon its own diplomats that immunity does not presuppose the right to violate laws of the receiving state and he presumed that other states followed a similar practice.[56] The Magistrate's Court of Buenos Aires was even

---

[54] Barnes, *DSB,* XLIII, 179.

[55] See, for example, Oppenheim I, 802; *In re Ledoux* (Uruguay, 1941), *AD* (1943–1945), Case No. 75.

[56] U.S., Department of State, *Press Releases,* XIII, No. 323 (December 7, 1935), 497. Former Governor E. F. Morgan of West Virginia was even more explicit: "I would most respectfully suggest that the innocent action of an untutored police is less deserving of admonishment than the willful defiance of speed regulations by such an important personage as an ambassador." Chesney Hill, "Sanctions Constraining Diplomatic Representatives to Abide by the Local Law," *AJIL,* XXV, (April, 1931), 266, fn.

more outspoken when dealing in 1958 with diplomats' infractions of municipal traffic regulations. The court declared that while traffic violators may be representatives of foreign countries, this "does not put them in a privileged position, so that they may freely violate the law."[57]

It is difficult to determine at present the extent to which diplomats abuse this privilege since most cases are not publicly reported. However, diplomats who normally accord full respect to local laws and regulations are less constrained in their attitude toward parking and traffic rules.[58] For example, a British report in 1955 indicated that the percentage of diplomats involved in minor offenses such as speeding was double that of British drivers.[59] The situation apparently has not appreciably improved since that time. A Labor party newspaper, the *Daily Herald,* in a 1964 editorial, charged that the "public understandably are fed up with the way people employed by foreign embassies get away with breaches of our laws. They resent motorists with CD plates freely committing offenses for which anyone else is punished."[60] The newspaper based its complaints against what it called "motorists above the law" on the numbers escaping punishment for illegal parking.[61] Along similar lines, the U.S. Department of State reported a sharp increase from 1961 to 1962 in parking violations by diplomats in Washington, D.C.[62]

Ultimately, if a diplomat habitually engages in breaking the law or if the breach is of shocking magnitude to the host state, good grounds would exist for his recall.[63] The host government normally communicates information concerning such violations to heads of missions and persistent violators are dismissed or transferred, a technique distinct from the more publicized device of declaring a diplomat *persona non*

---

[57]*In re N* (Argentina, 1958), *ILR* (1958-II), p. 535.

[58] The wayward diplomatic driver has long plagued local police. As an example, the District of Columbia Superintendent of Police listed in 1929, at the request of the U.S. Senate, thirty-five cases in which diplomats (in several instances the same person was named twice) between January 8, 1917, and May 23, 1929, were stopped or warned for operating vehicles while under the influence of liquor or for other violations. Hill, *AJIL,* XXV, 267.

[59] In a report to the House of Lords, Earl Jowett, Under Secretary for Foreign Affairs, noted that during a previous undefined period four per cent of the 2,500 diplomatic personnel in Great Britain were involved in such offenses, compared with two per cent of the association members. *The Times* (London), November 17, 1955, p. 5.

[60] As reprinted in *The Arizona Daily Star,* March 15, 1964, p. A-11.

[61] The *Herald* reported that during 1963 in London 2,078 embassy drivers escaped receiving parking tickets and fifty drivers avoided prosecution on other road offenses by invoking diplomatic immunity. *Ibid.*

[62] The Department of State reported that for the five months ended February 28, 1962, there were 2,256 violation notices placed on cars in Washington bearing diplomatic tags; this compared with 2,504 similar tags issued for the entire 1961 fiscal year ended June 30, 1961. *Ibid.,* April 23, 1962, p. B-6.

[63]Hill, *AJIL,* XXV, 256–258, 263.

grata.[64] The United States has now systematized its expulsion process for errant diplomatic drivers,[65] although it had effectively coped with the situation as early as the days when Elihu Root was Secretary of State (1905–1909) and the motor car was only beginning to replace the horse.[66]

In general, nations do not arrest or prosecute diplomats for disregarding traffic rules. Nonetheless, there is some support for a policy of subjecting diplomats to legal action under these conditions on the basis that driving privileges are granted, not as a legal right, but as an act of international courtesy.[67] This approach is contrary to accepted rules of diplomatic immunity and could pose a serious problem except for the fact that the number of diplomats wilfully violating police regulations[68] appears to be relatively small in proportion to the thousands assigned to diplomatic posts.[69] One might presume that the diplomat seriously believes that it is incumbent upon him not to abuse his privileges since intelligent restraint probably would prevent involvement with local officers.[70] This appears to be the general rule guiding diplomatic conduct.

---

[64] Denys P. Myers, "Contemporary Practice of the United States Relating to International Law — Diplomatic Immunity," *AJIL,* LIV (July, 1960), 649.

[65] Pedro San Juan, the Department of State's Assistant Chief of Protocol, reported that his office advises the ambassador of the country involved whenever a diplomat gets more than three traffic tickets. If the violation is especially serious or is repeated, the diplomat is summoned to the Department and warned that continued violations could result in his recall. *The Arizona Daily Star,* April 23, 1962, p. B-6.

[66] At the time, District of Columbia and neighboring authorities were plagued by diplomats who disregarded speed and traffic regulations. Root let it be known that habitual violators would become candidates for recall, a policy which apparently worked as "an effective check." George E. Anderson, "Diplomatic Immunities," *The Commonweal,* X (July 17, 1929), 290.

[67] See, for example, *In re N* (Argentina, 1958), *ILR* (1958-II), p. 535, in which the Magistrate's Court declared: "The rules of international courtesy which have been invoked in the various cases before us have been observed by our local authorities, in that they have provided reserved parking places for diplomatic personnel in front of the buildings occupied by their respective missions. But it does not follow that the rules of international courtesy authorize diplomats to park their cars wherever they please, drive at excessive speeds, violate traffic laws, obstruct traffic, disobey signals, or otherwise drive in disregard of traffic regulations. . . . It cannot be denied that when such offences are brought before a court, that court has a right to hear the charges."

[68] Except for the disregard for parking regulations as noted above. Speeding also has posed a problem. New Jersey officials in June, 1965, instituted a practice which, while falling short of legal proceedings, did mark a departure from the usual privileged treatment of diplomats. In keeping with a new policy, a speeding diplomatic automobile was escorted off the New Jersey Turnpike. *New York Times,* June 28, 1965, p. 27.

[69] Postwar security and espionage cases pose quite another problem.

[70] Declares Professor Hyde: "It is hardly to be anticipated . . . that a diplomatic officer accredited to the United States, if conscious of the nature of his mission and of the likelihood of rendering it abortive by contempt for law, would fail to take the customary precautions to respect regulations, or would intentionally give occasion to municipal authorities to hold him in restraint." Hyde, II, 1284.

Herschel V. Johnson, a U.S. Foreign Service Officer for thirty-three years and an ex-ambassador, declared that "individuals who respect the laws and customs governing foreign diplomatic agents . . . are uniformly treated with courtesy and generosity, and have no real trouble unless they are the cause of it themselves."[71]

Although it appears that diplomats do not engage in flagrant violation of laws of the host states, in the postwar period many have invoked their immunity from police jurisdiction in traffic cases to escape minor fines, to avoid prosecution for more serious offenses, or perhaps to avoid larger financial obligations.[72] This does not mean that injured persons are without recourse when the offending party is protected by diplomatic immunity. Compensation is frequently paid either by the government involved[73] or by the insurance company if the offending diplomatic agent is so covered.[74] But the fact that settlement has often been less than satisfactory is indicated in an analysis by Chesney Hill of twelve traffic cases between 1925 and 1931 involving foreign diplomats in the United States.[75] The demands were satisfied only in a small percentage of the cases.[76]

----

[71] Ambassador Johnson served in Switzerland, Bulgaria, Honduras, Mexico, Great Britain, Sweden, and Brazil as well as in Washington and at the United Nations before his retirement in 1953. Foreign Service Survey. Mrs. Eleanor Clark French, New York City's Commissioner to the United Nations, also claims that parking violations by diplomats has been "blown up all out of proportion by the press." *New York Times,* September 16, 1962, p. 37.

[72] The question has often been debated in the British Parliament and at one time prompted a Member of Parliament to ask if C.D. plates on diplomatic cars means "corps diplomatique" or "chauffeur dangereux." *The Times* (London), June 30, 1955, p. 10. Also see Chapter 8 for traffic cases involving members of the diplomatic staff and suite.

[73] For example, in 1957 a car driven by Joza Brilej, Yugoslav Ambassador to the United Nations, was involved in an automobile accident in which a pedestrian was killed. The driver of the other car charged that Brilej caused the accident by proceeding through a red traffic light. The Ambassador was immune from prosecution but the Yugoslav Government reportedly made a "substantial cash payment" to the victim's survivors. *The Arizona Daily Star,* November 25, 1962, p. A-8.

[74] For example, a Washington woman was killed on November 11, 1959, by a car driven by David Hearne, son of the Irish Ambassador to the United States, and a financial settlement was arranged by Hearne's insurance company. Letter to the writer from the Honorable Thomas J. Kiernan, Ambassador of Ireland to the United States, August 9, 1962.

[75] Hill, *AJIL,* XXV, 252–269.

[76] Two of the traffic victims made no attempt to obtain damages; one diplomat waived immunity and the insurance company was held liable; one diplomat was sued after his immunity ceased; one diplomat was transferred following a fatal accident; and five of the American nationals appealed directly to the ambassador involved. Of the five, one received a payment at the traffic scene but a demand for its return was made later; one received full satisfaction from the ambassador; and three were referred to insurance companies. Of the three, the insurance company repudiated liability on one case; offered one-fourth the amount requested in another; and paid three-fourths of the amount in another. *Ibid.*

Some attempts have been made to close these legal loopholes. In 1930 Senator McKellar introduced a bill to strip the diplomat of his immunity in traffic cases. The bill was introduced two days after a car driven by a Chilean naval attaché collided with another vehicle, seriously injuring the driver.[77] A year earlier, the District of Columbia Superintendent of Police had listed, at the request of the U.S. Senate, thirty-five cases in which diplomats (in several instances the same person was listed twice) between January 8, 1917, and May 23, 1929, were stopped or warned for operating vehicles while under the influence of liquor or for other violations.[78] However, a practice less drastic than removing immunity has evolved to protect individuals who have claims in respect of injuries by motor vehicles. It is an accepted practice that persons possessing diplomatic immunity obtain automobile liability insurance against third-party risks and that immunity be waived in cases of suit arising from accidents. This rule has been in effect in Great Britain since 1931 and has been accepted by diplomatic missions.[79] The procedure was illustrated in *Dickinson v. Del Solar*,[80] in which the court rejected a defense based on diplomatic immunity raised by the insurance company when the head of the diplomatic mission waived immunity. Formal waiver of immunity is anticipated if the matter cannot be settled out of court, and there is "every indication that such waiver will be forthcoming," as in the *Del Solar* case.[81] A more recent indication that settlement is usually reached in injury cases is seen in a statement by British Justice McNaughten in 1947 that no nation could afford to have any question arise with respect to discharge of obligations by their diplomatic representatives.[82] The jurist said he could not recall any case where any such question had arisen. He added:

> So meticulous in such matters are members of embassies in this country that I think I am right in saying that all of them undertake the obligation of taking out third-party insurance with regard to their motor cars, although, if they could be said to be negligent, they could not be sued. If there is an accident, I do not think that any foreign embassy seeks to raise the question of immunity. They allow the question of liability to be determined.[83]

---

[77] *Ibid.*, p. 265.
[78] *Ibid.*, p. 267.
[79] Great Britain, Parliamentary Papers *(Reports)*, Cmd. 8460, p. 4.
[80] [1930] 1 K.B. 376.
[81] Great Britain, Parliamentary Papers *(Reports)*, Cmd. 8460, p. 4.
[82] *Parker v. Boggan*, [1947] 1 All E.R. 46; *AD* (1946), Case No. 75, p. 160.
[83] *AD* (1946), 160.

On the other hand, an American lawyer, who was angered over the extension of immunities to those connected with international organizations,[84] demanded in 1946 that compulsory insurance and financial responsibility laws be made binding on the diplomat and his official and unofficial staff.[85]

In all fairness it should be noted that diplomats are not always to blame in these incidents; some have claimed that they are the object of special police harassment in traffic cases. A retired United States Foreign Service officer who served in Venezuela in the 1950's reported that

> traffic police used to seem to take particular delight in picking up U.S. and other foreign diplomatic officers (including wives) on minor traffic violations, taking them to police headquarters and holding them two to three hours before allowing them to contact their Embassy or releasing them.[86]

Traffic violations may be the most persistent jurisdictional problem, but by no means are the only type with which police are forced to cope. And, as a result, police departments in larger cities such as Washington and New York City have become extremely skilled in handling these situations within the framework of international law. Codes of procedure have been adopted; the New York model is an example of judicious restraint.[87] The police are cautioned not to subject diplomatic personnel to any restraint and to settle the question of identity on the spot and not by bringing the diplomat to a station house.[88] Discourtesy also is discouraged.[89] The envoy, his staff, or families are not to be arrested, issued a summons, or detained after their identity has been established.[90]

Police in the major cities often exercise this restraint, sometimes

---

[84] U.S. Congress, International Organizations and Immunities Act, Public Law 291, 79th Cong., 1st Sess., 1945.

[85] Luther N. Hussey, "The Negligent Diplomat," *Journal of the Bar Association of the District of Columbia,* XIII (April, 1946), 153. Hussey asked: "Did you ever have a negligence case against a diplomat? If he is insured, the Insurance Company will set itself up as both Judge and Jury and you will very likely accept their verdict whether or not you like it. If he is not insured, your only remedy is his generosity, if any." *Ibid.,* p. 152.

[86] Foreign Service Survey.

[87] New York City, Police Department, *Diplomatic Immunity,* p. 2.

[88] *Ibid.,* pp. 2–3.

[89] For example, a New York City patrolman was reassigned to a beat in Harlem for allegedly insulting a Syrian diplomat whose car was double parked. *New York Times,* February 12, 1965, p. 25. However, the policeman was reinstated to his former post the following month. *Ibid.,* March 24, 1965, p. 43.

[90] New York City, Police Department, *Diplomatic Immunity,* p. 1. However, the New York City Fire Department will tow away diplomatic vehicles if they are parked too close to fire hydrants and the public safety is endangered.

under trying conditions. The Washington police were confronted by a difficult situation in 1958 when one Haitian diplomat shot and killed another in the Haitian Embassy. The accused was not taken into custody, but police surrounded the embassy all day and escorted the ambassador and the accused to the airport where the latter enplaned for Haiti.[91] In 1959, New York police were forced to disarm a Venezuelan colonel, traveling on a diplomatic passport, who had jabbed a loaded pistol into the stomach of a stranger on a Manhattan street.[92] In 1960, Chicago police stopped a car which was traveling too slowly on a high-speed highway near an anti-aircraft missile base. The trooper issued only a warning ticket when the driver of the car identified himself as an assistant military and air attaché of the Hungarian Legation in Washington.[93] The same year Washington police investigated a complaint by a Cuban diplomat that he was physically attacked by his superior when he refused to return to Havana, but no charges were filed because all participants were covered by diplomatic immunity.[94]

However, the actions of police in some nonmetropolitan areas who are less well versed in the intricacies of diplomatic immunity have prompted State Department intervention to avoid international incidents. One earlier case which attracted considerable attention and which still is often cited involved Ghaffar Khan Djalal, Minister from Iran, who was arrested in Elkton, Maryland, for speeding and reckless driving. The charge was dismissed but costs were assessed against the chauffeur. The protesting minister ultimately received apologies from Secretary of State Hull and the governor of Maryland, and the offending police officer was dismissed.[95] The difficulties encountered by officers unversed in protocol were illustrated by one report which claimed that the driver tried to explain Djalal's status as Minister of Iran and that Chief Town Officer Jacob Biddle allegedly replied: "I've heard of Baptist ministers and Presbyterian ministers but never of Iranian ministers."[96]

---

[91] Myers, *AJIL,* LIV, 649.

[92] *Minneapolis Tribune,* December 15, 1959, p. 5. "Immunity" was one of the few English words the colonel knew and he shouted it time and again as he was led into a police station. He escaped arrest by pleading diplomatic immunity.

[93] *New York Times,* December 1, 1960, p. 18.

[94] *Ibid.,* December 7, 1960, p. 25.

[95] U.S., Department of State, *Press Releases,* XIII, No. 323 (December 7, 1935), 497; Hackworth, IV, 515–516. For other cases which support the immunity of diplomats from police jurisdiction, see Hackworth, IV, 516–533.

[96] Charles W. Thayer, *Diplomat* (New York: Harper & Brothers, 1959), p. 204. See also J. S. Reeves, "The Elkton Incident," *AJIL,* XXX (January, 1936), 95–96; "Speeding Diplomat: Persian Envoy . . . Claims Immunity," *Literary Digest,* CXX (December 7, 1935), 9; "Maryland Policeman Is No Respecter of Persians," *Newsweek, VI* (December 7, 1935), 13, and "On the Loose," *Newsweek,* LIV (November 23, 1959), 37.

Local officers also have been involved with the State Department in other diplomatic incidents. According to reports, the Department intervened on two separate occasions to obtain the release of diplomats who apparently had been drinking in Midwestern bars and in another case allegedly convinced a sheriff he should not march on an ambassador's New Jersey summer home in order to drag the diplomat's son before a court on a traffic charge.[97]

While in some cases since 1945, such as those noted above, the diplomat may have been inconvenienced or his pride and dignity wounded, his position does not seem to have been adversely affected by a lack of immunity from police jurisdiction. Irresponsibility at this level could greatly weaken the rights and privileges of diplomats, rights which are essential for the conduct of relations among states. It would appear that local officers who fail to grasp the vital character of diplomatic privileges and lawmakers who would like to curb what seems to them to be unwarranted excesses have been frustrated. In most cases where the diplomatic agent has been offended, protests by the sending state have resulted in redress and in acknowledgment of the covering rule of international law.[98] Professor Hill, in a study made some years ago, found that "for the most part, sanctions constraining diplomatic representatives to abide by the local law are effective in rendering justice to individuals and the receiving state."[99] He found that the precautionary and preventive measures are used chiefly to enforce police regulations and that most offenses are handled through diplomatic channels, and result in apologies, out-of-court settlements, waiver, or immunity. In some cases resort has been made to suits and expulsion.[100]

The situation today appears to be somewhat the same. Immunity from police jurisdiction is generally accepted. Diplomats apparently as a rule are treated with courtesy and restraint. In turn, except for some traffic excesses, they usually do not abuse local laws. Disputes are normally resolved through waiver or submission to arbitration.[101] Additional protection for non-diplomatic parties to traffic accidents is provided by third-party insurance. The problem is somewhat different when the dip-

---

[97] *New York Times,* June 4, 1954, p. 8; Abramson, *Coronet,* XLVIII, 123.

[98] William W. Bishop, Jr. (ed.), *International Law* (2d ed.; Boston: Little, Brown and Company, 1962), p. 593.

[99] Hill, *AJIL,* XXV, 268.

[100] *Ibid.*

[101] F. M., "The Diplomatic Immunities Restriction Act, 1955," *Law Journal,* CVI (February 10, 1956), 86. A similar observation is made by J. C. Arnold, "State and Diplomatic Immunity," *The Solicitor,* XIX (March 19, 1952), 70.

lomat acts with express or tacit approval of his government in abusing his privileges or when the local police merely serve as the arm of state policy to curb what appears to be involvement by diplomats in internal affairs or in espionage activities.[102] This is an offense of state against state and recourse should be had to arbitration or to some international tribunal. In fact, the violation is usually terminated through mutual recrimination, expulsion of diplomats, severance of diplomatic relations or reciprocal curbs on diplomatic activities.

---

[102] See Chapter 3.

CHAPTER 5

Immunities From
Civil Jurisdiction

ONE OF THE MORE INVOLVED areas of diplomatic privileges and immunities is that of civil jurisdiction. It is the purpose of this chapter to assess the doctrine by an analysis of a number of practices — especially those relating to the private acts of diplomats — since World War I but with emphasis on developments since World War II.

State Practices

Exemption from jurisdiction on civil questions is the only diplomatic immunity "conclusively established" by judicial decision.[1] Not until after nations universally extended to envoys immunities from criminal jurisdiction did a similar immunity covering civil actions become firmly established. Moreover, the establishment of this legal sanctuary aroused considerable opposition and, as a United Nations study puts it, the rule was not adopted "without a struggle."[2]

The concept was entrenched in European practice by the mid-seventeenth century. Courts in The Netherlands claimed jurisdiction over foreign diplomats until a States General edict altered the practice in 1679; in Great Britain, the rule apparently was established as early as 1657.[3] It has been restated in numerous British cases. A century ago, Lord Campbell in *Magdalena Steam Navigation Co. v. Martin* observed that while it had not previously been decided whether a foreign diplomatic agent was exempt from all civil actions "we think that this follows from well-established principles."[4] A British court fifty years later, in

---

[1] D. C. Holland, "Diplomatic Immunity in English Law," *Current Legal Problems,* IV (1951), 94.

[2] United Nations, Secretariat, "Memorandum on Diplomatic Intercourse and Immunities" (A/CN.4.98), International Law Commission, *Yearbook: 1956,* Vol. II (A/CN.4.SER.A/1956/Add.1), p. 164. Cited hereafter as ILC Secretariat Memorandum.

[3] *Ibid.,* pp. 164–165.

[4] (1859), 2 E. & E. 94; 121 Eng. Reprint 36; cited in ILC Secretariat Memorandum, p. 164.

In re the Republic of Bolivia Exploration Syndicate Ltd., was even more emphatic when it concluded that "a diplomatic agent accredited to the Crown by a foreign state is absolutely privileged from being sued in the English courts."[5] This judgment still seems to be the rule in Great Britain. The same principle was established in the French case of *Errembault de Deedzeele*.[6]

An American official has observed that

the prevailing interpretation of international law and the one which has been followed in American practice is that complete immunity from civil process should be granted under all circumstances.[7]

This has not always been the accepted doctrine in the United States. As late as 1874, Secretary of State Hamilton Fish disapproved a claim by John Jay, American Minister to Austria-Hungary, for diplomatic immunity from a civil process arising from his termination of a residential lease.[8] The current attitude of the U.S. Department of State is that the exercise of jurisdiction over a diplomat, whether the case stems from the exercise of his public or private activities, would "interfere with and hamper him in the performance of his official functions."[9] The rule, followed in executive and judicial practice,[10] also has been reinforced by writers of international law.[11]

---

[5] [1914] 1 Ch. 139.

[6] ILC Secretariat Memorandum, p. 165.

[7] William Barnes, "Diplomatic Immunity from Local Jurisdiction," *DSB,* XLIII (August 1, 1960), 179.

[8] John Bassett Moore, *A Digest of International Law* (Washington: Government Printing Office, 1906), IV, 637. In his instructions to Jay, Secretary Fish declared: "The assertion of these immunities should be reserved for more important and delicate occasions, and should never be made use of when the facts of the particular case can expose the envoy to the suspicion that private interest or a desire to escape personal or pecuniary liability is the motive which induced it. . . ." This citation is also used as an illustration by Barnes, *DSB,* XLIII, 179.

[9] Barnes, *DSB,* XLIII, 179.

[10] In 1939, when officials considered the attachment of property possessed by the Minister of Costa Rica in Washington, the State Department's Legal Adviser held that writs or processes in civil actions (as well as criminal) could not properly be served on diplomatic representatives. Green Haywood Hackworth, *Digest of International Law* (Washington: Government Printing Office, 1942), IV, 534. In 1956, a New York district court declared that it was clear that a court may not issue a process against a defendant as long as he has diplomatic immunity. *Arcaya v. Paez,* 145 F. Supp. 464 (1956). Cf. *Carrera v. Carrera,* 174 F. 2nd 496 (1949) in which the court declared: "It has long been a settled rule of law that foreign diplomatic representatives are exempt from all local processes in the country to which they are accredited. *Kent's Commentaries,* I, 15, 38"; cited in *Annual Digest* (1949), 288–289, fn.

[11] L. Oppenheim, *International Law,* Vol. I: *Peace,* ed. H. Lauterpacht (8th ed.; London: Longmans, Green and Co., 1955), p. 799. See, for example, *In re Nazare Agha* (France, 1921), *AD* (1919–1922), Case No. 203; *In re The Amazone,* [1940] 1 All. E.R. 269. Also 7 Anne Ch. 12; 22 U.S.C. 252.

However, some courts and a few publicists still maintain that diplomatic agents should not enjoy civil immunity for private acts. In addition, diplomats do not always receive this favored treatment in specified legal areas such as inheritance claims and estate cases. On the other hand, foreign offices subscribe to the general rule that a civil action cannot be brought against the diplomat and that the mere issue of a writ or summons commencing proceedings is null and void.[12] This doctrine of immunity from civil jurisdiction not only has become crystallized in customary international law but is found in both domestic legislation and international conventions.[13]

Giving Evidence

Traditional international law maintains that a diplomatic agent is not compelled to give evidence as a witness,[14] even if his testimony is essential to obtain conviction. This is the current view of the United States,[15] and the rule seems to have been subject to little challenge by

---

[12] For a statement of this doctrine, see *Musurus Bey v. Gadban,* [1894] 2 Q.B. 352. Also, an envoy is not responsible for contracted obligations of his predecessor. *Ortiz v. Hamad* (Argentina, 1956), *ILR* (1957), p. 526.

[13] For examples of domestic legislation, see Great Britain, Act of Parliament for Preserving the Privileges of Ambassadors and Other Publick Ministers of Foreign Princes and States, 7 Anne Ch. 12, 1708, I British and Foreign State Papers 903; 22 U.S.C. 252, 253, 254; Rev. Stat. 4063, 4064, 4065, 4066; and United Nations, Secretariat, *United Nations Legislative Series,* Vol. VIII: *Laws and Regulations Regarding Diplomatic and Consular Privileges and Immunities* (New York, 1958), *passim.* Cited hereafter as *U.N. Laws and Regulations.* For examples of international conventions, see Article 19 of the Convention on Diplomatic Officers, Adopted at Havana, February 20, 1928, reprinted in *AJIL,* XXVI (April, 1932), Supp., 175–177, from English text in *Sixth International Conference of American States: Final Act* (Habana, 1928), pp. 142–150, and Article 31 of the Vienna Convention on Diplomatic Relations, in United Nations, Conference on Diplomatic Intercourse and Immunities, 2 March–14 April, 1961, *Official Records,* Vol. II: (A/CONF.20/14/Add.1) (New York, 1962), pp. 82–88. Cited hereafter as Vienna Convention.

[14] Professor Moore states: "A diplomatic representative can not be compelled to testify, in the country of his sojourn, before any tribunal whatsoever." Moore, IV, 642, quoting 1897 Instructions to United States Diplomatic Officers. See also *ibid.,* 642–646; Hackworth, IV, 551–555; Charles Cheney Hyde, *International Law: Chiefly as Interpreted and Applied by the United States* (2d rev. ed.; Boston: Little, Brown and Company, 1947), II, 1270; Sir Ernest Satow, *A Guide to Diplomatic Practice,* ed. Sir Neville Bland (4th ed.; London: Longmans, Green and Co., 1957), pp. 201–202; Lauterpacht-Oppenheim, I, 717–718. The rule does not necessarily apply to subordinate personnel. For example, see *Juan Ysmael & Company v. S.S. Tasikmalaja* (Hong Kong, 1952), 1952 Hong Kong Law Reports 242; *ILR* (1952), Case No. 94, in which a diplomatic courier was required to testify.

[15] Barnes, *DSB,* XLIII, 179. Barnes also notes that this immunity may be waived.

writers of international law.[16] The U.N. Secretariat, in a Memorandum prepared for the International Law Commission, maintained that in general both authorities and earlier draft codes on diplomatic immunity support the view that while a diplomatic agent is not required to appear as a witness, he must give evidence in the embassy building before a duly appointed commissioner if the request is made through diplomatic channels.[17] On the other hand, even though his immunity protects him from prosecution for perjury, an envoy or staff member is competent to testify as a witness.[18]

Taxation

Of the various fiscal immunities, taxation is perhaps one of the most vexing in terms of theoretical justification and state practice. On the one hand, it is commonly held that immunity from taxation "is not strictly necessary for the exercise of diplomatic functions" and is granted only as a matter of international courtesy.[19] On the other hand, while this "non-essential" prerogative of diplomats has no lengthy tradition in international law, the exemption from taxation is well established in modern times and is supported by the jurisdictional immunities granted diplomats.[20] The United Nations Secretariat, after a recent survey of state practice, attempts at codification, judicial decisions, etc., in the area of diplomatic immunities and privileges, states flatly that there is "no doubt" that the diplomatic agent and his family are exempt from

---

[16]For example, one wrote in 1958: "No envoy can be compelled or even asked to appear as a witness in a criminal, civil or administrative court." Patrick Stirling, "The Immunities of Diplomatic Agents," *Law Journal,* CVIII (April 18, 1958), 244.

[17]ILC Secretariat Memorandum, pp. 167–168. However, the Secretariat admits that at present there is no generally accepted rule on the matter and determination of each case on its merits must be made by the governments involved. *Ibid.,* p. 168.

[18]*Diehl v. United States,* 265 F. 2d 344 (1959). In a criminal prosecution for housebreaking, the court admitted the testimony of a military attaché, the complaining witness, and of a domestic servant in his household, over an objection that diplomatic immunity would prevent prosecution of the witnesses for perjury. The court observed: "These witnesses took the oath, and moreover the diplomatic immunity from punishment for perjury can be waived by superior diplomatic officials." *Ibid.,* p. 345.

[19]Report of the League of Nations Committee of Experts for the Progressive Codification of International Law (Questionnaire No. 3 on Diplomatic Immunities) (C.196.M.70.1927.V, p. 299), cited by A. B. Lyons, "Personal Immunities of Diplomatic Agents," *BYIL,* XXXI (1954), 309, fn.

[20]Harvard Law School, "Research in International Law: I. Diplomatic Privileges and Immunities," *AJIL,* XXVI (April, 1932), Supp., 115ff. Cited hereafter as Harvard Draft.

all taxes levied by the host state "upon their person, their salary, and, as a rule, their personal property."[21]

However, divergent approaches and diverse practices in earlier periods[22] have not entirely disappeared, and conflicting policies still mark this phase of diplomatic immunities.[23] Since usage varies extensively among states, it would seem impracticable to attempt to determine, by a study of state legislation and rules, an absolute minimum of exemptions.[24] Among the reasons why it has been difficult, if not impossible, to establish general rules are (1) the varied opinion as to the existence of such a right[25] and (2) disagreement among those who agree on (1) as to the basis for granting the immunity.[26] However, there is agreement that exemption from taxation is important[27] and that failure to extend this immunity might well hamper the performance of the diplomatic function. Changes in this aspect of diplomatic immunity in the postwar period have been modest in comparison with those of other categories.

One controversial area involves income received by the diplomatic agent and his staff. Professor Lyons suggests that exemptions from income taxes on salary, while possibly not based on any rule of international law, are a matter of municipal law in that nationals of the receiving states are generally excluded from the privilege.[28] He also notes that there is "room for the view that it could be said to offend the sense of what is fitting" for one state to tax salaries paid by another state and it may be this fact "under the guise of comity or courtesy," rather than functional necessity, which provides the basis for exemption from taxation of diplomatic salaries.[29] Professor Hurst also supports this view.[30]

---

[21] ILC Secretariat Memorandum, p. 169.

[22] See, for example, E. R. Adair, *The Exterritoriality of Ambassadors in the Sixteenth and Seventeenth Centuries* (London: Longmans, Green and Co., 1929), pp. 93–100.

[23] See Lyons, *BYIL*, XXXI, 305–306.

[24] Harvard Draft, p. 115; see pp. 117–118 for a review of state practices. For similar recent summaries, see Satow, pp. 230–241, and *U.N. Laws and Regulations, passim.*

[25] See Lyons, *BYIL*, XXXI, 307, for examples.

[26] Lauterpacht-Oppenheim, for example, bases exemption from taxes on the *dictum,* exterritoriality of envoy, without citing supporting authorities. Oppenheim, I, 802–803.

[27] Professor Lyons maintains that exemption from taxation is "perhaps the privilege of the greatest day-to-day importance enjoyed by diplomatic envoys." Lyons, *BYIL*, XXXI, 305.

[28] *Ibid.,* p. 308.

[29] *Ibid.,* pp. 308–309.

[30] Sir Cecil Hurst, *International Law: Collected Papers* (London: Stevens & Sons Limited, 1950), p. 119.

Although the theoretical basis for granting such immunities may be obscure, implementation of the rule through domestic legislation is widespread.[31] For example, Great Britain, the United States, and the U.S.S.R. all extend this privilege through laws which were brought up to date in the 1950's.

The British Income Tax Act of 1952,[32] the "relevant provisions" of which have been found to be "somewhat verbose and obscure, and not always helpful,"[33] does not specifically exempt diplomatic agents from the income tax. However, Professor Lyons finds a general exemption by implication in the Act,[34] and contends, as a result of his extensive analysis, that the Act contains a "clear implication that the income of diplomatic representatives is exempt" from taxation both as a result of legislative interpretation and the application of general rules of international law.[35] The British Foreign Office is more specific and excludes direct application of the Act of 1952. In a memorandum to foreign diplomats, the Foreign Office points out that, except for special tax relief for heads of missions on interest and dividends from British government securities, exemptions from income tax payments rest, not on municipal legislation, but on considerations of international law.[36] The exemption extends to clerks, typists, and domestic servants as well as to official members of the diplomatic staff as long as they are not citizens of the United Kingdom and its colonies.[37]

---

[31] As are immunities from other forms of taxation. See *U.N. Laws and Regulations, passim.*

[32] 15 & 16 Geo. 6 and 1 Eliz. 2, Ch. 10, cited in part in *U.N. Laws and Regulations,* p. 358.

[33] Lyons, *BYIL,* XXXI, 310.

[34] *Ibid.* Lyons refers to Section 461(2) where certain categories of non-diplomats are granted "the same immunity from taxation as that to which a member of the staff of an accredited minister of a foreign state is entitled whether by virtue of any Act or otherwise."

[35] He reasons that in Section 461(2) "any Act" refers to the International Organizations (Immunities and Privileges) Act of 1950 which extends tax exemptions, of the type accorded diplomatic envoys and staffs, to similar personnel connected with international organizations and that "or otherwise" refers to the general law as ascertained from writers of international law. *Ibid.,* p. 311.

[36] Great Britain, Foreign Office, Protocol Department, *Diplomatic and Consular Immunities and Privileges.* (Memorandum describing the practice of Her Majesty's Government in the United Kingdom) (September, 1957), pp. 10, 11. The Protocol Department emphasized that this Memorandum is "compiled for information only" and "does not commit Her Majesty's Government in any way, nor does it purport to constitute an authoritative statement of the legal position." Nonetheless it might be reasonably assumed that this income tax interpretation reflects the official British attitude.

[37] Great Britain, *Diplomatic and Consular Immunities and Privileges,* p. 10.

In the United States, Section 893(a) of the Internal Revenue Code of 1954 (26 U.S. Code) excludes from taxation the wages, fees or salary of a diplomatic officer if such person is not a United States national, if his functions are of a character similar to that of United States agents abroad, and if his government grants similar exemptions to United States personnel.

The Soviet Union, by an executive order in 1956,[38] exempts, subject to reciprocity, nonnational members and employees of foreign diplomatic missions from tax on "remuneration received from the sending organization." Legislation adopted or revised by other nations since World War II reflects a similar policy.[39] Diplomatic representatives and their staffs assigned to the United States are generally exempt from the payment of federal excise taxes, federal income tax on their official salaries, and taxes on their automobiles and other personal property, either tangible or intangible, and on income derived from sources other than from business carried on by them in this country. Under the principles of reciprocity, members of U.S. diplomatic missions can claim immunity from the payment of similar taxes at their overseas posts. The exemption in the U.S. does not apply to citizens of this country although exceptions are made in certain cases for those who hold dual nationality.[40]

One point at issue concerns income derived from the private business or other non-official activities in the country to which the agent is assigned. The authors of the Harvard Draft note that authorities who attempt to distinguish between the official and non-official action of the envoy are not inclined to exclude such income, at least that derived from private sources in the receiving state.[41] Article 34(d) of the Vienna Convention lists as an exception to tax exemption "dues and taxes on private income having its source in the receiving State and capital taxes on investments made in commercial undertakings in the receiving State."

---

[38] Instruction No. 20 of 16 January 1956 of the Ministry of Finance of the U.S.S.R. concerning income tax, paragraph 4, as cited in *U.N. Laws and Regulations,* p. 341.

[39] For example, see Income Tax and Social Services Contribution Assessment Act 1936–1954 of Australia, cited *ibid.,* p. 10; Income Tax Ordinance (Chapter 188) as amended by Income Tax (Amendment) Act No. 1 of 1949 of Ceylon, cited *ibid.,* pp. 59–60; and Decree of 26 October 1950 Concerning Income Tax of Poland, cited *ibid.,* p. 254. For a summary of Canadian law and practice see Ernest H. Smith, "Tax Immunities of Diplomats Under Canadian Law," *Canadian Tax Journal,* VIII (September–October, 1960), 318–324.

[40] U.S., Department of State, Foreign Service Institute, *Diplomatic and Consular Immunities* (November, 1960), p. 2.

[41] Harvard Draft, p. 115. "Here, as in many other situations, there is a confusion between the liability of a diplomat with respect to taxation of his property, and the immunity of the diplomat from any coercion on the part of the receiving State to assert a lien upon property or to force the person to pay the tax." *Ibid.*

U.S. policy, as noted above, appears clear on this point. The Department of State emphasizes that income tax exemption for foreign diplomats does not apply to "any compensation received . . . from other sources [than official income] for services performed" or "from investments" in this country.[42] The problem should not face U.S. diplomats abroad since Foreign Service regulations prohibit them from engaging in private business in the country in which they are stationed.

A 1955 case which involved a Belgian, with diplomatic status, who had also served as vice president of a U.S. candy company, illustrates the American approach.[43] At issue was his company salary for the first six months of 1946, the period before he became ambassador to Portugal and when it was alleged that he rendered no service to the company. Under Section 211(b), as amended, Internal Revenue Code (26 U.S. Code), he was taxed as a nonresident alien engaged in trade or business. He contended that he was not so engaged and that in any event he was not subject to capital gains realized after his departure from the United States. On appeal from a decision of the Tax Court adverse to the petitioner the Court of Appeals held that the Tax Court decision must be affirmed. The court observed:

> The taxpayer never decided to quit as vice president of the company until he was called away to become Ambassador to Portugal. Up to that time he was receiving pay for services or for a call on his services. Hence he was "engaged in business" within the United States. He was an alien, and because of his diplomatic status, was a nonresident alien, despite his presence in this country.[44]

In Great Britain, no exemptions are granted to earnings other than official income (e.g., company directorships) unless the income is derived from sources outside the United Kingdom.[45]

Courts have tended to take a restrictive view on taxation of income

---

[42] *U.N. Laws and Regulations,* p. 371.

[43] *Van Der Elst v. Commissioner of Internal Revenue,* 223 F. 2d 771 (1955); *ILR* (1955), 543.

[44] The court referred to *Jamvold v. Commissioner,* 11 T.C. 122; Treas. Reg. 111, Section 29.111-2(b)

On the matter of the diplomat as a nonresident alien, cf. *In re Société Anonyme des Grands Garages Parisiens* (France, 1930), *AD* (1929–1930), Case No. 192. The firm sold seven motor cars to various diplomatic agents and contended, *inter alia,* that under the fiction of exterritoriality the cars could be considered exported out of France. The court rejected this view.

[45] Great Britain, *Diplomatic and Consular Immunities and Privileges,* p. 10; J. L. Brierly, *The Law of Nations* (5th ed.; Oxford: At the Clarendon Press, 1955), p. 215; Lyons, *BYIL,* XXXI, 311. Professor Lyons contends that "on principle it would seem that income . . . from . . . sources external to the individual's employment in the Embassy should be taxed." *Ibid.,* p. 309.

other than official salary, both in cases during the interwar period and since World War II, although the number of illustrations is somewhat limited. In a German case in 1929, the court reasoned that while an envoy was immune from administrative penalties and from taxation in general, he might be subject to taxation "for special reasons" (not identified), the collection of which could be barred only if it interfered with his official duties.[46] This legalistic circumlocution apparently implied that part of the diplomat's income was taxable for special reasons and could be enforced by means short of disrupting his diplomatic duties.[47] This restrictive view on the immunity from taxation was also reflected in a series of court cases from 1924 to 1940 which held that a diplomat was not immune from a luxury tax except by statutory provision,[48] from professional license fees or taxes on business property,[49] from taxes for public services, land taxes, and inheritance and contract taxes,[50] or from purchase and sales taxes.[51] While there is no federal sales tax in the United States, special provisions providing for diplomatic exemption have been made by local and state taxing units such as the District of Columbia, New York City, and the State of Maryland.[52] On the other hand, some indirect taxes are payable by diplomats assigned to the United States when the tax does not fall directly on the buyer.

These diplomatic taxation policies appear to be universal although states differ in methods of determining liability, the types of income which are taxable, and methods of collection.

Movable and Immovable Property

Post-World War II judicial decisions have in general supported the rule of international law that diplomatic agents enjoy immunity from

---

[46] *Diplomatic Envoys, Exemption from Taxation Case* (Germany, 1927), *AD* (1927–1928), Case No. 248.

[47] See Lyons, *BYIL, XXXI,* 313.

[48] *In re J. N.* (Hungary, 1924), *AD* (1923–1924), Case No. 171.

[49] *Thams v. Minister of Finance* (France, 1930), *AD* (1929–1930), Case No. 191.

[50] *Gobierno de Italia en Svc. v. Consejo Nacional de Educación* (Argentina, 1940), *AD* (1941–1942), 196. Lyons contends that the imposition of legacy and other death taxes cannot by a "stretch of the imagination" constitute a hindrance to a diplomatic envoy in the discharge of his functions. Lyons, *BYIL, XXXI,* 319; see also *ibid.,* pp. 316–318.

[51] *Gobierno de Italia en Svc. v. Consejo National de Education; In re Société Anonyme des Grands Garages Parisiens* (France, 1930), *AD* (1929-1930), Case No. 192. See Lyons, *BYIL, XXXI,* 315–316.

[52] *U.N. Laws and Regulations,* pp. 369–370.

suits involving their personal property. It is generally contended that courts have jurisdiction over private immovable property held by the diplomat,[53] except in regard to such immovable property as is devoted to the official use of the embassy or legation, although there are few cases to illustrate this point.[54] The principle that only immovable property utilized for private pleasure or profit is subject to jurisdiction of the host state is incorporated into the Vienna Convention of 1961.[55]

On the other hand, Sir Cecil Hurst takes issue with this claim that exemption from local jurisdiction does not extend to actions connected with immovable property held by the envoy in a private capacity in the receiving state.[56] He bases his argument, in part, on the difficulty in drawing a clear distinction between immovable property occupied by the agent in his private capacity and that occupied in his official capacity. The foreign representative "is not sometimes an ambassador and sometimes a private individual."[57] However, the trend appears to be, at least in some states, toward making this distinction.

Diplomats are protected from jurisdiction in the rental of immovable property even when leases are obtained under conditions which would be grounds for legal action against non-diplomatic personnel. For example, the Paris Court of Appeal in 1950 held that the cultural counsellor of Spain could not be evicted from an apartment even though the party from whom he had subleased the property had entered into the agreement in violation of her lease.[58] The apartment administrator unsuccessfully contended that diplomatic immunity should not apply since in effect the counsellor had appropriated by force something to which he had no legal right. The same court in 1959 rejected another landlord's plea that immunity should be denied in a transaction which was executed in the form customary for leases between private individuals where the

---

[53] "The local courts also have jurisdiction as regards immovable property held within the boundaries of the receiving State by an envoy, not in his official character but as a private individual." Oppenheim, I, 799.

[54] *Montwid-Biallozor v. Ivaldi* (Poland, 1925), *AD* (1925–1926), Case No. 245. There are few cases illustrating this point; Lyons pointed out in 1953 that this was the only case covering private property of a diplomat reported since 1919 in the *Annual Digest* (A. B. Lyons, "Immunities Other Than Jurisdictional of the Property of Diplomatic Envoys," *BYIL*, XXX (1953), 137).

[55] Article 31(1,a) lists as an exception to immunity "a real action relating to private immovable property situated in the territory of the receiving State, unless he holds it on behalf of the sending State for the purposes of the mission."

[56] Hurst, pp. 223ff.

[57] *Ibid.,* p. 234.

[58] *Martelly et Admin. des Domaines v. Díez del Corral* (France, 1950), ILR (1951), Case No. 111. The court noted that even if the sublease charge were true, it still did not prevent the diplomatic agent from "invoking his immunity from jurisdiction in a personal, civil action."

premises had been leased to a "commercial department," in this case the Commercial Department of the Spanish Embassy.[59]

In other postwar decisions, courts have not questioned this basic premise.[60] The rule was well stated by the Supreme Court of Chile in another rental case, *In re Chayet,*[61] when it declared that the diplomat's "inviolability protects not only his person but his house and the movable property for his personal use or necessary for the performance of his duties."

As for movable property, there are few cases concerning the seizure or other interference with goods belonging to diplomatic envoys. However, it is clear that protection extends to all property which is necessary for the fulfillment of the diplomatic function.[62] The test as to whether the property is necessary for the convenience of the envoy as applied by the courts in *Novello v. Toogood*[63] apparently still stands.[64] The question is whether such immunity extends to all of the property owned by the diplomat. This may be doubted. Lyons observes the basic difference between the approach of Sir Cecil Hurst who would extend immunity to all such goods wherever found and whether or not they are needed to fill the functions of a mission, and Sir Ernest Satow who would grant immunity only if goods of the envoy or the premises are used for diplomatic purposes or occupied by the envoy.[65] There might be some question about the status of diplomatic goods left in pawn or

---

[59] *Laforest v. Commercial Department of the Spanish Embassy* (France, 1959), 28 *ILR* 357 [1959]. Cf. *Parker v. Boggan,* [1947]1 All E.R. 46; *AD* (1946), Case No. 75, in which the court struck down a landlord's refusal to approve a sublease to the counsellor of the Turkish Embassy in London. The ground for the refusal was that the Turk had diplomatic status and thus could not be sued in English courts. See also *De Miglio v. Paez,* 18 Misc. 2d 914, 189 *N.Y.S.* 2d, 593 (1959).

[60] For example, *Acuña de Arce v. Solórzano y Menocal* ([Chile, 1956], *ILR* [1956], 422) in which immunity was invoked after execution of the court's order, and *Ribeiro v. Chinatti* ([Brazil, 1954], *ILR* [1954], 249). Cf. *Demoiselle B. v. D.* (France, 1927), *AD* (1927–1928), Case No. 249. For a contrary view, see *Minister of Belgium v. Judge of Second Court of First Instance in Civil Matters of Santiago* (Chile, 1952), *ILR* (1952), Case No. 88.

[61] (Chile, 1932), *AD* (1931–1932), Case No. 181.

[62] Lyons, *BYIL,* XXX, 149.

[63] (1823), 107 E.R. 204.

[64] Although the case involved a servant, Lyons maintains that it "would probably guide an English court in a case where the goods of an envoy had been seized." Lyons, *BYIL,* XXX, 121.

[65] *Ibid.,* pp. 119–120. The Soviet Union apparently follows the Satow approach, one Russian publication noting that "the property rights of a diplomatic envoy are not considered inviolable when they are not linked with the fulfillment of his official functions." Y. A. Korovin and Others, *International Law* (Moscow: Foreign Languages Publishing House, [1961]), p. 303.

a vehicle in a garage for repairs.[66] Developments in the postwar period apparently have not carried the rule past this point.

The expression by Professor Lyons that intangible property of an envoy probably must be regarded as covered by diplomatic immunity seems reasonable, since restriction of his enjoyment of this income[67] might seriously inconvenience him, make it difficult for him to maintain his proper status and diplomatic appearance, and hinder him to such an extent as to be a violation of international law.[68] A court in Uruguay approached the problem from this same point of view when it held that bank deposits of a diplomatic secretary and an attaché of the French Legation must be released despite a judicial moratorium which suspended all transactions by the bank. The court, in considering the case of *In re Ledoux,*[69] emphasized the judicious caution which is essential to avoid infringement of the diplomat's activities:

> The immunity of diplomatic agents from civil jurisdiction rests upon a logical and simple base. As diplomatic agents they do not acquire legal domicil in the place where they discharge their mission; there is no ground which justifies the intervention of our tribunals with respect to their persons or their property. On the other hand, diplomatic agents cannot be obliged to appear before our tribunals without infringing their inviolability and without disturbing gravely the exercise of their function.[70]

Immunity, the court added, would be useless unless it were extended to "everything necessary for him [the diplomat] to live with dignity." Everything which belongs directly to him in his official capacity; everything which he uses; everything which serves for his maintenance or that of his house is "absolutely exempt" from jurisdiction.[71] There appears to be a general rule that the diplomat's intangible property is protected by his immunity.

Exceptions to Immunity

There are a number of exceptions to immunity from civil jurisdiction, some of which are incorporated into the Vienna Convention,

---

[66] Lyons, *BYIL,* XXX, 149.

[67] "It has to be remembered that the dividends, interests, or royalties arising therefrom may constitute a part — it might be embarrassing to inquire how considerable a part — of his income." *Ibid.,* p. 150.

[68] *Ibid.* But note the section on Private Acts of diplomats in this chapter for evidence of an opposing philosophy.

[69] (Uruguay, 1941), *AD* (1943–1945), Case No. 75.

[70] *Ibid.,* pp. 241–242.

[71] *Ibid.,* p. 242.

and most of which do not seem to have been altered significantly during the postwar period. Under the Vienna Convention, exceptions to the diplomatic immunity from taxation include, in addition to private income, direct taxes, taxes on private immovable property, estate and inheritance duties, service charges, registration and court fees.[72]

It is also recognized that an exception to tax immunity arises when an envoy enters an action against himself and allows it to proceed without pleading immunity.[73] But even where he has waived his immunity down to judgment, he can plead immunity to bar execution of the judgment for as long as his mission continues and for a reasonable period afterward. Judgments cannot be executed against the diplomatic agent except in exceptional cases (e.g., estate, immovable private property) and where the measures do not infringe upon the inviolability of the diplomat.[74]

A number of decisions during the interwar period were concerned with counterclaims and setoffs; however, the rule stated in Oppenheim still seems to stand as a reasonable guide:

> If he himself [a diplomatic agent] brings an action under the jurisdiction of the receiving State, whereupon [sic] the courts of the latter have civil jurisdiction over him to the extent, it is submitted, of enforcing the ordinary incidents of procedure, including a setoff or counterclaim by the defendant arising out of the same matter, but even then not so as to enable the latter to recover from the envoy an excess over and above the latter's claim.[75]

There appeared to be some deviation from this rule when the Court of Rome, in *Cholam Samsani v. Società Urbe,*[76] held that a diplomatic representative, as plaintiff in an original suit, may plead exemption from jurisdiction if he should become a defendant in a counterclaim. The court observed that in bringing the action, the diplomat accepted jurisdiction "only within the strict limits of the action brought by himself" and that "the new counterclaim on the part of the defendant goes beyond the limits of the principal action and gives rise to a new judgment."[77] The United Nations Secretariat, in reviewing the case as part

---

[72]Article 34. An indication of agreement on general principles might be reflected in the brevity of discussion when the International Law Commission considered the article on taxation. United Nations, International Law Commission, *Yearbook: 1957,* Vol. I (A/CN.4/SER.A/1957), pp. 118–119.

[73]Oppenheim, I, 799. *In re Suarez, Suarez v. Suarez,* [1917] 2 Ch. 131.

[74]See Article 31(3), Vienna Convention. Cf. *Dickinson v. Del Solar,* [1930] 1 K.B. 376.

[75]Oppenheim, I, 799–800.

[76](Italy, 1940), *AD* (1941–1942), Case No. 111.

[77]*AD* (1941–1942), 373.

of a general survey of diplomatic privileges and immunities, observed:

> The Court concluded that a diplomatic representative may plead exemption from jurisdiction even in the case of a counterclaim, that such a plea is well founded and that the counterclaim brought by the defendant cannot therefore be entertained.[78]

The Secretariat concluded, however, that "this view . . . is not generally accepted."[79] For example, Sir Cecil Hurst observed that both English and French courts have assumed jurisdiction in counterclaims against diplomats arising out of the same facts as those found in the original action.[80] Hersch Lauterpacht, as editor of the *Annual Digest,* pointed out that English courts "allow counterclaims as a defense, but not if they constitute substantially independent actions in respect of other and entirely distinct matters."[81] This view that counterclaims must be confined within the general limitations of the original action appears to be the accepted one. For this reason, courts study the merits of each particular case[82] and extraneous charges cannot be included in counterclaims.[83]

Another exception to civil jurisdiction which finds authorities and practices at odds concerns professional, commercial, and private trading activities of the diplomatic agent. While many publicists and jurists appear to support the view that exemption from jurisdiction should be respected even where an agent engages in commercial activities,[84] the signatory powers of the Vienna Convention appear to have moved from codification to progressive development of international law by including as an exception from civil immunity "an action relating to any professional or commercial activity exercised by the diplomatic agent in the receiving State outside his official functions."[85]

---

[78] ILC Secretariat Memorandum, p. 165.

[79] *Ibid.* The facts as presented in the *Annual Digest* would indicate that the court considered that a second lawsuit arose as the result of the lodging of the counterclaim. This also would appear to be the interpretation of the United Nations Secretariat and would differ from the not unusual practice of disallowing a counterclaim on the grounds it relates to a separate cause of action.

[80] Hurst, pp. 242–244.

[81] *AD* (1941–1942), 374, fn. Lauterpacht observed that the Court of Rome's approach "conforms with that held by English courts," thus apparently viewing the counterclaim as relating to separate matters from the original suit. If this were the case, then the decision would not, as the U.N. Secretariat noted, reflect a generally unacceptable view.

[82] *Chinese Embassy (Immunities) Case* (Germany, 1925), *AD* (1925–1926), Case No. 243; cf. *Drtilek v. Barbier* (France, 1925), *AD* (1925–1926), Case No. 242.

[83] *High Commissioner for India and Others v. Ghosh,* [1959] 3 All E.R. 659; *AJIL,* LIV (1960), 412.

[84] ILC Secretariat Memorandum, p. 167.

[85] Article 31(1,c).

This may reflect the movement from absolute to limited immunities concerning the governmental and business activities of states and their instrumentalities. The Vienna Convention is compatible with earlier draft codes which were analyzed by United Nations experts in connection with preliminary work leading up to the 1961 agreement. These codes reportedly upheld the principle that a diplomatic agent who engages in private commercial transactions or holds real property in the receiving state is not immune to a suit resulting from such private business.[86] The International Law Commission noted that these activities are normally inconsistent with the position of a diplomatic agent, and many customs conventions limit the duty-free privilege to those persons who engage solely in official activities. The sage advice of Satow quite possibly is heeded by most diplomats: "It will be better for more reasons than one, to eschew all speculation and commercial transactions of whatever nature in the country where he is accredited."[87] Nevertheless, persons with whom the agent has had commercial or professional relations cannot be deprived of their ordinary remedies.[88]

This view is supported by a 1930 French case, *Thams v. Minister of Finance*[89] in which the counsellor of the Legation of Monaco in Paris, who represented a number of business firms there, was held liable for taxes on commercial premises.[90] This approach is also taken by some writers. For example, Charles Dupuis states that exemption from jurisdiction would not extend to a diplomatic agent who engages in commercial transactions in the host country. However, he adds that "in doubtful cases, it would be the function not of the local courts but of the sending State to determine the dividing line."[91] The most important judicial expression of this restrictive point of view has been made

---

[86] ILC Secretariat Memorandum, p. 164. The documents analyzed were Bluntschli's Draft Code, 1868; Fiore's Draft Code, 1890; Pessoa's Draft Code, 1911; Phillimore's Draft Code, 1926; Strupp's Draft Code, 1926; Draft Code of the Japanese Branch of the International Law Association and the Kokusaiho Gakkwai, 1926; Project of the International Commission of American Jurists, 1927; Resolution of the Institute of International Law, 1929; Harvard Draft Code, 1932. Cited *ibid.*, pp. 146–152.

[87] Satow, p. 192.

[88] United Nations, International Law Commission, "Report to the General Assembly Covering the Work of Its Tenth Session, 28 April–4 July, 1958" (A/3859), *Yearbook: 1958,* Vol. II (A/CN.4/SER.A/1958/Add.1), p. 98.

[89] (France, 1930), *AD* (1929–1930), Case No. 191.

[90] Cf. *Van Der Elst v. Commissioner of Internal Revenue,* 223 F. 2d 771 (1955).

[91] Charles Dupuis, "Liberté des voies de communications. Relations internationales," *Recueil des cours de l'Académie de droit international* (Paris: Librairie Hachette, 1924), I, 303, cited in ILC Secretariat Memorandum, p. 167.

by Italian courts and is considered below in its broader context of immunities for private acts.[92] A more liberal interpretation has been taken by Britain where it is "well established" that immunity from jurisdiction is still granted even though the ambassador engages in trade.[93] British courts seem to have been rather consistent in holding that suits involving business activities would hamper the diplomat's activities as much as other types of civil actions.[94]

Despite these conflicting developments, one may accept Professor Gould's view that "a rule of general international law will sustain a diplomat's plea of immunity while in office in actions brought against him in consequence of his business activities";[95] however, the trend may be toward a more restrictive approach to this exemption from civil jurisdiction.

A final comment on exceptions to jurisdictional immunity overlaps some of those previously considered, but raises the basic point of state treatment of the diplomat concerning public (or official) and private (or nonofficial) acts — which might be connected with business activities or with a variety of other matters, e.g., traffic violations, contracts, etc. The established rule of international law that a diplomatic agent, while undertaking a mission for his country, is exempt (excluding acceptable exceptions) from the jurisdiction of the receiving state, both with respect to public and private acts, is compatible with the concept that immunity is extended not for the benefit of the individual but for the benefit of the state so that he may fulfill his diplomatic duties with dispatch and independence.

However, he is not exempt from the local law for acts performed in a private capacity, since his immunity in this case is merely an immunity from the jurisdiction of local courts and other authorities. For example, see *Dickinson v. Del Solar*[96] which is notable more for the "suggestive dicta" of Lord Hewart, than for the decision per se. He suggested that diplomatic privilege does not impart immunity from legal liability from local jurisdiction and that the diplomat may be sued in his own or a third state in actions arising before or during his tenure

---

[92] See following section on Private Acts.

[93] Holland, *Cur. Leg. Prob.,* IV, 96. For similar views, see Hurst, p. 241ff, and Oppenheim, I, 716.

[94] See, for example, *Taylor v. Best* (1854), 14 C.B. 487; *In re Republic of Bolivia Exploration,* [1914] 1 Ch. 139; and *Magdalena Steam Navigation Company v. Martin* (1859), 2 E. & E. 94, discussed in Satow, pp. 184–185.

[95] Wesley Gould, *An Introduction to International Law* (New York: Harper & Brothers Publishers, 1957), pp. 272–273.

[96] [1930] 1 K.B. 376.

of office.[97] The distinction is important. Immunity for official acts is permanent; the host state may never bring action in its courts with regard to these acts.[98] On the other hand, legal liability may be imported for unofficial acts in cases of waiver and termination of mission.

Private Acts

In legal theory, the diplomat has immunity from jurisdiction regardless of the public or private nature of the act. However, it is in this field of diplomatic immunity that courts have labored diligently in the modern period (a) to find that elusive line between public and private acts and (b) to determine whether diplomats may be hailed before local courts when only a private aspect of their conduct is involved. The decisions bridge the gap from the concept of absolute immunity from jurisdiction (liberal or Anglo-American interpretation), to the limited (or restrictive view) which would bar immunity from jurisdiction for acts of a private character.

Although Italy has traditionally been the nation most sympathetic toward the restrictive view, Italian courts have moved from one pole to the other, and without complete consistency, in a series of cases dating from 1922 to 1953. While the significant decisions for purposes of this study were rendered in the 1950's, a review of the earlier cases is helpful in placing the recent developments within a proper historical framework.

In 1922, the Court of Cassation of Rome (Combined Division) decided in *Comina v. Kite*[99] that diplomatic agents are subject to the jurisdiction of Italian courts in accordance with the rules of Italian common law for private acts and obligations and not for those committed as representatives of their governments. In this case, the proceedings had been brought against an employee of the American Embassy in Rome to compel him to release an apartment which he had rented from

---

[97] See Horace E. Read, "Case and Comment," *Canadian Bar Review*, IX (June, 1931), 444–447, and James W. Garner, "Introductory Note — Decisions of National Tribunals Involving Points of International Law," *BYIL*, XI (1930), 227. Cf. *Parker v. Boggan*, [1947] 1 All E.R. 46, and *Norton v. General Accident, Fire and Life Assurance Company* (Erie, 1940), *AD* (1938–1940), Case No. 163, in which Maguire, J., accepts the reasoning of Lord Hewart.

[98] For this reason, a diplomat is entitled to immunity for his official acts even after the termination of his duties. See for example, *Zoernsch v. Waldock*, [1964] 2 All E.R. 256 where Diplock, L.J., comments (p. 266): "An envoy's immunity from suit and legal process in respect to acts done in his official capacity was permanent, unless waived by his government. . . ." See also comment on Article 18, Harvard Draft, pp. 97–99.

[99] (Italy, 1922), *AD* (1919–1922), Case No. 202.

the plaintiff.[100] The court declared that "the absolute immunity put forward from historical times is now ended" since it was "contrary to justice and to legal logic." It was contended that private acts have no relation to the exercise of sovereignty or to the functions of the sending government; nor do they impair the dignity and effectiveness of the mission; hence there is no need for protection by the principle of immunity. Furthermore, the court maintained that a diplomatic agent should not use his legal protection to avoid debts, invoke Italian laws only for his own advantage, etc.

The decision, which Professor Briggs calls an "aberration,"[101] may have been just that as far as general international law is concerned, but perhaps it was not such an aberration in Italian judicial circles. According to the editor of the *Annual Digest,* the view that diplomatic agents do not enjoy immunity in matters of a private law nature apparently was first expressed by the Court of Cassation of Naples in a decision of March 16, 1886,[102] and then by the Court of Cassation of Rome in a decision of April 20, 1915.[103] In the period between these two decisions, the Court of Appeals in Rome[104] and the Court of First Instance of Rome,[105] both in 1912, declared themselves in favor of absolute immunity.

This liberal interpretation of 1912 was reversed by *Comina v. Kite,* and the decision was sharply criticized by the United States and the Diplomatic Corps in Rome. The Department of State noted that the effort on the part of a diplomat to procure living quarters did not mean engaging in private business, and it noted further that under similar circumstances an Italian diplomat in the United States would be "entirely exempt" from judicial process. The French ambassador, as dean of the Diplomatic Corps, informed the Italian government that the decision was contrary to the accepted practice of all states.[106] In addition, a League of Nations expert observed that Italian law was unsettled on this point and that the restrictive approach had drawn much criticism

---

100 See also Hackworth, IV, 548–549.

101 Herbert W. Briggs (ed.), *The Law of Nations* (2d ed.; New York: Appleton-Century-Crofts, Inc., 1952), p. 783.

102 *Typaldos v. Lunatic Asylum of Aversa, AD* (1938–1940), 426, fn.

103 *In re Rinaldi, AD* (1938–1940), 426, fn.

104 *Avedo Diaz v. Loschiavo, AD* (1938–1940), 426, fn.

105 *Rampa v. Minister for Foreign Affairs, AD* (1938–1940), 426, fn.

106 "Cette décision est en contradiction avec la règle communément, admise jusqu'ici et suivie en pratique par tous les États; Cette régle est, qu'en principe les Agents diplomatiques sont exempts de la juridiction non seulement pénale mais civile, dans les pays où ils sont accredités." Harvard Draft, p. 105.

from within the country.[107] The principle followed in *Comina v. Kite* was rejected in a series of later decisions, the principal ones being *Harrie Lurie v. Steinmann*,[108] *De Meeus v. Forzano*,[109] and *Lagos Carmona v. Baggianini*.[110] However, there were some intervening cases which were not compatible with the new interpretation.

In *Harrie Lurie v. Steinmann,* the court held that immunity applied to the private acts of the ecclesiastical counsellor of the German Embassy accredited to the Holy See and that such immunity was not limited to the head of mission but applies to the "whole of the official staff of the Embassy or Legation." The court contended, in response to plaintiff's argument, that the Law of Guarantee of 1871 (Article 11), which provided for diplomatic immunity for representatives of foreign governments, specifically applied to private acts since no question of immunity arises when diplomats act as agents of the state. The court ruled categorically that diplomats were outside the jurisdiction of the host country.

Although *Harrie Lurie v. Steinmann* was clearly distinguished from *Comina v. Kite,* there followed a series of cases in the Courts of Rome and Florence which reverted to the restrictive theory. In the first of these, *Perrucchetti v. Puig y Cassauro*,[111] the court held that it had jurisdiction over the Mexican ambassador who had pleaded immunity in a dispute arising from the purchase of property to be used as an embassy building. The court contended that diplomatic immunity as secured under international custom could not be extended beyond activity relating to the fulfillment of the main diplomatic functions since "the case of political relations constitutes the real scope of a diplomatic mission." Under this theory, diplomatic privilege normally could not be claimed by a state in its economic and juridical (private law) relations, such as the acquisition of property, and the fact that a contract is concluded by a diplomatic agent and that the foreign state is summoned in the person of the diplomat is immaterial.[112]

---

[107] M. Diena, rapporteur of the subcommittee on diplomatic privileges and immunities of the League of Nations Committee of Experts for the Progressive Codification of International Law, in his report to that committee, said: "These judgments of the Courts [*In re Rinaldi and Comina v. Kite*] have been strongly criticised, however, even in Italy, from the point of view of international law as it exists to-day, and it cannot be said that in Italy the law is definitely settled in this sense." League of Nations pub. (C.196.M.70.1927.V/1927.V.1/p.80); cited in Hackworth, IV, 551.

[108] (Italy, 1927), *AD* (1927–1928), Case No. 246.

[109] (Italy, 1940), *AD* (1938–1940), Case No. 164.

[110] (Italy, 1953), *ILR* (1955), 533.

[111] (Italy, 1928) *AD* (1927–1928), Case No. 247.

[112] See Editor's Note, *AD* (1927–1928), p. 366.

Two years later, the Rome court issued a similar ruling in *Cimino Bosco v. Luijano Escheverri*.[113] The court held that it had jurisdiction over the wife of a diplomatic agent of Colombia accredited to the Holy See, who was involved in a contract action, because the act was of private law nature. The reasoning differed slightly from that followed in the *Perrucchetti* case since the court maintained in its *dictum* that a doctrine of immunity modified by territorial sovereignty had replaced the old concept of extraterritoriality.[114]

A third case, following the same pattern, involved a car, owned by the diplomatic secretary of the Chilean Embassy to the Holy See, which ran over an Italian national who brought action against the ambassador as a representative of Chile. In this case, *Balloni v. The Ambassador of Chile to the Holy See*,[115] the court held that the embassy's plea to its jurisdiction was ineffective. The reasoning seemed to be little more than a refinement of the sovereignty concept followed in the *Bosco* case. Jurisdictional immunity, the court contended, is accorded to diplomatic agents under international custom. Since customary rules stem from the need for full freedom by the diplomats to carry out the functions of their mission, immunities can be determined from the nature of the mission, and exemption from jurisdiction would not apply to any acts committed by agents or members of their suite outside the sphere of their official functions.

The *Perrucchetti, Bosco,* and *Balloni* cases illustrated the "predominant tendency" (restrictive) of the Italian courts during this period — 1928 to 1934 — in dealing with jurisdictional immunity for private acts.[116] On the other hand, Italian writers tended to favor the extension of diplomatic immunity to purely private acts,[117] as did the Court of Cassation in *De Meeus v. Forzano* in 1940.[118] The court held that immunity from civil jurisdiction covered acts of a private law nature lying out-

---

[113] (Italy, 1930), *AD* (1929–1930), Case No. 196.

[114] The court observed: "The old theory of extraterritoriality of diplomatic agents has been abandoned and replaced by another, more correct, doctrine which reconciles the principle of territorial sovereignty with that of immunity which the representatives of foreign States must enjoy in the sense that not only the families but also the diplomatic agents themselves are subject to the territorial laws and to the jurisdiction of our courts in regard to all questions of private law concerning their persons, except when the agents have acted as representatives or at the order of the foreign State." *AD* (1929–1930), p. 304.

[115] (Italy, 1934), *AD* (1933–1934), Case No. 164.

[116] See Editor's Note, *AD* (1933–1934), 384.

[117] *Ibid.*

[118] (Italy, 1940), *AD* (1938–1940), Case No. 164. Cf. *Cholam Samsani v. Società Urbe* (Italy, 1940), *AD* (1941–1942), Case No. 111, in which the lower court, in granting diplomatic immunity also in respect to acts of a private law nature, followed this decision of the United Sections of the Court of Cassation.

side the sphere of diplomatic functions. The facts in the case are not clear, but it appears that a Belgian diplomat appealed from a decision of the Court of Rome of December 15, 1937, which had rejected his invocation of diplomatic immunity in respect to acts of a private law nature. He also argued that since Belgium granted immunity in such instances, Italian courts had to allow his plea by way of reciprocity.[119]

The Court of Cassation based its reversal of the Court of Rome's decision on reasoning somewhat as follows: Firstly, the principle that diplomats are inviolable is derived from the ancient rule of *jus gentium* and became firmly established with the spread of permanent missions. Secondly, this inviolability requires freedom of action on the part of the diplomat, action which would be diminished by exercise of jurisdiction by the host state. Thirdly, there was never any question of immunity in public activity; the only problem concerned immunity from civil jurisdiction for private transactions.

In this latter case, if immunity is based on the "inherent quality" of the diplomatic agent, then it would be difficult to grant it in part and deny it in part;[120] on the other hand, if immunity is of a personal nature, it is by nature indivisible. And finally, the court observed that in order to exercise public functions freely, the diplomat must be exempt from jurisdiction even in respect of acts concerning his private life. The court also referred to a number of precedents to support its view that immunity from civil jurisdiction is extended to transactions of a private law nature.

While there were no special provisions in Italian law, the court referred to a law of May 27, 1929, No. 810[121] (which implemented the Lateran Treaty), in which reference is made to privileges and immunities enjoyed by diplomatic agents, according to international law, without inclusion of any restrictive definition of the terms. Express agreements also lend force to this policy and the court cited The Hague Agreement of May 22, 1928, concerning the status of members and officials of the

---

[119] It is interesting to note that an Italian court was unmoved by a similar United States plea in *Comina v. Kite, supra,* p. 114. Cf. *Società Arethusa Film v. Reist* (Italy, 1953), *ILR* (1955), 549.

[120] The court observed: "It would be difficult and arbitrary to indicate any limit in the matter without creating the possibility of suspicion that artificial restrictions are being imposed upon that special liberty which is the ultimate reason for immunity and which the authorities of the receiving State intended to guarantee to the agent." *AD* (1938–1940), 424.

[121] Treaty between the Vatican and Italy, signed at Rome, February 11, 1929, cited in *AJIL*, XXIII (July, 1929), Supp., 187–195.

Permanent Court of International Justice,[122] the Lateran Treaty, and the Havana Convention.

The restrictive theory of diplomatic immunity seemed to be well on its way out of Italian jurisprudence by 1953 when the Tribunal of Rome, in a civil action involving the third secretary of the Chilean Embassy in Italy, reversed a lower court and again held that Italian courts had no jurisdiction in an action against a foreign diplomatic agent whether or not the action arose out of acts of a private character. In this case, *Lagos Carmona v. Baggianini,*[123] the appellate court held that the lower court had returned to earlier case law which had "long been discredited"[124] instead of following the "generally accepted rule" acknowledged by the United Chambers of the Court of Cassation.[125]

The court traced the origin and historical evolution of the institution of diplomatic immunity,[126] then said that the phrase *ne impediatur legatio* explained the modern *ratio* as well as the sphere within which immunities are to be granted. The nonrestrictive approach was also supported by more practical reasons: e.g., the difficulty in distinguishing between public and private acts; the different stages of civilization among nations which necessitates full jurisdictional immunity, and the impairment of international relations which might result if coercive action is taken against foreign diplomats.[127]

After establishing that full jurisdictional immunity from civil suits existed in international law, the court found evidence that the interna-

---

[122] The court observed that The Hague Agreement expresses what at that time were held to be the rules of international law in force with respect to diplomatic immunities and privileges. "It confirms the absolute immunity appertaining to the person of the diplomatic agent with special reference to exemption from the jurisdiction of the receiving State." *AD* (1938–1940), 425.

[123] (Italy, 1953), *ILR* (1955), 533.

[124] *ILR* (1955), 534; see *Comina v. Kite, supra,* p. 114.

[125] *ILR* (1955), 534; see *De Meeus v. Forzano, supra,* p. 117. Sir Hersch Lauterpacht, editor of the *Annual Digest,* apparently viewed the *De Meeus* case as the significant reversal in Italian judicial practice and reproduced the court's reasoning at some length.

[126] The court declared the reasons for the existence of diplomatic immunity can be attributed to: (1) "The representative character of the envoy" who "brings abroad with him the marks of the absolutism of his sovereign *legibus solutus* with respect to the legal system of his own state." (2) "The function in *jus gentium* of considering *extra territorium,* and therefore withdrawn from local sovereignty, the person of the envoy." (3) "The necessity of granting the envoy a protection greater than that granted to the ordinary alien, to ensure the performance of his diplomatic mission." (4) "The necessity — which arose with the development of the constitutional form of the modern State — of maintaining peaceful relations in the international community." *ILR* (1955), 535–536.

[127] *Ibid.,* p. 536.

tional rules were adapted to the Italian system.[128] Furthermore, nations have signed numerous multilateral agreements declaring their willingness to exempt diplomatic agents from civil suits in respect of acts connected with their official duties.[129] These conventions and laws "leave no room for doubt as to the existence of a *consensus gentium* and of an international custom, the binding force of which is recognized by the family of nations, and which ensures full jurisdictional immunity to diplomatic agents in the States in which they carry out their duties."[130]

The trend in the cases supporting a liberal approach to jurisdictional immunity is compatible with the generally accepted rules of international law, especially as found in Anglo-American practice. However, in recent cases, Italian courts have again appeared to challenge this liberal interpretation which had been clearly endorsed by Italian jurists.

In *Castiglioni v. Federal People's Republic of Yugoslavia,*[131] the Tribunal of Rome held that immunity is extended to the agent as a person and not as an organ of his state. When the Yugoslav minister was summoned to answer for acts done in a private law case brought against Yugoslavia, the question of jurisdiction no longer involved diplomatic immunity but the ability of a state to exercise jurisdiction over another state.[132] In other words, the diplomat wears two hats: one as

---

[128] Reference was made to Article 10 of the Italian Constitution: "The Italian legal system conforms to the generally accepted rules of international law and to Article 12 of the Lateran Treaty which grants foreign diplomats accredited to the Holy See the benefit within Italy and privileges and immunities conferred on diplomatic agents by international law." The court also found similar enactments in other nations: The Austrian Decree Laws of 1811, German legislation of 1925, the Civil Code of Colombia, Decree of the Soviet Socialist Republics of June 30, 1921, and the Constitution of the United States. *Ibid.*

[129] *Ibid.* Cited were the Havana Convention of 1928 (Articles 19 and 20), the Agreement of September 20, 1926, between the Swiss Federal Council and the League of Nations (for English translation, see Martin Hill, *Immunities and Privileges of International Officials* [Washington: Carnegie Endowment for International Peace, 1947], pp. 138–142); Agreement of May 28, 1928, between the Netherlands and the Permanent Court of International Justice (for English translation, see *ibid.,* pp. 199–202); and a Convention between Roumania and the European Commission for the Danube, which granted "full immunity from jurisdiction to the Heads of Service of the Commissions and their deputies who did not possess Roumanian nationality, while for all other officials the immunity was limited to their official acts." *ILR* (1955), 536–537.

[130] *ILR* (1955), p. 537. *Cf. Società Vivai Industriali Roma v. Legazione dell' Arabia Saudita* (Italy, 1953), *AJIL,* XLIX (1955), 585, which upheld the immunity of the Saudi Arabian minister in Rome from suit in the Italian courts, and *Cholam Samsani v. Società Urbe* (Italy, 1940), *AD* (1941–1942), Case No. 111, which ruled in a civil case involving the first secretary at the Persian Legation in Italy that the privilege of immunity extends to acts of a private law nature.

[131] (Italy, 1952), ILR (1952), Case No. 43.

[132] *AJIL,* XLIX (1955), 100. Cf. *Perrucchetti v. Puig y Cassauro* (Italy, 1928), *AD* (1927–1928), Case No. 247.

the political representative of the state at which time he is immune from civil jurisdiction; the other as a representative of his state in a private law matter, at which time he is not immune.

In a 1953 case, *Società Arethusa Film v. Reist,* [133] the court agreed with the newly emerging Italian practice against restrictive immunities but held that such immunity did not apply to subordinate staff members, in this case Wilbur H. Reist, Chancellor of the United States Embassy in Rome. The court noted that many prior decisions defined civil immunity for diplomatic agents but that the Court of Cassation had not previously been concerned with regard to retinue and subordinate staff. However, the same court in 1927 had observed in its *dicta* that immunity for private acts applied to the "whole of the official staff." [134]

In its 1953 decision, the court, accepting the representational theory of diplomatic immunity, claimed that submitting subordinate personnel such as secretaries and clerks to jurisdiction for their private actions would not restrict their freedom of action relative to functions connected with their mission. The court found support for this point of view in Article 7 of the 1926 agreement between the League of Nations and the Swiss Federal Council. [135] The court, in rejecting Reist's plea of reciprocity, contended that United States practice was irrelevant since it was only a lone instance from which no customary rule of international law could be deduced. [136]

Six years later, the court in Rome narrowed the list of diplomatic agents entitled to immunity for private acts by excluding attachés on the grounds that they were technical personnel whose functions were not concerned with the diplomatic representation of a state. [137] Also in 1959, the Italian Court of Cassation held that a contract between the Venezuelan Naval Mission to Italy and Italian citizens employed

---

[133] (Italy, 1953), *ILR* (1955), 544.

[134] *AD* (1927–1928), Case No. 202.

[135] *Supra,* fn. 129. Article 7 established the liberal principle of immunity (including private acts) for diplomatic agents of the first category, then stated: "Le personnel de second catégorie jouit des mêmes privilèges pour les acts accomplis officiellement et dans la limite de ses attributions. Il reste soumis aux lois et à juridiction locale pour les actes de sa vie privée." Similar stipulations were noted in the 1938 European Danube Commission-Roumanian agreement. *Ibid.*

[136] *ILR* (1955), 549; cf. *De Meeus v. Forzano, supra,* p. 117 for a contrary conclusion by the Court of Cassation.

[137] *Mariana v. Adel el Labban and Pierucci* (Italy, 1959), 28 *ILR* [1959], 366. The defendant was a commercial attaché at Egyptian Embassy and apparently was acting in a private capacity. However, the court distinguished all attachés (military, naval, commercial and air) as well as consuls from diplomatic agents.

as servants in the mission's mess was a contract of a private and not of a public character and thus the mission could not invoke immunity to gain exemption from jurisdiction in a breach of contract action.[138]

If one were to divide the Italian "private act" cases into historical periods — pre-World War I, the interwar period, and post-World War II — a fairly equal division of cases supporting the restrictive theory (or limited immunity), on the one hand, and the liberal approach (or absolute immunity), on the other, would be found in each period. Or, reviewing the cases in another way, the Italian court decisions would fall into two patterns — the "restrictive" extending from *Typaldos v. Lunatic Asylum of Aversa* (1886) through *Comina v. Kite* (1922) to *Società Arethusa Film v. Reist* (1953) and *Mariana v. Adel el Labban and Pierucci* (1959) and the "liberal" from *Avedo Diaz v. Loschiavo* (1912) through *Harrie Lurie v. Steinmann* (1927) to *De Meeus v. Forzano* (1940) and *Lagos Carmona v. Baggianini* (1953). However, despite this apparent inconsistency, Italian courts and writers appear to have rejected the concept that the diplomatic agent does not have immunity from civil jurisdiction in acts of a private law nature. For example, the decision in *Lagos Carmona v. Baggianini* that diplomatic agents have complete immunity from civil jurisdiction (except for acts of the type included as exceptions in Article 31 of the Vienna Convention) seems compatible both with the trend in Italian jurisprudence and the view of Italian writers.

The practice in Italy now is to extend immunity to diplomatic agents for private acts with some possible exceptions. These would include (1) an agent who is acting on behalf of his state in a matter which falls outside the political scope of his diplomatic function, (2) military, naval, air, and commercial attachés even though they are universally recognized as diplomatic agents, (3) subordinate staff members such as clerks, stenographers, *et al.,* and (4) members of non-diplomatic agencies such as military missions. Insofar as diplomatic personnel are concerned (and the Court of Rome's decision relative to attachés may not stand in future cases), the Italian movement has been away from the restrictive theory.

This development is both logical and commendable — logical since the practice rested both on a questionable theoretical base and a weak practical foundation and commendable since it brings Italian practice into line with the general rules of international law. In essence, the

---

[138] *Venezuelan Naval Mission v. Bernardini and Others* (Italy, 1959), 28 *ILR* [1959], 413.

Italian courts based the "restrictive" decisions on the concept that interference with the diplomat in his private capacity somehow would not affect his function as the official representative of his country or, as the court in *Perrucchetti v. Puig y Cassauro* held, economic/juridical relations could be divided from political relations. These concepts are quite incompatible with the essential inviolability of the diplomat.

The restrictive theory also linked the problem of diplomatic immunity with the sovereign immunity of the state and exempted states from jurisdiction in respect to acts performed by their organs *jure imperi* but not *jure gestionis*. Under this theory, it would be the state and not the agent to which immunity extended. The desire to close loopholes in the legal structure by making diplomats liable in these situations is understandable since the private law activities of states are much more extensive and diverse than they were in the past. In the light of this practice, the obligation of states to recognize each other's immunity is tending to disappear or to be confined within more restricted limits. If, however, the state and the diplomat are linked, the immunity extended to the latter would also tend to diminish, a most unfortunate development.

Another disturbing factor in the Italian cases is the apparent rejection of the principle of reciprocity. The reasoning that the practice in a single state does not in itself make international customary law may have missed the point, since custom develops through the practices of one or more states by means of bilateral or multilateral arrangements and the idea of reciprocity has long been one of the essential elements in the development of international law.

Italian jurists, on the other hand, have presented an extremely able line of argument as to why diplomatic immunity for private acts should be accepted in international law, as it has now been accepted by Italian courts. Immunity is founded upon functional necessity, the need for the agent to carry out his functions undisturbed by restrictions imposed by the receiving state. By its very nature, diplomatic immunity is indivisible; it cannot be limited; it must apply to all interests, state and private. The diplomat cannot carry out his public functions if he is harassed by litigation for acts performed in his private character. This viewpoint was stated in the "classic pleading" of Desjardins, the Advocate General, before the French Court of Cassation in the case of *Errembault de Deedzeele* in 1891. Desjardins declared:

> The court will at least have to dispose of the point whether a distinction should be made, with regard to exemption from jurisdiction, between acts performed by the diplomatic agent as a representative of his Government and acts which he performs merely as a private individual. I respectfully submit that such a distinction would be

erroneous. If a diplomatic agent were to be subject to the jurisdiction of French courts whenever he acted as a private individual, such creditors as he might have would pursue him mercilessly and their litigious manoeuvres — whether legitimate or merely vexations — might hinder him in the discharge of his duties; this would lead to the very situation which the law of nations sought to avoid in propounding the maxim: *ne impediatur legatio!* [139]

The court endorsed these conclusions.

While the principle of extending immunity to cover private acts seems to have been accepted in Italy, a few recent cases in South America, chiefly in Chile, revealed a strong undercurrent of support for the restrictive theory. Three of the cases came before courts in Chile. In *Castillo v. Zalles,* [140] it was held that the economic counsellor of the Bolivian Embassy at Santiago de Chile could not claim immunity in a suit concerning servitude on water rights of real property. *In re Areco León (Minors),* [141] the plea of the first secretary of the Uruguayan Embassy in France to jurisdiction on the grounds that he was immune for his personal acts (alimony payments) was rejected. The third case, *Minister of Belgium v. Judge of Second Court of First Instance in Civil Matters of Santiago,* [142] involved a rental collection action against the former diplomatic secretary of the Belgian Legation.

The court reflected the assumptions underlying each of the cases in noting that "when diplomatic functionaries enter into contracts in their private capacity, without regard to their status as public representatives, the local courts may take jurisdiction over the matter." [143]

The Chilean courts referred to customary international law but also based their decisions, with a certain amount of inconsistency, on the Code of Private International Law of 1928 (Bustamante Code). [144] The Bustamante Code provides that an American diplomatic officer shall be exempt from civil jurisdiction in an American country to which he is accredited in regard to personal or real actions brought against him in his official capacity (Articles 333 and 334). However, if he

---

[139] As cited in the ILC Secretariat Memorandum, p. 165.

[140] (Chile, 1955) *ILR* (1955), 540.

[141] (Chile, 1955), *ILR* (1956), 425.

[142] (Chile, 1952), *ILR* (1952), Case No. 88.

[143] *ILR* (1952), 384. Cf. *In re Ledoux* (Uruguay, 1941), *AD* (1943–1945), Case No. 75.

[144] Code of Private International Law, annexed to the Convention adopted at Habana, February 20, 1928, from text in Manley O. Hudson (ed.), *International Legislation* (Washington: Carnegie Endowment for International Peace, 1931), IV, 2283–2354; also in 86 L.N.T.S. 111.

has acted in a private capacity, then he is subject to the local jurisdiction in regard to real or mixed actions brought against him (Article 335).

In the case involving a Bolivian diplomat *(Castillo v. Zalles),* the court held that he was subject, under the Code, to local jurisdiction since he had acted in a private capacity. There was some inconsistency in the other two cases since in one *(In re Areco León [Minors])*[145] the Code was held not to apply since it had not been ratified by the sending state (Uruguay) while in the other the Code was held to be binding on a European diplomat (minister of Belgium).[146] Little else in judicial reasoning beyond that already reported in the Italian cases was included in the *Annual Digest/International Law Reports* abstracts; however, the court *In re Areco León (Minors)* did cite several authorities to the effect that the diplomat is not entitled to traditional protection for private acts.[147]

While this extension of jurisdiction, as based on an analysis of cases in the *Annual Digest/International Law Reports,* is confined primarily to Italy and Chile, two Anglo-American decisions during the period are of minor interest. A British court in *Juan Ysmael & Company v. S.S. Tasikmalaja*[148] held that a diplomatic courier must appear as a witness. The court noted that a diplomatic courier "has no official recognition and is granted exemption from civil and criminal jurisdiction and afforded special protection only during the exercise of his office" and that there was no reason why he should not appear in court for cross-examination.[149] Of perhaps greater significance was a decision by a New York court in *Agostini v. De Antueno* that immunity did not apply in a suit for recovery of real property occupied by an

---

[145] This case was complicated by a "third state" factor, since the diplomat, Don Alberto Areco Pittaluga, while in Chile, was assigned to a diplomatic mission in France. The court declared that "personal actions" must be brought against him in his official capacity in order for him to claim immunity but that the advance notice given to the Ministry of Foreign Relations of Chile said nothing about any diplomatic duties. *ILR* (1956), 427. It would appear from this reasoning that the applicability of the Code would have been immaterial.

[146] A report by the Fiscal, approved by the court, noted: "Although the provisions of the Code . . . are binding only on the American States which have ratified it, nevertheless they may be considered as real and definitive principles of international law which may properly be applied in situations arising in Chile regarding the diplomatic agents of non-American States." *ILR* (1952), 384.

[147] The court cited Miguel Cruchago Tocornal, Fernando Albónico and Germán Vallejos Friere. ILR (1956), 428. It is perhaps significant that all of those quoted are Latin publicists who support a view found primarily in Italy and in Latin American nations.

[148] (Hong Kong, 1952), 1952 Hong Kong Law Reports 242, 288; *ILR* (1952), Case No. 94.

[149] *ILR* (1952), 405.

accredited foreign representative to the United States and "not pertaining to his diplomatic status."[150]

An incident in the U.S.S.R. also indicated that the Soviet officials adhered to the concept of civil jurisdiction in the case of private acts. The Soviet Union, in the name of the National Hotel in Moscow, started a civil action against a Brazilian diplomat to recover damages to hotel property as the result of an altercation between Brazilian and Soviet citizens and the police. The diplomat apparently was allowed to leave the country before the suit was pressed to conclusion.[151]

Despite these instances, the review of *International Law Report* cases since 1945 does not lend general support to the notion that the restrictive theory has gained general acceptance outside of the Latin areas, and in Chile, as in Italy, the attitude of the courts is not free from uncertainty. In 1956, a year after the two restrictive decisions, a higher court in Chile reversed a lower court and accepted a report from the Fiscal that the principle of exemption from jurisdiction of lower courts covers all the civil acts of a diplomat.

In this case, *Acuña de Arce v. Solórzano y Menocal,*[152] the Fiscal cited with approval the French writer, Professor Charles Rousseau, who in a 1953 edition of a treatise on international law,[153] contended that diplomatic immunity would cover any civil act since immunity from jurisdiction was indivisible. The decision noted that this contemporary opinion is supported by the opinions of earlier writers (Bello, Andre Weiss, Franz von Liszt, and Julio Diena) who were in general agreement that diplomatic officers are completely exempt from the jurisdiction of the state to which they are accredited because they personify the sovereignty of the state which sends them.[154]

---

[150] N.Y.S. 2d 245, 248 (1950), digested *AJIL,* XLV (1951), 201. Although jurisdiction was asserted against the third secretary of the Argentinian delegation to the United Nations, the court noted that he was entitled to the same privileges and immunities as diplomatic agents accredited to the United States subject, of course, to corresponding duties and obligations. The court declared that the recovery of such realty was a matter of local concern subject to local laws and that the local court's jurisdiction was essentially *in rem* and not *in personam.* See David R. Deener, "Some Problems of the Law of Diplomatic Immunity," *AJIL,* L (January, 1956), 118–119, fn. The court apparently relied extensively on the case of *State of Ohio ex rel. Popovicic v. Agler,* 280 U.S. 379, 50 S. Ct. 154, 74 L. Ed. 489 (1930) although this action for divorce involved, not a diplomat, but the vice consul of Rumania.

[151] *New York Times,* January 21, 1947, p. 2; February 24, p. 21.

[152] (Chile, 1956), *ILR* (1956), 422.

[153] Charles Rousseau, *Droit international public* (Paris: Recueil Sirey, 1953), pp. 345–346.

[154] *ILR* (1956), 424–425.

This view is supported by a 1959 U.S. decision upholding diplomatic immunity in a suit arising from private transactions.[155] Other cases before United States courts also follow this line of reasoning.[156] In addition, this liberal interpretation was upheld in a Brazilian decision in 1954, *Ribeiro v. Chinatti,*[157] in which the court declined jurisdiction in a rental dispute involving an attaché at the Austrian Embassy. In an earlier rental case, a French court had ruled along similar lines.[158] A British writer, in commenting on the recent case of *Ghosh v. D'Rozario,*[159]

---

[155] The Supreme Court of New York noted: ". . . the vesting in the Supreme Court of the United States of original and exclusive jurisdiction of 'All actions or proceedings' against ambassadors and other public ministers of foreign States excludes by implication the right to maintain any action or proceedings in a local court, whether *in personam* or *in rem,* against a foreign diplomatic representative duly accredited to this country." *De Miglio v. Paez,* 18 Misc. 2d 914, 189 N.Y.S. 2d 593, 597 (1959). A district court judgment denying the defendant, the Consul General of Venezuela and its alternate representative to the United Nations with the rank of Envoy Extraordinary and Minister Plenipotentiary, adjournment to obtain evidence of his diplomatic and consular immunity, was reversed and a new trial ordered. The municipal court was held to be without jurisdiction in any proceeding against a foreign diplomatic representative. In *Arcaya v. Paez,* 145 F. Supp. 464, affirmed 244 F. 2d 958 (1956), an action for libel aganst the defendant in the above case was stayed on the ground of diplomatic immunity when he was appointed as alternate representative to the U.N. In this case, the court held that immunities and privileges accorded to ambassadors and ministers have been extended to include, among others, an accredited resident representative to the United Nations, with the rank of minister plenipotentiary. In this case the court observed that diplomats were "absolutely immune" from suit even though it is based on private transactions. Cf. *Magdalena Steam Navigation Company v. Martin* (1859), 2 E. & E. 94.

The New York Supreme Court also observed in the *Agostini* case (át p. 596): "Particularly apposite to the situation at hand is the case of *Bliss v. Nicolaeff,* 1st Dept., 191 Misc. 798, 79 N.Y.S. 2d 63, involving a summary proceeding to recover possession of premises leased as a school for children of Soviet officials and as a residence. The court there indicated that it would have rejected jurisdiction if it had satisfactorily appeared that the proceeding was against the Consul of a foreign Government. The same conclusion must apply with even greater force as regards a tenant who has the rank of ambassador or minister of a foreign State."

[156] See *Knocklong Corp. v. Kingdom of Afghanistan,* 6 Misc. 2d 700, 167 N.Y.S. 2d 285 (1957), where the Nassau County Court upheld a claim of immunity in an action brought by the holder of a tax deed to determine title to property owned in fee by the Kingdom of Afghanistan; *Carrera v. Carrera,* 84 U.S. App. D.C. 333, 174 F.2d 496 (1949), where the U.S. Court of Appeals held that the rule of diplomatic immunity applies in the field of domestic relations; and *Tsiang v. Tsiang,* 194 Misc. 259, 86 N.Y.S. 2d 556 (1949), where the court affirmed that a third-state national employed as an embassy butler and chauffeur was immune from process.

[157] (Brazil, 1954), *ILR* (1954), 249.

[158] "Diplomatic agents enjoy an absolute immunity from jurisdiction in civil and commercial matters; their voluntary submission to the territorial jurisdiction of the country to which they are accredited must be authorized by their government." *Demoiselle B. v. D.* (France, 1927), *AD* (1927–1928), 368. Cf. *Consular Premises (Greece) Case* (Greece, 1931), *AD* (1931–1932), Case No. 187, and *Afghan Minister (Consular Activities) Case* (Germany, 1932), *AD* (1931–1932), Case No. 179.

[159] [1962] 2 All E.R. 640.

observed that "the decision is clearly, on the authorities, in accord with the established view that . . . the immunity extends to all acts, whether official, private or professional."[160]

A Yugoslav court in 1956 ruled that an embassy was a juridical person and could not be sued since the real defendant in the case was the foreign state which the embassy represented. In this case, *Claim Against Foreign Embassy Case,*[161] the plaintiff had been knocked down by an auto owned by a military mission of a foreign embassy and brought action against the embassy, not the mission, for damages. The lower court had held that diplomatic missions were "granted exterritoriality" and were exempt from jurisdiction. The Supreme Court apparently carried the reasoning a step further by ruling that the real defendant was not the military mission personnel involved, nor the embassy to which the mission was attached, but rather the state itself which could not be sued without voluntary submission.[162]

In similar litigation, the Court of Appeals of Paris in a 1959 decision, *Laforest v. Commercial Department of the Spanish Embassy,*[163] held that the Spanish Embassy was entitled to immunity from the jurisdiction of French courts "even in matters concerning the performance of private contracts."[164] Finally, a Luxembourg court also observed in a 1957 case, *Bolasco v. Wolter,* that diplomatic representatives are entitled to full diplomatic immunity both from civil and criminal jurisdiction not only for official acts "but also proceedings arising out of acts performed in a private capacity."[165] This *dictum* appears to reflect current international practice and most nations tend to reject the restrictive Italian and South American precedents.[166]

Conclusions

Although developments in international law over such a restricted period as the post-World War II era might be of limited significance

---

160 K. R. Simmonds, "The 'Rationale' of Diplomatic Immunity," *International and Comparative Law Quarterly,* XI (October, 1962), 1208.

161 (Yugoslavia, 1956), *ILR* (1956), 431.

162 Cf. *Caja Nacional de Ahorro Postal v. Legacion de Polonia* (Argentina, 1952), *AJIL,* XLIX (1955), 100.

163 (France, 1959), 28 *ILR,* 357–359.

164 *Ibid.,* p. 358.

165 (Luxembourg, 1957), *ILR* (1957), 526.

166 For example, the United States Court of Appeals for the Allied High Commission in Germany declared that "Italy, unlike other countries," has followed a "highly rigid application of the restrictive theory of sovereign immunity." *Hartje v. Yugoslav Military Mission and Another* (1954), *ILR* (1954), 119. See also *De Miglio v. Paez,* 18 Misc. 2d 914, 189 N.Y.S. 2d 593 (1959) and *Carrera v. Carrera,* 84 U.S. App. D.C. 333, 174 F. 2d 496 (1949).

in long-range speculation, evidence indicates that the diplomat's position has not changed appreciably insofar as his immunities from civil jurisdiction are concerned. However, evolution of these rules has not followed uniform patterns. On the one hand, a restrictive tendency is seen in regulations pertaining to professional, commercial, and private trading activities of the diplomatic agent; on the other hand, the Anglo-American tradition of granting full immunity, at least for diplomatic agents, for private as well as public acts appears to have made considerable inroads into the practice of some Latin nations.

The extension of immunity from taxation, although a relatively recent development, is now firmly established in international practice with respect to the salaries and, in general, the property of diplomatic agents despite considerable divergency in practice. Immunities from payment of taxes by diplomatic agents, at least on their official emoluments, is embedded in the legislation of many nations and is supported by customary practice. Conversely, nations appear to be reluctant to waive taxes assessed on incomes of diplomats from investments and private activities.

Immunity extends to movable property insofar as is necessary for the fulfillment of the diplomatic mission. Immovable property not used for official purposes probably is subject in many cases to host state jurisdiction, although lease and rental court actions have emphasized that the diplomat's home is his inviolable castle. He also enjoys general immunity from giving evidence.

Practice since 1945 also has clarified to a degree some of the exceptions to immunity from civil jurisdiction. These include certain taxes (on private income, estates, inheritances, etc.), counterclaims arising out of the same set of facts and not exceeding the original claim, and professional, commercial, and private trading activities. While the diplomat's plea for immunity probably would be sustained today if an action were brought against him as a result of his commercial endeavors (certainly in Great Britain), the trend now appears to be toward the exclusion of these activities from the immune category.

The general rule of international law pertaining to private acts has been reinforced and extended in the postwar period. It still follows the Anglo-American tradition in that the diplomat is protected from judicial proceedings both for his official and his unofficial activities. Italian and Latin American courts have often denied this immunity for private acts; however, the practice in these countries now appears to be that the diplomatic agent, if not the subordinate staff member, is entitled to this privilege.

CHAPTER 6

Customs Privileges
and Courtesies

DURING THE POST-WORLD WAR II PERIOD diplomatic agents have continued to enjoy the privileges of duty-free imports and other customs courtesies although abuses such as excessive purchases of automobiles, attempts to smuggle currency, watches, etc., have on many occasions strained relations among nations. Retaliatory action has often followed the most flagrant abuses of the customary practices. The impact of political developments on these customs, privileges, and courtesies will be considered below.

Rules, Regulations, and State Practices

Even though nations allow this duty-free import of goods by the ambassador and his staff and their families, most writers agree that such an immunity rests on international comity or courtesy, and is not a mandatory rule of international law.[1] This is not to discount the suggestions that the practice has hardened into a rule of law,[2] or less

---

[1] L. Oppenheim, *International Law*, Vol. I: *Peace*, ed. H. Lauterpacht (8th ed.; London: Longmans, Green and Co., 1955), p. 803; United Nations, Secretariat, "Memorandum on Diplomatic Intercourse and Immunities" (A/CN.4.98), International Law Commission, *Yearbook: 1956*, Vol. II (A/CN.4.SER.A/1956/Add.1), p. 170; *U.S. Foreign Service Manual*, Vol. I, Part I, Section 252, as cited in United Nations, Secretariat, *United Nations Legislative Series*, Vol. VIII: *Laws and Regulations Regarding Diplomatic and Consular Privileges and Immunities* (New York, 1958) pp. 374ff, cited hereafter as *U.N. Laws and Regulations;* A. B. Lyons, "Personal Immunities of Diplomatic Agents," *BYIL*, XXXI (1954), 326; Hall, Gauchille, Genet, Strisower, and Diena, as cited in Harvard Law School, "Research in International Law: I. Diplomatic Privileges and Immunities," *AJIL*, XXVI (April, 1932), Supp., 107. Cited hereafter as Harvard Draft.

[2] Resolution of the Institute of International Law, Section 11, as cited in *AJIL*, XX (1926), Spec. Supp., 155. Lyons questions whether, since the liability to pay customs dues does not hinder diplomatic activity, exemptions could be regarded as more than concessions based on international comity. Lyons, *BYIL*, XXXI, 326.

strongly stated, international law imposes an obligation to grant such extensions to diplomatic agents.[3] This concept is reflected in efforts to codify the rules of diplomatic privileges and immunities with customs exemptions included both in the Havana Convention of 1928[4] and the Vienna Convention of 1961.[5] The Vienna accord, which appears to stand as an acceptable general rule, provides that receiving states, in accordance with local laws, shall grant exemption from customs duties, taxes, and similar charges on articles for the official use of the mission and for personal use of the diplomatic agent or members of his family, including articles intended for his establishment.[6]

This immunity from payment of customs fees as well as the privilege of free movement of diplomatic shipments, also is based largely on reciprocity, "strict reciprocity" in the case of the United States,[7] a two-way proposition as emphasized by the Department of State in its successful plea in 1956 for the International Longshoreman's Association to "recommend" to its members that diplomatic consignments to delegations from the Soviet Union and Eastern European countries be exempted from an informal boycott of Iron Curtain freight.[8]

Even though these reciprocal arrangements, treaties, development of customary practices, etc., are apparently reducing the differences among states, a wide divergency still is found in state practice with respect to the classes of diplomats to whom privileges are extended, the kind and value of articles excluded, and methods by which customs formali-

----

[3] *In re Serventi* (Italy, 1921), *AD* (1919–1922), Case No. 211. One writer noted that while the privilege of imports rests on a somewhat different basis than the right of inviolability and freedom from criminal and civil law, it is as fully established as these rights. George E. Anderson, "Diplomatic Immunities," *The Commonweal,* X (July 17, 1929), 290.

[4] Convention on Diplomatic Officers, Adopted at Havana, February 20, 1928, reprinted in *AJIL,* XXVI (April, 1932), Supp., 175–177, from English text in *Sixth International Conference of American States: Final Act* (Habana, 1928), pp. 142–150. Article 18(3) reads: "Diplomatic officers shall be exempt . . . from customs duties on articles intended for the official use of the mission, or for the personal use of the diplomatic officer or of his family."

[5] Vienna Convention on Diplomatic Relations, in United Nations, Conference on Diplomatic Intercourse and Immunities, 2 March – 14 April, 1961, *Official Records,* Vol. II: *Vienna Convention on Diplomatic Relations* (A/CONF.20/14/Add.) (New York, 1962), pp. 82–88.

[6] *Ibid.,* Article 36.

[7] *U.S. Foreign Service Manual,* Vol. I, Part I, Section 251.1, as reproduced in *U.N. Laws and Regulations,* pp. 374ff.

[8] *New York Times,* December 18, 1956, p. 62. Department representatives earlier had warned of possible "grave" results if Eastern European countries should retaliate by refusing to handle shipments to United States diplomatic personnel in their countries.

ties are waived or modified.[9] Some of these variations are found in British, Russian, and American legislation which also reflects the general rules of customs courtesies.

Exemption from duties on baggage on first arrival and on goods thereafter imported for personal use by diplomats serving in Great Britain is (a) on a general basis for heads of mission and higher ranks (counsellors, secretaries, attachés); and (b) on a particular basis of reciprocal agreement with certain countries for all personnel.[10] Diplomatic baggage is admitted on showing a pass, and supplies for official use of the family are also admitted without examination. It is assumed that quantities will not be excessive although no restrictions are applied.[11] Bilateral agreements have been concluded with some countries whereby members of diplomatic staffs below the rank of attaché (excluding domestic servants) enjoy, conditionally, the same privileges.[12]

The Soviet Union also permits the entry of personal hand and heavy baggage, subject to reciprocity, of ministers and staff members of the counsellor, secretary and attaché ranks and their families.[13] The Soviet Union sets a separate annual ceiling, in ruble value, on the custom-free goods which can be shipped in by the embassy or legation itself, the head of mission, for counsellors and attachés, and for other members of the diplomatic corps.[14]

The privilege of free entry has not always been granted by the United States to representatives of foreign countries.[15] For example, the *Personal Instructions to the Diplomatic Agents of the United States* (1885) stated that "the diplomatic privileges of importing goods for personal use is not accorded to a foreign Secretary of Legation in the United States or in any foreign country, so far as is known."[16] In addition, the exemption of diplomats from the prohibition laws of the United

---

[9]Lyons, *BYIL*, XXXI, 326; U.S., Department of State, *United Nations Conference on Diplomatic Intercourse and Immunities: Report of the Delegation of the United States*, Department of State Publication 7289 (Washington: U.S. Government Printing Office, 1962), p. 19.

[10]Lyons, *BYIL*, XXXI, 322–323. Great Britain, Protocol Department, *Diplomatic and Consular Immunities and Privileges* (Memorandum describing the practice of Her Majesty's Government in the United Kingdom) (September, 1957), p. 13.

[11]Great Britain, *Diplomatic and Consular Immunities and Privileges*, p. 13.

[12]*Ibid.*

[13]Order No. 110 of 26 October 1948 concerning the Central Customs Administration, *U.N. Laws and Regulations*, p. 342.

[14]*Ibid.*, p. 343.

[15]John Bassett Moore, *A Digest of International Law* (Washington: Government Printing Office, 1906), IV, 678.

[16]Harvard Draft, p. 112.

States also met some opposition,[17] although it would have been difficult to find a precedent for a blanket ban on liquor imports for diplomatic personnel.[18] However, diplomats stationed in the United States probably did not seriously abuse this import privilege,[19] and some nations, such as Great Britain and Mexico, voluntarily curbed imports of alcoholic beverages. Great Britain, for example, was a little touchy over reaction to smuggling activities,[20] and desired to avoid clouding a respected diplomatic position by abusing a privilege which was denied to residents of the host country.[21]

However, United States policy at present appears to be compatible with general practice, and diplomatic agents accredited to the United States receive a number of customs concessions, provided their governments accord reciprocal privileges to corresponding officials of the United States.[22] Foreign diplomatic officers, their families, suites, and servants may import baggage and effects free of duty.[23] The United States also grants duty-free import of articles for personal and family use during the official residence in this country of diplomatic officers and, like the British but unlike the Russians, there is no quota system.[24] Also authorized is the importation of articles for official use — costumes, regalia, office supplies, etc. — under the "usages of international courtesy" on the basis of reciprocity; packages containing official documents if accompanied by a certification of contents; and articles to be used in

---

[17] Professor Preuss contends that this exemption should not have been made for the following reasons: customs exemptions for diplomats are not based on international law, diplomats are not exempt from the substantive law of the receiving state, diplomatic privilege would not be violated by a refusal to grant customs exemption, and importation of diplomatic liquors would in most cases involve third persons in unlawful acts which authorities were legally bound to prevent. Lawrence Preuss, "Foreign Diplomats and the Prohibition Laws," *Michigan Law Review,* XXX (January, 1932), 333–348.

[18] Rules regulating the purchase and import of wines into seventeenth-century Turkey may have been the only direct precedent in international practice to the Eighteenth Amendment and the Volstead Act. A. H. Feller, "A Seventeenth Century Problem in the Application of Prohibition Laws to Foreign Diplomats," *AJIL,* XXVIII (1934), 349–351.

[19] One writer maintains that "investigation has shown no serious breach of privilege." Anderson, *The Commonweal,* X, 290.

[20] For example, see *I'm Alone,* digested from documents published in the U.S. Department of State Arbitration Series, No. 2 (1–7), 1931–1935, by Herbert W. Briggs (ed.), *The Law of Nations* (2d ed.; New York: Appleton-Century-Crofts, Inc., 1952), pp. 385–388.

[21] For an analysis of the decision by Sir Esme Howard, British Ambassador to Washington, to curb liquor imports, see Anderson, *The Commonweal,* X, 289–290.

[22] *U.S. Foreign Service Manual,* Vol. I, Part I, Section 200, as reproduced in *U.N. Laws and Regulations,* pp. 374ff.

[23] *Ibid.,* Section 251.1.

[24] *Ibid.,* Section 255.1.

exhibits.[25] Articles sent through the mails to heads of missions are delivered without submission to customs; similar items sent to other diplomatic representatives as well as articles sent to chiefs of missions in any manner other than mail are subjected to the usual customs inspection.[26]

These regulations have at times hampered the work of the mission. In postwar Russia, embassy operation was made more difficult by high duties on diplomatic imports, said by United States Ambassador Walter Bedell Smith to stem from the application of a law hitherto loosely enforced, as part of a campaign to obtain more dollars.[27] In another instance, the United States Embassy in London cancelled an order for several thousand dollars worth of cutlery and silverware from Sheffield, England, which was to have been used in United States European missions, when the British government insisted on the payment of a 33 1/3 per cent export tax.[28]

Diplomats also reported import problems with currency behind the Iron Curtain. One noted that insofar as he knew, the Soviet Union was the only country where a person of diplomatic rank was not permitted to export or import local currency; it was the practice to check rubles at the border and retrieve them on re-entry.[29] Another ex-Foreign Service officer reported that following annexation by the Soviet Union of the Baltic States in 1940, diplomats remaining briefly in Latvia were unable legally to exchange foreign currencies for local currency.

A number of retired Foreign Service officers reported instances of difficulties and delays due to the attitudes and practices of individual customs house officers (Brazil, for example) rather than governmental policy, or as one officer put it, changes were always taking place depending "upon the whim of local officials." Measures for correction have taken place at the same level since minor customs officials are "susceptible to education on rights" and to "friendship." The tactics have ranged from bringing pressure to bear on "petty customs officials" and continual "vigilance," to utilizing personal diplomacy — inviting the officials to diplomatic and consular affairs and, in one case, assisting an official to obtain a travel grant to the United States where he studied customs

---

[25] *Ibid.*, Sections 252, 253, 254.

[26] *Ibid.*, Section 255.2.

[27] *New York Times,* October 8, 1947, p. 14. Ambassador Smith gave this example: a pack of typewriter paper which cost less than $2 in the United States was taxed about $25.00 when imported for embassy use.

[28] *Ibid.*, May 26, 1948, p. 15.

[29] Information and comments in this and the following two paragraphs are taken from the Foreign Service Survey.

procedures. In Latin America, for example, much can depend on personal relations and being "simpático," and, in some backward areas, personal gifts have been quite persuasive.

Diplomats in the postwar period have been bothered in a few cases by petty fees which often, but not always, cost more in irritation than in cash. One ex-diplomat explained that "local authorities seemed to be primary movers — and the method favored was by levying these fees, miscellaneous charges or costs on the customs brokers who cleared import shipments and who could not easily contest the actions."

However, some incidents since World War II have been of a more serious nature and have somewhat marred relations among nations. In one well-publicized case, Nikola V. Novikov, the Soviet Ambassador to the United States, claimed among other things that he had been held by customs for an hour at La Guardia Airport in New York and that his baggage was sent through the usual formalities as if he did not have immunity.[30] The collector of the port of New York countered that no attempt was made to inspect the baggage, but that Novikov refused to sign a customs form for record purposes. In the words of Secretary of the Treasury John W. Snyder, "All that was asked of him was the same as that asked of President Roosevelt, Prime Minister Churchill, all the Kings and Queens and everybody else that has been here."[31] The State Department said it regretted the incident but blamed it on lack of advance warning and crowded port conditions.[32] Despite Soviet protests, there appeared to be little more in the incident than perhaps a case of mismanagement.

There have been other cases which may not have breached international law (since customs rules stem from municipal regulations) but which at least have strained the guidelines of international comity. The United States in 1948 protested the stripping and search of three Americans, including an embassy clerk, for no apparent reason.[33] The Polish Embassy in Istanbul complained that Turkish officials stripped a commercial attaché of his belongings, which were returned several days later.[34] According to news reports in 1948, Swiss customs authorities violated the immunity of a number of delegates to a meeting of the United Nations Economic and Social Council, including United States

---

[30] *New York Times,* October 9, 1946, pp. 1, 19; October 11, p. 3.

[31] *Ibid.,* October 9, 1946, p. 19; October 10, p. 12; October 11, p. 3.

[32] *Ibid.,* October 16, 1946, p. 10; "Investigation of Incident Relating to Arrival of Soviet Ambassador," *DSB,* XV (October 20, 1946), 726.

[33] *New York Times,* December 24, 1948, p. 5.

[34] *Ibid.,* September 17, 1948, p. 11.

Assistant Secretary of State Willard Thorpe, from whose trunk films and cigarettes were allegedly taken.[35] These cases illustrate a trend which has become obvious since the end of World War II, that is, the inspection of diplomatic articles by customs officials under special circumstances.

Smuggling

One of the principal reasons for searching diplomats and diplomatic baggage is to prevent smuggling. Scattered cases reported by the news media[36] lend credence to the contention by governments that diplomatic abuse of the customs privilege warrants a more restrictive approach, especially in the inspection of diplomatic baggage. The smuggling incidents were not confined to lower ranking personnel — two of them involved heads of missions. In 1953, Eduardo de Arteaga, Uruguayan Minister to Belgium, was fined for trying to smuggle $38,592 worth of diamonds out of England. He pleaded guilty but said he had agreed to carry the diamonds as a favor for a friend and was to receive no pay.[37] Customs officials reported a large amount[38] of Egyptian and American currency and jewels seized from Don Luis F. de Almagro, Cuban Minister to Egypt, Lebanon and Syria, as he prepared to board a plane for Beirut at the Cairo airport. According to the *New York Times,* customs officials for some time had suspected Señor de Almagro of smuggling money and jewels from the country under cover of diplomatic immunity. The minister, who reportedly said he was not aware that it was illegal for him to take out cash and jewels, was dismissed from the service.[39]

Watches were the downfall for two other foreign representatives. Georges Geoffroy, French Consul at Dusseldorf, refused to be searched, and claimed immunity when he arrived at a London airport. Customs officials persisted and found 290 watches sewn into the lining of his waistcoat.[40] Customs officials at Belfast charged Ricardo Ernest Soto, variously identified as an attaché and a Panamanian consular officer in London, with smuggling 1,680 watches from the Republic of Ireland.[41]

---

35 *Ibid.,* July 21, 1948, p. 5.

36 Presumably these cases represent only a portion of the total number of incidents.

37 *New York Times,* May 1, 1953, p. 3. His attorney said de Arteaga had been dismissed from the Foreign Service and now was "ruined, dishonored and despised."

38 The original news report listed the total at about $15,000. *Ibid.,* December 31, 1953, p. 3. A later United Press report gave the figure of $142,500. *Ibid.,* January 1, 1954, p. 6.

39 *Ibid.,* January 1, 1954, p. 6.

40 *Ibid.,* December 27, 1947, p. 27.

41 *The Times* (London), February 25, 1954, p. 6.

Sometimes the attempted smuggling has more serious consequences. As discussed in Chapter 4, two Latin American ambassadors were stripped of their immunity and sentenced for using the diplomatic pouch to smuggle heroin into the United States. They were members of an international operation which utilized diplomats to slip drugs valued at millions of dollars into this country. In 1958 in another case, officials in Lebanon inspected a car driven by a Belgian consul general who was stationed in Syria and found, according to press reports, 33 submachine guns, 28 pistols, 32 revolvers, 16 hand grenades, 1,800 rounds of machine gun ammunition, 1,500 rounds of other ammunition, several time bombs, and some demolition equipment.[42]

Smuggling of currency, jewels, watches, drugs, bombs, etc., is only one of the problems faced by customs officials in their dealings with privilege-abusing diplomats; they also have been called upon to police the import (in bulk lots) of propaganda supporting a rival political ideology.

In one instance, the Italian Foreign Ministry refused to permit thirty-five packages of Communist propaganda to be delivered to the Czechoslovakian Legation in Rome. It had apparently been mailed by the Italian section of the Cominform in an attempt to avoid customs inspection and import tax.[43] A similar case the same year resulted in the severance of diplomatic relations between Cuba and the Soviet Union following an exchange of charges and counter-charges as to whether diplomatic rules had been violated.[44]

While most of the customs cases have involved the movement of goods, currency or propaganda, some writers have viewed the practice of noninspection as a threat to national security. A Boston lawyer pointed out that, as it now stands, a hostile country could smuggle in

---

[42] *New York Times,* May 13, 1958, p. 4.

[43] *Ibid.,* June 22, 1952, p. 6.

[44] Two Soviet couriers, arriving from Mexico with packages of documents not covered by permit, refused inspection and returned by the same plane. Cuban Ministry of State officials claimed that the Soviet government had no official relations with the new government of Major General Fulgencio Batista (Batista seized power in a coup on March 10, 1952); thus, the act was not a violation of diplomatic procedure. Cuba had no mission in Moscow at the time, but the Russians maintained a Legation in Havana under the Soviet Embassy in Washington. The U.S.S.R. broke the remaining diplomatic relations, charging that the action had "deprived the U.S.S.R. Legation of normal diplomatic communications" and violated "generally recognized diplomatic rules." *Ibid.,* March 22, 1952, p. 4; April 4, p. 1. *New York Times* writer R. Hart Phillips claimed that Soviet couriers, heavily laden with luggage, had been making frequent trips to Cuba, reportedly bringing in a considerable amount of gold to exchange for U.S. currency in the black market. *Ibid.,* April 6, 1952, p. 21.

an atomic bomb, piece by piece, then reassemble it for use when desired.[45] His solution would be to hold an international conference to reach agreement on elimination of whatever present practices "make such a national disaster possible."[46] It is difficult to see how agreement on such restrictions could be reached if the piecemeal smuggling of a bomb is possible, without virtually eliminating traditional customs privileges.

The nations assembled for the diplomatic conference in Vienna in 1961 acknowledged that exemption from inspection is only a relative privilege. They incorporated into Article 36 a provision that a diplomat's baggage is not exempt from inspection when there are "serious grounds" for presuming that it contains articles not intended for his personal use or that of his family, or articles the import or export of which is prohibited by law or controlled by the quarantine regulations of the receiving state. The action is compatible both with American and Russian practice. In commenting on the Vienna Convention, the United States delegation observed that the provision "should dispel the popular misconception that a diplomat's baggage is exempt from inspection."[47] The Russians already have included such a ruling in their customs regulations. Article 2 of Order No. 110 of 26 October 1948 provides that in "exceptional circumstances" diplomatic baggage may be inspected by special order of the Central Customs Administration.[48]

"Duty-free" Privileges

While concern over smuggling, the importation of propaganda, and security matters may have contributed to the tightening of import restrictions and inspection procedures for diplomats in the postwar period, another factor has been the violation (rather flagrant at times) of privileges by agents who managed to remain within the letter of the law if not within the dictates of good taste. It might be noted that the installation of mission commissaries did alleviate to some extent the need for import of personal items by diplomats and introduced an element of what ex-diplomat William R. Langdon called "physical as well as legal extraterritoriality." Mr. Langdon observed that "it would seem as if carloads [of personal goods] are imported under mission

---

[45] Thomas A. Mahoney, "Total Disaster in Washington — What Then?", *America*, XCV (September 29, 1956), 614–616.

[46] *Ibid.,* p. 616.

[47] *U.S. Delegation Report,* p. 19.

[48] *U.N. Laws and Regulations,* p. 342.

request so that all American personnel enjoy a general extraterritorial privilege in respect to daily necessities."[49]

Despite this new convenience, diplomats still have managed to abuse their duty-free entry privileges by bringing in automobiles, furniture, refrigerators, liquor, luxury goods, and other items for resale "at a good profit on the local market." The abuse may be attributed, at least in part, to the great increase in numbers of diplomatic personnel, many in borderline capacities, and, in part, to the human desire to do a favor or to return a profit. The problem was well stated by Gerald A. Mokma, who spent thirty-one years in the diplomatic and consular service:

> I have personally known many diplomats who have abused the privileges to which they were entitled. Many of them have enriched themselves by doing so and in countries where an honest effort is made by the authorities to control the conduct of the people the natural result has been a closer scrutiny of the activity of the diplomats.

Supporting cases are legion — both from the Survey and from other sources. Philip Ernst, a retired Foreign Service officer, told of the United States navy captain (an embassy attaché) who walked off a ship with a diplomatic bag which he said was filled with "official mail." Customs officials inspected the bag and found it laden with canned goods. Mr. Ernst observed: "Individuals such as the captain often ruin in five minutes our work of many years." The diplomatic pouch apparently is put to many uses not originally contemplated, such as importing watches, nylon stockings, and cameras to sell on the black market, and even for shipping forbidden paintings, antiques, and other art treasures across frontiers.[50]

Another former United States diplomat reported that the right of diplomats to sell personal possessions — usually on leaving their post — was curtailed after an ambassador of a small country was found bringing in substantial quantities of furniture for profitable sale through a commercial outlet — "in effect a fence."[51] The accredited minister of a European nation, also serving in South America, reportedly imported eleven pianos in the course of less than two years.[52] The diplomat, after

---

[49] Foreign Service Survey. Many respondents to the Survey noted this development. One declared: "I expect that with commissaries in most missions, the question of customs and excise privilege no longer arises," while another noted that "entry free . . . food supplies for the staff was . . . no longer necessary as these were obtained from SHAEF [Supreme Headquarters, Allied Expeditionary Forces] which greatly eased the situation."

[50] Charles W. Thayer, *Diplomat* (New York: Harper & Brothers, 1959), p. 212.
[51] *Ibid.*
[52] Anderson, *The Commonweal,* X, 290.

receiving a leave of absence, departed in a carnival-like atmosphere, with a small flotilla following his ship out of the harbor to the cacophony of shrieking whistles and blowing horns. Later the piano import activities came to light, and he never returned to his post.[53]

However, it is the automobile, the mid-twentieth century status symbol, which seems to have been the center of this particular brand of diplomatic irresponsibility. Formerly in most countries, the diplomat could import an automobile free of duty and sell it at his pleasure without payment of tax or duty; in recent years, there has been a tightening of controls. The reason is obvious — abuse of the privilege by the diplomatic agent. In Canada, in 1951, several Latin American diplomats allegedly bought expensive American cars at wholesale prices and imported them free of duty, then sold them to Canadians who were unable to import them under any conditions.

In Iraq at the end of World War II, even automobile tires were commanding fabulous prices — as high as $400. As a result of these abuses, nations have tended to be less lenient. While practice varies, the policy has been to retreat from the free-import, unregulated sale. One step was to permit the diplomat to sell the car only on transfer from the country, and Canada permits the importation of cars only with written approval and certification of necessity by the chief of mission. Now, in many countries, the diplomat must pay duty if he sells the car in less than two or three years from the date of importation regardless of transfer. In France, he is not permitted to sell his car at all, but must export it at the time of transfer.[54]

In Great Britain, the diplomat is permitted to import one motor car within three months of his first arrival if the vehicle has been in his possession — and in case of a British-made car, his use — prior to his diplomatic assignment to the United Kingdom. The importer must also agree that the car will not be sold but will be exported on the termination of his tour of duty or earlier.[55] Over the years, there definitely has been a worldwide tightening of controls over import and disposal of the diplomats' private cars.[56]

---

53 *Ibid.*

54 Information in this paragraph is based on the Foreign Service Survey.

55 Great Britain, *Diplomatic and Consular Immunities and Privileges*, p. 13.

56 Sending nations have often cooperated in these efforts. For example, Jack E. McFall, as United States Ambassador in Finland, reported: "With my concurrence, the Finnish government tightened its regulations on motor car importation and resale. Some minor abuses of privilege had been detected at the cost of increased revenue to the Finns, so as Ambassador I encouraged the tightening up procedure and then personally policed it carefully to ensure 100 per cent adherence to the revised procedures." Foreign Service Survey.

One example of wholesale abuse of the duty-free import privilege, with items ranging from rock-and-roll records and old shoes to freezers and automobiles, involved United States and other diplomatic personnel in Pakistan.[57] By selling at prices three to four times above what owners paid for the goods in the United States,[58] many were able to realize thousands of dollars in profits when their duty tours ended. While the practice was not illegal, it was regarded as "cheap and undignified" and presented Americans as "moneygrubbers."[59] Although Americans were not the only ones who did this, there were about ten times more of them involved than the total for any other country.[60] The State Department curbed the profiteering by restricting such total sales to 500 rupees (about $105) and by requiring that a list of the goods to be sold be cleared with the embassy.

In 1964, the United States Embassy in Brazil imposed restrictions on the sale of automobiles by employees of U.S. Government agencies after an auto dealer in Recife brought legal action against two employees of the Agency for International Development. They were accused of failing to sell their automobiles to the dealer, under an alleged prior agreement, after the vehicles had been in Brazil for two years, when they were not subject to any resale duty payment. At the time, a 1962 medium-priced American car reportedly was worth at least $6,000. The U.S. Embassy imposed a restriction stating that cars could be sold by American government employees only with prior Embassy approval.[61]

A short time later, in February of 1965, the United States Government issued a circular designed for all overseas posts, forbidding personnel from selling their automobiles and other personal property at a profit. It was believed that the profiteering tended to tarnish the desired image abroad of a dedicated and ethical U.S. public servant. Disciplinary action, including possible dismissal, was threatened. The circular was greeted by anguished wails on the part of a large segment of the official American community in Latin America, according to a *New York Times* survey, and only a small minority interviewed

---

[57] As reported by A. M. Rosenthal in the *New York Times,* April 5, 1958, pp. 1, 4.

[58] For example, a two-year-old Chevrolet brought between $4,100 and $5,000; a $300 refrigerator, $600. *Ibid.,* p. 4.

[59] *Ibid.,* p. 1.

[60] About 505 United States officials and 1,100 wives and children in Karachi. *Ibid.,* p. 4.

[61] *Ibid.,* December 21, 1964, p. 24.

defended the new policy.[62] The sale of autos and other duty-free goods could net a person before returning to the United States a tidy profit of several thousand dollars. This may have been part of the lure of the overseas appointment in the first place.

Similar profiteering in Washington prompted the State Department in 1958 to crack down on foreign diplomats who were selling tax-free autos, liquor, and cigarettes. The Department said the most flagrant case involved an embassy employee who imported five or six cars in as many weeks and offered them in classified advertisements to anyone meeting his price.[63] In a circular sent to the heads of foreign missions in Washington, the Department warned that if the abuses continued, "the Government of the United States will find it necessary to re-examine its liberal policy of according exemptions from customs duties and internal revenue taxes on articles obtained for the personal use of members of embassies and legations."[64] Five years later, the Department circulated a note to all foreign missions requesting that the tax-free purchases of automobiles be restricted to one a year for each diplomat.[65]

It seems apparent from this evidence that abuse of the import privilege has been considerable although not necessarily widespread among the diplomatic personnel.[66] However, diplomatic missions of some nations admit that part of their maintenance costs are covered by the sale of duty-free goods.[67]

Recent Trends

Despite the numerous instances of abuse reported, a majority of the retired United States Foreign Service officers participating in the Survey did not detect significant changes during their tours of duty. Of the 176 who checked answers to the query asking whether they had noted changes in the treatment of the diplomat with reference to

---

[62] *Ibid.,* March 22, 1965, pp. 1, 15. The State Department speculated that one acceptable method to solve the problem would be through the organization of non-profit foundations by the ambassadors to dispose of the automobiles owned by U.S. Government employees. Profits could be used for scholarships or similar endeavors. *Ibid.,* March 24, 1965, p. 40.

[63] *Ibid.,* April 19, 1958, pp. 1, 8.

[64] *Ibid.*

[65] *Ibid.,* October 31, 1963, p. 1. The Department said some diplomats bought six to seven cars a year with the apparent intention of selling them at a profit.

[66] The U.S. State Department, in its 1958 warning, said it realized that "a large majority of diplomatic personnel" were careful not to abuse their privileges. *Ibid.,* April 19, 1958, p. 1.

[67] *Ibid.,* March 22, 1965, p. 1.

customs, fees, taxation, and similar privileges, 105, or 60 per cent, replied in the negative. Another 60, or 34 per cent, answered yes, and 11, or 6 per cent, declared they did not know.[68]

There was a further split among those who reported changes — some reported a more restrictive tendency on the part of customs and fiscal officials in receiving states; others detected a liberalizing development. The greater restrictions on customs, fees, and tax privileges seemed to be the result of two developments. The first was the great increase in clerical, administrative, ancillary, and quasi-diplomatic personnel. Many responses to the questionnaire illustrated this point. For example, one diplomat observed that "it is not so easy for foreign officials to be as generous in dealing with a mission comprised of a hundred persons as with one consisting of only a few." Another said: "Obviously [the addition of] . . . so-called diplomatic personnel . . . has caused a well-justified curtailment of privileges." The second cause of increased restrictions has been the irresponsibility of some diplomats in taking advantage of the courtesies extended. For example, an ex-Foreign Service officer said: "There were instances of tightening up the customs free privilege but these were possibly made necessary by abuses of privileges by individuals in the diplomatic corps."

The basic change does not seem to have been the result of any wholesale modification of municipal legislation, but rather in a "more exacting" interpretation of existing laws. One ex-diplomat explained it this way:

> I believe that the rights, privileges and immunities in this respect have changed little. What has changed is the administration of the formalities relating to them. There has been so much abuse of the diplomatic privilege that the authorities are more "sticky."

This reduction in privileges has taken the form of more rigid inspection, the application of quotas, the ban on some imports such as the "flat ruling" laid down by the old king, Ibn Saud, that no one, including diplomats, could import potables into Saudia Arabia, restrictions on the resale of items which were imported duty-free, etc.

A substantial, but smaller, number of respondents, in their general comments, indicated that privileges of this type had been extended, rather than reduced. One declared that "in recent years host governments have been more liberal in the matter of exemption from customs duties," and another declared that "the diplomat is much better treated with reference to fiscal privileges." This deviation from what appears

---

[68] This information and that following unless otherwise noted is taken from Foreign Service Survey.

to be a general consensus might be explained in part by wide geographical dispersal of the diplomatic corps and their career service concentration in different parts of the world, and by the fact that many referred not to a general extension but to a tendency for the differences between diplomats and consular officers and between various diplomatic categories to disappear as the result of revised consular conventions and commercial agreements, liberalized practices, etc.

Thus while perhaps some of the loopholes might have been closed by host governments, at the same time privileges were granted to new classes of governmental personnel — consular, clerical, non-diplomatic etc. The questionnaire comments indicated a steady and general improvement especially in the treatment accorded consular officers. One ex-Foreign Service officer observed: "My impression was that the privileges of diplomats changed little during my service, but that those of consuls were being steadily increased to catch up with the diplomats."

But of perhaps more significance was the extension of these privileges "way beyond the 100 per cent diplomat to include innumerable military and economic groups, etc." Fiscal privileges such as freedom from local taxation, customs duties, auto registration fees, drivers' license fees, etc., were accorded to non-diplomats as well as diplomatic personnel, a change which occurred in large part because of the numerous agencies from the United States which sought diplomatic privileges after World War II. Retired diplomat John M. Madonne observed that some agencies, such as the U.S.I.A., enjoy more or less the same privileges as are extended to diplomatic and consular officers.

A network of international agreements, reflecting both a crystallization of customary practices and the extension of free entry privileges, etc., to new categories, is becoming a more important source for these privileges, especially since the end of World War II. For example, the United States and Nicaragua extended on a reciprocal basis free entry of goods upon first arrival in the country, and free importation of items needed for personal use during official residence for both diplomatic and consular officers, and employees and families. Liberia permitted duty-free entry of goods and the local purchases from United States navy stores by employees of the United States Legation and the United States Public Health Mission.[69]

---

[69] Customs Privileges for Foreign Service Personnel, exchange of notes between the United States and Nicaragua, December 3, 1951, and October 9, 1952, 184 U.N.T.S. 106, and Duty Free Entry of Goods and the Purchase Locally from U.S. Navy Stores by Employees of the U.S. Legation and the U.S. Public Health Mission, exchange of notes between the United States and Liberia, May 2 and July 22, 1949, 232 U.N.T.S. 283. Scores of similar agreements may be found in the United Nations Treaty Series (U.N.T.S.) and the United States Treaties and Other International Agreements (U.S.T.).

Obviously, there are differences, rather marked in some cases, between countries, and these differences account for exceptions to any generalizations about fiscal and custom privileges. The Survey results did indicate, in a very general way, some of these divergencies which might be attributed to historically different practices, divergent political systems and geographical area, etc., and to the diplomatic atmosphere existing between two countries at a given time.

Several general conclusions can be drawn from the answers in the Survey. First, customs privileges accorded lower-ranking personnel are somewhat more limited than those given to the chiefs of mission. British practice provides a good example. However, there appears to be an easing of the policy requiring all shipments to be addressed to the head of mission. Second, as has been noted, differences exist among nations, apparently stemming from variations in forms of government, in size, and in geographical location. Totalitarian governments may tend to be more strict in dealing with diplomatic personnel, one retired Foreign Service officer noting that quotas were often placed on import privileges by Iron Curtain nations, and another claiming that he had been treated in a generous and friendly manner in all nations except the Dominican Republic.

Another respondent found a difference between the large and small nations, with the latter more prone to assert a right of baggage inspection. Still another contended that diplomats seemed to receive less consideration in Latin American than in European countries. However, these are random observations, and in no way reflect any consensus of the retired Foreign Service officers and staff. Certainly restrictive practices are not the monopoly of dictatorships or small or Latin countries; more than one Survey respondent asserted that the Swiss were less generous than many other nations in their customs policies, and one referred to Great Britain as being "parsimonious" in affording customs and kindred privileges.

Third, in extreme cases anyway, nations apparently tended to be more generous at the point-of-entry with diplomats representing friendly powers than those representing enemy or unfriendly nations. Retired Foreign Service officer H. T. Mooers observed that nations receiving aid from the United States generally afforded more favored treatment to our representatives than to diplomatic personnel from countries giving little or no aid. In Spain at the time of World War II, no privileges were extended until United States armies landed in North Africa, and the government saw that the tides of war had shifted in our favor.[70]

---

[70] The diplomat reporting this fact in the Foreign Service Survey added: "No doubt today with our aid to Spain the situation is quite satisfactory."

Here one sees that the "cold war" also has had its impact upon an area of diplomatic practice. The work of the mission has been hampered by currency and other regulations or (and this does not always involve ideological protagonists) by stringent application of the law on the part of border officials for personal as well as official reasons. Instances of mistreatment of diplomats, with wounds at least to their dignity, also have been reported at customs stations.

On the other hand, diplomats have abused their rights through outright smuggling, through illegal imports by way of the diplomatic pouch, and by the excessive purchases of items, especially automobiles, and their resale, often at a handsome profit. In part because of these developments, as well as the security problems of the atomic age, the practices of inspection of diplomatic baggage or shipments, if there is reason to believe that a law is being violated, is more fully accepted.

Finally, while variations in practice, as well as continued abuses by diplomats, complicate the problem of granting exemption from customs regulations, nations through treaties, internal legislation, and the development of custom appear to be moving closer to uniform practices in this area of diplomatic privileges and immunities.

CHAPTER 7

The Official
Diplomatic Staff

IT HAS BEEN INDICATED in the previous chapters that some of the general rules of personal inviolability, jurisdictional immunities, and customs privileges and immunities which are applicable under international law to diplomatic personnel have been modified since World War II. However, since these rules differ for the various categories of personnel, the emerging international law of privileges and immunities for the official diplomatic staff, the retinue and family of diplomatic agents, local nationals in the employ of diplomatic missions, and non-diplomatic personnel will be considered separately in the remaining part of this study.

Diplomatic Agents

The upper echelon members of diplomatic establishments (ambassadors, ministers, and counsellors) are covered by the general rules of diplomatic immunity, and their position is determined on the basis of diplomatic status rather than rank. Thus the previously discussed guidelines almost universally apply to these persons. The immunity of ambassadors and ministers is absolute except in rare instances such as involvement in war crimes[1] or when the diplomat acts as an agent of the state, and immunity is held to attach to him as a person and not as an organ of the state.[2] Jurisdiction also has been exercised in Italy over diplomats in general in matters involving other private acts,[3] and presumably the rule still stands that a diplomat is not immune in case

---

[1] *In re Best and Others* (Denmark, 1949, 1950), *ILR* (1950), Case No. 146, and *In re Abetz* (France, 1950), *ILR* (1950), Case No. 89. See discussion of these war crimes cases in Chapter 4.

[2] See *Castiglioni v. Federal People's Republic of Yugoslavia* (Italy, 1952), *ILR* (1952), Case No. 43, and *Perrucchetti v. Puig y Cassauro* (Italy, 1928), *AD* (1927–1928), Case No. 247. Cf. *Case of Castiglioni* (Italy, 1951), *AJIL,* XLIX (1955), 100.

[3] See section on Private Acts in Chapter 5.

of any attack which he himself provokes.[4] However, these minor exceptions to immunity as enjoyed by heads of missions, including chargés
d'affaires in charge of missions,[5] would not seem to have weakened
their traditional claim to absolute immunity. Although rare exceptions
may be found,[6] state practice in the post-war period also has reinforced
the traditional position of the counsellor of the embassy.[7]

Since the rules covering other diplomatic agents vary, the
positions of secretaries, attachés and "part-time" diplomats will be
analyzed by categories.

Secretaries

While the decisions dealing with diplomatic privileges and immunities for secretaries of embassies have not been uniform, usually
diplomats in this category are in a favored position. Thus, in some
cases in which immunities for secretaries have been questioned, courts
have been criticized for deviating from general international practice.
For example, in 1926 the Court of Appeals of Santiago, Chile, in *Pacey
v. Barroso*[8] rejected the plea of immunity submitted by Barroso, Secretary of the Brazilian Embassy in Chile, who had been charged with
fraud. The court contended that diplomatic immunity extended only to
ambassadors, ministers, and chargés d'affaires, and that secretaries and
employees of embassies or legations were subjected to the laws of the
host country. The Court of Appeals, acting as a court of first instance in
criminal cases involving diplomatic agents, established a new doctrine
on the case, a doctrine which the editor of the *Annual Digest* found "at
variance with the weight of judicial and textual opinion in Latin
America."[9] Twenty years later, another writer contended that the
extension of jurisdiction over the secretary of a legation was still at
variance with Latin American doctrine,[10] and apparently also at variance
with the practice in other nations.[11]

---

[4]See *The State v. Acuña Araya* (Costa Rica, 1927), *AD* (1927–1928), Case
No. 243.

[5]See *Caceras v. Areco* (Paraguay, 1938), *AD* (1938–1940), Case No. 165.

[6]See *Castillo v. Zalles* (Chile, 1955), *ILR* (1955), 540.

[7]See *Bolasco v. Wolter* (Luxembourg, 1957), *ILR* (1957), 525–526; *Mongillo
v. Vogel*, 84 F. Supp. 1007 (1949); *Parker v. Boggan*, [1947] 1 All E.R. 46; and
Martelly et Admin. des Domaines v. Diez del Corral (France, 1950), *ILR* (1951),
Case No. 111.

[8]*AD* (1927–1928), Case No. 250.

[9]*Ibid.*, p. 370.

[10]Joyce A. C. Gutteridge, "Immunities of the Subordinate Diplomatic Staff,"
BYIL, XXIV (1947), 155.

[11]The name of the third secretary of the Spanish Embassy in London was struck
out as a co-respondent in a 1925 divorce suit on a plea of diplomatic immunity.
Chesney Hill, "Sanctions Constraining Diplomatic Representatives to Abide by the
Local Law," *AJIL*, XXV (April, 1931), 268.

However, in 1950 a United States court in *Agostini v. De Antueno*[12] asserted jurisdiction in a suit to recover realty against the third secretary of the Argentinian delegation to the United Nations even though according to the *Headquarters Agreement,*[13] he was entitled to the "same privileges and immunities, subject to corresponding conditions and obligations" as diplomatic envoys accredited to the United States. The court reasoned that the federal treaty power was limited in matters of "historical local concern" such as suits for recovery of realty, and that real property of a diplomat not connected with his official capacity is subject to local law.[14] Essentially, the court's jurisdiction was "basically *in rem,* and not *in personam.*"[15] The Italian courts also denied immunities to secretaries of the Chilean Embassy, one in 1934 and the other in 1953, in taking the restrictive approach to private acts of diplomats.[16]

On the other hand, international practice in the postwar period appears to have followed more closely the conclusion reached by the Court of Appeal of Brussels in *M.C. v. Société Foncière du Nouveau Parc*[17] that the appellant, as secretary to the U.S. Embassy in Belgium, was a diplomatic agent entitled to "the privilege of exterritoriality." The principle, so declared the court, was generally accepted by the law of nations and reflected "settled Belgian practice," according to the editor of the *Annual Digest.*[18] The doctrine was supported by later decisions such as those by the Supreme Court of Uruguay which held *In re Ledoux*[19] that the secretary and the attaché of the French Legation could withdraw bank funds despite a moratorium suspending bank transactions, and by the Supreme Court of Argentina which declined jurisdiction over the agricultural secretary of the Canadian Embassy in Buenos Aires in the case of *In re Hillhouse.*[20]

---

[12] 99 N.Y.S. 2d 245 (1950).

[13] Agreement between the United Nations and the United States Regarding the Headquarters of the United Nations of June 26, 1947. U.N. Doc. A/519, 11 U.N.T.S. 11.

[14] David R. Deener, "Some Problems of the Law of Diplomatic Immunity," *AJIL,* L (January, 1956), 118–119, fn.

[15] *Ibid.,* p. 119.

[16] See *Lagos Carmona v. Baggianini* (Italy, 1953), *ILR* (1955), 533, and *Balloni v. The Ambassador of Chile to the Holy See* (Italy, 1934), *AD* (1933–1934), Case No. 164.

[17] (Belgium, 1934), *AD* (1933–1934), Case No. 162.

[18] *Ibid.,* p. 381, fn. Cf. *Deposit (Land in Czechoslovakia) Case* (Czechoslovakia, 1936), *AD* (1938–1940), Case No. 167, and *Carrizosa v. Meyers* (Argentina, 1938), *AD* (1938–1940), Case No. 166.

[19] (Uruguay, 1941), *AD* (1943–1945), Case No. 75.

[20] (Argentina, 1955), *ILR* (1955), 538. Cf. *Greek State v. X* (Greece, 1953), *ILR* (1953), 378.

Attaches

Proliferation in the attaché category of diplomatic agent has been one of the most significant developments in foreign representation since World War I, and especially since World War II. Since the attaché is included along with the counsellor and secretary in the diplomatic agent group entitled to basic privileges and immunities, this category has not raised special problems as such. However, military attachés, because of their activities during the "cold war," have been declared *persona non grata* on a rather regular, methodical basis. Their surreptitious snooping is now part of accepted international procedures, and flows from the recognized function of the attaché as a "diplomatic spy."[21]

Attachés might also be distinguished in another respect in that they (in their various roles ranging from military to food and shipping attachés) were not fully accepted as members of the diplomatic family until well after World War I.[22] While counsellors and secretaries were enjoying full diplomatic status, some types of attachés were still being treated as non-diplomatic persons. The development of the American attaché corps illustrates this phase of diplomacy. By the eve of World War II, the United States had developed a specialized corps of attachés. In 1939, President Roosevelt integrated the attaché program by placing the overseas personnel of the Departments of Agriculture and Commerce under the Department of State. The Department of the Treasury and the military departments have continued to appoint their own attachés, who are generally linked to the United States missions overseas. Under the Eisenhower administration, the Department of Agriculture again assumed direction of the agricultural attachés. The State Department also assigns cultural and scientific attachés although the latter category, first organized in 1949, had been virtually terminated by 1954 when it was again revived.[23]

---

[21] The Poles apparently had a different concept of the military attaché from that accepted by Western nations. Under the Polish definition, the attaché should attend parties in full dress uniform as a decoration for his ambassador and watch occasional parades and military activities. Anything beyond this was apparently superfluous and dangerous. *New York Times,* April 13, 1948, p. 7. Also see Hanson W. Baldwin's observations on the mission of the attaché, *ibid.,* October 10, 1964, p. 5.

[22] However, it might be noted that the first military and naval attachés were sent, as observers and intelligence officers, to U.S. missions abroad in the 1880's (Allen Dulles, *The Craft of Intelligence* [New York: Harper & Row, Publishers, 1963], p. 40), and that in 1924 the diplomatic list in Washington included attachés, military attachés, naval attachés, commercial attachés, air attachés, and agricultural advisers (Tracy Hollingsworth Lay, *The Foreign Service of the United States* [New York: Prentice-Hall, Inc., 1925], p. 152.

[23] Elmer Plischke, *Conduct of American Diplomacy* (2d ed.; Princeton, N.J.: D. Van Nostrand Company, Inc., 1961), pp. 157–158.

This expansion into such "non-diplomatic" areas as agriculture and commerce aroused resistance both from established foreign service personnel and host governments. While commercial attachés were classed as diplomatic officers with attendant privileges and immunities by the United States Foreign Service in the early 1920's,[24] they were regarded by some colleagues as "interlopers."[25]

A United States court in 1932 appeared to be at least mildly concerned about the diplomatic nature of the commercial attaché functions. In considering a civil action involving the commercial attaché of the Royal Italian Embassy in *Girardon v. Angelone*,[26] the court raised a question as to whether there was sufficient proof to require it to hold that such an attaché was a diplomatic official entitled to immunities. The court noted that it had been very difficult to determine just what were the duties of a commercial attaché. While the grant of immunity was based on executive determination, the case does illustrate both judicial perplexity about proliferation of attachés and the practice of extending immunities to various types of attachés.[27]

Some nations also were reluctant to accept new types of attachés as full-fledged members of the diplomatic family. When the United States in 1925 wanted to appoint treasury officials as customs attachés to collect tariff information in Great Britain, the Foreign Office promptly refused to authorize diplomatic status. The British government reasoned that duties of these officials stemmed from domestic legislation, and were of an administrative and fiscal nature.[28] The fact that an Act of Congress of January 13, 1925,[29] stated that these officers were entitled to diplomatic

---

[24] Green Haywood Hackworth, *Digest of International Law* (Washington: Government Printing Office, 1942), IV, 407.

[25] A retired American Foreign Service officer commented that commercial attachés in Asia in the early 1920's "were rather regarded as interlopers by consular personnel who were responsible for the development of our commerce abroad." Foreign Service Survey.

[26] 254 N.Y.S. 657 (1932).

[27] Cf. *In re Alberto Grillon (Hijo)* (Argentina, 1929), *AD* (1929–1930), Case No. 194, and *In re Chayet* (Chile, 1932), *AD* (1931–1932), Case No. 181, both involving commercial attachés, and *Case of Ito* (Argentina, 1934), *AD* (1933–1934), 383, fn., involving a naval attaché. Also, U.S. Supreme Court Justice Frank L. Young in November, 1929, held that the court lacked jurisdiction in a suit against the commercial attaché of the Argentine Embassy in the United States for alimony and counsel fees. Reported by Hill, *AJIL*, XXV, 268. See also a report on the attack upon Colonel Krastitch, Yugoslav military attaché at Sofia, in Clyde Eagleton, "The Responsibility of the State for the Protection of Foreign Officials," *AJIL*, XIX (April, 1925), 299.

[28] S. H. Brookfield, "Immunity of the Subordinate Personnel of a Diplomatic Mission," *BYIL*, XIX (1938), 155.

[29] 43 Stat. 748.

privileges made no difference to the British. In fact, foreign governments almost universally refused to accept these attachés.[30]

The British government also resisted acceptance of labor and cultural attachés primarily because the functions assigned to these officials would interfere with the domestic affairs of Great Britain.[31] The British rationale was succinctly expressed by Sir Cecil Hurst, who noted that the "principle which should be adopted is that a government can refuse to accord diplomatic privileges to an agent who is sent to its territory by a foreign government on business which only concerns the internal affairs of the latter."[32] Even though the dynamic character of diplomatic privileges and immunities and the need to extend them into new spheres of governmental activity were recognized by British jurists as early as 1737 in *Barbuit's Case*,[33] it was not until recent years that the British fully accepted these categories.

A convincing illustration of the change in British attitude is found in the officially listed personnel attached to the British Embassy in Washington, which includes, in addition to military, air, and naval attachés, the following categories: attachés for defense research, civil air, shipping, atomic energy, agriculture and food, colonial affairs, petroleum, and finance — all of whom are entitled to diplomatic privileges and immunities.[34] Even small diplomatic missions are often dominated by attachés. For example, of Guinea's three officials listed for its Washington diplomatic staff, two were attachés: cultural and commercial.[35] The Soviet Union also has a strong attaché contingent in its Washington embassy but designates specifically only the military, air, and naval attachés. The remainder bear only the simple attaché title.[36]

Immunities for these attachés, no matter their specific designation, have not been uniformly applied in diplomatic practice. Again, a restrictive approach is found in the Latin nations of Argentina and

---

[30] Hackworth, IV, 407. Treasury Department representatives were known as "special commissioners" before 1919 when they were designated "treasury attachés" and attached to legations and embassies. In 1923, their title was changed first to "customs attaché" and then to "customs representative" and back to "customs attaché" with the Act of 1925. After the general rebuff by other nations, these attachés adopted the former title of "customs representatives" and after 1930 they were again known as "Treasury attachés." *Ibid.,* pp. 407–408.

[31] Brookfield, *BYIL,* XIX, 154–155.

[32] Sir Cecil Hurst, "Course on Diplomatic Immunities," *Recueil des Cours,* XII (1926), 155; cited by Brookfield, *BYIL,* XIX, 155.

[33] 25 Eng. Reprint 777.

[34] U.S., Department of State, *Diplomatic List,* Department of State Publication No. 7395 (Washington: U.S. Government Printing Office, June, 1962), pp. 24–25.

[35] *Ibid.,* p. 27.

[36] *Ibid.,* pp. 57–58.

Italy. An Argentine court indicated in a 1943 case, *Bregante v. Souviron,*[37] that the agricultural attaché of the United States Embassy in Buenos Aires did not have a diplomatic character.[38] The lines between the attaché rank and other diplomatic personnel were more clearly drawn in a 1959 case in Italy, *Mariana v. Adel el Labban and Pierucci.*[39]

While most jurists and writers consider that the diplomatic rank extends down through the attaché level, the Prefecture of Rome held that a commercial attaché at the Egyptian Embassy was not a diplomatic agent within the accepted meaning of that term and thus was subject to the jurisdiction of Italian courts.[40] The court followed the rather odd reasoning that military, naval, commercial and air attachés are technical personnel, and thus differ in nature and function from diplomatic agents. Only the latter, who are accredited by the sending to the receiving state by a "special international legal act known as 'credentials,'"[41] are entitled to immunity from jurisdiction.

This concept of non-immunity for attachés deviates from general practice which has strongly favored including these diplomats within the privileged group. The approach was seen in the liberal interpretation of the Act of Anne[42] in *Parkinson v. Potter*[43] and cited *In re The Amazone* a half century later.[44] An action had been brought on a lease against an attaché of a foreign embassy, and it was contended that the Act of Anne contained no mention of attachés. To this Mathew, J., responded:

---

[37] (Argentina, 1943), *AD* (1943–1945), Case No. 76.

[38] The action was brought against a governess employed by the attaché and involved a determination of the jurisdiction of the Supreme Court of Argentina, which has original jurisdiction over persons enjoying diplomatic immunity. The mere fact that the defendant was a governess in the family of the agricultural attaché was found to be no reason to submit her case to the original jurisdiction of the Supreme Court; "neither did it appear that her employer had the character of a diplomatic envoy." *Ibid.,* pp. 242–243.

[39] (Italy, 1959), 28 *ILR* 366.

[40] While the report did not indicate the nature of the action brought against the attaché, it was assumed that he was acting in a private capacity and not in the course of performing his official functions. *Ibid.*

[41] The court apparently referred to the "letter of credence" which diplomatic envoys present to the head of state of the receiving country. It is doubtful if this test, rather than that of functional necessity, is considered by many as a valid basis for extending immunities. For a brief comment on "diplomatic credentials" see Plischke, pp. 295–297.

[42] Great Britain, Act of Parliament for Preserving the Privileges of Ambassadors and Other Publick Ministers of Foreign Princes and States, 7 Anne Ch. 12, 1708, I British and Foreign State Papers 903.

[43] (1885), 16 Q.B.D. 157.

[44] [1940] 1 All E.R. 269.

It appears from the authorities that the privilege of the embassy is recognized by the common law of England as forming a part of international law, and according to that law it is clear that all persons associated in the performance of the duties of the embassy are privileged, and that an attaché is within that privilege.

Courts of other nations in the postwar period have followed a similar reasoning concerning the status of attachés. For example, courts in Argentina[45] and Brazil[46] have refused to take jurisdiction over attachés in the absence of waivers. Also, in a 1955 decision, the Supreme Court of Ceylon in *Appuhamy v. Gregory*[47] reasoned that the test of immunity is apparently whether the attaché in question was performing duties in the embassy to assist the ambassador. The court cited Slessor, L.J.,[48] in rejecting the contention that the military or naval attaché was not one of the ambassador's staff. The fact that an attaché's salary came from the military and not from the foreign office was not considered a determining factor in the Ceylon case. Rose, C.J., reasoned:

It seems to me that the fact than an attaché is not paid by the Embassy but is paid in fact by the United States Navy in whose employ he is does not remove him from the immunity, if in fact he is doing work on behalf of the Ambassador and is working in the Embassy.[49]

A French court, in a 1959 decision opposite to the *Mariana* case discussed above, extended immunity to the commercial section of a foreign embassy in Paris. The dispute in this case, *Laforest v. Commercial Department of the Spanish Embassy,* involved a lease entered into by a French citizen and the Commercial Department of the Spanish Embassy represented by the commercial attaché.[50] The owner of the house contended that as the lease had been executed in the form customary for leases between private individuals, and as the premises had been leased to a "commercial" department, the Spaniards were not enti-

---

[45] *Mazo de Stagni v. Stagni* (Argentina, 1956), *ILR* (1956), 430. Compare the Supreme Court decision in this case with *Bregante v. Souviron* noted above.

[46] *Ribeiro v. Chinatti* (Brazil, 1954), *ILR* (1954), 249.

[47] (1953), 55 New Law Reports (Ceylon) 235; *ILR* (1955), 541.

[48] *In re The Amazone,* [1940] 1 All E.R. 269.

[49] *ILR* (1955), 543. While the case involved the immunity of the attaché's assistant, the court based its decision on the fact that the assistant was entitled to immunity on the basis of his superior's status.

[50] (France, 1959), 28 *ILR* 357–359. The lease actually was signed by Antonio Mosquera whose name appeared on the diplomatic list as "Minister Plenipotentiary, Commercial Counsellor." However, the court identified him as the "commercial attaché" and clearly implied that immunity extended to diplomatic attachés engaged in trade and commercial activities.

tled to claim immunity from the jurisdiction of French courts. The Court rejected these arguments on the grounds that the Commercial Department had no independent legal personality and therefore formed part of the Spanish Embassy.

The court distinguished between a commercial department which operated as a legal part of an embassy and a separate commercial or trading service which would not enjoy privileges and immunities. In essence, the court ruled that persons attached to embassies and engaged in "technical" functions of a contractural, commercial, and financial nature are entitled to diplomatic immunity.

"Part-Time" Diplomats

Diplomatic missions occasionally procure the services of a professional expert either in a functional or advisory capacity to serve on a part-time basis. Recent cases support the view that immunity should be denied to such persons. One, *In re Norell*,[51] involved the civil attaché of the Swedish Legation in Buenos Aires whose duties appeared to be of a part-time nature only. In an action for tort against him, he failed to produce a required certificate from the Swedish government authorizing his diplomatic status. The Supreme Court declared that it did not have original jurisdiction. In commenting on the case, the editor of *Revista Jurídica Argentina la Ley* observed: "A person must be a member of an embassy or legation. It is not sufficient that a person serve part time or that he not be in close association with the mission. . . ."[52] Hackworth reports a similar decision which stemmed from a 1937 traffic accident in Cuba.[53] The suit was instituted against a part-time employee of the American Embassy, a "Legal Translator," who was a Cuban citizen, for whom the State Department did not in fact claim diplomatic immunity.

The Argentine Federal Supreme Court also ruled that a person who served as legal and commercial adviser to a legation did not come under its original jurisdiction over diplomatic personnel. The case, *In re Giménez*,[54] arose out of criminal proceedings against an Argentine national who was juridical and commercial adviser of the consulate-general of Paraguay and who assumed a similar position with the Lega-

---

[51] (Argentina, 1955), *ILR* (1955), 539.
[52] *Ibid.*
[53] Hackworth, IV, 540–541.
[54] (Argentina, 1941), *AD* (1941–1942), Case No. 113.

tion of Paraguay while the case was on appeal. In denying a claim to diplomatic status, the court observed:

> The character of legation lawyer, which is comparable to a juridical adviser, does not give its holder a diplomatic status. Consequently, whether as adviser of the Consulate or of the Legation of Paraguay, the accused has no right to the original jurisdiction of the Supreme Court.[55]

The court referred to an earlier case, *In re Berkman,*[56] in which it held that an Argentine national who called himself "Legal Counsellor of the Polish Embassy" lacked diplomatic status since he was merely the lawyer for the embassy.

The issue of "part-time" diplomats also arises from the modern trend toward the amalgamation of consular and diplomatic services. The British Attorney General in the frequently quoted case of *Engelke v. Musmann*[57] declared that His Majesty's government was not prepared to accept the view that merely because the services were amalgamated a nation could claim immunity for persons performing purely consular functions. On the other hand, if such a person were a member of the diplomatic staff and performing diplomatic functions, then the overlap of duties into consular affairs does not, in the eyes of the British government, deprive him of his diplomatic immunity. In this case, the German diplomat, Herman Gustav Constantine Engelke, performed "some service on the right side of the line between consular service and ambassadorial service."[58] A German court in 1932 reasoned along similar lines in the *Afghan Minister (Consular Activities) Case*[59] when it held that diplomatic immunity extends to the acts of the minister when he is functioning in his dual role as consular agent.

Presumably the official involved must perform more than token diplomatic services. The problem arose again in Great Britain in *Price v. Griffin*[60] in considering the dual status of Griffin, Vice Consul in the amalgamated American Foreign Service. Apparently no check was made to determine whether Griffin's duties were primarily diplomatic, or for that matter if they were diplomatic at all. The court accorded him full diplomatic privileges on the basis of the Foreign Office statement that

---

55 *Ibid.,* p. 375.
56 (Argentina, 1933), *AD* (1933–1934), 383, fn.
57 [1928] 1 K.B. 90.
58 *Ibid.,* p. 95.
59 (Germany, 1932), *AD* (1931–1932), Case No. 179.
60 (1948), *AJIL,* XLIII (1949), 187.

he was a member of the staff of the United States ambassador.[61]

On the other hand, the Supreme Court in Hong Kong in 1952 in the case of *Juan Ysmael & Company v. S.S. Tasikmalaja*[62] ruled that a consul general in Hong Kong who claimed to have performed duties usually performed by diplomatic officers was not entitled to diplomatic immunities. The court rejected *Parkinson v. Potter*[63] and *Engelke v. Musmann*[64] as precedents on the grounds that, in the former, the consul general had the additional character of an attaché and that the same principle applied to Engelke, who was an accredited member of the ambassador's staff.

It may be presumed then that there is no rule of international law extending immunities to part-time embassy workers such as legal advisers or to consular agents unless the latter are performing diplomatic functions as a principal, and not an incidental, part of their duties.

Administrative and Technical Agents

The variegated pattern of immunities extended to the administrative and technical staff[65] at the end of World War II indicates that the problems pertaining to immunities in this area are still far from resolved, although nations may be moving toward a greater uniformity in practice.

In a study published in 1947, Joyce A. C. Gutteridge observed that although recognition of the jurisdictional immunity extended to minor officials and servants, the practice was not universal and their position was far from well defined.[66] At one end of the scale were Germany and Austria who extended full immunities to minor officials and servants unless they were nationals of the receiving states; at the other end were the Soviet Union which excluded both minor officials and servants, and Greece which would not extend in principle jurisdictional immunity in either criminal or civil matters. Italy and France tended to be conservative in their approach to the problem; both the United States and Great Britain were inclined to be more generous.[67] Gutteridge concluded:

---

[61] For comments on this case, see A. B. Lyons, "Note: Claims of Diplomatic Immunity: Some Special Aspects," *BYIL*, XXVI (1949), 433–437.

[62] (1952), Hong Kong Law Reports 242, 288; *ILR* (1952), Case No. 94.

[63] (1885), 16 Q.B.D. 152.

[64] [1928] 1 K.B. 90.

[65] Included in this category are such functionaries as chancellors, archivists, clerks, secretaries, stenographers, messengers, guards, couriers, porters, dragomans, and interpreters.

[66] Gutteridge, *BYIL*, XXIV, 155.

[67] *Ibid.*, pp. 152–156.

Reluctantly we are driven to the opinion that on this matter the Law of Nations speaks with many tongues, and if we seek guidance from the writers and authorities on international law we are still without a clear light on our path.[68]

Because of the impossibility of drawing rules either from state practice or from viewpoints expressed by publicists, Miss Gutteridge turns to the Harvard Draft[69] and to an agreement covering United Nations officials.[70] The Harvard group, observing that no universal principle exists and that in usage many countries depart from general practice, concludes that immunity to the lower categories should be granted only to the extent necessary to avoid undue interference with the mission. The ILC Convention also stresses that diplomatic privileges and immunities are granted, not for the personal benefit of the individual, but so that the work of the mission is not impeded. This criterion, according to Miss Gutteridge, makes it possible to draw a distinction between the head and the diplomatic staff of a mission, on the one hand, whose criminal and civil immunity are universally recognized, and clerical and service staff members to whom immunity is not always conceded.[71]

Miss Gutteridge suggests two guidelines to govern the extension of privileges and immunities to personnel ranking below the diplomatic staff. First, the receiving state would not exercise jurisdiction over a minor official or servant for any act done by him in the performance of his official duty. Second, in all other cases the receiving state should exercise jurisdiction only when this would not constitute undue interference with the conduct of the mission's business.

This "progressive development" philosophy is also found in the 1958 Draft Articles on Diplomatic Intercourse and Immunities, in which the International Law Commission went even further in suggesting immunities for this category.[72] Under Article 36, the administrative and technical staffs of a mission, together with the members of their families forming part of their households, were extended full diplomatic immuni-

---

[68] *Ibid.*, p. 156. He cites Rivier (complete immunity to servants) and Fauchille (no immunity to this group whatsoever) as extremes, with Oppenheim, Hall, and Pradier-Fodéré ranged between.

[69] Harvard Law School, "Research in International Law: I. Diplomatic Privileges and Immunities," *AJIL* XXVI (April, 1932), Supp., 91, Article 23.

[70] Section 20, General Convention on the Privileges and Immunities of the United Nations of February 13, 1946. 1 U.N.T.S. 15.

[71] Gutteridge, *BYIL*, XXIV, 157–158.

[72] United Nations, International Law Commission, "Report to the General Assembly Covering the Work of Its Tenth Session, 28 April-4 July 1958" (A/3859), *Yearbook:1958*, Vol. II (A/CN.4/SER.A/1958/Add. 1).

ties and privileges. An exception was made for such persons if they were nationals of the receiving state.

The commission noted that there was a lack of uniformity in state practice and that it could either work "on the principle of a bare minimum," a course it rejected, or attempt to establish a general rule based on what would appear to be "necessary and reasonable," a course it followed.[73] The commission rejected, as being too restrictive, suggestions that these categories should qualify for immunity from jurisdiction solely in respect of acts performed in the course of their duties. Admitting that it was taking a "progressive step," the commission justified its liberal rule on the following grounds: the diplomatic mission must be considered as an organic whole and immunities extended on the basis of actual duties performed.

In some instances, the work of administrative and technical personnel might even be of greater importance than that carried out by diplomatic personnel. Some in this category, such as an archivist or the ambassador's secretary, may be privy to as much confidential information as are members of the diplomatic staff. In addition, it would be difficult to distinguish between various members or categories of the administrative and technical staffs.[74]

Sir Gerald Fitzmaurice of Great Britain maintained in the 1958 discussions that even though the extension might not reflect current practice in going beyond existing international law, it should be adopted because of functional necessity. He pointed to the difficulty in maintaining a distinction between diplomatic personnel and administrative and technical personnel, noting that functions performed by the latter had formerly been performed by the diplomatic staff before the embassy workload forced the change. The function, he argued, still remained diplomatic.[75] Earlier the British Interdepartmental Committee had reached a similar conclusion. After noting that many persons in this category perform work of a highly confidential and secret nature, the committee concluded that any withholding of immunity from this group "would, or at any rate might, be contrary to International Law."[76] The

---

[73] *Ibid.,* p. 101.

[74] *Ibid.,* pp. 101–102.

[75] United Nations, International Law Commission, *Yearbook: 1958,* Vol. I (A/CN.4/SER.A/1958), p. 162.

[76] Great Britain, Foreign Office, Parliamentary Papers *(Reports),* Cmd. 8460, January, 1952, "Report on Diplomatic Immunity by an Interdepartmental Committee of State Immunities," p. 5.

British Foreign Office contended that a majority of states granted such immunity.[77]

When the 1958 draft article was discussed at the Vienna Conference, it quickly became apparent that many states were not yet ready to accept such an extension of diplomatic privileges and immunities. A number of nations flatly charged that the extension was far too drastic.[78] While most of the nations opposed the article, which was modified, a number of smaller nations, such as Tunisia, Vietnam, Venezuela, and the United Arab Republic, categorically rejected the entire concept of extension. Venezuela was not able to accept even a modified version of the article since its laws barred extension of privileges and immunities to administrative, technical, and service staff personnel.[79] Support for the ILC draft came primarily from the two major powers, the United States and the Soviet Union, and a few of their allies. Other delegations, i.e., India and Austria, wanted modifications such as exclusion of customs privileges.

The discussion indicated that the smaller nations were concerned about the increase in numbers of administrative and technical personnel stationed in their countries. The Tunisian delegate said that extension of immunities to these persons might place a "crushing burden" on the receiving states.[80] The Burmese delegate wanted to avoid the creation of a "privileged class" of foreign residents.[81] It was argued that the ILC had shown "unexpected boldness" in going "far beyond" the limits of the rules of international law,[82] and that the conference should remain on the "solid ground" of codifying existing law rather than developing new rules.[83] The Russians and the Americans, whose inflated diplomatic staffs included an assortment of personnel under this category, pleaded for rentention of the ILC article, using arguments along the lines of those expressed by the commission.[84]

---

[77] *Ibid.*

[78] For the debate on this article, see United Nations, Conference on Diplomatic Intercourse and Immunities, *Official Records* Vol. I: *Summary Records of Plenary Meetings and of Meetings of the Committee of the Whole* (A/CONF.20/14) (Geneva, 1962), pp. 193–201.

[79] As noted in the Venezuelan reservation to acceptance of this provision. See United Nations, Secretariat, *Status of Multilateral Conventions* (ST/LEG/3.Rev.1) (New York, 1959), p. III-34.

[80] United Nations, Conference on Diplomatic Intercourse and Immunities, *Official Records,* Vol. I, p. 194.

[81] *Ibid.,* p. 195.

[82] *Ibid.,* p. 194.

[83] *Ibid.,* p. 195.

[84] *Ibid.,* pp. 197–198.

The conference, unswayed by the arguments of the two major powers, amended Article 36 so that privileges and immunities would be extended (except in criminal cases) to administrative and technical personnel only for their official acts. In addition, customs privileges were restricted to articles imported at the time of their first installation.[85]

It appears, from the Vienna debate, that a number of Asian and African states officially oppose extension of immunities to administrative and technical personnel; the United States and the Soviet Union support such an extension; and a number of other European and non-European nations endorse such an extension, but with limitations. In addition, it is apparent that divergencies exist also in state practice.

As noted previously, an Italian court in *Società Arethusa Film v. Reist*[86] distinguished administrative from diplomatic personnel by holding that the former were not entitled to diplomatic immunity for unofficial acts. Some thirty years earlier a German court had distinguished between diplomatic and subordinate personnel by declaring that the latter lose their privileges when the receiving state no longer wishes to receive them and so notifies the sending state.[87] Other courts in the post-World War II period have taken a restrictive view of the immunities extended to subordinate personnel. The Supreme Court in Hong Kong ruled in a 1952 case, *Juan Ysmael & Company v. S.S. Tasikmalaja*,[88] that a diplo-

---

[85] Compare the pertinent sections:

Article 36(1) (ILC Draft): "Apart from diplomatic agents, the members of the family of a diplomatic agent forming part of his household, and likewise the administrative and technical staff of a mission, together with the members of their families forming part of their respective households, shall, if they are not nationals of the receiving State, enjoy the privileges and immunities specified in Articles 27 to 34." United Nations, International Law Commission, *Yearbook: 1958,* Vol. II, p. 43.

Article 37(2) (Vienna Convention): "Members of the administrative and technical staff of the mission, together with members of their families forming part of their respective households, shall, if they are not nationals of or permanently resident in the receiving State, enjoy the privileges and immunities specified in Articles 29 to 35, except that the immunity from civil and administrative jurisdiction of the receiving State specified in paragraph 1 of Article 31 shall not extend to acts performed outside the course of their duties. They shall also enjoy the privileges specified in Article 36, paragraph 1, in respect of articles imported at the time of first installation." United Nations, Conference on Diplomatic Intercourse and Immunities, 2 March–14 April, 1961, *Official Records.* Vol. II: *Vienna Convention on Diplomatic Relations* (A/CONF. 20/14/Add. 1) (New York, 1962), pp. 82–88 for text; also in *AJIL,* LV (October, 1961), 1064–1077. Cited hereafter as Vienna Convention.

[86] (Italy, 1953), *ILR* (1955), 544.

[87] *Diplomatic Immunities (German Foreign Office) Case* (Germany, 1926), *AD* (1925–1926), Case No. 244. However, in criticizing this decision, Professor Karl Strupp noted: "It may well be doubted whether this judgment can be approved. It is believed that such persons enjoy the privileges of exterritoriality so long as they are employed by the foreign state, whose declaration is alone relevant." *Ibid.,* p. 323.

[88] (1952), Hong Kong Law Reports 242, 288; *ILR* (1952), Case No. 94.

matic courier "has no official recognition and is granted exemption from civil and criminal jurisdiction and afforded special protection only during the exercise of his office."[89] The Argentine Supreme Court held in 1955, in *Cabañez v. Ramírez*[90] and again in 1958, *In re Haidar*,[91] that administrative employees of foreign embassies were not invested with diplomatic status and thus did not come under the court's original jurisdiction.[92]

While these cases tend to lend credence to a restrictive extension of immunities to such subordinate personnel, other judicial decisions indicate that the practice is far from uniform. For example, in 1941 an Italian court rejected the contention of tax authorities that exemptions applied only to heads of mission.[93] The court held that diplomatic immunities must be granted not only to heads of mission but also to their official staff. In its opinion, the court declared:

> According to the *communis-opinio* the legal reason for extending immunity to the staff of the legation is to be found in the relationship of direct collaboration which exists between the diplomatic representative and his highest officials. Therefore, the considerations which justify the grant of immunity to diplomatic agents must, according to international law, apply also to justify the same concession in respect of the official staff of the diplomatic missions.[94]

Professor Lyons, in his 1954 survey of British practice, reached a similar conclusion, that all persons, of whatever rank (including British subjects engaged prior to August 27, 1952), are entitled to certain income tax exemptions.[95] A non-national clerk or typist, for example, is entitled to the same income tax immunities as is a counsellor, secretary, or attaché. An exception is made in case of any individual engaged in a trade or business.[96]

The problem of extension of immunities to these lower ranking members of the diplomatic establishment was considered rather extensively in *Appuhamy v. Gregory*[97] in which the court endorsed an approach

---

[89] *Ibid.*, p. 405.

[90] *ILR* (1955), 538.

[91] *ILR* (1958-II), 539.

[92] For a discussion of the position of commercial and trade representatives and other quasi-diplomatic personnel, see Chapter 11.

[93] *In re DiSorbello (Marchese)* (Italy, 1941,) *AD* (1941–1942), Case No. 108.

[94] *Ibid.*, p. 356.

[95] A. B. Lyons, "Personal Immunities of Diplomatic Agents," *BYIL,* XXXI, (1954), 311.

[96] *Ibid.*

[97] (1953), 55 New Law Reports (Ceylon) 235; *ILR* (1955), 541.

followed by the major powers at the Vienna Conference. James Ashley Gregory, a clerk and assistant to the United States Naval Attaché in Colombo, had been sued for wages allegedly owed to a personal servant. The court held that diplomatic immunity extended not only to the ambassador but to the family, suite, and servants, and if the attaché is immune then such immunity would extend to his assistant. The functional test was applied since the duties and not the source of income (e.g., the military services) was the determining factor in ascertaining immunity.

The court drew its rule that immunity extends to the lower ranking personnel from the case of *Assurantie Compagnie Excelsior v. Smith*[98] in which immunity was granted to Tom Smith, a United States Embassy clerk. Smith served as chief of the Mail Department of the embassy in London in a position of "great confidential importance." He handled outgoing dispatches and was in charge of the embassy seal. Lord Justice Scrutton held that a position entailing such responsibilities came within the class of persons who were privileged.[99]

In a later incident in Britain, diplomatic immunity was successfully claimed for seven United States Embassy marine guards who were court-martialed for selling cigarettes and whisky that had not gone through customs.[100] In these cases, officials applied the pragmatic test of function and based immunity on whether or not the activity of the person involved was part of the mission's diplomatic endeavors. Or as one writer put it, the privilege attaches to the staff only insofar as it is necessary for the "convenience" of the ambassador and insofar as it is "actual, *bona fide* service."[101]

While it would be difficult to make a convincing case that full diplomatic immunities have been extended to administrative and technical personnel, there appears to be a trend toward accepting these persons as "diplomatic agents," in part because of the difficulty in drawing a clear line between the diplomatic and subordinate personnel and in part because these lower ranking employees have taken over functions of confidence and trust, some of which formerly were handled by the diplomatic ranks.

Both the United States and Russia, as well as Great Britain, which

---

[98](1923), 40 T.L.R. 105.

[99]Cf. *Demoiselle B. v. D.* (France, 1927), *AD* (1927–1928), Case No. 249, and *In re Mrs. J.* (Holland, 1933), *AD* (1933–1934), Case No. 165, in which immunity was successfully pleaded for chancellors in foreign legations.

[100]*New York Times*, February 2, 1960, p. 3.

[101]Patrick Stirling, "The Immunities of Diplomatic Agents," *Law Journal,* CVIII (June 13, 1958), 375.

have more at stake in protecting their swollen diplomatic establishments, support the extension of immunities to these categories. It is not uncommon to find this view expressed among the publicists. [102] In addition, customs and other fiscal privileges have been extended during the postwar period to clerical, administrative, ancillary and quasi-diplomatic personnel despite the action taken at Vienna.[103] It would not be surprising if this liberalizing trend were to continue.

---

[102] For example: "In addition to counsellors, secretaries, attachés and other senior officials, whose position is clear, it would seem that all office staff, however humble their official standing, even the officeboy if one should be employed, would be protected." J. T. Taylor, "Diplomatic Immunity," *Criminal Law Review* [n.v.] (April, 1955), 231.

[103] Vienna Convention, Article 37.

CHAPTER 8

The Retinue
And Families

ALTHOUGH DIPLOMATIC PRACTICE HAS CHANGED in the post-World War II period, traditional rules of diplomatic privileges and immunities provide a relatively uniform and universally accepted body of international law. These rules, as discussed in earlier chapters, are less clearly defined when applied to servants, subordinate staff members and families of diplomatic personnel. The prevailing tendencies, often of a liberalizing nature, have left their imprint on the status of those who enjoy a privileged position because of their peripheral association with the diplomatic mission.

Service and Unofficial Staff

Although the law of nations covering diplomatic privileges and immunities for the subordinate diplomatic staff "speaks with many tongues"[1] most governments recognize that servants, service personnel, and other "unofficial" employees of missions are entitled, at a minimum, to limited protection from jurisdiction. The absence of uniformity and the lack of universality in the application of these rules are reflected in judicial decisions and state practice. American experts on international law in 1932 reported that practice varied from the Anglo-American approach of extending substantially the same privileges and immunities to all classes of embassy employees to the Italian policy of refusing a privileged standing to lower ranking personnel.[2]

Similar conclusions were reached in two separate studies following World War II. In 1947, an English scholar found that on the one extreme Germany, Austria, the United States, and the United Kingdom granted generous immunities to servants and service personnel while on the other

---

[1]Joyce A. C. Gutteridge, "Immunities of the Subordinate Diplomatic Staff," *BYIL*, XXIV (1947), 155.

[2]Harvard Law School, "Research in International Law: I. Diplomatic Privileges and Immunities," *AJIL*, XXVI (April, 1932), Supp., 119. Cited hereafter as Harvard Draft.

extreme France, Italy, and the Soviet Union adhered to a restrictive policy.[3] In 1952, the British Somervell Commission observed that a number of states including the Soviet Union, in contrast with general practice, did not recognize the immunity of servants of any nationality.[4]

Not only is there a divergency in policy and practice among states, but each state itself must determine which subordinates in a mission or in an envoy's household are entitled to immunity. This determination is not easy to make with precision, as the International Law Commission, in laying the groundwork for codification efforts under United Nations auspices, discovered in 1958. The commission observed that there was "no uniformity in the practice of States in deciding which members of the staff of a mission shall enjoy privileges and immunities."[5] One writer has even suggested that each case must be considered on the basis of whether the nature of the office is sufficient to justify protection.[6] And the problem is further complicated by the question of whether diplomatic immunity is comprehensive enough to confer protection to a person who, though nominally employed by a diplomatic agent, is in the service of the wife or children — a maid or governess, for example.[7]

Agreement has been reached, however, on one basic rule — claims for immunity must be based on *bona fide* official service.[8] The trend was clearly established in earlier cases which refused to recognize as *bona fide* the employment of an ostler by a diplomat who kept no horses, a coachman by an envoy who kept no coach, a cook by a minister who kept no kitchen, a gardener by one who had no garden, and an English chaplain by the Moslem ambassador from Morocco.[9] That the subordi-

---

[3]Gutteridge, *BYIL,* XXIV, 156.

[4]Great Britain, Foreign Office, Parliamentary Papers *(Reports),* Cmd. 8460, January, 1952, "Report on Diplomatic Immunity by an Interdepartmental Committee on State Immunities," p. 6. Cited hereafter as the Somervell Report.

[5]United Nations, International Law Commission, "Report to the General Assembly Covering the Work of Its Tenth Session, 28 April–4 July, 1958" (A/3859), *Yearbook: 1958,* Vol. II (A/CN.4/SER.A/1958/Add.1), p. 101.

[6]Patrick Stirling, "The Immunities of Diplomatic Agents," *Law Journal,* CVIII (June 13, 1958), 375.

[7]J. T. Taylor, "Diplomatic Immunity," *Criminal Law Review* [n.v.] (April, 1955), p. 232.

[8]Stirling, *Law J.,* CVIII, 375.

[9]For a report on these cases, see John Bassett Moore, *A Digest of International Law* (Washington: Government Printing Office, 1906), IV, 655. John Westlake, *International Law* (2d ed.; Cambridge: At the University Press, 1910), I, 280, cites, *inter alia,* as supporting cases: *Triquet v. Bath* (1764), 3 Burrow 1478; *Heathfield v. Chilton* (1767), 4 Burrow 2016; *Fisher v. Begrez* (1833), 2 C. & M. 240; and *In re Cloete* (1891), 7 T.L.R. 565.

For a review of cases dealing with English law, see J. Mervyn Jones, "Immunities of Servants of Diplomatic Agents and the Statute of Anne 7, c 12," *Journal of Comparative Legislation and International Law,* XXII (February, 1940), 21–22.

nate must perform *bona fide* service to be eligible has emerged as a basic rule of diplomatic immunity, accepted by the experts in international law.[10] It is also generally agreed that subordinate staff members must be engaged on a permanent basis and not under a casual contract of service. For example, a taxi driver in the hire of a diplomat could not claim immunity.[11]

Although *bona fide* permanent service is accepted as a starting point, attempts to formulate other guidelines have been far more frustrating. However, some progress has been made in the attempts to codify the rules of diplomatic privileges and immunities for the lower ranking staff members. A comparison of codification efforts made before World War II with those made after the war clarifies this point.

The annotated code prepared by experts in international law under the supervision of the Harvard Law School — designed to serve as the American working paper for a League of Nations codification conference — illustrates the pre-war approach.[12] The Harvard Draft, while affording no immunities from jurisdiction to service personnel, or "servants" in a strict sense, did, under Article 23, permit a receiving state to exercise jurisdiction over service personnel "to an extent and in such manner to avoid undue interference with the conduct of the business of a mission."[13] Although the Harvard Draft was more "generous" in this respect than the earlier Havana Convention which did not even mention servants among categories covered by "inviolability,"[14] the end product was comparatively restrictive. The Harvard group could find no satisfactory theoretical base other than the out-moded *franchise du quartier* of earlier times under which the head of a mission punished his servants, a concept now obsolete.[15] As a result, the tendency at the time of the Harvard study was "undoubtedly in the direction of a curtailment of their [servants'] privileges and immunities, and *de lege ferenda* the

---

[10]See Gutteridge, *BYIL,* XXIV, 150; Richard Young, "Diplomatic Immunities," *American Bar Association Journal,* XXXIX (September, 1953), 840; D. C. Holland, "Diplomatic Immunity in English Law," *Current Legal Problems,* IV (1951), 101; and Stirling, *Law J.,* CVIII, 375.

[11]Taylor, *Crim. L. Rev.,* 1955, p. 232.

[12]The Harvard Draft. While the League's codification efforts were terminated by events leading to World War II, the work of the Harvard Law School still stands, at least for the American student of international law, as a major source of pre-World War II codification activity.

[13]*Ibid.,* p. 118.

[14]See Article 14, Convention on Diplomatic Officers, adopted at Havana, February 20, 1928, reprinted in *AJIL,* XXVI (April, 1932), Supp., 176, from English text in *Sixth International Conference of American States: Final Act* (Habana, 1928). Cited hereafter as Havana Convention.

[15]Harvard Draft, pp. 119–120. See also Gutteridge, *BYIL,* XXIV, p. 148.

governments of the world seem to be practically unanimous in the desire that all privileged standing be denied to this class."[16] This same tendency is found in the projects for codification of the law of diplomatic privileges and immunity which were drawn up between 1895, when the Institute of International Law adopted its Resolution on diplomatic privileges and immunities,[17] and the late 1920's.[18]

Under current practice, the concept of "functional necessity" could provide the rationale for determining the extension of immunities to service and unofficial personnel. This conclusion certainly was implied in the International Law Commission's call for "a general and uniform rule based on what would appear to be necessary and reasonable."[19] Post-World War II developments would indicate a more liberalizing tendency in state practice concurrent with the bypassing of the theoretical block raised by the old idea of *franchise du quartier*.

Portents of a fresh approach can be seen in a comparison of the Harvard Draft with the 1961 Vienna Convention on Diplomatic Relations,[20] which marked the first time in the history of the modern nation-state system that wide international agreement was reached on a comprehensive code regulating diplomatic relations.[21]

In contrast with the Harvard Draft group, the International Law Commission, in its preparatory work for the Vienna Convention, distinguished between the service staff (domestics in the employ of the mission) and private servants (domestics in the employ of the ambassador or member of a mission). Apparently this was on the basis that the former

---

[16] Harvard Draft, p. 120.

[17] Reprinted in *AJIL*, XXVI (April, 1932), Supp., 162–164, from text J. B. Scott (ed.), *Resolutions of the Institute of International Law Dealing with the Law of Nations* (New York, 1916), pp. 119–123.

[18] Harvard Draft, p. 120.

[19] United Nations, International Law Commission, *Yearbook: 1958,* Vol. II, p. 101.

[20] United Nations, Conference on Diplomatic Intercourse and Immunities, 2 March–14 April, 1961, *Official Records,* Vol. II: *Vienna Convention on Diplomatic Relations* (A/CONF.20/14/Add.1) (New York, 1962), pp. 82–88 for text; also in *AJIL,* LV (October, 1961), 1064–1077. Cited hereafter as the Vienna Convention.

[21] The Regulation signed at Vienna on March 19, 1815, between the eight powers signatory to the Treaty of Paris of 1814, Austria, France, Great Britain, Portugal, Prussia, Russia, Spain, and Sweden, with the annex added in 1818 at Aix-la-Chapelle by Austria, France, Great Britain, Prussia, and Russia, dealt with classification of diplomatic agents and not with their privileges and immunities For a text of the earlier Vienna regulation, see Herbert W. Briggs (ed.), *The Law of Nations* (2d ed.; New York: Appleton-Century-Crofts, Inc., 1952), pp. 749–750. For a general discussion of the Congress of Vienna, see Harold Nicolson, *The Congress of Vienna* (New York: Harcourt, Brace and Co., 1946), and Sir Charles Webster, *The Congress of Vienna* (London: Bell, 1937).

is entitled to immunity as a right for its official duties while the latter are not so entitled,[22] although the receiving state should treat private servants in a manner which would not unduly interfere with the conduct of the mission's business.[23]

The Vienna Convention, under Article 37 (3,4), specifically extends limited immunities to the service staff but fewer immunities to private servants of members of a mission, if they are not nationals or non-permanent residents of the receiving state. While the Harvard Draft extends immunities to servants only insofar as they are necessary not to interfere with a mission's activities, the Vienna Convention stipulates that the service staff shall enjoy immunity from civil and criminal jurisdiction with respect to official acts as well as exemption from taxes on their salaries and from local social security provisions. Private servants of mission members are exempt from income taxes. Beyond this, they are entitled to immunities and privileges only to the extent admitted by the host state, which also is warned against interfering unduly with the performance of the functions of the mission.

This more detailed consideration of the service and the unofficial staff constitutes a liberalizing trend, but it cannot be construed as the achievement of uniformity in state practice. Both the Harvard group and the International Law Commission recognized the absence of fully accepted rules, the former referring to its work as "an attempted and approximate recognition of modern international practice"[24] and the latter seeking a uniform rule which would be "necessary and reasonable."[25] Thus, the basic problem remains: the inevitable conflict between a liberal approach by most nations,[26] and the reluctance, since World War II, on the part of some states, including the Soviet Union, to recognize immunity of servants of any nationality.[27]

---

[22] Except for exemption from dues and taxes on the emoluments they receive by reason of their employment.

[23] United Nations, International Law Commission, *Yearbook: 1958*, Vol. II, p. 102. This distinction between "service staff" and "private servants" is difficult to ascertain in state practice; thus it might be considered to belong more in the realm of "progressive development of international law" (i.e., the formulation of new rules) rather than in the codification of international law (i.e., the restatement of accepted rules).

[24] Harvard Draft, p. 119.

[25] United Nations, International Law Commission, *Yearbook: 1958*, Vol. II, p. 101.

[26] As the British Interdepartmental Committee on State Immunities noted: "The majority of states recognize such immunity except where the servants are local nationals." Somervell Report, p. 6.

[27] *Ibid.*

Because of this conflict, relations between nations become more strained when some governments adhere to a liberal policy in the granting of immunities to the service and unofficial staff while others fail to reciprocate. Logically, since both reciprocity and retaliation are accepted principles of international law, the liberal states would tend to reduce the privileges and immunities for these lower ranking persons. It would be reasonable to contend that "restrictive" state A, which, for example, refused to accord certain immunities to chauffeurs and maids assigned to the embassy of "liberal" state B, should not expect state B to extend these immunities to similar personnel in the embassy of state A, even though it might be the general policy of state B to do so.

This situation plagued a number of states. The British government, which considered itself victimized by a number of restrictive states, counteracted forcefully with executive and legislative action in the 1950's, permitting the government to rescind personal immunities from any diplomatic category of any foreign government in Great Britain if it appeared that such personal immunity was not extended to the corresponding category of diplomats attached to Her Majesty's missions in the foreign country concerned.

The main problem involved the extension of immunities to servants in London missions of nations which did not grant the same courtesies and rights to such servants in British diplomatic establishments. Although authority was given to diminish immunities of envoys, families, and official and unofficial staffs, the chief problem was the legal position of servants and subordinate staff members assigned by the United Kingdom to certain countries.[28]

Judicial determination on the question sheds additional light on this problem. Possibly the "classic" restrictive case is that of the coachman of Mr. Gallatin, United States Minister to London, who was arrested

---

[28] The problem came to a head in a case not directly concerning diplomatic privileges and immunities, but which touched off a chain of events culminating in the first major amendment to the Act of Anne of 1708. The case was *Krajina v. Tass Agency* ([1949] 2 All E. R. 274) in which the Court of Appeals extended the doctrine of state immunity to a Russian news agency. As a result of the *Krajina* decision, the British government in 1950 appointed an Interdepartmental Committee on State Immunities under the chairmanship of Lord Justice Somervell to study the twin problems of state immunity and diplomatic immunity. The committee report of July 13, 1951, to the Foreign Office, was presented to Parliament in January, 1952. In its recommendation dealing with the subordinate staff, the committee recommended that "the Foreign Secretary should in the future refuse to accept any local national as holding any position in a foreign embassy in this country, including the position of a 'domestic servant,' except on the condition that such person shall not enjoy a personal diplomatic immunity." Somervell Report, p. 7. See Chapter 2 for a full discussion of this development.

in the stable of the legation and charged with assault.[29] While neither Gallatin nor the government "offered any protest" to the proceedings, the American minister did protest invasion of his property, but probably would have raised no objections had the servant been arrested off the premises.[30] In similar cases, in 1888, the Prussian coachman of the French ambassador in Berlin was condemned without protest from France, and in 1881 and 1894, Roman courts sent to jail or fined coachmen attached to diplomatic missions for failing to obey police orders.[31]

More recently, doubts as to the immunity of servants and service personnel were raised by courts in Italy, Brazil, and Argentina. In the *Case of Mohammed Lajed Ahmed*,[32] an Italian court rejected the claim of immunity by the servant of a diplomat who had been accused of running over a person while driving on an unofficial mission. The court reasoned as follows: with the abandonment of the "fictional and irrational" theory of exterritoriality, immunity has been based on whether its refusal would impede the function of a diplomatic agent. While the question of immunities to be extended servants finds states in disagreement, the "latest doctrine" holds that it is up to the state to determine whether a strict or a liberal interpretation should be followed. The court noted that only two states, the United States[33] and Austria,[34] grant total immunity to servants.

The handling of a similar case, *In re Jursitis*,[35] by the highest court in Brazil was less conclusive. Jursitis, a Lithuanian national employed as a driver by the Austrian Embassy in Rio de Janeiro, was involved on May 22, 1953, in a collision while driving an embassy car. He was convicted by a magistrate's court under the Brazilian Penal Code. An application for *habeas corpus* was made on his behalf on the ground that the magistrate had no jurisdiction because (1) Jursitis was a member of the embassy staff and (2) he was an alien. The lower court dismissed the application on grounds that Jursitis was not a diplomatic officer and thus not entitled to immunity and that, in any event, he was not an Austrian national.

---

[29] Sir Ernest Satow, *A Guide to Diplomatic Practice*, ed. Sir Neville Bland (4th ed.; London: Longmans, Green and Co., 1957), p. 214.

[30] "Diplomatic Immunity and the Criminal Law," *Law Journal*, LXVIII (October 12, 1929), 227.

[31] Clyde Eagleton, "The Responsibility of the State for the Protection of Foreign Officials," *AJIL*, XIX (April, 1925), 300.

[32] (Italy, 1951), *AJIL*, XLIX (1955), 100–101.

[33] Act of April 30, 1790 (1 Stat. 118; 22 U.S.C. 254).

[34] Penal Code of 1804.

[35] (Brazil, 1956), *ILR* (1956), 429.

In a split three-two decision, the Supreme Court dismissed the appeal, denying immunity to the driver. The court declared that "immunity must be limited to diplomatic agents, the official staff of the mission and members of their respective families residing with them." Jursitis was Lithuanian, not Austrian, and even if immunity extended to servants employed by an embassy, it covered only those who were of the same nationality as the head of mission. Despite the ruling, a strong case was made for the extension of immunity to service personnel. The two dissenting justices observed that the tendency of foreign states was to enlarge the scope of diplomatic immunity to "persons in the service of diplomatic agents, whatever their rank or nationality." In addition, both the Austrian Embassy and the Brazilian Minister of Foreign Affairs were recorded as favoring the recognition of such immunity.

The practice in Argentina is not entirely consistent since its Supreme Court appears to have followed both the liberal and the restrictive interpretations. The court, in two recent cases, clearly excluded chauffeurs from the privileged class of diplomatic persons. *In re Dorogoutsev,*[36] the chauffeur to the Soviet ambassador and defendant in an action for personal injury applied to have the case heard in the first instance in the Supreme Court, which in Argentina has original and exclusive jurisdiction over members of foreign missions who have diplomatic status. In a report to the court, the Procurator General held that the chauffeur was not a diplomatic officer and that the case did not come within the original jurisdiction of the court, a view in which the court concurred. Two years later *In re Fernandez,*[37] the court also refused to take jurisdiction when charges of reckless driving were brought against Alfredo Fernandez, chauffeur to a foreign embassy in Buenos Aires.

The Argentine Supreme Court in recent decisions also has denied diplomatic status to personal servants. *In re Rodríguez et al.,*[38] the court ruled that ordinary courts had jurisdiction over a case involving two domestic servants (nationality not indicated) of the American Embassy, who were charged with fighting within the premises of the embassy at Buenos Aires. The court agreed that the pair did not have the diplomatic status which would exempt them from the ordinary criminal court jurisdiction. The high Argentine tribunal reached a similar decision in *Bregante v. Souviron.*[39] A car owned by the agricultural attaché of the

---

36 (Argentina, 1956), *ILR* (1956), 430.
37 (Argentina, 1958), *ILR* (1958-II), 543–544.
38 (Argentina, 1958), *ILR* (1958-II), 546.
39 (Argentina, 1943), *AD* (1943–1945), Case No. 76.

United States Embassy in Buenos Aires and driven by the governess in his employ, the defendant, struck a bicycle ridden by Bregante and injured him.

In considering whether the case was within the original jurisdiction of the Supreme Court, the judge held that it must be remitted to a provincial court. It was reasoned that even if the attaché had diplomatic immunity[40] it did not follow that circumstances alone were sufficient to extend the principle of immunity to the governess. She was not part of the personnel of the embassy nor of the suite of the ambassador. However, if the opinion *In re Dorogoutsev* had been followed, it would have made no difference whether the governess had been employed by the ambassador or by a lower ranking diplomatic officer.

Of interest, but of less value in attempting to determine Argentine practice, was the case of *Fiscal v. Lanusse*.[41] An automobile driven by the chauffeur of the United States Embassy in Buenos Aires struck a car causing some personal injuries to a passenger and damage to the vehicle. Summary action against the chauffeur was commenced in an inferior criminal court, but the case was transmitted to the Supreme Court as being within the latter's original jurisdiction. The state Procurator recommended its return to the lower court on the rather strange ground that diplomatic privilege covered the vehicle but not the driver. The Supreme Court concurred, noting that there did not appear to be "any denunciation, accusation, or charge against any diplomatic agent or person of a legation or servant thereof to whom is attributed the commission of the crime." The case is inconclusive in that the Supreme Court did not clarify whether the chauffeur was not within the category of privileged persons, or whether its decision was due to some formal flaw in the action.[42]

While these cases reveal a reluctance on the part of certain courts to grant jurisdictional immunities to servants and service personnel in motor vehicle accident cases, a more substantial body of case material can be presented to illustrate the opposing tendency. A useful reflection of this liberal interpretation is found in Anglo-American practice, as well as in courts of other countries, both for the modern and earlier periods.

---

[40] However, the editor of the *Annual Digest* observed that "neither did it appear that her employer had the character of a diplomatic envoy," *AD* (1943–1945), 243.

[41] (Argentina, 1938), *AD* (1938–1940), Case No. 170.

[42] Editor's Note, *AD* (1938-1940), 435. Cf. *In re Roberto Tavellino* (Argentina, 1936), *AD* (1935–1937), Case No. 184, in which action for injuries in a motor car accident by the chauffeur of the American commercial attaché was started, then dropped since injuries were held to have been due to the fault of the victim.

Early United States precedents included decisions that the arrest of a runaway slave who was employed by the British minister violated diplomatic privilege,[43] and that criminal immunity extended to a cook in the employ of an embassy.[44] These cases are not exceptions since United States courts have consistently held that exemption of diplomatic representatives, including subordinates, family, and servants is a long-settled rule of international law. The case of *Carrera v. Carrera*[45] is possibly the most significant recent example. Rosa H. Carrera sued Amable H. Carrera for separate maintenance for herself and for custody and support of their fifteen-year-old son. The Carreras were nationals of Ecuador, and when the action was instituted both were domestic servants in the Czechoslovakian Embassy. The embassy requested immunity for Carrera, whose name was on the "White List." The court noted that not only foreign diplomatic representatives but their subordinates, family and servants as well, are exempt from all local processes in the host country.[46] In the same spirit, the State Department officially noted in 1960 that the extending of immunity to servants is accorded on the basis of "accepted principles of international law which have been incorporated in domestic legislation."[47]

A similar liberal interpretation may be found in Great Britain, where practice follows the Act of Anne, which is still in force, and which has always been regarded as declaratory of the extent of immunity under international law from civil process.[48] The Act followed the arrest of the Russian ambassador and appears to have been passed to appease the anger of the Czar.[49] The purpose of the Act makes it an offense to sue out or execute any writ or process whereby any ambassador or public minister or the domestic servant of such envoy may be arrested or imprisoned or his or their goods and chattels distrained. It is reasonable to infer from earlier British practice that in the case of servants, immunities were

---

[43] *United States v. Jeffers*, Fed. Cas. 15471 (1836).

[44] *United States v. Lafontaine*, Fed. Cas. 15550 (1831).

[45] 174 F. 2d 496 (1949).

[46] Citing *Kent's Commentaries*, I, 15, 38; *Harvard Law Review*, XXVII (1914), 489; and *Yale Law Journal*, XXVII (1917), 392.

[47] William Barnes, "Diplomatic Immunity from Local Jurisdiction," *DSB*, XLIII (August 1, 1960), 180; 22 U.S.C. 252–254. In the American Foreign Service, persons considered to be clothed with diplomatic immunity include "employees of the mission," which apparently covers such categories as chauffeurs, but includes only "personal servants" of the "Ambassador or other Chief of Mission," and not of diplomatic staff members. U.S., Department of State, Foreign Service Institute, *Diplomatic and Consular Immunities* (November, 1960), p. 2.

[48] Somervell Report, p. 6.

[49] See *The Mattueof Case* (1710), 10 Mod. 4; 88 Eng. Reprint 598.

limited to transactions arising from their official functions or where the comfort, convenience, or dignity of the envoy is interfered with.[50]

The "official function" rule is found in *Novello v. Toogood*[51] in which a British-born subject, employed by the Portuguese ambassador as chorister and by non-diplomatic interests as a theater prompter and music teacher, was involved in a trespass case. He was denied immunity on the grounds that the act in question was private and extraneous to the purposes of the mission.[52] In cases where the comfort, etc., of the envoy are not disturbed, the ambassador is not affected and thus the servant is not entitled to any privilege.[53] Later cases substantiate the British attitude toward immunities for subordinate personnel. For example, in 1906, immunity was extended to a chauffeur, employed by the United States Embassy, who was charged with dangerous driving,[54] and in 1908, a chauffeur for the Netherlands minister was not prosecuted on a charge of driving a car while under the influence of drink.[55]

A half-century later, in 1958, a British court allowed an even more liberal extension of immunities when in *Police v. Hitchcock*[56] immunity was extended to a non-diplomatic employee who at the time was in the *actual* service of non-diplomatic persons. The *Hitchcock* case, before the Bow Street Court in London on March 6, 1958, involved a low ranking employee who was not on the embassy payroll. The facts were as follows: Charles Thomas Hitchcock, a British subject who served as chauffeur for the Military Attaché Department of the United States Embassy in London, was cited for leaving a car in a restricted area for seventy-five minutes on October 11, 1957. The car was registered in the name of Mr. Mack, an administrative clerk in the office of the army attaché. Mack was on the diplomatic list; Hitchcock, who was paid by the United States army, was not. At the time of the incident, Hitchcock was driving a party of visiting United States congressmen. The United States claimed that Hitchcock was under the ambassador's direct line of command and should have immunity under the Diplomatic Restrictions Act of 1955[57]

---

[50] See Holland, *Cur. Leg. Prob.*, IV, 101.

[51] (1823), 1 B & C, 554; 107 E. R. 204.

[52] See Jones, *J. Comp. Leg. & Int. L.*, XXII, 24–25.

[53] Maule, J., in *Taylor v. Best* (1854), 14 C.B. 487; 139 Eng. Reprint 201. Also, see *Parkinson v. Potter* (1885), 16 Q.B.D. 152.

[54] *Law Times,* CXXI (1906), 309–320, cited by Gutteridge, *BYIL*, XXIV, 150.

[55] *South London Press,* April 22, 1938, cited by Gutteridge, *BYIL*, XXIV, 150. See also Jones, *J. Comp. Leg. & Int. L.*, XXII, 27. Cf. *Herman v. Apetz*, 224 N.Y.S. 389 (1927).

[56] Stirling, *Law J.,* CVIII, 375–376; *The Times* (London) *Law Report,* March 7, 1958, p. 7; March 13, 1958, p. 6; *The Times* (London), March 18, 1958, p. 6.

[57] 4 Eliz. 2, Ch. 21.

as being on official duty. The court held that it had no jurisdiction.

Sir Lawrence Dunne, Chief Metropolitan Magistrate, followed the rule pronounced by Justice Mathe in *Parkinson v. Potter*[58] that ". . . all persons associated in the performance of the duties of the embassy are privileged, and that an attaché is within that privilege." While the defendant was not an attaché, he did provide "transport and hospitality to such American citizens visiting these shores as the American government wants entertained," which was part of the ambassador's duties.[59] When asked whether this interpretation of diplomatic privilege was not a "bit haywire" and "out of hand," Ian Harvey, British Under-Secretary of State for Foreign Affairs, explained that only those persons entitled to diplomatic privileges and immunities receive it, clearly implying that Hitchcock was in this category.[60]

In a similar action, the Marlborough Street Magistrate's Court in London extended diplomatic immunity to a servant of the Saudi Arabian Embassy who was not on the diplomatic list.[61] The London decisions are consistent with the rule drawn from *Assurantie Compagnie Excelsior v. Smith* (1923)[62] that diplomatic immunity extends to family, suite, and servants.[63]

While this liberal interpretation in the common law countries of Great Britain and the United States does not constitute a general rule of international law, the practice of other states often concurs.[64] Decisions by courts in Italy and Argentina are indicative of this "liberalizing" approach.

The Court of First Instance of Rome, *In re Reinhardt*,[65] placed servants in the privileged class. A domestic servant, not an Italian national, of the second Secretary of the Swiss Legation to the Holy See[66]

---

[58] (1885), 16 Q.B.D. 152, 157.

[59] Stirling, *Law J.,* CVIII, 376.

[60] *The Times* (London), March 18, 1958, p. 6.

[61] "Diplomatic Privilege," *Journal of Criminal Law,* XVIII (April–June, 1954), 113–114.

[62] 40 T.L.R. 105.

[63] Cf. *Appuhamy v. Gregory* (Ceylon, 1953), 55 *New Law Reports* (Ceylon) 235; *ILR* (1955), 541–543.

[64] For a review of the earlier practices in non-Anglo-American states, see Gutteridge, *BYIL,* XXIV, *passim.*

[65] (Italy, 1938), *AD* (1938–1940), Case No. 171.

[66] The same immunities were extended to diplomatic personnel connected with the Vatican as to those stationed in Italy. Article 12(2) of the Treaty between the Vatican and Italy (Lateran Treaty) of February 11, 1929, as cited in *AJIL,* XXIII (1929), Supp., 187–195, states: "Envoys of foreign governments to the Holy See will continue to enjoy in the Kingdom of Italy all the privileges and immunities which pertain to diplomatic agents according to international law."

had been accused of infanticide committed in Italy. The court declined jurisdiction on the grounds that the immunities and prerogatives accorded to diplomatic agents must, by customary international law, be extended to servants, provided they are not nationals of the receiving state.

In a series of cases in the late 1930's and early 1940's, the Supreme Court of Argentina ruled that it had original jurisdiction under the Argentine Constitution over two cooks[67] and the Spanish chauffeur of the United States ambassador.[68] In the latter case, the court observed that the Constitution "does not require that the ambassadors or ministers be actual parties, but only that the action should refer to matters concerning them, as does a criminal action against a person of their official or personal staff." In such an action, the court declared, the privileges and immunities of the ambassador may be affected even though he is not a direct party to the action.[69] The court in 1934 *In re Taiolino*[70] held that civil proceedings against the chauffeur of the commercial attaché of the United States Embassy did not fall within the jurisdiction of any Argentine court since immunity had not been waived.

A number of conclusions emerge from this review. In the first place, state practice in extending diplomatic privileges and immunities to subordinate personnel is neither uniform — having wide divergency in approaches — nor universal,[71] since a vacuum exists in international law as far as fully accepted rules are concerned. Findings by both the British Interdepartmental Committee on State Immunities and the International Law Commission of the United Nations illustrate the diversity.

Secondly, it is impossible to classify subordinate personnel with precision because of the marked increase in both numbers and types. However, their service must be *bona fide,* part of the mission's operation, and on a regularized basis before immunity is considered by the host state.

Thirdly, states have liberally extended immunities in recent years

---

[67] *In re Kosakiewick* (Argentina, 1941), *AD* (1941–1942), Case No. 114, and *Fiscal v. Gallardo* (Argentina, 1939), *AD* (1938–1940), 428–429, fn.

[68] *Fiscal v. Sanjurio* (Argentina, 1938), *AD* (1938–1940), 428, fn.

[69] *Ibid.*

[70] (Argentina, 1934), *AD* (1933–1934), 383, fn.

[71] Nor, it would seem always logical. For instance, the Chinese chauffeur of a diplomat stationed in the People's Republic of China was involved in a traffic accident. The traffic court held that since the chauffeur was eighty per cent responsible for the accident, the diplomat would receive eighty per cent of the compensation. As told by Gerald Clark in *Impatient Giant* (New York: David McKay Company, Inc., 1959), pp. 120–121, who added: "The diplomat, so far as I know, is still trying to figure it out."

by placing servants and service personnel in a privileged position at least for acts connected with their public functions. The restrictive policy of denying a privileged status to this class has been less pronounced. Major codification efforts, the "landmark" British legislation, and judicial decisions lend credence to this conclusion. For example, the extension of limited immunities to the service staff and private servants under the Vienna Convention of 1961 is a liberal step forward from the Harvard Draft of 1932. Furthermore, the British government, through investigation and legislation, albeit of a restrictive nature, encouraged greater uniformity in state practice and, *inter alia,* forced modification of Soviet policies. The British, in effect, forcefully restated the long-accepted rule of international law that diplomatic privileges and immunities must be based on reciprocity.

Division of various court cases into liberal-restrictive categories also would find the bulk of the supporting evidence on the liberal side. While the famed Gallatin case is most widely quoted as an example of restrictive practice, modern cases of this type in the *Annual Digest/International Law Reports* are limited to Italy, Brazil, and Argentina. While it might be illogical, although necessary under this concept, to extend immunities to diplomatic agents for unofficial acts, it would be completely unreasonable to accord the same privileges to servants. However, all of the "restrictive" cases dealt with traffic incidents and, even if accepted as conclusive, would still leave a wide area for a differing interpretation.

The Anglo-American cases, as well as a scattering of decisions from other nations, support the rule that immunity should be extended to service personnel and servants, at least for their official acts. This would be true even though the release of servants (in a certain number of earlier cases, at least) may have been more a matter of courtesy than of obligation.[72] Even chauffeurs and drivers in traffic cases are included in the immune group. An extreme instance is found in *Police v. Hitchcock* where a non-diplomatic employee, not on the embassy payroll, driving a car registered to an embassy clerk, and in the service of non-diplomatic persons, was granted immunity. It was reasoned that his duties came under the ambassador's direct line of command. Broad immunities could be covered by this generous interpretation, and would extend to nationals of third states employed as servants.

In the United States, court decisions, statutes, and State Department policy make it clear that the exemption of servants is considered

---

[72] This point was made by Eagleton, *AJIL,* XIX, 300.

to be a settled rule of international law. Italian and Argentine courts concur, and even in Brazil a strong dissent in a three-two decision denying immunity to a servant left the ruling in doubt. The trend is logical since the activity of subordinate personnel is an integral part of the protected diplomatic apparatus.[73]

Families

It is a long-established rule in international law that privileges and immunities extend to families of diplomatic agents, although publicists have disagreed whether this should be "full"[74] or "limited"[75] immunities for the wife and children of only the head of mission, or whether immunities should extend to families of other diplomatic personnel.[76]

Extension of the privileged status at least to families of the diplomatic staff is a rule of international law universally accepted by jurists,[77] and by most writers,[78] although Satow would also include the wives and children of lower ranking personnel (e.g., archivists, clerks, and inter-

---

[73] Two accepted guidelines in international law for these categories might be: 1. Servants and service personnel are immune for their official acts. 2. In other cases, jurisdiction should be exercised only when such action will not interfere with the work of the mission. The two rules are stated by Gutteridge, *BYIL*, XXIV, 158–159. This study would tend to reinforce their applicability.

[74] "The same exemption from local jurisdiction, which the ambassador himself enjoys, is granted by the law of nations to his family." Theodore Dwight Woolsey, *Introduction to the Study of International Law*, ed., Theodore Salisbury Woolsey (6th ed. rev. and enl.; New York: Charles Scribner's Sons, 1898), p. 142.

[75] "Persons composing the family of the minister do not enjoy any other rights and prerogatives beyond those which are due them in accordance with propriety and diplomatic ceremonial. . . . These persons cannot enjoy the rights and prerogatives which, according to international law, belong to the representative of a foreign state." Pasquale Fiore, *International Law Codified*, trans. Edwin M. Borchard (New York: Baker, Voorhis and Company, 1918), 242.

[76] "Besides the persons who are on the diplomatic staff of the mission, immunity from the territorial jurisdiction, civil or criminal, is generally enjoyed by those who are living with them as part of their family or household." Westlake, I, 280.

[77] See *In re Jursitis* (Brazil, 1956), *ILR* (1956), 429, in which the Supreme Court observed that immunity extended to "the official staff of the mission and members of their respective families residing with them." Cf. *Carrera v. Carrera*, 174 F. 2d 496 (1949).

[78] For example, "members of the families of diplomatic officers," in Kurt von Schuschnigg, *International Law* (Milwaukee: The Bruce Publishing Company, 1959), p. 247; "members of the diplomat's immediate family, the officials attached to his mission and their families," in Elmer Plischke, *Conduct of American Diplomacy* (2d ed.; Princeton, N.J.: D. Van Nostrand Company, Inc., 1961), p. 346; and "families" of "foreign diplomats" in Oscar Svarlien, *Introduction to the Law of Nations* (New York: McGraw-Hill Book Company, Inc., 1955), pp. 246–247. Hyde, in addition to heads of missions, refers only to embassy secretaries. Charles Cheney Hyde, *International Law: Chiefly as Interpreted and Applied by the United States* (2d rev. ed.; Boston: Little, Brown and Company, 1947), II, 1273.

preters).[79] The rule is also reflected in codification efforts and state practice. The framers of the widely-quoted Harvard Draft[80] and of the only multilateral instruments signed to date dealing with "traditional" diplomatic privileges and immunities[81]— the Havana Convention[82] and the Vienna Convention[83]— concur in this minimum rule.

The codes reflect widely accepted state policies. The United Nations Secretariat, in a survey of state rules and regulations, found numerous examples supporting the doctrine, stated both in general terms of extending immunities to the families of the official staff[84] or in specific terms of similar extensions to dependents of "first category" personnel (counsellors, secretaries, and attachés).[85] The practice in the Soviet Union, the United States, and Great Britain is compatible with this doctrine. The Soviet Union grants full immunity to families of a more generously conceived "first category" which includes charges d'affaires and trade representatives in addition to counsellors, secretaries, and attachés.[86] The United States designates families of "duly accredited" diplomatic officers.[87]

In Great Britain, jurisdictional immunities "are customarily regarded

---

[79] Satow, pp. 192–193.

[80] The Harvard Draft refers throughout to mission members and members of their families with the member of mission (Article 1) defined as a person "authorized by the sending state to take part in diplomatic functions."

[81] As contrasted with immunities for personnel of and representatives to international organizations.

[82] In the Havana Convention (Article 14) reference to "members of the respective families" follows reference to "all classes of diplomatic officers" and "the entire official personnel of the diplomatic mission."

[83] Under the Vienna Convention (Article 37), members of the families of diplomatic agents "forming part of . . . [their] household[s]" enjoy full immunities and members of the families of administrative and technical staffs enjoy the same extensive but limited immunities as are extended to those staffs (Articles 26, 37). No reference is made in the Vienna Convention to families of service staff or private servants.

[84] New Zealand: "A member of the family of a member of the official staff of a chief representative shall be entitled to . . . immunity from suit and legal process as would be accorded to him if the chief representative were an envoy." New Zealand, Diplomatic Immunities Act, 1952, cited in United Nations, Secretariat, *United Nations Legislative Series*, Vol. VIII: *Laws and Regulations Regarding Diplomatic and Consular Privileges and Immunities* (New York: 1958), p. 217. Cited hereafter as *U.N. Laws and Regulations.*

[85] Swtizerland: "Les femmes et les enfants de ces personnes [lere catégorie] bénéficient des mêmes prérogatives pour autant qu'ils vivent sous le même toit et n'exercent pas d'activité lucrative." Règles appliquées par le Département politique fédéral en matière d'immunités et privileges diplomatiques et consulaires. Cited in *U.N. Laws and Regulations*, p. 304.

[86] Y. A. Korovin and Others, *International Law*, trans., Dennis Ogden (Moscow: Foreign Languages Publishing House [1961]), p. 304.

[87] Barnes, *DSB*, XLIII, 180.

as extending to the wife of a head of mission or member of his official staff and also to those members of their families who are dependent upon them."[88] The British policy statement is supported by judicial interpretation of the Diplomatic Privileges Act of 1708 (Act of Anne)[89] and by later legislation,[90] including the Diplomatic Immunities (Commonwealth Countries and Republic of Ireland) Act, 1952, dealing with High Commissioners,[91] and the Diplomatic Immunities Restriction Act, 1955, dealing with diplomatic personnel in general.[92] Furthermore, the British Interdepartmental Committee on State Immunities contends that these immunities ordinarily granted in Great Britain "are either certainly or probably required by international law."[93]

The designation "family" as used by many writers of international law with reference to this category of diplomatically immune persons,[94] obviously includes the diplomat's wife, even perhaps if she is estranged,[95] and children.[96] Most writers do not distinguish between the two categories, although the highly respected Oppenheim-Lauterpacht work[97]

---

[88] The official British attitude was defined for the House of Commons in 1958 by Ian Harvey, Parliamentary Under Secretary for Foreign Affairs. *The Times* (London), April 10, 1958, p. 6.

[89] The word "domestick" in the act has been interpreted to mean a member of the ambassador's household (by Lord Dunedin in *Engelke v. Musmann,* [1928] A.C. 433, 447) and to mean both his "diplomatic family" and his personal family (by Lord Phillimore, *ibid.,* p. 450). It is generally accepted that the act is not exhaustive but is merely declaratory of common law.

[90] O. M. Stone, "Families Personal and Diplomatic," *Modern Law Review,* XXII (March, 1959), 193–194.

[91] 15 & 16 Geo. 6 and 1 Eliz. 2, Ch. 18, cited in *U.N. Laws and Regulations,* pp. 348–350. Article 1(1) (c) extends immunity to "members of the family of a chief representative or of a member of the official staff of a chief representative entitled to immunity. . . ."

[92] 4 Eliz. 2. Ch. 21. Article 1 (1) refers to "the personal immunities conferred by law on the envoys of foreign sovereign powers accredited to Her Majesty, their families and servants, and members of the official staff of such envoys and their families. . . ."

[93] Somervell Report, p. 7.

[94] Harvard Draft, *passim;* Svarlien, p. 247; von Schuschnigg, p. 247; Wesley Gould, *An Introduction to International Law* (New York: Harper & Brothers Publishers, 1957), p. 270; William F. Bishop, Jr. (ed.), *International Law* (2d ed.; Boston: Little, Brown and Company, 1962), p. 593.

[95] Satow's *Guide* contends that this immunity extends even to wives living apart. Satow, p. 193, fn., which cites supporting English and French decisions: "*Cottenet v. Rafalovitch,* Clunet (1908), 153; *Macnaghten v. Coveridias,* Annual Practice, etc. (1923), Vol. I." See also Charles Thayer, *Diplomat* (New York: Harper & Brothers Publishers, 1959), p. 204; and Taylor, *Crim. L. Rev.* (1955), p. 231.

[96] For example, "wives and families" in Satow, p. 193; "sa famille (femme et enfants)" in Charles Rousseau, *Droit International Public* (Paris: Recueil Sirey, 1953), p. 345, and "immediate family" in Plischke, p. 346.

[97] L. Oppenheim, *International Law,* Vol. I: *Peace,* ed. H. Lauterpacht (8th ed.; London: Longmans, Green and Co., 1955), p. 812.

does grant full inviolability only to the wife and limited immunities to the children and other relatives.[98] Hyde,[99] whose analysis centers on United States practice, also disagrees with the majority of publicists and is on the opposite extreme from Oppenheim. He claims that the minister's exemption extends, not only to his wife and children, but to his parents and other family members, such as brothers[100] and nieces, and possibly household guests.[101] In practice, the Soviet Union also provides for extension of immunities beyond the diplomat's wife and children. While these two categories (if the children are in their minority) enjoy "complete immunity," other members of the family are immune on the basis of reciprocity.[102]

Despite these minority viewpoints, which are undoubtedly reflected in the practice of some states, in general, wives and children of the diplomat are entitled to immunity. In addition, these family members presumably must either live "under the same roof" as the diplomatic agent[103] or, more broadly speaking, form part of his household,[104] and, in some cases at least, also be dependent upon the diplomat for support.[105] Thus, at a minimum, diplomatic privileges and immunities extend to the envoy's wife and dependent children who are domiciled in the diplomatic household. It is far less certain whether immunities are enjoyed by relatives other than the "immediate" family."

In addition, it is also a fully crystallized rule of international law that immunity extends to the wife and dependent children of official diplomatic agents as well as to the family of the head of mission. There is some dispute as to whether families of administrative and technical staff members should enjoy these rights and courtesies.

Finally, the theoretical basis of family immunity might be explained

---

[98] *Ibid.*

[99] Hyde, II, 1273.

[100] This contrasts with the case of Don Pantaleon Sa, brother of the Portuguese ambassador in London and a member of his suite, who in 1653 killed an Englishman. He was arrested, tried in England, found guilty, and executed. Woolsey, p. 146.

[101] Hyde, II, 1273.

[102] Korovin and Others, p. 304.

[103] Havana Convention, Article 14; Bishop, p. 593; Gould, p. 270; Hyde, II, 1273; Oppenheim, I, 812; and Holland, *Cur. Leg. Prob.*, IV, 101.

[104] The terminology used in the Harvard Draft (Article 1) and the Vienna Convention (Article 37); both imply a family unit and the difference in practice probably has no significance. However, logically, the latter would not require physical proximity of the privileged group although an extension of the term to "common household" (von Schuschnigg, p. 247) no doubt would.

[105] Barnes, *DSB*, XLIII, 180. The United States extends this immunity to families on the basis of "universally accepted principles of international law" which have been incorporated into domestic legislation (22 U.S.C. 252–254). *Ibid.*

as an act of international courtesy[106] or as "the exercise of common humanity"[107] rather than as an extension of the theory of functional necessity which explains the granting of privileges and immunities to diplomats.

The theoretical basis, but not the practical application, of family immunity might be questioned. As the following materials will illustrate, states since 1945 have consistently applied these rules in cases pertaining to wives and children of heads of missions and, with less consistency, to the families of subordinate diplomatic agents.

Wives of Diplomatic Agents

In the post-World War II period, state practice (based on the cases and incidents examined) followed with some deviation the general minimum rule: the wife is entitled to the same type of immunities which are granted to her diplomatic husband. The rule applies to the wife of an ambassador; it is questionable if its extension to the wives of other diplomatic agents is as universally accepted.

The doctrine was stated in *Friedberg v. Santa Cruz et al.,*[108] in which the Appellate Division of the New York Supreme Court applied traditional rules of diplomatic immunity to the wife of the Chilean ambassador to the United Nations. The court ruled that under United States law[109] a permanent representative to the United Nations with the rank of ambassador or minister plenipotentiary is entitled to the same privileges and immunities in the United States as are accorded to diplomatic envoys to the United States. Thus, in adhering to doctrine applicable to traditional diplomats, the court granted the ambassador's wife immunity as a "domestic" of the envoy.[110]

This immunity also probably protects the wife of an ambassador from legal action even for liabilities incurred prior to her marriage. This was the ruling of the French Court of Cassation in *Époux Y v. Société Centrale de Construction*[111] in which the decision of an appeals court

---

106 The Soviet view. See K. Baginyan and M. Lasarev, review of D. B. Levin, *Diplomatic Immunity* (Moscow: U.S.S.R. Academy of Sciences Publishing House, 1949), in *Soviet State and Law* (February, 1951), pp. 91–92, in *Current Digest of the Soviet Press,* No. 15 (May 26, 1951), p. 5.

107 An American view. Eagleton, *AJIL,* XIX, 299.

108 86 N.Y.S. 2d 369 (1949). Action was brought as a result of an auto accident.

109 U.S., Congress, Public Law 357, 80th Cong., 1st Sess., 1947.

110 See also *People v. Von Otter,* 114 N.Y.S. 2d 295 (1952), according immunity to the wife of the counsellor of the Swedish delegation to the United Nations when charged with unlawful parking of a motor vehicle.

111 (France, 1958), *ILR* (1958-II), 542–543.

was overruled.[112] The high court held that the wife of a diplomat was immune from jurisdiction in the matter of a debt contracted prior to her marriage. The underlying premise[113] was that the "person of an envoy of a foreign Government must not be in any way interfered with."

In contrast to the American and French decisions, the Supreme Court of Argentina, in *Re D'Athouguia da Rocha Fontes,[114]* denied a privileged status to Francisca D'Athouguia, wife of the first secretary of the Portuguese Legation at Buenos Aires, who was involved in a traffic accident. The court decided that its exclusive and original jurisdiction granted by the Constitution over cases involving diplomatic officers[115] did not extend to members of their families. The phrase "or to the personnel of the embassy or legation who have diplomatic status" in the applicable Argentine statute[116] could not be construed so as to extend the jurisdiction of the court to families of such persons. Thus she was subject to the ordinary jurisdiction of the lower courts.

However, the *D'Athouguia* case is distinguished from the French and American cases by (1) the involvement of the wife of a legation secretary and not of an ambassador and by (2) the restrictive approach often taken by the high court in Argentina. It might be more closely compared with an Italian case, *Cimino Bosco v. Luijano Escheverri.[117]* The court claimed jurisdiction over the wife of a foreign diplomatic agent because the litigation involved an act of private law. However, Italian courts now tend to reject this restrictive concept[118] and wives of diplomats probably would be extended immunity even in private law cases.[119]

While wives do enjoy a privileged status,[120] they are expected to

---

[112]In 1955, a court of appeals concluded that there was no reason to believe that the functions or independence of the diplomat would be "compromised" by legal action against his wife. This discredited doctrine is found in *Société de Construction à Paris v. Guiroye, Wife of De Ayala* (France, 1955), *ILR* (1955), 549–. 550.

[113]As stated by the Civil Court of the Seine in *Société Centrale Construction v. De Ayala* (France, 1950), *ILR* (1951), 348.

[114](Argentina, 1957), *ILR* (1957), 529.

[115]See Article 101, *Anales de Legislación Argentina,* 1852–1880, p. 79, cited in *ILR* (1957), 529, fn.

[116]Article 24(1) of Law 13.998, *Anales de Legislación Argentina,* X-A, p. 222, cited in *ILR* (1957), 529, fn.

[117](Italy, 1930), *AD* (1929–1930), Case No. 196.

[118]See, for example, *Harrie Lurie v. Steinmann* (Italy, 1927), *AD* (1927–1928), Case No. 246; *De Meeus v. Forzano* (Italy, 1940), *AD* (1938–1940), Case No. 164; and *Lagos Carmona v. Baggianini* (Italy, 1953), *ILR* (1955), 533.

[119]See also, for example, *Victor Eastman Cox v. Teresa Vandivieso* (Ecuador, 1930), *AD* (1929–1930), Case No. 195.

[120]Although the Argentina decision clouds the status of wives of lower ranking diplomatic agents, national legislation, diplomatic codes, and the work of publicists leave little doubt that most states would extend full privileges and immunities at least to the wives of counsellors, secretaries, and attachés. This record is a product of post-World War II activity and thus reflects current practice.

observe local laws, customs, and regulations meticulously.[121] When this courtesy is abused, the end result is the expulsion from the country, not only of the wife, but also of her diplomat husband.

The most widely-publicized postwar case of this type involved Mrs. Karl E. Sommerlatte, wife of the second secretary of the United States Embassy in Moscow, who was charged with "hooliganism" following an incident in a Moscow factory workers club.[122] Soviet and United States versions of the incident differed but Mrs. Sommerlatte and a companion were detained by police and later she was labeled "undesirable," in effect, a demand that she be sent home. She departed from Moscow with her husband about ten days later.[123] A more serious, but comparable earlier case, occurred in Peking in 1921 when an alleged attack on another Italian woman by the wife of the Italian minister, was followed by the suicide of an attaché in the legation. The incident led to the recall of the minister.[124] A Persian diplomat to the United States suffered a similar fate in 1927.[125] Few wives are involved in these incidents, or at least few cases have been publicly reported.[126]

Since only a limited number of cases or complaints involving wives appear in the records,[127] it may be assumed that these women have been granted privileges and immunities from local criminal and civil jurisdiction. The only major exception appears to have been the restraints placed upon diplomatic wives of Russian nationality by the Soviet Union during a brief period following World War II. The violation of diplomatic practice, which took the form of emigration bans, was an aberration rather

---

[121]See, for example, the statement by Secretary of State Hull, in connection with the arrest of the Iranian minister at Elkton, Maryland, U.S., Department of State, *Press Releases,* XIII, No. 323 (December 7, 1935), cited by Briggs, pp. 773–774.

[122]*New York Times,* October 27, 1954, p. 13; October 28, p. 13.

[123]See also *ibid.,* October 29, 1954, p. 3; October 30, p. 2; November 4, p. 6; November 6, p. 4.

Senator Margaret Chase Smith, touring in Europe at the time, said she would not be "surprised" if United States-Soviet diplomatic relations were broken, although she declined to link this statement with the Sommerlatte case. *Ibid.,* October 29, 1954, p. 4.

[124]Chesney Hill, "Sanctions Constraining Diplomatic Representatives to Abide by the Local Law," *AJIL,* XXV (April, 1931), 267.

[125]The third secretary of the Persian Legation in Washington was transferred to duty in the Persian Foreign Office after his wife had been involved in an auto accident in which the occupant of the other car was fatally injured. *Ibid.,* p. 263.

[126]However, in 1959, the wife of the assistant Russian naval attaché in Washington was accused of shoplifting a $2.56 cut of meat from a supermarket. The woman, Mrs. Galina Glinsky, was detained briefly, but the Russian Embassy apparently did not lodge a complaint nor did the food store press charges. *Minneapolis Tribune,* January 10, 1959, p. 1.

[127]E.g., British and United States law reports; the *Annual Digest/International Law Reports; The Times* (London); the *New York Times;* and indexes of legal and learned journals.

than evidence of changing patterns of immunity. However, at least one of the cases became an international incident, and the practice in general illustrates one of the major themes of this study: the politicizing of diplomatic relations in the cold war.

One of the "Russian wives" incidents sent the Legal Committee of the United Nations General Assembly into a lengthy, spirited, and, at times, bitter debate. The Soviet Union had refused to issue an exit visa to the Russian daughter-in-law of David Cruz Ocampo, Chilean Ambassador to the Soviet Union. The Soviet action was criticized before the committee as a violation of human rights and of the rule of international law on diplomatic immunity. The action was defended as being a matter of domestic jurisdiction over which the United Nations had no competence.[128] The General Assembly later adopted a resolution declaring that "measures which prevent or coerce the wives of citizens of other nationalities from leaving their country of origin are *inter alia,* contrary . . . to diplomatic practices and to the principle of reciprocity. . . ."[129]

Two other similar incidents involving wives of diplomats were reported during the same period. In one, George E. Power, attached to the Canadian Embassy in Moscow, married a Russian ballet dancer in 1945, the same year he was transferred back to Ottawa. She reportedly sought a divorce in Moscow in 1947 after being denied a total of seven visa requests made by the Canadian government.[130] Also in 1947, Athanase G. Politis, the Greek Ambassador to Moscow, reported that the Soviets refused to permit his Russian-born wife to accompany him when he left Moscow on sick leave.[131]

This Russian policy, which finds its precedent in Czarist times,[132] apparently has been eased; at least no other cases were noted for the years following 1947. However, the security aspect of having "Communist" wives connected with Western missions apparently continued to be a problem. The British Foreign Office adopted a policy of removing For-

---

[128] United Nations, General Assembly, *Official Records,* Third Session, Sixth Committee (1948), pp. 718–781.

[129] United Nations, General Assembly, Resolution 285, *Official Records,* Third Session (1949), pp. 34–35.

[130] *New York Times,* September 27, 1947, p. 3.

[131] *Ibid.,* July 4, 1947, p. 4.

[132] Ernest A. Gross, Alternate United States Representative to the General Assembly, reported that in the sixteenth century the Danish government requested the Russian Foreign Office to allow the wife of the Danish ambassador, whom he had married in Moscow, to leave for Denmark. The Russian Foreign Office, in rejecting the request, observed that "it would be unseemly to give that woman in bondage to your man Sider." Ernest A. Gross, "Discussion of Chilean Proposal Relating to Soviet Wives of Foreigners," *DSB,* XIX (December 26, 1948), 798.

eign Service personnel who married Russian citizens from its Moscow embassy to avoid their being "blackmailed" into passing information to the Soviet government.[133]

Children of Heads of Diplomatic Missions

Even though children of the heads of diplomatic missions may not be entitled to complete inviolability,[134] a general rule of international law would grant them exemption from civil and criminal jurisdiction. The materials of international law are limited in their evidence supporting this rule. For example, the thoroughly documented Oppenheim-Lauterpacht work refers only to the Carlos Waddington case of a half century ago to illustrate the doctrine.[135] Three postwar cases in the United States would indicate that the rule still stands. The most flagrant of these cases involved David Hearne, twenty-one-year-old son of the Irish ambassador to the United States, John J. Hearne, whose antics culminated in the death of a Washington widow and his parental banishment from America.[136] Young Hearne was the driver of a car which on November 11, 1959, killed Mrs. Jossie Hamlin, a domestic worker, as she crossed a Washington street. The youth was charged with homicide, colliding with a pedestrian, and failing to have Washington, D. C., license plates on his car — charges which were dropped when diplomatic immunity was invoked.

Although there was never a question of immunity, the United States Department of State made it clear that the responsibility for the youth's actions rested with the Irish government and his father, who was described as being apprehensive over U.S. public opinion. In Ireland, an independent member of the Dáil Eireann (Chamber of Deputies) questioned the right of Hearne to claim diplomatic immunity. The Irish government noted that the problem was not raised since the United States automatically applied the rule of diplomatic immunity.

---

[133] *New York Times,* May 8, 1954, p. 3. Four such staff members, all in junior clerical grades, were subjected to this purge procedure between 1948 and 1954. *The Times* (London), May 8, 1954, p. 4.

[134] According to Oppenheim, I, 812–813.

[135] When in 1906, Carlos Waddington, son of the Chilean envoy in Brussels, killed the secretary of the Chilean Legation, he was not immediately arrested. Two days later the Chilean envoy waived the immunity of his son, an action later endorsed by his government. He was tried for murder by a Belgian jury and acquitted. *Ibid.*

[136] *New York Times,* October 13, 1959, p. 20; November 12, p. 8; November 13, p. 11; November 14, p. 7; November 16, p. 39; November 18, p. 25; November 22, Sec. IV, p. 4; November 26, p. 3; November 28, p. 12. *Minneapolis Tribune,* November 13, p. 3; November 14, p. 3; November 18, p. 9.

Before the death case, Hearne had figured in four instances of disorderly conduct (1957 to 1959), the last requiring the efforts of eight policemen to subdue Hearne and two companions.

The Irish government, in response to some questions raised, met at least the minimum international standards applicable in such cases. In the first place, the elder Hearne ordered his son to attend the inquest, which may have been a moral but was not a legal obligation. Secondly, both of the Hearnes attended funeral services for the victim at which time the ambassador informed the congregation that a financial settlement would be made. The settlement was arranged by Hearne's insurance company and the state of Ireland was not directly involved.[137] Finally, Ambassador Hearne removed his son from American University and sent him back to Ireland to continue his schooling.[138]

United States authorities maintained that the Hearne case constituted an exception to normal conduct by diplomatic families. State Department officials were quoted as saying that they could recall no similar case involving a member of an ambassador's family. However, circumstances were somewhat the same in the fatal injury on January 7, 1928, of a girl hit by a car driven by the son of the British ambassador to the United States.[139]

Two other post-World War II cases, less serious but still reinforcing the rule of diplomatic immunity for sons of ambassadors to the United States, involved young drivers from Paraguay and Pakistan. In the first, Carlos Platé, seventeen, was released on December 29, 1959, by police in Fairfax County, Virginia, when his father, Ambassador Juan Platé of Paraguay, identified him as having diplomatic immunity. The boy had been arrested following a high-speed chase through two counties. However, the ambassador waived the son's immunity and paid $100 for damages to a lawn on which the car had skidded.[140]

The second case involved Hamad Ali, the seventeen-year-old son of the Pakistani ambassador, who allegedly would not appear in a Wall

---

[137] Letter to the writer from the Honorable Thomas J. Kiernan, Ambassador of Ireland to the United States, August 9, 1962, who also reported that the elder Hearne later left the United States and was reassigned to diplomatic duty in Accra, Ghana.

[138] The son of an American diplomat in Ireland was also sent home after a girl told authorities that she had been attacked. Michael H. Cardozo, "Diplomatic Immunities, Protocol and the Public," *Journal of International Affairs,* XVII (No. 1, 1963), 62.

[139] Officials decided that the English chauffeur was responsible since he was in charge of the car at the time and the son was under age and had no permit. No legal proceedings were instituted. Satisfaction apparently was given by the ambassador who offered to have the girl sent to a hospital, put his car and personal surgeon at the disposal of the family, and called on the family. Hill, *AJIL,* XXV, 264–265.

[140] Denys P. Myers, "Contemporary Practice of the United States Relating to International Law," *AJIL,* LIV (July, 1960), 649; *Minneapolis Tribune,* December 31, 1959, p. 10.

Township, New Jersey, court on a charge of reckless driving. The chief of police of Wall Township said he and his three-man force would march to the ambassador's summer home and take Hamad before a judge to show that traffic laws were not to be "sneezed at." The State Department reportedly intervened, and the "marching orders" were cancelled.[141]

The Hearne, Platé and Ali cases would indicate that there has been no postwar deviation from the United States policy, stated in 1938, that the son of a foreign ambassador or minister, as a member of the diplomatic household, may not be penalized for traffic and more serious violations.[142] No cases to the contrary were found, and the rule might be reinforced by a similar British interpretation in a 1927 traffic incident involving the son of the Spanish ambassador.[143] It may be presumed that at least the children (as well as the wife) of the chief of mission, living under his roof, enjoy the same immunities from civil and criminal jurisdiction as the father.

Children of Other Diplomatic Agents

While postwar practice is compatible with, and thus supports, the general rule extending privileges and immunities, at least from jurisdiction, to the wives and children of chief envoys, the situation becomes far more cloudy when materials dealing with the families of other diplomatic agents are considered.

The accepted doctrine is that wives and children of diplomatic agents, at least down through the official ranks to the attaché level, should enjoy immunities similar to those extended to the families of mission heads. However, the practice of states in the postwar years has not been uniform and has not always been in keeping with the doctrine. Thus it would be a risky generalization either to assert the universality of the rule or to specify classes of diplomatic families covered.

The courts, as well as executive departments, have considered doctrinal questions in the period under study. Fortunately, in one case, *Re C. (An Infant),*[144] decided by the Chancery Division in Great Britain on

---

[141] Martin Abramson, "Scofflaws in Striped Pants," *Coronet,* XLVIII (August, 1960), 123–124.

[142] As noted by the chief of the State Department's Division of Protocol to L. C. Day of the Montgomery County Police, October 7, 1938, cited by Green Haywood Hackworth, *Digest of International Law* (Washington: Government Printing Office, 1942), IV, 521.

[143] Hill, *AJIL,* XXV, 262.

[144] L.R., [1959] Ch. 363; [1958] 3 W.L.R. 309; [1958] 2 All E.R. 656. For additional details, see also *AJIL,* LIII (January, 1959), 188, and *The Times* (London) *Law Reports* (June 11, 1958), p. 5.

June 10, 1958, a British court for the first time dealt directly with the extension of immunities to the personal family of an ambassador's "diplomatic family." The facts were these: The infant was born in 1943 in Greece of Greek parents and in 1947 his mother was killed in an automobile accident. The father studied at the London School of Economics from 1945–1950 and worked in Greece from 1950–1955. In 1951, he married in Greece an Englishwoman who, in 1952, brought the youngster to Great Britain with the father's consent. In 1955, the father came to Great Britain. In 1956, he obtained employment in the Greek Embassy and separated from his wife at about the same time. He was a member of the Greek Diplomatic Service and acknowledged as such by the British Foreign Office with the inclusion of his name on the diplomatic list.

The father desired to send the boy back to Greece to continue his education; the wife (stepmother of the child) objected to the interruption of his British schooling and commenced proceedings to make the boy a ward of the court. The father asked the court to set aside the proceedings on grounds that both he and the lad were entitled to diplomatic immunity. The proceedings were set aside, Justice Harman ruling that as the father had not surrendered parental rights the boy should be considered a member of the family and a person to whom diplomatic immunity should be extended.

For the first time, two questions arose for decision:[145]

(1) Whether the personal families of a foreign envoy's "diplomatic family" are immune from jurisdiction in English courts;

(2) If so, whether a child not resident with his father is a member of that father's personal family.

With reference to the first question, the extension of immunities to personal families of the "diplomatic family" was based on the Diplomatic Act of 1708 (Act of Anne) as well as on postwar legislation in Great Britain. Justice Harman noted that while nothing is said in the Act of Anne about the family of the ambassador, he "cannot doubt that the immunity does extend to the family."[146] Harman referred to a speech by Lord Phillimore in the House of Lords to that effect in *Engelke v. Musmann:*[147]

> The ambassador further requires, in order that he may effectually do his Sovereign's business, that there should be a like immunity for his personal family, that is to say, his wife and his children if living with him, his diplomatic family, as it is sometimes called, that

---

[145] See Stone, *Mod. L. Rev.,* XXII, 193.
[146] L.R., [1959] Ch. 363, 366.
[147] [1928] A.C. 433, 450.

is to say, his counsellors, secretaries and clerks, whom I take to be intended by the word "domestic" in the statute of Anne, and his ordinary servants, described in the statute as "domestic servants."

Justice Harman said he "cannot doubt" that this immunity of the "personal family" also extends to the "personal family" of the staff of the ambassador, and by staff he included those persons carried on the Foreign Office lists as diplomatic personnel, which would cover the present case.[148] Additional evidence is found in *Halsbury's Laws of England* which puts it thus: "The immunities of a diplomatic agent are extended to his family 'living with him,' and that is because it is considered that the ambassador or his staff ought not to be harassed so as to disturb them in the important duties which they have to perform."[149] In addition, both the Diplomatic Immunities (Commonwealth and Republic of Ireland) Act, 1952, and the Diplomatic Immunities Restriction Act, 1955, extend immunities to the families of members of the "official staff of an embassy."

In view of these laws and the preceding evidence, Justice Harman concluded that the boy was "entitled to the immunity which the law throws over diplomatic representatives."[150] It has been suggested that this question had not come before a British court prior to 1958 since (1) it was unlikely that proceedings against a family member would not affect the immunity of the diplomat himself and (2) that while some areas of immunity have been the cause of concern, these have not affected the family lives of embassy members.[151]

At least one British writer, A. B. Lyons, takes sharp exception to the above decision and charges that Justice Harman "unnecessarily broke fresh ground" in deciding that the child himself was entitled to immunity.[152] Lyons bases his argument on the general contention that prior to and apart from the Diplomatic Acts of 1952 and 1955 there is little authority supporting this type of immunity. Lyons claims that "virtually none" of the modern writers extend "family immunity" beyond the ambassador himself. He dismisses Satow's *Guide* which includes wives and families down to the clerical level among those entitled to immunity[153]

---

148 L.R., [1959] Ch. 363, 366.

149 *Halsbury's Laws of England,* ed. Lord Simonds (3rd ed; London: Butterworth & Co. [Publishers] Ltd., 1954), VII, 272.

150 L.R., [1959] Ch. 363, 367.

151 Stone, *Mod. L. Rev.,* XXII, 194.

152 A. B. Lyons, "Decisions of British Courts during 1958–59 Involving Questions of . . . Public International Law," *BYIL* XXXV (1959), 262–263.

153 Satow, p. 193.

as not being a "prime authority" on legal matters. He also contends that one has to go back to Westlake in 1910 to find support for general enjoyment of immunity by families.[154]

Further, he notes that the *Annual Digest/International Law Reports* lists no cases since 1919, when the publication was started, in which immunity from jurisdiction was granted to members of families of one of the staff of a mission. Finally, he finds that in *Carrera v. Carrera*,[155] a United States court dealt with the claim for custody of a child from the point of view of the immunity from process of the child's parent. For Lyons, this is the "correct view" since the father unquestionably was entitled to diplomatic immunity, and proceedings were instituted against the father. Thus, *In re C.* could have been decided on the grounds of the father's immunity without considering the child's status.

Lyons' reasoning on the *Carrera* case is logical, reasonable, and convincing since the facts are roughly comparable. However, his other contentions are not as compelling. He might reject Satow as an authority, but it is questionable whether he should dismiss in the same cavalier fashion the judicial interpretation of the Act of Anne, major postwar legislation on the problem of immunities in Great Britain, municipal legislation in other nations including the United States and the Soviet Union, the Havana Convention, the Harvard Draft, and a number of modern text writers. As for the *Annual Digest/International Law Reports,* the question of immunities for families of the diplomatic staff has not often come before the courts for decision.

State practice therefore must be explored to determine what rules, though they may be shadowy, now exist. *In re C.* stands in splendid isolation as a groundbreaking case and whether or not the court should have dealt with the child's immunity, apart from that of his father, there is opinion both inside and outside Great Britain to support the decision. However, such opinion does not mean that the decision necessarily reflects international practice, since incidents discussed below would lend some credence to a contrary viewpoint. But it does mean that authority exists to support the opinion.

Returning to the second question raised in the decision, the ruling indicates that a dependent child would not actually have to dwell "under the same roof" as the privileged person in order to enjoy immunity. Although the child was principally under the control of the stepmother

---

154 Westlake, I, 280.
155 174 F. 2d 496 (1949).

since 1952 and largely educated in Great Britain, and before joining the Greek Embassy in 1956 the father had neither maintained nor educated the child, he had never surrendered his parental rights.[156] Also he did maintain and educate the child when he became financially able to do so after 1956, and the son did remain a member of his family.

The British case is not without precedent. For example, when the son of the commercial counsellor of the British Embassy in Washington was charged with operating a motor vehicle without registration and insurance, the Department of State called to the attention of Massachusetts authorities the pertinent United States Statutes (4062–4064) and asked that the summons be withdrawn. The matter was settled satisfactorily by the court clerk.[157]

In contrast, in other cases governments have taken a more restrictive view on extension of immunities to sons of sub-ambassadorial diplomats. The question was raised recently by both the Greek and the United States governments.

In the Greek case, legal experts of the Foreign Ministry in Athens decided that Robin Johnson, twenty-one, could not benefit from the immunity of his father, Brigadier James Johnson, British Military Attaché.[158] Johnson, driving his father's car, was involved in an accident with a motorcycle on April 5, 1958, in which the cyclist was killed and a passenger injured. Johnson was not arrested immediately since there was some uncertainty in Greek law regarding immunity for families. However, on April 9, the Public Prosecutor held that Johnson might be charged with responsibility for the accident.

Legal experts at the Greek Foreign Ministry and the British Foreign Office attempted to work out the extent to which families are entitled to diplomatic privileges and immunities. The point in doubt involved the meaning of the word "domicile," or in this case whether a visiting student is domiciled with his father. Young Johnson, an electrical engineering student in Great Britain, was on Easter holiday to Greece and was not permanently residing with his father.

The Times diplomatic correspondent said that the Greek Code of Criminal Procedure "is not clear. It includes among those immune heads of missions and their families . . . 'and other persons who enjoy immunity' in virtue of treaties of international usage commonly ac-

---

[156] Stone, *Mod. L. Rev.,* XXII, 194.

[157] Hackworth, IV, 520–521.

[158] Lyons, *BYIL*, XXXV, 264; *The Times* (London), April 9, 1959, p. 7; April 10, p. 6; April 14, p. 9.

cepted."[159] Eventually, the legal experts of the Greek Foreign Ministry decided that the granting of immunity to all members of families was not required by international usage; thus young Johnson could not benefit from his father's immunity. He was charged with manslaughter by negligence.

While the Greek case apparently turned on the question of domicile, the United States the following year denied immunity to the son of a lower ranking member of an embassy staff who did have immunity. The decision clearly hinged upon the father's status rather than upon the fact that the son, like Johnson, was a student not physically present "under the diplomatic roof."

Police in Washington, D. C., dropped a charge of simple assault against seventeen-year-old Farhad Adjoodani, after he invoked his diplomatic immunity as the son of Mahmoud Adjoodani, an educational officer at the Iranian Embassy. Young Adjoodani had admitted slapping his sixteen-year-old American girl friend because she had dated others while he was away in college at Youngstown, Ohio. Police also said Adjoodani fired two shots in the air with a pistol capable of shooting only blanks.[160] Although the girl's father, a Lutheran minister, declined to press charges, the Department of State left the way open for possible prosecution by announcing that the youth was not immune to prosecution as police had originally stated. The Department stated that "as Assistant Director of the Iranian Student Exchange, the boy's father . . . has diplomatic immunity from prosecution but this does not extend to members of his family."[161]

In 1930, the State Department had also denied immunity to the son of a military attache. The Department said that since the name of the son had not been registered in the Department and since he did not appear to be in the service of the ambassador, there seemed to be no reason why process should not be served on him, provided that it was not done on the premises of the embassy or of the military attaché.[162]

On the other hand, two municipal court judges in Oakland, California, claimed that the State Department had tried to influence a traffic case involving the grandson of Generalissimo Chiang Kai-shek, head of the Nationalist Chinese government on Formosa. Although the sentence

---

[159] *The Times* (London), April 10, 1958, p. 6.

[160] *Minneapolis Tribune,* November 30, 1959, p. 1.

[161] *New York Times,* December 1, 1959, p. 36. Adjoodani was not listed in any issue of the *Diplomatic List* (Washington: U.S. Government Printing Office) during 1959.

[162] Hackworth, IV, 521.

was suspended, it was done on grounds other than diplomatic immunity. It would appear that the reported pressure stemmed from the possibility of international repercussions and not from any exaggerated notion of diplomatic immunity extending to the youngster.[163]

In summary, under existing international law, based both upon state pronouncements and practice, wives and children of heads of mission are entitled to immunity, at least from civil and criminal jurisdiction, while the families of lower ranking mission members may be in a less advantageous position.

Wives of ambassadors appear to be immune from jurisdiction for acts committed either prior to or during their marriage, and offspring[164] enjoy a similar immunity at least during their minority or while they are part of the diplomatic household. An Argentine court did deny diplomatic status to the spouse of a first secretary, but a decision from a nation which has professed an affinity for the restrictive interpretation of diplomatic immunities does not support a universal exception to the rule. Family members, of course, are obligated to obey local laws and regulations or face explusion (which includes the diplomat himself in the case of wives who are found by the receiving state to be undesirable). The sending state also is obligated to take corrective measures when children violate local laws.

The practice covering families of diplomatic agents other than the chief envoy is not uniform, especially for children, and the rule of international law for this category is not settled. However, the landmark British decision would indicate that personal families of the "diplomatic family" do enjoy immunity. Furthermore, extenuating circumstances are found in the deviant cases (e.g., the sons of a military attaché stationed in Greece and of an educational officer assigned to an embassy in the United States).

If the child of a diplomat has reached his majority, if he resides away from the household, and if his dependency upon the father for support is questioned, immunity might not be extended. However, this does not necessarily violate the basic rule that children to whom such exceptions do not apply, are immune from jurisdiction. Also the fact that the son of an educational officer is not in the privileged category does not mean that children of counsellors, secretaries, and attachés would not be included under the protective rule.

---

[163] *Minneapolis Tribune,* March 20, 1960, p. 17A.

[164] While pertinent cases involved only sons of diplomatic persons, it might be assumed that similar rules would apply to daughters.

CHAPTER 9

Nationals

As in the case of service and unofficial personnel, there is not complete agreement in the codes, cases and treaties as to the privileges and immunities of nationals of the receiving state employed by a diplomatic mission.[1] While the United States continues to be rather liberal in extending such immunities, a growing number of other states appear to be narrowing the immunities accorded their nationals.

International Practice

In United States law, once a national assumes a diplomatic position with a foreign power, he is regarded as immune[2] except in cases of suits brought for debts contracted before he entered the service of a foreign envoy.[3] The United States has consistently protested when nationals of other countries, employed by U. S. diplomatic missions, have been subjected to local jurisdiction. For example, Czechoslovakia, China, and Switzerland failed to grant immunities to local nationals employed as chauffeurs in American missions despite the fact that the United States nationals employed by these nations in their American diplomatic estab-

---

[1]See Green Haywood Hackworth, *Digest of International Law* (Washington: Government Printing Office, 1942), IV, 526–530, for examples of varied state practice.

[2]According to Hackworth, the United States appears to have followed the rule given by Halleck: "It was at one time contended that the subjects of the State to which a public minister is accredited, do not participate in his rights of ex-territoriality, but are justiciable by the tribunals of their country. But the better opinion seems to be that, although such State may very properly prohibit its subjects from becoming the employees or servants of a foreign minister, if it does not so prohibit them, they are, while so employed, to be considered without the limits of its jurisdiction." Henry W. Halleck, *International Law* (3rd ed.), cited by Hackworth, IV, 526–527.

[3]22 U.S.C. 254. A similar provision is found in the municipal legislation of the Philippines. See the Republic Act No. 75 of 21 October 1946 (Section 5) as cited in United Nations, Secretariat, *United Nations Legislative Series*, Vol. VIII: *Laws and Regulations Regarding Diplomatic and Consular Privileges and Immunities* (New York, 1958), p. 234. Cited hereafter as *U.N. Laws and Regulations*.

lishments did enjoy a privileged status. The Department contended that, although not a general rule of international law, the practice of including such nationals on privileged lists is "almost universal" and is justified "on the ground of practical necessity and conveniences," as well as reciprocity and comity.[4]

Although the United States is lenient to nationals during their period of privileged employment, it does not hesitate to claim jurisdiction *immediately* upon termination of their employment, for prior offenses, or to deny immunity to persistent law violators. A case in point involved an American, Walter C. Hook, Jr., chauffeur to the ambassador from Saudi Arabia, who was arrested for speeding in Hyattsville, Maryland. The Department of State took the "unusual action" of stripping him of his diplomatic immunity, claiming that he "created a hazard to the safety of the lives of others," and noting that he had a record of at least thirteen traffic violations ranging from speeding to illegal parking.[5]

In a 1939 case, *District of Columbia v. Paris,* the police court took a restrictive attitude. Paris, an American citizen who had been charged with ten traffic violations from 1937–1939 while employed as a butler to the Japanese ambassador, was named defendant in an action brought as he left that embassy's employ. The court decided that the defense of immunity is not available to a national after the termination of his official duties for offenses alleged to have been committed during the period of his employment, and that Paris was not entitled to the traditional "reasonable period" of immunity following such termination.[6]

Postwar developments in Great Britain have been somewhat different. British authorities, apparently convinced that most countries, in granting immunities, distinguish between their own nationals and those of a foreign embassy, have tightened restrictions on British domestics employed by foreign diplomats. Their object has been to achieve a uniform rule for all such nationals, domestics as well as non-domestics. It has long been settled that British nationals serving a foreign mission in an official, administrative, or technical capacity have immunity only for

---

[4] Hackworth, IV, 526–529. France also follows the policy of granting immunity to embassy servants even those "who are French citizens." Great Britain, Foreign Office, Parliamentary Papers *(Reports),* Cmd. 8460, January, 1952, "Report on Diplomatic Immunity by an Interdepartmental Committee on State Immunities," p. 5. Cited hereafter as the Somervell Report.

[5] *New York Times,* August 1, 1952, p. 5; August 7, p. 3; Cf. *People v. Roy,* 200 N.Y.S. 2d 612 (1959), in which Justice of the Peace Van Horn denied immunity to the chauffeur of the Indonesian ambassador to Canada, declaring that diplomatic persons share in the responsibility of maintaining safety on the public highways.

[6] *AD* (1938–1940), Case No. 169; *AJIL,* XXXIII (1939), 787. See Harvard Law School, "Research in International Law: I. Diplomatic Privileges and Immunities," *AJIL,* XXVI (April, 1932), Supp., 137.

official acts.[7] The *Hitchcock* case is evidence that the rule still prevails since a British court granted immunity to a British national, who as a United States Embassy chauffeur had been arrested for a traffic violation.[8] However, those nationals accepted by the British government as servants in foreign diplomatic establishments were granted full personal immunities, not merely protection, for their official acts.[9]

The British Interdepartmental Committee on State Immunities, in noting this anomalous situation, recommended in January, 1952, that no local national should be accepted for any position at a foreign embassy, including the position of "domestic servant," except on the condition that "personal diplomatic immunity" not be granted.[10] A uniformity in practice covering both diplomatic and clerical positions, on the one hand, and domestic servants, on the other, was achieved by administrative action on August 27, 1952, when immunity of British subjects employed as servants ended. The order was implemented three years later through the Diplomatic Immunities Restriction Act, 1955.[11]

A similar restrictive action was taken at about the same time by Denmark. The Danish Ministry of Foreign Affairs ruled that in the future no objections would be raised against the submission of subordinate staff members of Danish nationality (clerks, typists, and janitors) and the Danish domestic staff (servants and chauffeurs) to criminal proceedings.[12] The British action, and presumably the Danish, were caused by the failure of other states to extend immunities to local national servants.

Other nations in their legislation have gone beyond the British modification as immunities are apparently denied to nationals even for actions connected with their diplomatic functions. The record shows a tendency on the part of many nations, particularly Italy, to apply municipal law

---

[7]Somervell Report, p. 5. See also Sir Ernest Satow, *A Guide to Diplomatic Practice,* ed. Sir Neville Bland (4th ed.; London: Longmans, Green and Co., 1957), p. 139. The rule was established by proclamation in 1786 as the result of abuse of privileges under the Act of Anne by British nationals who escaped legal responsibilities by obtaining appointment in foreign missions.

[8]See Chapter 8.

[9]The position was stated by Lord Phillimore in *Engelke v. Musmann,* [1928] A.C. 433, 451: "When we come to the ordinary domestic servant, it may well be, that if he be a British subject, the Foreign Office may intimate that they cannot accept him so as to give him privilege. But according to English law (which may in respect of the domestic servant who is a national go somewhat beyond general international law) once the man is tendered as a domestic servant, and the tender is accepted, the status is created and the privilege attaches."

[10]Somervell Report, pp. 5, 7.

[11]4 Eliz. 2, Ch. 21, Section 2(1). See Satow, p. 139.

[12]Circular Concerning the Criminal Prosecution of Diplomatic Mission Personnel of Danish Nationality, dated 14 January 1955, cited in *U.N. Laws and Regulations,* p. 98.

to their own nationals who are in foreign diplomatic establishments.[13] For example, local nationals are not immune in Colombia, Nicaragua, or South Africa, while in Thailand nationals working in diplomatic missions are subject to local jurisdiction, and in Argentina a national is not eligible to partake of privileges and immunities unless employed by the chief of mission or consul.[14]

One of the more helpful articulations of the restrictive approach was that of a Belgian court which claimed that it was necessary for Roman law countries to hold nationals employed by foreign missions liable to local civil and criminal jurisdiction. The Court of Appeals of Brussels (1957), in *Public Prosecutor v. Sluys*[15] ruled that Belgian nationals who were members of the retinue of a diplomatic agent did not enjoy immunity from jurisdiction. The appellant was a Belgian national charged with homicide by negligence as a result of a highway accident. His plea for immunity on the ground that he was employed as a chauffeur by the United States Embassy was rejected by the court. The court, in discussing the immunity almost unanimously accorded the envoy's family, official staff and even his personal retinue, observed that this rests on the doctrine that sending states are in a position to punish offending diplomats:

> Indeed, while a Government may inform a foreign State of the offence committed by one of its agents or a member of the retinue and expect that State to institute appropriate proceedings, it would be powerless in relation to one of its own nationals, whose criminal activity would accordingly go unpunished.[16]

The court noted the differences between the Belgian and United States practice, but emphasized that the U. S. in fact considers that an offending national remains subject to local jurisdiction during his employment, and merely postpones proceedings until his position is terminated. This practice is possible, the court added, since Anglo-Saxon law "does not know the concept of prescription." In contrast, "complete reciprocity cannot be granted by Roman Law countries, where that concept would rule out the possibility of any sanction [against an offending national]."[17] This "fundamental difference" in principles prevents the extension of complete reciprocity, and thus, the court said, nationals employed by diplomatic establishments in Belgium cannot be granted the same privi-

---

[13]Wesley Gould, *An Introduction to International Law* (New York: Harper & Brothers, 1957), p. 274.

[14]*U.N. Laws and Regulations*, pp. 3, 65, 224, 332, 325.

[15](Belgium, 1957), *ILR* (1957), 529.

[16]*Ibid.*, p. 530.

[17]*Ibid.*, p. 531.

leges and immunities as nationals employed in a similar capacity in the United States.

In a similar case, a Hungarian, Otto Fernbach, was arrested on April 17, 1951, following a minor traffic accident in which he was involved while acting as official chauffeur for the American Legation in Budapest. The legation later learned that Fernbach had been sentenced to fifteen days imprisonment, but he then disappeared for a two-year period. He reappeared "unexpectedly" on April 20, 1953, stating only that he had been in prison, and was re-employed by the legation. However, in view of the treatment of nationals in the East European countries after World War II, it is not entirely unlikely that other charges against him had been made.[18]

The restrictive rule was discussed in greater detail earlier, in 1941, by the Central Commission for Direct Taxes in Italy. In deciding the case of *In re Di Sorbello (Marchese),* the commission held that Di Sorbello, an Italian citizen who served as counsellor of the Nicaraguan Legation to the Vatican, was not entitled to income tax exemptions since he was an Italian national whose diplomatic office was only honorary; his main occupation was administering his three estates in Italy. The commission's *dicta* were stronger: No agents of local origin, whether their functions be substantive or honorary, would be exempt from these taxes. It was noted that the term "envoy" both literally and from "constant uniform repetition" means a diplomat who originates with the sending state. Since the diplomatic agent is an "organ" of the appointive state, he must be, under general principles of municipal law, a national of such state. Furthermore, under customary law, the diplomatic agent is not a citizen of the state where he is to perform his functions. It would be difficult, the commission reasoned further, for a local national to carry out certain functions (e.g., in case of war or in negotiations affecting vital interests). There is also the technicality that Di Sorbello was not an Italian representing a foreign state in Italy but rather a diplomatic agent of Italian nationality sent by a foreign state to Italy (e.g., Vatican City). [19] The commission supported its

---

[18]"Restriction on Hungarian Legation's Information Activities," *DSB,* XXXIII (September 19, 1955), 461. Fernbach was one of twelve Hungarian employees of the United States Legation in Hungary who were arrested, detained, or tried during the period 1950–1955.

[19]*AD* (1941–1942), Case No. 108, pp. 358–362. Article 12(2), Treaty between the Vatican and Italy (Lateran Treaty) of February 11, 1929, in *AJIL,* XXIII (1929), Supp., 187, stipulates: "Envoys of foreign governments to the Holy See will continue to enjoy in the Kingdom of Italy all the privileges and immunities which pertain to diplomatic agents according to international law. Their embassies or legations may still be located in Italian territory, possessing the immunity due to them according to the provisions of international law, even though their Governments may not have diplomatic relations with Italy."

conclusion by citing many examples in international law to the effect that the national of the host state is not entitled to full diplomatic privileges and immunities.[20]

The decision was in agreement with the *dicta* of the Court of First Instance of Rome which in a 1938 case, *In re Reinhardt,* noted that nationals of a receiving state may not enjoy the prerogatives and immunities customarily accorded by international law.[21]

Sometimes the application of local laws to nationals employed by foreign diplomatic establishments results in inequities. In *Regele v. Federal Ministry of Social Administration,* an Austrian citizen employed by the United States Embassy in Vienna was bound, under United States law, to make contributions to an American retirement fund, and upon retirement thus be entitled to a U.S. pension. At the same time, the Austrian national insurance office assessed her for compulsory contributions, payable under Austrian law by all citizens employed in Austria, for sickness, unemployment and accident insurance, and retirement benefits. She sought relief from the Austrian contributions by contending that the United States Embassy in Vienna was "exterritorial" and thus she was not employed in Austria within the relevant meaning of Austrian social insurance legislation. The court rejected the outmoded "exterritoriality" concept and held that the employment was "in Austria," which made her fully liable to pay all contributions under Austrian law.[22]

Despite these inconsistencies in the interpretation of rules of international law covering local nationals, there appears to be agreement in some areas. One example was the endorsement in Article 38 of the Vienna Convention of a rule that local nationals in diplomatic service are immune from jurisdiction only in respect to official acts performed in the exercise of

---

[20]Agreement between the League of Nations and the Swiss Federal Council Concerning Diplomatic Immunities of September 20, 1926, League of Nations, *Official Journal* (1926), pp. 1422–1444, cited in Martin Hill, *Immunities and Privileges of International Officials* (Washington: Carnegie Endowment for International Peace, 1947), pp. 138–142; and Agreement Concerning the Privileges and Immunities of Personnel of the European Commission of the Danube between the European Commission and Rumania of August 18, 1938, in Manley O. Hudson (ed.), *International Legislation* (Washington: Carnegie Endowment for International Peace, 1949), VIII, 98–100. As an illustration, under Article 3, commission officials of Rumanian nationality were granted immunity only for "acts performed in their official capacity within the scope of their duties."

[21](Italy, 1938), *AD* (1938–1940), Case No. 171. Argentine courts have also held that a national serving as a commercial adviser *(In re Gimenez* [1941], *AD* [1941–1942], Case No. 113) or as a legal counsellor *(In re Berkman* [1933], *AD* [1933–1934], 383, fn.) was not entitled to immunities. However, these decisions were based primarily on the character of the function, and not on the fact that Gimenez and Berkman were local nationals.

[22](Austria, 1958), *ILR* (1958-II), 544.

diplomatic functions.[23] This has been the spirit of recent British practice, as shown in the Somervell Report, and reflected in the legislation of other nations.[24] It is also not uncommon to hold such nationals liable for the payment of various taxes. In West Germany, locals in the service of other diplomatic and consular missions "in all cases" remain fully liable to taxation. In the United States, diplomatic personnel must be non-citizens in order to enjoy exemptions from federal excise taxes, the District of Columbia sales and use tax, and the federal income tax.[25]

Furthermore, nations have the right to state the terms under which they will accept their nationals in diplomatic capacities to be employed by other nations.[26] Lord Phillimore stated the rule in *Engelke v. Musmann*,[27] when he pointed out that the receiving state may indicate that an ambassador or other diplomatic agent may not be agreeable to it and thus refuse accreditation; "when the person tendered is a subject of the receiving country, conditions may be made." This interpretation is also found in *Macartney v. Garbutt* in which it was stated that, when a British subject is received by the Crown as an accredited representative of a foreign power, the British government can deny him full diplomatic immunity.[28]

It is not definitely established in international law whether a "third state" national — of neither the sending nor the receiving state — employed in a diplomatic establishment is immune from jurisdiction. The Supreme Court of Brazil held *In re Jursitis*[29] that a Lithuanian national employed as a driver by the Austrian Embassy in Rio de Janeiro was not entitled to immunity from the jurisdiction of the courts in criminal matters.

---

[23]United Nations, Conference on Diplomatic Intercourse and Immunities, *Official Records*, Vol. II: *Vienna Convention on Diplomatic Relations* (A/CONF. 20/14/Add.1) (New York, 1962), pp. 82–88 for text.

[24]For example, Canada in Section 5(4), Diplomatic Immunities (Commonwealth Countries) Act, 1954, and New Zealand, Section 5(c)(i), Diplomatic Immunities Act, 1951, cited in *U.N. Laws and Regulations*, pp. 58 and 218, respectively.

[25]For Germany, Article 4, Administrative Order of 13 October 1950, and for the United States, Section III (C,D,E), Memorandum from the Secretary of State to Chiefs of Mission, dated 25 July 1955, on Rights and Privileges Accorded Representatives of Foreign Governments in the United States, cited in *U.N. Laws and Regulations*, pp. 126 and 367–370, respectively.

[26]Satow, p. 139; Lawrence Preuss, "Capacity for Legation and the Theoretical Basis of Diplomatic Immunities," *New York University Law Quarterly Review*, X (December, 1932), 175–176.

[27][1928] A.C. 433, 450.

[28]*L.R.*, [1890] 24 Q.B.D. 368. The court observed: "An examination of the works of writers of international law confirmed the view that the only mode of escaping from the doctrine of exemption was to impose on an envoy, when received, that he shall be subject to the local jurisdiction." Cited by Satow, p. 140.

[29](Brazil, 1956), *ILR* (1956), 429.

The court, in the face of strong dissent, declared that even if diplomatic immunity extended to servants employed by an embassy, it covered only those servants who were of the same nationality as the head of mission. By comparison, the United States contends "that by international usage" immunity covers employees who are "nationals of third states."[30] The statement referred to a traffic case in which action had been brought in Austria against a Czechoslovakian national who was serving as chauffeur for an American military attaché. The Austrian Ministry of Justice expressed the opinion that the chauffeur was immune from Austrian jurisdiction in a civil action. In a later case, *Carrera v. Carrera*,[31] a United States court of appeals granted immunity in a domestic relations suit to an Ecuadorian national, employed as a servant in the Czechoslovak Embassy.

In summary, while there is no basic agreement on the international rules, nations do distinguish between local nationals and other nationals in determining the scope of diplomatic immunities. While the local national has never enjoyed the same privileged position as the diplomat who is domiciled in the host state, developments since the end of World War II point to an even slightly wider gap between the two categories, at least for domestics.

States range from liberal to restrictive both in their legislation and in their executive and judicial interpretation of the rules governing nationals. At one extreme, the national occupies a similar position to the non-national; at the other extreme the national is extended few privileges and immunities.

Despite the differences, most nations accept the general rule that nationals have immunity for their official acts. It is doubtful if many states would grant local nationals any period of grace from jurisdiction following termination of their employment. The host state also has the right to establish basic regulations under which its own nationals will be received in positions with foreign diplomatic establishments, and these rules do contain restrictions, such as non-waiver of taxes.

Impact of the Cold War

As noted above, the local national employed by a foreign diplomatic establishment enjoys immunity for his official acts although some states in the post-World War I period have tightened regulations affecting these

---

[30]Hackworth, IV, 531.
[31]174 F. 2d 496 (1949).

persons through legislative and judicial actions. These modest restrictions have been compatible with the changing rules of international law.

Nations in East Europe and the Soviet Union, however, departed significantly from tradition in their treatment of local nationals employed by Western diplomatic missions, and especially those on the staffs of United States and British missions. Scores of East Europeans and Russians have been harassed out of their diplomatic jobs, detained, imprisoned, executed or denied citizenship privileges. The fact that these persons held diplomatic or subordinate positions in embassies and legations gave them little or no protection.

The Soviet-East European position is difficult to justify or rationalize within the framework of traditional international rules. On the other hand, this position would be justified when activities of local nationals violate local laws and regulations or are inimical to the interests of the host state. While no sending nation would publicly reveal the personnel of its espionage apparatus, it is not unlikely that some of the local nationals may have had assignments going beyond those of innocent interpreter, clerk, or janitor.

Furthermore, the mistreatment of local nationals may be better understood, if not justified, if it is kept in mind that (a) the Communist interpretation of international law differs from the traditional interpretation[32] and (b) harsh methods (such as the elimination of hostile elements) are needed to establish and maintain a totalitarian regime in a society with traditions antithetical to the new dogma. If postwar treatment of nationals is further analyzed within the broad spectrum of the cold war of the late 1940's and 1950's, the calculated action against nationals employed by certain foreign governments emerges as an aspect of

---

[32]For a complete and recent text on international law from the Soviet point of view, see Y. A. Korovin and others *International Law*, trans., Dennis Ogden (Moscow: Foreign Languages Publishing House [1961]). Other discussions are found in Hans Kelsen, *The Communist Theory of Law* (London: Stevens & Sons Limited, 1945), pp. 148–192; Rudolf Schlesinger, *Soviet Legal Theory: Its Social Background and Development* (New York: Oxford University Press, 1945), pp. 273–290; Arthur Nussbaum, *A Concise History of the Law of Nations* (Rev. ed.; New York: The Macmillan Company, 1954), pp. 285–290; T. A. Taracouzio, *The Soviet Union and International Law* (New York: The Macmillan Company, 1935); Gould, pp. 86–100. Also see W. W. Kulski, "The Soviet Interpretation of International Law," *AJIL*, XLIX (October, 1955), 518–534; John N. Hazard, "Cleansing Soviet International Law of Anti-Marxist Theories," *AJIL*, XXXII (April, 1938), 244–252; Y. Korovin, "On General Norms of International Law," *Soviet State and Law*, No. 7 (1950), pp. 14–26, condensed in *Current Digest of the Soviet Press* (February 9, 1952), pp. 9–10; Y. Korovin, "International Law Today," *International Affairs* (Moscow), (July, 1961), pp. 18–22; and O. J. Lissitzyn, "Recent Soviet Literature on International Law," *The American Slavic and East European Review*, XI (1952), 257–273.

internal political control rather than as a defiance of international norms. It is a fact of international political life that national interest and national security are prime motivating forces for nations — Western as well as Communist — in formulating and adjusting to accepted rules of international conduct.[33] Nonetheless, while the Soviet satellite practice may be considered an aberration resulting from internal tensions when compared with Western-oriented rules of international law, it still has affected a significant number of diplomats. In some ways, the treatment of local nationals employed by foreign missions in East Europe and the Soviet Union has been one of the more meaningful trends since 1945.

The actions taken against local employees of diplomatic missions by governments almost exclusively Communist, fall conveniently for analysis into two general categories: (1) Types of "Crimes" and (2) Methods of Control.

Types of "Crimes"

"Crimes against the state," offenses dealing chiefly with charges of espionage for a foreign power and violation of state security, involved numerous local nationals. More than twenty of these persons employed by British and American diplomatic and informational missions in Bulgaria, Hungary, and Czechoslovakia, primarily between 1950 and 1955, suffered penalties ranging from detention and arrest to torture and execution. Hungary appeared to have the greatest number penalized; Bulgaria meted out the most severe treatment.

The U.S. Department of State reported that two Bulgarian employees were executed, a third died after mistreatment by police, and others were arrested and tortured in what the Department called a "campaign of persecution" against local nationals employed by the American Legation in Sofia. Another dozen local nationals employed by the United States at its legation in Hungary fell into the hands of security police between 1950 and 1955. Two of these received severe sentences on charges of espionage, others were arrested, and some were convicted on a variety of charges.

In 1955, the State Department catalogued twelve cases of "disap-

---

[33]As an illustration, and on another level of international law, witness the present conflict among nations over the extent of territorial waters, or the basic conflicts in matters of expropriation. For recent discussions of the impact of world politics on international law, see Morton A. Kaplan and Nicholas DeB. Katzenbach, *The Political Foundations of International Law* (New York: John Wiley & Sons, Inc., 1961); C. Wilfred Jenks and Others, *International Law in a Changing World* (Dobbs Ferry, N.Y.: Oceana Publications Inc., 1963); B. V. A. Röling, *International Law in an Expanded World* (Amsterdam: Djambatan, 1960); and Wolfgang Friedman, *The Changing Structure of International Law* (New York: Columbia University Press, 1964).

pearing" local employees in Budapest, and requested, without success, that either charges against those detained be made known to the legation or those persons accused be permitted to return to their employment. The following year, the Department reported that the whereabouts of seven of these nationals was still unknown. Charges of smuggling also went on record in the widespread actions against Hungarian employees.[34]

The Czechoslovakian government, like its Hungarian and Bulgarian neighbors, also handed down stiff prison sentences to nationals employed by both the American[35] and British[36] missions charged with espionage activities. Although the locale of virtually all the postwar espionage cases involving nationals was in East Europe, a few occurred outside the area.[37]

Publicly stated policies of Eastern European nations are quite clear. In the minds of Czechoslovakian, Hungarian, and Rumanian officials, untrustworthy local nationals engaged in espionage and other activities on behalf of foreign powers against their native countries. Thus the basis for any immunity was destroyed and the courts, exercising ordinary jurisdiction over nationals of the country, assessed penalties ranging from execution and long imprisonment to detention and loss of citizenship.

Western powers, especially the United States, took an opposite viewpoint. In the first place, it was claimed that local nationals performed only the specific duties required of them as employees of the Western diplomatic mission. Indicative of the United States stand was a denial, in connection with a Czechoslovakian spy case, that the State Department had ever suggested that the accused "should perform services disloyal or inimical to their country." Furthermore, with reference to arrests of Bulgarians, the Department maintained that these national employees were

---

[34]See "Bulgaria Warned Actions Threaten Normal Relations with U.S.," *DSB*, XXII (January 30, 1950), 159; "Contributing Factors Leading to Withdrawal of Relations with Bulgaria," *DSB*, XXII (March 6, 1950), 353–355; Donald R. Heath, "Flagrant Communist Activities in Bulgaria Produced Break," *DSB*, XXII (March 20, 1950), 442; "Harassment of Legation Employees and Correspondents in Budapest," *DSB*, XXXIV (February 13, 1956), 246–248. See also *DSB*, XXXIII, 461, *DSB*, XXXIV, 247. *New York Times*, February 22, 1950, p. 4; June 24, 1951, p. 27; June 29, p. 1; January 15, 1956, p. 1; February 4, p. 1; September 7, 1958, p. 16.

[35]*Ibid.*, October 22, 1949, p. 1; October 23, p. 1; October 24, p. 8; October 25, p. 4; October 26, p. 3; October 27, p. 8; October 30, p. 1; November 4, p. 2; November 9, p. 20; April 13, 1950, p. 7; April 14, p. 3; April 20, p. 1; April 15, 1959, p. 4; "Attack Against USIS Work at Praha Protested," *DSB*, XXII (April 24, 1950), 633.

[36]*New York Times*, January 3, 1947, p. 11; January 31, p. 1; March 24, 1949, p. 18; March 27, p. 15; April 3, p. 14; April 16, p. 4; June 8, p. 5; July 19, p. 7; *The Times* (London), March 23, 1949, p. 4; March 24, p. 4; March 25, pp. 4, 6; March 26, p. 4; March 28, pp. 3, 4; March 29, p. 3; April 4, p. 3; April 6, p. 5.

[37]For an example of such an incident in the Middle East, see the *New York Times*, March 31, 1958, p. 12.

engaged "only in such routine duties as are accepted as normal diplomatic practice in diplomatic missions through the civilized world."[38]

Secondly, the United States contended that local nationals had been "singled out as special targets, falsely accused of subversion, and subjected to cruel and wholly unwarranted punishment."[39] The execution and death in prison of the Bulgarians were prime examples The United States also questioned police methods used in obtaining anti-American statements.[40]

Thirdly, the United States maintained that, in reality, the "crime" committed by local nationals was one of maintaining normal contacts with foreign diplomats with whom they worked in embassies and legations. The actions taken against them were not connected with the exercise of justice, the Department of State claimed, but rather the nationals were victimized in order to "terrorize" the people, "discredit" the United States diplomatic establishment, and "undermine" the prestige of the United States.

Finally, the United States raised the question whether employment by an American embassy or legation makes local nationals traitors per se. For example, the United States asked that the Czechoslovakian government publicly state that it had no objection to such employment and that it would not discriminate against or penalize such nationals for their embassy employment.[41]

It is interesting to note that the American case rested not so much on the violation of diplomatic immunities but on the contention that basic rules of justice and humanity had been violated in the filing of false charges, the mistreatment of individuals, and the severe penalties accorded by the courts.

The United States did take some retaliatory action. The mistreatment of nationals constituted one of many elements in a chain of events[42] which culminated in the forced recall of United States Minister, Donald R. Heath, from Bulgaria in 1950 and the severance of diplomatic relations

---

[38] See *ibid.*, April 15, 1950, p. 4; "Bulgaria Warned . . . " *DSB,* XXII, 159.

[39] "Harassment of Legation . . . ,"*DSB,* XXXIV, 247.

[40] "U.S. Closes Information Libraries in Czechoslovakia," *DSB,* XXII (May 1, 1950), 684–685.

[41] "Contributing Factors . . .," *DSB,* XXII, 353; "Attack Against USIS . . .," *DSB,* XXII, 633; "Harassment of Legation . . .," *DSB,* XXXIV, 247.

[42] Others included an anti-American propaganda campaign, travel restrictions, hampering administrative tactics, from the American point of view, and interference in domestic affairs and espionage activities on the part of United States diplomats, from the Bulgarian side.

by the United States. The closure of consulates and libraries both in Czechoslovakia and the United States was one by-product of the disputed events involving nationals. The reaction of the United States in Hungary was less extreme. Travel by American citizens to Hungary was banned, and orders were issued for Hungary to stop all information activities in the United States, including dissemination of *New Hungary* and other publications.[43]

While most of those arrested or forced to abandon their jobs were accused of crimes relating to espionage or violation of state security, many faced other accusations. Some were charged with attempting to depart from their native countries or helping others do so. Nationals employed by the British Information Office in Bucharest were among the nine persons arrested on charges of organizing an illegal mass exodus from Rumania to Vienna. As noted earlier, Roderick Sarell, British Embassy First Secretary, was declared *persona non grata* for his alleged connection with the affair. The following year, four former employees of the United States Embassy in Prague were charged with attempting to flee the country after losing their jobs as the result of a general personnel reduction order affecting the Embassy. The cutback resulted from orders issued by the Czechoslovakian government. In 1956, a translator for the U.S. Embassy in Belgrade was sentenced to eight years on a charge of having helped a wartime member of General Draja Mihailovic's partisans in his attempt to flee the country.[44]

Another group of local nationals received stiff sentences for currency dealings. Four of five Rumanians sentenced on April 28, 1950, for "black market currency deals" on behalf of their "Anglo-American masters," had been employed by the British and United States information services. One was sentenced to life imprisonment; the others received fifteen-year sentences. United States Legation employees in Hungary and Poland were also accused of unlawful fiscal maneuvers. In the Hungarian case, a criminal court in Budapest sentenced Impra Deri, a journalist employed by the U.S. Legation, to ten months, and deprived him of political rights for three years. Deri was indicted for failing to report an American bank account of $1,000 and for mailing another $1,000 to his wife during her visit to the United States. Protests by U.S. Minister

---

[43]See "Bulgaria Warned . . . ," *DSB*, XXII, 159; "U.S. Suspends Diplomatic Relations with Bulgaria," *DSB*, XXII (March 6, 1950), 351–352; Heath, *DSB*, XXII, 442–443; *New York Times*, April 20, 1950, p. 1; "U.S. Closes Information . . . ," *DSB*, XXII, 684–686; "Harassment of Legation . . . ," *DSB*, XXXIV, 248; "Restriction on Hungarian . . . ," *DSB*, XXXIII, 462.

[44]*New York Times*, July 28, 1949, p. 3; July 29, p. 6; August 14, p. 30; October 6, 1950, p. 12; November 9, 1955, p. 6; April 22, 1956, p. 10; *The Times* (London), July 29, 1949, p. 5; August 3, p. 4; August 15, p. 4; September 24, p. 3.

Selden Chapin against the arrests were rejected by the Hungarian government. In the Polish case, police arrested Janina Dabrowska. She and her husband were accused of operating a racket to extort money from visa applicants. A Polish newspaper reported that Mrs. Dabrowska was able to obtain a list of emigration applicants through her clerical job in the consulate section of the United States Legation.[45]

Many local employees of foreign missions were taken into custody for reasons which either were never made public or not included in the reports. It is not unusual for foreign offices of sending states to be uninformed of charges in the arrest of local nationals,[46] and governments are often reluctant to provide details.[47] The British lost at least five East Europe employees in the "unknown category" in 1957 and 1958.[48] Three Polish women employees of the United States and two smaller western embassies — Sweden and Belgium — were arrested in 1947 on undisclosed charges. While American and British embassies had previously been harassed by security police, the case marked the first time that the smaller missions had been targets.[49]

These detentions of nationals also plagued United States and British missions in areas other than East Europe. The Middle East is an example. In Iran, the British mission closed temporarily because of alleged mistreatment of nationals employed there. In a brief period in 1957, three employees of the American Embassy in Damascus were seized or detained by Syrian authorities.[50]

---

[45]*New York Times,* November 26, 1947, p. 2; November 27, p. 18; March 5, 1960, p. 8; *The Times* (London), April 27, 1950, p. 5; April 29, p. 6; "Rumanian Trial of Local Employees Aimed at Discrediting U.S. Mission," *DSB,* XXII (May 15, 1950), 755.

[46]See, for example, the State Department's account of the arrest of twelve employees at the U.S. Hungarian Legation. "Restriction on Hungarian . . . ," *DSB,* XXXIII, 461.

[47]Few of the inquiries sent by the writer to various governments were answered.

[48]One, George Balica, Rumanian employee at the British Legation in Bucharest, disappeared after battling five men who arrested him at his home. *New York Times,* February 15, 1958, p. 3. Four others — an interpreter, an administrator, a head mistress at the Legation school and a telephone operator — were arrested in 1957 in what a British spokesman described as a "deliberate attempt to sabotage the work of the Legation." *Ibid.,* September 6, 1957, p. 3; *The Times* (London), September 6, 1957, p. 10; October 10, p. 7; October 23, p. 8.

[49]The women were identified as Sofie Michalowska, a consular clerk in the U.S. Embassy; Countess Janina Czarnewska, a translator at the Swedish Embassy; and Halina Abakanowicz, an employee of the Belgian mission. *New York Times,* December 11, 1947, p. 21.

[50]The curb on diplomatic activity in Iran followed British protests against attacks on Iranians working at the British Embassy which included, according to the British Foreign Office, an incident in which two Iranian workers were "manhandled." See *ibid.,* July 26, 1952, p. 3, and for Syria, October 29, 1957, p. 2; November 3, p. 2; November 5, p. 6.

Movement of citizens and fiscal operations are properly regulated under civil codes of host nations, and it is not incomprehensible that some nationals attempted to flee or to increase their income through black market activities and illegal currency dealings. These fiscal practices were not peculiar to East Europe and were found in other parts of the world during the period under study. If the nationals employed by diplomatic establishments did violate local laws, then they were subject to prosecution, although the penalties, such as a life sentence or the loss of political rights, appear somewhat severe.

Some arrests for unknown causes might have been "crimes against the state" since authorities do not always publicize this type of prosecution. It is conceivable that some of those detained were harshly penalized. However, it is difficult to judge these incidents, although they do provide further evidence of the assiduous efforts of authorities to control deviant nationals.

Methods of Control

The freedom of diplomatic missions to conduct their official business without harassment is one of the pillars supporting the concept of diplomatic privileges and immunities. This principle extends to nationals insofar as their work at an embassy or legation is concerned. Any attempts to diminish the effectiveness of the diplomatic establishment through exigent demands, direct or indirect, on employees, including local nationals, violates a basic rule of international law.

Thus, while legal action against a local national employed by a mission would be compatible with international practice if the national was a lawbreaker or a spy, such proceedings, if essentially based on an intent to intimidate the individual or the mission, clearly violate accepted diplomatic practice. The Western powers maintained that this intent to intimidate has been the moving force behind the vexatious actions of East Europe. Motives aside, the basic methods utilized to regulate and manipulate the local national contingent of the diplomatic family have been (1) arrest, detention, and (at times) legal proceedings, (2) regulations of the size of diplomatic missions, (3) police surveillance of diplomatic missions, (4) prior clearance and security checks of local nationals, (5) direct pressure on local nationals, and (6) indirect pressure on local nationals.

The record abounds with statements by American and British officials charging that "legalized mistreatment" of local nationals is designed not to enforce municipal laws or protect the state from internal enemies but rather to hamper the operation of diplomatic missions The arrest of nationals has been labeled by British spokesmen as a "crude attempt to terrorize" local employees for associating with foreigners, and as attempted sabotage of the legation's work — a "slow buildup" to render the mission completely ineffective.[51] The American attitude is similar. The Department of State said that the trial of British and American information service local employees was designed not only to discredit the Western diplomatic missions, but "to intimidate Rumanians from employment by or association with these missions."[52] More direct results were reported by United States Minister Heath, who noted that as a result of tactics used against nationals in Bulgaria, many employees resigned without giving reasons and were even fearful of bringing their letters of resignation to the embassy.[53]

The policy of forcing diplomatic missions to reduce the size of their staffs appeared to be part of a well-defined pattern in East Europe in the period following World War II. For example, in the summer of 1950 the United States government dismissed forty-seven nationals under orders from the Polish government to reduce the United States staff by half.[54] At about the same time, half of the Czech citizens employed by the United States Embassy in Prague received severance notices.[55] This technique of staff depletion was viewed by the U.S. Department of State as a failure on the part of East Europe to maintain "a decent regard for the conventions of the community of nations."[56]

Legations were also placed under surveillance, with the movements of both diplomatic personnel and mission visitors carefully watched as a more indirect but also repressive method of control. Possibly the greatest impact was upon visitors to the Western legations and embassies. For example, the United States claimed that in a period of one month at least one hundred visitors to the United States Legation in Hungary were detained.[57] In Czechoslovakia, many nationals in the late 1940's were reportedly afraid to go near Western diplomatic establishments, and conducted their business through intermediaries. On the other hand, the indi-

---

[51]*Ibid.,* December 11, 1957, p. 21; *The Times* (London), October 23, 1957, p. 8.

[52]"Rumanian Trial . . .," *DSB,* XXII, 755.

[53]Heath, *DSB,* XXII, 442.

[54]*New York Times,* August 1, 1950, p. 2. Some of the local nationals in Poland reportedly demonstrated "undisguised relief" that the severance decision was not placed on them and noted that relatives had been in "constant difficulties" because of their connection with the United States Embassy. *Ibid.*

[55]*Ibid.,* May 12, 1950, p. 7. Including drivers, cleaning women, and translators, there were about eighty local employees. Some thirty resigned following the conviction of two U.S.I.S. employees on charges of spying.

[56]"Czechoslovak Demand to Cut U.S. Staff Follows Isolation Pattern," *DSB,* XXII (June 12, 1950), 974–975. A similar development preceded the break in American-Cuban relations following the Castro revolution.

[57]*New York Times,* September 2, 1955, p. 2.

rect effect on nationals employed by the missions is obvious. For instance, after police were stationed in the vicinity of the United States Embassy in Prague, a number of Czechoslovakian employees reportedly became afraid and hastily quit their jobs.[58] Also effective as a control over local nationals has been the direct regulation of personnel by the host state through prior clearance and security checks. For example, a Rumanian decree in 1948 divested Rumanians of their citizenship if they accepted employment with foreign governments without the consent of the Rumanian government.[59]

The government of India used a slightly different approach in 1954 when it instituted a system of checking Indian employees of the United States Embassy to uncover possible security risks. About 300 clerks, stenographers, and employees of technical and informational divisions, and private household servants were affected.[60] India, of course, could find a precedent in the United States where a campaign was waged during the McCarthy period to remove United States nationals believed to be "security risks" from the United Nations Secretariat.[61] Procedures were devised for establishing loyalty,[62] and extensive hearings were held to probe the activities of United States citizens employed by the United Nations.[63]

Direct government pressure, aside from legislation or dossier checks, has also been cited as a method of harassment of local nationals employed by foreign governments in diplomatic missions. The British encountered this problem in the Soviet Union. British Ambassador Sir Maurice Peterson, in a memorandum of April 28, 1949, addressed to the Soviet Foreign Ministry, complained that seven Russian staff members in the British mission left their jobs under pressure of "Soviet organs," and retaliated by withholding a visa from a Soviet attaché stationed in London.[64] Two years later, an American delegate to the United Nations sounded a similar

---

[58]*Ibid.,* March 18, 1948, p. 19.

[59]*Ibid.,* July 8, 1948, p. 8.

[60]*Ibid.,* March 19, 1954, p. 6.

[61]For accounts of the critical 1952–1954 period when American staff members of the United Nations were under fire, see Inis L. Claude, Jr., *Swords into Plowshares* (New York: Random House, 1956), pp. 206–211, and Trygve Lie, *In the Cause of Peace* (New York: Macmillan, 1954), Chapter XXI.

[62]See U.S., President, Executive Orders 10422 of January 9, 1953 (18 Federal Register 239) and 10459 of June 2, 1953 (18 Federal Register 3183). Also in U.S., Senate, Subcommittee on the United Nations Charter, *Review of the United Nations Charter: A Collection of Documents,* 83d Cong., 2d Sess., 1954, pp. 232–238.

[63]See U.S., Senate, Subcommittee to Investigate the Administration of the Internal Security Act and Other Internal Security Laws, *Hearings, Activities of United States Citizens Employed by the United Nations,* 83d Cong., 2d Sess., Parts 1–6, *passim,* and *Second Report, Activities . . . ,* 83d Cong., 2d Sess., 1954, *passim.*

[64]*New York Times,* May 25, 1949, p. 4; May 26, p. 3.

complaint. John Sherman Cooper, speaking before the Ad Hoc Political Committee of the General Assembly, charged that local employees in the Soviet Union, Czechoslovakia, Poland, Rumania, Bulgaria, Hungary, and Albania were "intimidated or forced to leave us."[65]

It is apparent that local nationals were placed under considerable pressure as a result of the aforementioned methods of control and as a result of the "constant danger and sometimes death" which threatened them.[66] It was also indicated that native citizens employed in missions received subtle but pointed hints on the desirability of terminating their employment.

Many local nationals dropped from sight, their departures unexplained. George V. Allen, Assistant Secretary of State, told a Senate Appropriations Subcomittee in 1948 that "a number of Russians" working for the United States Information Service in Moscow had disappeared. The United Press also reported that Russian translators and clerks employed by the American Embassy in Moscow "have gradually drifted away without explanation."[67]

These methods of control, whether based on political expediency or legal necessity, were effective in reducing the numbers of local nationals on diplomatic lists and in making it more difficult for missions to fulfill their functions. On the other hand, the nations of East Europe viewed the entire process as an internal matter with the involvement in the question by other nations as a presumptuous infringement on sovereign prerogatives.[68] East Europeans voiced another complaint. They charged that Western governments recruited local personnel from among persons who were unfriendly to the regime. For example, the Hungarian Foreign Office claimed that the United States kept in contact with "high ranking officials, princes and barons" of past Hungarian regimes.[69] The Hungarian premier added that in general it would be better if Western legations did not invariably recruit their employees from classes hostile to Hungarian regimes.[70]

---

[65]John Sherman Cooper, "Discussion of Tensions between Yugoslavia and U.S.S.R.," *DSB,* XXV (December 17, 1951), 987.

[66]As noted by the *New York Times* (Editorial), April 6, 1950, p. 28.

[67]*Ibid.,* April 8, 1948, p. 3; April 17, p. 4.

[68]When queried why former Hungarian employees of the United States Legation who had been detained were not freed in order to improve relations with the United States, Erno Gero, the Communist party chief in Hungary, told newsmen that these nationals had been tried as Hungarian citizens and thus their cases were an internal issue. *Ibid.,* August 15, 1956, p. 4.

[69]*Ibid.,* September 16, 1955, p. 5.

[70]To which one Western diplomat retorted: "Some of our employees have been with us over twenty years. Is it their fault that conditions in Hungary have changed." *Ibid.,* November 3, 1955, p. 12. It may be noted that living in the past is risky in any state where the political system has changed.

While the protest against meddling in internal affairs and recruiting among elements antagonistic to host regimes is important, the basic complaint was that Western missions utilized the nationals for nondiplomatic activities, such as collecting data, working with anti-regime movements, espionage, etc. The Communist governments would probably cite as evidence the discharge by the United States Embassy in Warsaw of a Polish employee who declared to security police that she was a participant in the Polish underground.[71]

An overall view of the postwar developments in East Europe may leave the impression that the basic issue had been a waging by Western foreign offices of a determined and dedicated campaign to assure the employment of as many foreign nationals as possible in overseas diplomatic posts, a campaign conducted in the face of a multi-pronged, and sometimes ruthless, effort by host nations to force these nationals to leave their lucrative jobs. This oversimplified blueprint was only part of the diplomatic battle. In theory, and sometimes in fact, the positions of the protagonists were reversed and the sending nations applied this constraining force. There was always the nagging possibility that the receiving nation might have positioned a spy among the locals on the foreign mission's payroll. This has happened. In 1960, a Cuban employee of the United States Embassy in Havana was discharged because she was suspected of informing for the secret service of the Castro regime.[72]

A decade earlier, this possibility worried the U.S. Congress which sent Senators Theodore F. Greene and Henry Cabot Lodge on an eleven-day tour of overseas diplomatic posts to determine what precautionary measures had been taken by the Department of State against Communist espionage. The senators promptly recommended the discharge of 13,000 aliens in the United States missions and their replacement by American citizens in order to diminish the possibility of national secrets slipping into the wrong hands.[73] However, the total number of these aliens remained at 10,076 in 1962.[74] While the security or political aspect of hiring local

---

[71]The woman was identified by Warsaw newspapers as Mrs. Anny Naimska, "the American Embassy's principal liaison with the underground." The embassy said that she was an accounting clerk who had worked for the United States before the war and who had been rehired in 1945. *Ibid.*, April 30, 1947, p. 8.

[72]*Ibid.*, July 20, 1960, p. 6.

[73]*Ibid.*, June 15, 1950, p. 1; for a friendly editorial on the senators' recommendation, see *ibid.*, June 16, 1950, p. 24.

[74]U.S., Senate, Committee on Government Operations, Subcommittee on National Security Staffing and Operations, *Hearings, Administration of National Security*, 88th Cong., 1st Sess., 1963, Part 2, Exhibit III. The total included 306 aliens employed by the Department of State in East Europe: Bulgaria, 22; Czechoslovakia, 30; Hungary, 30; Poland, 117; Rumania, 19; and Yugoslavia, 88. No Russian nationals were listed in the Moscow embassy. *Ibid.*

nationals abroad may have dominated consideration of this question, a moral issue also arose. Although there is no question that the employment of local nationals as translators, servants, clerks, etc., is both economical and efficient, it might be asked whether a nation should place these persons in constant danger and, in some cases, under the threat of death. The record clearly reveals that many have died or been imprisoned, and probably others were at least ostracized because of their employment by foreign powers.[75] Apparently the pressures sometimes mounted to intolerable limits. Newsman John MacCormac reported that servants in Western diplomatic missions in East Europe were compelled by the secret police to spy, and that "several servants have committed suicide because of this pressure."[76]

However, history may have provided the answer. The public recording of these cases against local nationals fell sharply after 1950 and virtually disappeared from public reports after 1955. This apparently happened without wholesale removal of nationals, perhaps because of eased political tensions, the achieving of greater political stability by the regimes involved, or the attrition of anti-regime personnel through the effective techniques of persuasion.

---

[75]The *New York Times* in an editorial asked "whether the United States can in good conscience continue to employ nationals of the Iron Curtain countries in its diplomatic missions at the increasing risk of imperiling their freedom and their lives?" April 14, 1950, p. 22.

[76]*Ibid.*, August 21, 1953, p. 4.

CHAPTER 10

Non-Diplomatic Personnel: Part I

THE GROWTH OF GOVERNMENT REPRESENTATION — diplomatic and non-diplomatic alike — has been one of the major political phenomena of the post-World War II period. Although increasing numbers of commissioners, agents of various types, representatives to international organizations and meetings, and persons within the diplomatic structure representing economic and social interests, were reported in the 1920's,[1] most pre-World War II diplomatic establishments, even for larger nations, were comprised of small, select numbers of professional diplomats. This situation changed with the World War II expansion of both diplomatic[2] and non-diplomatic operations,[3] resulting in a "general anxiety in many people's minds about the growing army of civilians receiving diplomatic immunity."[4]

---

[1]As early as 1925, one writer sounded a warning which has become familiar today: "The personal immunities granted to the diplomat cannot . . . be extended to the swelling number of governmental agents of all sorts, nor are they now needed for his subordinates." Clyde Eagleton, "The Responsibility of the State for the Protection of Foreign Officials," *AJIL*, XIX (April, 1925), 313. Eagleton suggested that special agents should have protection only for their official acts, a policy followed in a number of nations.

[2]For example, in 1926 the American Legation in Athens consisted of 5 persons on the diplomatic list (the minister, first secretary, third secretary, military attaché, and commercial attaché). In 1960, the Foreign Service list included the names of 50 State Department employees under the United States Embassy at Athens and 56 under other departments, or 106 United States government employees in all. Foreign Service Survey.

[3]For example, in 1960 more than 6,000 American technicians were assigned overseas in 58 countries. (These economic aid agents alone totalled more than the number of Americans in all United States diplomatic missions.) U.S., Department of State, *International Cooperation Administration,* Department of State Publication No. 6803, Economic Cooperation Series 51 (Washington: Government Printing Office, 1959), p. 9.

[4]A statement by Alfred Robens, a Laborite Member of Parliament from Blyth, before the House of Commons. *The Times* (London), June 30, 1955, p. 5.

A New Dimension in Diplomacy

Developments in the United States are indicative of this new era of "diplomacy." The proliferation of personnel has had an impact on the conduct of our foreign relations in two ways: first, the activities of foreign agents in the U.S. have greatly increased; and, second, United States Foreign Service has been vastly expanded, and so have non-diplomatic functions — economic, military, and information. The U.S. Foreign Service, in contrast to the period before World War II, is now a minority group in our overseas structure. Government agencies abroad include the United States Information Agency, Agency for International Development, the Central Intelligence Agency and presumably other intelligence units, the Departments of Defense, Commerce, Health, Education and Welfare, Interior, Justice, Agriculture, and Labor, the General Accounting Office, the General Services Administration, the Atomic Energy Commission, the Smithsonian Institution, the Panama Canal Company, the Peace Corps, Treasury Department, American Battle Monuments Commission, Federal Aviation Agency, and the National Aeronautics and Space Administration.[5] Even state and city departments have representatives abroad. For example, the Port of New York Authority assigned a direct representative to Zurich, Switzerland, a country without a navy, or a merchant marine.[6]

The expansion of American personnel abroad is primarily due to the expansion of "non-diplomatic" agencies. Of the 127,352 paid federal government civilian employees in foreign countries as of June 30, 1962 (including 30,803 United States citizens and 96,549 non-citizens), the State Department employed only 16,789, or slightly more than 13 per cent. The percentage would be even lower if intelligence personnel, on which statistics are never released, were added. The State Department's total payroll was dwarfed by the 44,154 hired by the army and was smaller than the navy (18,053) and the air force (24,017). There were more *civilian* army employees in Korea, or 20,000, than State Department workers in more than 120 posts throughout the world. In West Germany, the U.S. Information Agency employed 1,096, and the army 2,861, compared to 1,355 working for the State Department. (See Table 1.)

---

[5] From listings in American Assembly, *The Representation of the United States Abroad* (New York: Graduate School of Business, Columbia University, 1956), p. 14, and U.S., Senate, Committee on Foreign Relations, Subcommittee on National Security Staffing and Operations, *Hearings, Administration of National Security,* 88th Cong., 1st Sess., 1963, Part 2, Exhibit III.

[6] Foreign Service Survey.

TABLE 1

PAID CIVILIAN EMPLOYEES OF ALL FEDERAL AGENCIES[7]

(June 30, 1962)

	Total	Citizens	Non-Citizens
Department of State	16,789	6,713	10,076
Agency for International Development	12,794	4,076	8,718
U.S. Information Agency	8,076	1,213	6,861
Army	44,154	9,184	34,970
Navy	18,053	2,222	15,831
Air Force	24,017	5,431	18,586
Treasury	189	150	39
Justice	191	164	27
Interior	322	320	2
Agriculture	647	183	464
Commerce	533	425	108
Health, Education & Welfare	214	149	65
American Battle Monuments Commission	435	41	394
Atomic Energy Commission	26	26	—
Federal Aviation Agency	191	190	1
National Aeronautics & Space Administration	12	12	—
Total, All Agencies	127,352	30,803	96,594

The reasons for the increase of non-diplomatic United States personnel abroad are apparent. The U.S. has a treaty network with more than forty other nations. Thousands of Americans are assigned to economic and technical aid missions and to military advisory groups. Information and propaganda have become an accepted branch of foreign policy. Private investment and annual excursions abroad by millions of tourists require government assistance. All this involves a new group of non-diplomats and necessitates new rules in the extending of privileges and immunities. The rules covering these personnel are not uniform: some have been incorporated into diplomatic establishments and thus enjoy most of the traditional rights; others are covered by special treaty provisions; still others benefit from courtesies extended under expanding general rules of international law. The extension of privileges and immunities to these thousands of non-diplomatic personnel has had an adverse effect on the prerogatives of regular diplomats, whose ranks are also greatly swollen. At least such was the consensus of the retired Foreign Service personnel polled by the writer.

---

[7] The figures are taken from Exhibit III attached to U.S., Senate, Committee on Foreign Relations, Subcommittee on National Security, *Hearings,* 1963, Part 2. The paid civilian employees of all federal agencies are listed.

This question was asked: Do you believe that the great increase in non-diplomatic government personnel abroad, or the character of their activities, since World War II, has in any way adversely affected diplomats with respect to their traditional enjoyment of privileges and immunities? The results were as shown in Table 2.

TABLE 2

RESPONSES, GROUPED BY DATE OF RETIREMENT

OF PERSONNEL QUERIED

	1960–1955	1954–1950	1949–1945	1944–1940	1939 & Earlier	Unclassified	TOTAL
Yes	30	39	17	5	7	8	106 (53%)
No	16	19	6	1	0	2	44 (22%)
Don't Know	9	10	13	3	1	1	37 (19%)
No Answer	3	3	3	1	1	1	12 (6%)
Total	58 (29%)	71 (36%)	39 (19%	10 (5%)	9 (5%)	12 (6%)	199

More than two-thirds of those expressing an opinion (106 of 150) said they believed the expanding overseas activities of governments were making their own positions less advantageous in terms of privileges and immunities. However, fewer of those who retired during the later period expressed this concern.[8] (The references in the analysis which comprises the balance of this section are to comments taken from the Foreign Service Survey. In many cases, the respondents requested they not be quoted or have information attributed to them.)

Three of the major complaints expressed were that non-diplomatic personnel made excessive claims of immunity, abused their privileges, and frequently were unprepared for their assignments.

The excessive demands by non-diplomatic personnel was described by Eugene H. Dooman, whose thirty-two years of foreign service were spent in four key posts — Tokyo, London, Paris, and Moscow:

> With each of our embassies a microcosm of the government in Washington, and with every department and agency pressing the

---

[8] Of the 150 retired Foreign Service officers and staff members who voiced an opinion, about 70% believed that their rights and privileges had been adversely affected. Those whose service had been largely during the recent period of inflated missions seemed less inclined to note such an adverse effect. Although the number responding is too small to be significant, 100% of those who retired before 1939 answered in the affirmative when asked about the adverse effect. The percentage of "yes" answers declined progressively by five-year retirement groups between 1940 and 1960: 1940–1944, 83%; 1945–1949, 74%; 1950–1954, 67%; and 1955–1960, 65%.

State Department for the securing of rights and privileges for its own representatives abroad, it was inevitable that there . . . resulted an extension by some process of osmosis of privileges to clerks and others at lower levels. Our pre-war diplomatic officers were meticulous in guarding the sanctity of their privileged position — and for all I know that may be the case with the diplomatic officers of today; but . . . those who have not had an opportunity to absorb the traditions of diplomacy are disposed to deal rather lightly with their privileges and with their corresponding obligation to guard them scrupulously . . . those who have real or fancied claim to some degree of extraterritorial status has so vastly increased, resulting in frequent instances of corruption and abuse, that the public generally, abroad as well as here, is increasingly disposed to question the need, from the point of view of transaction of diplomatic business, of granting privileges to those not within the immediate entourage of an ambassador . . . .

A number of the Survey respondents voiced this complaint of "excessive claims" by non-diplomatic personnel which often strained the privileges extended to regular diplomats.[9] According to Philip Ernst, from 1929 to 1959 a consular and diplomatic officer in South America, the Middle East, Europe, and other areas, this zeal on the part of non-diplomats adversely affected the diplomat "because of the embarrassing incidents they [the non-diplomats] are bound to create."

Retired diplomats also found "too much abuse of privileges by the Johnny-Come-Latelys" and especially by the "one-time-abroad employee." Edward D. McLaughlin, who served in numerous diplomatic and consular positions from 1929 to 1956, declared that "diplomatic privileges have been flagrantly abused, and frequently, for profit," a complaint also voiced by others.[10] The non-diplomats, "not brought up in the traditions, responsibilities, character and *esprit de corps* of the real Foreign Service . . . are rarely either careful or tactful enough to avoid unpleasant squabbles with the authorities," and some "persistently antagonize" nationals of the receiving state.[11]

---

[9] Two comments are illustrative: "Too often those persons of a non-diplomatic character claimed rights and privileges to which they were not entitled and which the average fully accredited diplomatic personnel would rarely, if ever, claim;" and "Non-diplomatic personnel invariably make an all-out effort to acquire every form of diplomatic privilege. Inevitably this puts a strain on such privileges, since they are demanded by a large number of officials instead of a handful of diplomats."

[10] For example: "[There are] too many 'operators,' some of them out 'to make a fast buck' by selling autos, etc., and riding hard on their 'diplomatic' status and privileges while paying too little attention to their responsibilities and obligations."

[11] One Survey respondent attributed their conduct to inexperience: "Much of the personnel of diplomatic establishments today has of course nothing to do with diplomacy. High titles are held by persons with no experience or even knowledge of foreign affairs. Their work is so specialized that they frequently have no contact with officials or residents of the country to which they are accredited."

The result has been that many host governments have been confused as to the "authority and rule" of this "flood" of assorted American personnel, regarding them as "neither fish, flesh, nor fowl." Considering the great variety of their titles and the number of different government agencies represented, this reaction is understandable. Large colonies of Americans living apart in conditions vastly superior to those of many local nationals cause foreign governments to "resent the extension of special privileges" to numerous information, economic, and similar personnel.

Such resentments have caused a "loss of prestige" by diplomatic officers and a "cheapening of the diplomatic title," two complaints most often voiced.[12] A substantial number of the retired Foreign Service officers and staff members agreed that these attitudes had adversely affected the position of many Americans. Some noted only the withdrawal of minor courtesies and privileges, but others, including ex-diplomat Gerald A. Mokma, observed "drastic restrictions," and ex-Ambassador Jack K. McFall observed:

> If for no other reason than sheer weight of numbers in the areas where we have multitudinous U.S. Government operations, it is understandable that the foreign government concerned would be disposed . . . to withhold . . . privileges that they would otherwise willingly bestow.

The Foreign Service Survey is not as conclusive as these observations might indicate. There are two reasons: (1) As noted, a substantial number of retired diplomats did not detect an appreciable lowering of privileges and immunities, at least for official embassy and legation personnel; and (2) the adverse effect on American personnel abroad is due in part at least to the great proliferation not only of non-diplomatic but of diplomatic personnel, a fact pointed out in several Survey answers.[13] One outspoken critic of the "new" Foreign Service summarized this point:

> In former years, the diplomatic profession was "aristocratic;" today it has not only become "democratic" but highly "vulgarized." "Ministers" and "Third Secretaries" are about a "dime a dozen,"

---

[12] Other examples: "The absurd increase in numbers of personnel in the U.S. Foreign Service and the multiple dilutions through the Wristonizing nonsense must cause [a] . . . reduction in prestige. . . ."

"I believe that prestige has suffered, partly because a diplomat is no longer the *rara avis* that he was; and because there is the ever-present suspicion of espionage."

[13] It should be noted that the Survey answers represent a one-sided view as questionnaires were circulated only among persons who had served in the U.S. Foreign Service and who might well be piqued and resentful over the granting to hordes of non-diplomatic personnel those privileges and immunities which so long had been the exclusive preserve of traditional diplomats.

many of them representing small countries — and very inexperienced — prone in none too few cases, to abuse their position to blackmarket in currency, alcohol, etc., which tends to cheapen the profession. While this is more true of the representatives of small countries, our own service and even the staid old British service is not free from this taint.

Merwin L. Bohan, who held responsible commercial diplomatic posts in several missions and who served as United States delegate at numerous international conferences, declared that "even the title of Ambassador has become so common that it no longer carries the prestige it once did while such titles as minister, counsellor, secretary, and attaché are no longer the magic words they were before World War II." He contended that "the United States is particularly to blame for the proliferation of such titles."[14]

Some respondents believed that while the expansion of overseas activities might be an irritant, the overall impact was not necessarily deleterious. Tigner Ogletree, who served from 1924 to 1955, stated:

> In most of the countries in which I served, the activities of non-diplomatic and "extracurricular" personnel were regulated by special arrangements between the United States and the respective countries covering such personnel. Hence, while the additional staff at times aggravated the problems of the diplomatic representative, it did not necessarily have an adverse effect on his privileges and immunities.

While the reactions of the old-line diplomat might range from sophisticated tolerance to shocked disbelief and resentment, international practice in the post-World War II period is clear: (a) the incorporation by a majority of nations of so-called non-diplomatic functions is a permanent part of overseas representation and (b) there is extension of some privileges and immunities to these "upstarts" of diplomacy. The easy generalizations end at this point since practices vary not only among nations but among categories of non-diplomatic personnel. These practices, especially as they have evolved since 1945, will be considered separately for commissions and special agents, economic and commercial agents, military agents, and information agents.

Commissions and Special Agents

Nations historically have dispatched agents and commissioners on a wide variety of assignments. Because of the absence of accepted rules

---

[14] Others noted this increase in diplomatic categories but held that the State Department was not entirely responsible since it was forced to yield to the "irresistible" pressure from other government departments and agencies.

of international law governing these agents who are not an integral part of foreign ministries, policies respecting immunities have been neither uniform nor consistent. To an extent, some general themes based on treaty arrangements and municipal legislation have emerged. It may be that some accepted guidelines of international law covering these non-diplomatic groups are in the formative stage.

One aspect of this phase of international intercourse recently came before a United Nations agency. The International Law Commission, which prepared the draft proposals for the successful Vienna conference of 1961, also has considered the problem of *ad hoc* diplomacy. The commission's effort included diplomatic conferences and the activities of itinerant envoys and special missions sent to states for limited purposes. In its annual report to the General Assembly in 1960, the ILC proposed draft articles covering special missions. It found no reason to exclude them, thus applied the articles formulated in 1958 which defined privileges and immunities for permanent diplomatic missions.[15]

However, the International Law Commission was considering official missions and individuals carrying out special diplomatic assignments in a foreign state such as ceremonial functions (e.g., coronations, weddings, funerals, etc.) or negotiating agreements on special diplomatic matters. These missions, in effect, are temporary extensions of the sending nation's permanent diplomatic staff and are generally, but not always, headed by a professional diplomatic officer. Thus, the proposed draft code, even if adopted by a majority of nations, would apply only in small part to the categories of agents discussed in this chapter. It would not apply to non-diplomatic commissions of a permanent or semi-permanent nature or to the host of political, economic, military, and informational personnel who do not always fit neatly into diplomatic categories.

Within these non-diplomatic classifications, it is easier to find precedents for commission members than for other types of state agents. Actually, public political agents who are not invested with diplomatic character and who are dispatched for negotiations or other purposes apparently do

---

[15]United Nations, International Law Commission, "Report to the General Assembly covering the Work of Its Twelfth Session" (A/4425), *Yearbook: 1960,* Vol. II (A/CN.4/SER.A/1960/ADD.1) pp. 179–180. The commission defined a special mission as "an official mission of State representatives sent by one State to another in order to carry out a special task. It also applies to an itinerant envoy who carries out special tasks in the States to which he proceeds." *Ibid.,* p. 179. For the Report and Draft Articles on Ad Hoc Diplomacy by A. E. F. Sandstrom, Special Rapporteur, and Memorandum by Jiménez de Arechaga. ILC member from Uruguay, see *ibid.,* pp. 108–117. See also, United Nations, ILC "Report . . . Covering the Work of Its Tenth Session" (A/3859), *Yearbook: 1958,* Vol. II (A/CN.4/SER.A/1958/ADD.1), pp. 89–105, 108.

not have either the position or the privileges of diplomatic envoys. Although "their persons and personal papers are probably inviolable," international practice has not provided "distinct rules . . . concerning the special privileges to be granted such agents.[16] The same might be said for non-political agents, who also do not have a diplomatic status or who are not covered by treaty provisions.

The uncertainty of the position of the special agent, as one type of non-diplomat, is ably described by Maurice Waters in his careful scrutiny of foreign office opinions, court decisions, and scholarly observations on the position of the *ad hoc* diplomat.[17] It is obvious from his study that the special agent does enjoy certain privileges and immunities, apparently on the basis of courtesy and reciprocity rather than by right. However, international practice, to say the least, is diverse.

Despite these indistinct rules and the non-diplomatic character of agents, commission members, etc., a foundation for immunities to be granted one category — commissions and commission members — was laid during the period following World War I. At that time, as later, the emphasis was on treaty arrangements.

There are ample numbers of international agreements to illustrate this growth and development, even though before 1920 the extension of immunities to commissions was "clearly an exception" to accepted rules of international conduct.[18] For example, when a British commissioner to the United States under the Jay Treaty of 1794, between the United States and Great Britain, was prosecuted in a Philadelphia criminal court, his government did not complain. American commissioners to Britain under the same treaty asked for but were refused diplomatic privileges and

---

[16]L. Oppenheim, *International Law*, Vol. I: Peace, ed. H. Lauterpacht (8th ed., London: Longmans Green and Co., 1955), p. 860; see pp. 859–863. Oppenheim divides non-diplomatic missions into six categories. His three main classes of agents are the public political agents; commercial agents such as members of trade delegations and managers of state industries who are "fully subject to the jurisdiction of the State in whose territory they are" unless covered by agreements; and members of commissions for which no distinct rules have emerged but who should be entitled to personal inviolability and protection of their papers. His other categories are couriers, spies and secret political agents.

[17]Maurice Waters, *The Ad Hoc Diplomat: A Study in Municipal and International Law* (The Hague: Martinus Nijhoff, 1963), pp. 112–155. As Waters observes (in citing Elmer Plischke), agents who enjoy the confidence and intimacy of a president (e.g., Colonel Edward M. House, Harry Hopkins, and Averell Harriman) probably occupy a more favorable position insofar as status, privileges and immunities are concerned than does the average diplomat. However, the rules for the legions of lesser lights are still fuzzy.

[18]Joseph L. Kunz, "Privileges and Immunities of International Organizations," *AJIL*, XLI (October, 1947), 829.

immunities[19] Commissioners in the pre-World War I period enjoyed such rights only under statutes and international agreements;[20] otherwise immunity was not granted. The same principle prevailed during the 1920–1939 period, and the granting of privileges and immunities, especially to the newly created river commissions following the conclusion of World War I, was "greatly extended," but through treaty arrangements.[21] An early example of this practice was a 1921 multilateral agreement under which the property of the International Danube Commission and members of the commission were "entitled to privileges and immunities which are accorded in peace and war to accredited diplomatic agents."[22]

In 1922, the delegates, secretary general, and his assistants on the Elbe Commission, were extended the "usual diplomatic privileges,[23] and in 1923, the diplomatic privileges were granted to persons on the Oder Commission in their official functions.[24] More detailed privileges and immunities were incorporated into the Danube Commission Treaty of 1938.[25] Under Article 1, the chief and deputy chiefs were granted immunity from civil and criminal jurisdiction; the rest of the personnel were

---

[19]John Bassett Moore, *A Digest of International Law* (Washington: Government Printing Office, 1906), IV, 428–429.

[20]Kunz gives several examples (citations omitted): Mexico invested its commissioners on the Mixed Claims Commission under the U.S.-Mexico Convention of April 11, 1839, with diplomatic character; diplomatic privileges were granted members of the International Finance Commission by Greece in 1898; the privilege of "independence and neutrality" was given to the Central Commission for the Navigation of the Rhine by the German-French Treaty of August 15, 1804, and to the European Danube Commission under the Treaty of the Congress of Paris of March 30, 1856; and "inviolability" was extended to the International Congo Commission by the Berlin Congo Act of 1885. Kunz, *AJIL*, XLI, 828–829.

[21]*Ibid.*, p. 830. While commissioners in the earlier period were not entitled to diplomatic or consular privileges, they were "usually accorded such courteous treatment" as would "facilitate the performance of their functions." George Grafton Wilson, *Handbook of International Law* (St. Paul, Minn.: West Publishing Company, 1910), p. 190.

[22]Convention Instituting the Definitive Statute of the Danube of July 23, 1921 (Belgium, Great Britain, France, Greece, Italy, Rumania, and the Kingdom of Serbs, Croats, and Slovenes), 26 L.N.T.S. 173, Article XXXVII.

[23]Convention Instituting the Statute of Navigation of the Elbe of February 22, 1922 (Germany, Belgium, Great Britain, France, Italy, and Czechoslovakia), 26 L.N.T.S. 219, Article VIII.

[24]Article 19 of the Convention of October 27, 1923, extended diplomatic privileges to the president, delegates and other assistants, the members and personnel of the secretariat, "dans l'exercise de leurs fonctions." Kunz, *AJIL,* XLI, 831.

[25]Agreement Concerning the Privileges and Immunities of Personnel of the European Commission of the Danube between Rumania and the European Commission of August 18, 1938, cited in Manley O. Hudson (ed.), *International Legislation* (Washington: Carnegie Endowment for International Peace, 1949), VIII, 99–100.

extended the same immunity with respect to official acts but were subject to local laws with respect to private acts. Higher ranking personnel were also granted fiscal immunities. Under Article 3, commission officials of Rumanian nationality were declared immune from "the jurisdiction of the local courts in respect of acts performed in their official capacity within the scope of their duties."

Non-diplomatic agents and members of other commissions shared in these expanding grants of immunity. Reparations commissions are one example. Under the Treaty of Versailles, the German government agreed to accord to members of the Interallied Reparation Commission and its authorized agents "the same rights and immunities as are enjoyed in Germany by duly credited diplomatic agents of friendly powers.[26] Members of boundary commissions also were entitled to a protected status.[27] In 1938, when a suit was pending against Enrique Arroyo-Delgado, Secretary-General of the Ecuadoran Boundary Commission (which had met in Washington with the Peruvian Boundary Commission to settle the boundary dispute between Ecuador and Peru), the Department of State informed the presiding judge that Arroyo had been received by the United States government in a diplomatic capacity and that he was entitled to diplomatic immunity.[28] In 1937, the chief administrator, administrators, and their subordinates who were to prevent intervention into Spanish politics by manning observation posts in France and Gibraltar were granted "the immunities normally accorded to diplomatic officers" under a pact signed by twenty-seven nations.[29] Immunities also were granted during the inter-war period to the Interallied Rhineland High Commission, the Ambassadors Conference, the Polish-Danzig Harbor Board, agents executing the Dawes Plan, and international plebescite commissions.[30]

Various other agents also enjoyed privileges and immunities during the pre-1940 period. Representatives of fallen governments and special envoys on temporary missions who often had diplomatic titles were among

---

[26] Treaty of Versailles in *The Treaties of Peace: 1919–1923* (New York: Carnegie Endowment for International Peace, 1924), I, Article 240. See also Hajo Holborn, "Diplomats and Diplomacy in the Early Weimar Period," in Gordon A. Craig and Felix Gilbert (eds.), *The Diplomats: 1919–1939* (Princeton, N.J.: Princeton University Press, 1953), pp. 123–171.

[27] Kunz, *AJIL,* XLI, 831.

[28] Green Haywood Hackworth, *Digest of International Law* (Washington: Government Printing Office, 1942), IV, 536.

[29] International Committee for the Application of the Agreement Regarding Non-Intervention in Spain, "Resolution Relating to the Scheme of Observation of the Spanish Frontiers by Land and Sea," adopted at London, March 8, 1937, British White Paper, Spain No. 1 (1937), Cmd. 5399, cited in *AJIL,* XXXI (1937), Supp., 165 (Annex I, Section 5).

[30] Kunz, *AJIL,* XLI, 831.

the agents in this category.[31] At times even an outright political agent apparently was granted immunity despite general international practice to the contrary. General Plutarcho Calles, former President of Mexico, who was threatened with arrest in Laredo, Texas, in connection with the June 7, 1922, murder of two anti-regime Mexican army officers, enjoyed this distinction. Calles was in the United States as a private citizen but was involved in some state activity. Secretary of State Stimson said Calles enjoyed diplomatic immunity which would exempt him from arrest and prosecution. The Department of State argued that Calles had a diplomatic passport and that he aided the Mexican ambassador in negotiations with the United States, thus giving him the status of diplomat. A more compelling reason might have been that through international custom Calles, as an ex-president, was entitled to a privileged position.[32]

Thus substantial groups of non-diplomats — primarily members of commissions — were granted immunities during the inter-war period. One highly respected writer on international law claimed that prior to 1941 only the United States took "a negative attitude" toward granting immunities to members of international commissions, and this was on the grounds that "under international law diplomatic privileges were due only to members of diplomatic missions."[33] In the United States, members of special missions and commissions, although entitled to "special protection and courtesies," did not acquire diplomatic status unless they were attached to a regular diplomatic mission.[34] Actually the United States was not alone in its reluctance to grant immunities to representatives and staff members of international commissions. For example, a Greek court in 1934 in *X v. Y and the Greek State* ruled that members of the Greco-Bulgarian Mixed Emigration Commission were not entitled to diplomatic immunities.[35]

---

[31] For example, immunity was granted by the United States to Serge Ughet, the financial attaché of the Embassy of the Russian Provisional Government. Hackworth, IV, 418. In 1938, Myron Taylor served on an intergovernmental committee to facilitate the emigration of refugees from Austria and Germany with the rank of ambassador extraordinary and plenipotentiary. For other such instances, see Hackworth, IV, 412–414.

[32] Paul K. Walp, "Sovereign Immunities for Officers of Popular Institutions," *Southwestern Social Science Quarterly,* XII (March, 1932), 305–307.

[33] Kunz, *AJIL,* XLI, 830.

[34] The State Department in 1933 observed: "It is believed that the general principles of international law with respect to diplomatic immunity do not extend to persons with such status unless the members of such commissions are attached to the regular diplomatic mission in Washington of their respective countries and thereby they become entitled to diplomatic privileges in the regular way. They are, however, considered to be entitled to special protection and courtesies as distinguished citizens of their Governments." Hackworth, IV, 419–420.

[35] (Greece, 1934), *AD* (1933–1934), Case No. 167.

Governments have hesitated even more in extending immunities to agents further removed than commission members from the diplomatic realm. Both the United States and Mexico have refused to grant diplomatic status to agents of unrecognized governments,[36] and representatives of governments given *de facto* and not *de jure* recognition do not appear to enjoy diplomatic privileges and immunities in English law.[37]

Earlier European cases illustrate this reluctance to give non-diplomatic agents immunity. In 1898, the Belgian Court of Cassation, in considering the plea for immunity by the official representative of the Dutch government for the fine arts section of the Brussels International Exposition of 1897, held that administrative-type agents who are carrying out governmental directives rather than advising policy-makers or negotiating, are not entitled to diplomatic immunity.[38] In 1907, France refused to accord diplomatic status to an agent sent to Europe by the Isthmian Canal Commission to recruit laborers during the construction of the Panama Canal even though the Department of State had designated him as an attaché in the United States Embassy in Paris. The French Foreign Office noted that diplomatic immunities would be incompatible with the functions of a labor recruiting agent.[39] In 1925, the Supreme Court of Poland held in *Warsaw Mission of the International Red Cross Committee v. City of Warsaw* that a Red Cross committee did not enjoy the "exterritoriality" which would entitle it to immunity from judicial proceedings.[40]

Although nations may disagree on the general rules for special agents, commission members, and representatives, the treaty-based rules devised for the older commissions (rivers, boundaries, etc.) differ little from those

---

[36] With reference to the status of Ludwig C. A. K. Martens, who purported to represent the Russian Socialist Federated Soviet Republic which was not recognized by the United States, the State Department commented: "It appears that although the right of legation is accorded full Sovereign States and may be, in a limited sense, accorded Semi-Sovereign States, ... a deposed Sovereign or a community recognized as a belligerent can act only through political agents, who are not entitled to diplomatic privileges." Hackworth, IV, 415. In 1959, a majority of the heads of diplomatic missions in Mexico City, including U.S. Ambassador Robert C. Hill, accepted an invitation to a reception planned by Onos de Plandolit, representative of the regime of Generalissimo Francisco Franco. Mexico had not had diplomatic relations with the Spanish Government since 1939 when she refused to recognize Franco's victory in the Civil War. The reception was cancelled when Mexican Foreign Minister Manuel Tello ruled that Senor de Plandolit occupied the same position as any other visitor to Mexico and had no diplomatic status. The Foreign Ministry recognized only the Spanish Loyalist representatives who occupied the Spanish Embassy. *New York Times,* July 19, 1959, p. 2.

[37] *Fenton Textile Association Ltd. v. Krassin* (1922), 38 T.L.R. 259.

[38] Cited by Waters, p. 128. The case is *Taco Mesdag v. Heyermans* (Belgium, 1898).

[39] Hackworth, IV, 408.

[40] (Poland, 1925), *AD* (1925–1926), Case No. 248.

designed for similar agencies today. For example, the United States and Mexico, in creating an International Boundary and Water Commission in 1945, adhered to the traditional pattern that designated persons are granted the same privileges and immunities as diplomats.[41] Although a new agreement for the Danube was reached by the Soviet Union and East Europe in 1948, it is regarded as invalid by the United States, Great Britain, and France who still consider the treaty of 1921 in force.[42] An agreement in 1945 between the United States, Great Britain, and Western European nations provided for the Central Commission of the Rhine to resume its pre-war functions.[43] Provisions for immunities to be granted members of commissions also have been incorporated into numerous treaty proposals in the post-war period.[44]

The practice of extending diplomatic status to governments-in-exile, followed during World War I, still prevails. Then the State Department included in the *Diplomatic List* the names of members of special missions, not regularly connected with the diplomatic services of their respective countries. Members of the exiled Belgian government enjoyed diplomatic immunities in France.[45] Great Britain made similar provisions for the large numbers of foreign representatives in London during World War II, and

---

[41] The United States-Mexican Water Utilization Treaty of February 4, 1944, T.S. 994, 59 Stat. 1219. Article 3(4) provided that "each government shall accord diplomatic status to the Commissioner designated by the other government. The Commissioner, two principal engineers, a legal advisor, and a secretary, designated by each government as members of its Section of the Commission shall be entitled in the territory of the other country to the privileges and immunities appertaining to diplomatic officers."

[42] Oppenheim, I, 469–470.

[43] Agreement Providing for Participation by the United States in the Central Commission of the Rhine, Effected by Exchange of Notes of October 4 and 29 and November 5, 1945. 60 Stat. 1932; T.I.A.S. 1571, 138 U.N.T.S. 75. The agreement included an understanding that the Commission would "exercise the powers and functions accorded to the pre-war Rhine Commission." U.S. Note of October 29, 1945, 138 U.N.T.S. 80.

[44] This has been true of proposals submitted both by governments and by writers. For an example of the former, see provisions for privileges and immunities to be extended to members of the Control Commission in the Western Draft Treaty on the Discontinuance of Nuclear Weapons Tests, April 18, 1961, in U.S., Department of State, *Geneva Conference on the Discontinuance of Nuclear Weapon Tests: History and Analysis of Negotiations,* Department of State Publication No. 7258 (Washington: U.S. Government Printing Office, 1961), pp. 512–519. For an example of a private proposal, see section dealing with privileges and immunities of resident commissioners in the Draft of a Treaty Establishing a World Disarmament and World Development Organization as proposed by Grenville Clark and Louis B. Sohn in *Current Disarmament Proposals* (New York: World Law Fund, 1964), p. 170.

[45] Hackworth, IV, 414; John Sand, "Diplomatic Immunity," *Free Europe,* IV (October 31, 1941), 254; Egon Schwelb, "The Diplomatic Privileges (Extension) Act, 1944," *Modern Law Review,* VIII (March, 1955), 50–51; and "Diplomatic Privileges," *Law Journal,* XCI (March 15, 1941), 107.

at one time there were eight diplomatic corps in London besides the one accredited to the Court of St. James.[46] The Diplomatic Privileges (Extension) Act, 1941,[47] extended privileges and immunities, identical with those accorded regularly accredited diplomats, to members and high officials of foreign and provisional governments if they were allied with Great Britain.

Similar authority was extended to foreign national committees in the United Kingdom which were capable of maintaining armed forces in association with British forces. On these staffs, privileges and immunities were accorded only those persons whose status was equivalent to diplomatic secretary or higher. A list of them was compiled by the British government and officially published to identify those entitled to diplomatic status. The act actually meant that top officials of exiled governments enjoyed in law greater protection than the British Prime Minister, members of his government, and their staffs. But the precedent had been established during World War I, and, furthermore, members of host governments never share in the privileges accorded members of the regular diplomatic corps.[48]

It was clearly established in 1952 that High Commissioners and their entourage from Commonwealth countries were entitled to diplomatic status. The British High Court of Justice had held in 1925 in *Isaacs & Sons v. Cook*[49] that High Commissioners from the Dominions do not enjoy diplomatic status and thus are not entitled to immunity either under common law or the Act of Anne. However, in 1952, the British Parliament extended the same immunities to High Commissioners, their official staff, members of their families, and members of the commission's domestic staff as are accorded to corresponding categories connected with diplomatic establishments.[50]

On the other hand, non-diplomatic agents who are not included in treaty-regulated commissions or statute-governed groups have not necessarily enjoyed diplomatic privileges and immunities in the recent period.

---

[46]A. B. Lyons, "Personal Immunities of Diplomatic Agents," *BYIL,* XXXI (1954), 333, fn. See also F. E. Oppenheimer, "Governments and Authorities in Exile," *AJIL,* XXXVI (October, 1942), 568–595.

[47]4 & 5 Geo. 6, Ch. 7, as amended by the Diplomatic Privileges (Extension) Act, 1944, 7 & 8 Geo. 6, Ch. 44.

[48]Sand, *Free Europe,* IV, 254; Schwelb, *Mod. L. Rev.,* VIII, 51.

[49][1925] 2 K.B. 391.

[50]Great Britain, Diplomatic Immunities (Commonwealth Countries and Republic of Ireland) Act, 1952, 15 & 16 Geo. 6 & 1 Eliz 2, Ch. 18; also cited in United Nations, Secretariat, *United Nations Legislative Series,* Vol. VIII: *Laws and Regulations Regarding Diplomatic and Consular Privileges and Immunities* (New York, 1958), pp. 348–350. See also D. C. Holland. "Diplomatic Immunity in English Law," *Current Legal Problems,* IV (1951), 93–96.

The United States attitude was expressed in *Trost v. Tompkins,*[51] a case involving a shipping and immigration agent.

The decision reached in this regard states a widely accepted view, pertinent at this point, that special agents do not have diplomatic character. In the *Trost* case, the U.S. Court of Appeals observed that immunity extends only to ambassadors and other diplomatic personnel and that no court has ever held that everyone acting on behalf of a foreign state enjoys immunity from local jurisdiction. In *U.S. v. Coplon and Gubitchev,*[52] the court ruled that a person becomes clothed with immunity only under specific agreement if he is not attached to a permanent diplomatic mission.

In 1945, the Zurich Tax Appeals Commission, *In re the Turkish Inspector of Students,*[53] denied immunity from taxation to a Turkish national employed by his government as inspector of Turkish students in Switzerland. The court held that both under Swiss law and international practice the only foreign representatives entitled to privileges and immunities were members of diplomatic missions or consular officers. The overseeing of students was considered an educational and not a diplomatic or consular function. The fact that the Turkish agent carried a diplomatic passport was also immaterial insofar as establishment of diplomatic status was concerned, a view which is compatible with accepted practice under international law. Another example was the special representative of Generalissimo Francisco Franco who was admitted into Mexico under a "courtesy" resident's permit — apparently without diplomatic status — to conduct negotiations for the Spanish government.[54]

The position of the special agent, and the implications of his at least quasi-diplomatic status, became the center of a three-year international dispute following the ill-fated invasion of Egypt by Great Britain and France during the 1956 Suez crisis. Egypt severed diplomatic relations with the invading nations and sequestered British and French property.[55]

---

[51]44 A. 2d 226 (1945).

[52]88 F. Supp. 915 (1950).

[53](Switzerland, 1945), *AD* (1946), Case No. 80, Cf. the U.S. State Department opinion that an Assistant Director of the Iranian Student Exchange had diplomatic immunity from prosecution. However, the Iranian was attached to the Embassy of Iran in the United States. See Chapter 8.

[54]*New York Times,* May 5, 1955, p. 4. The two nations had no formal diplomatic relations at the time.

[55]Egypt and Syria united to form the United Arab Republic on February 1, 1958. The designation "Egypt" will be used for references prior to that date; the designation "United Arab Republic" will be used for reference after that date. The United Arab Republic resumed diplomatic relations with Great Britain in December 1959, and with France in April, 1963.

Later, under an international agreement, Great Britain and France dispatched missions to Cairo to assist in the liquidation of seized assets. In the case of both missions, a controversy arose over the extent to which diplomatic privileges and immunities should be extended. While basic issues were also raised in the U.A.R.-British altercation, the U.A.R.-French dispute, which culminated in a public trial of French diplomats, provided excellent opposing viewpoints on the position of a mission member who is not attached to a diplomatic establishment.[56]

The facts in the France-Egyptian controversy are as follows:[57] On August 22, 1958, France and the United Arab Republic entered into the Zurich Agreement[58] providing for the appointment of a Commission on French Interests in Egypt to be sent to Cairo to assist in the property settlement.

The nations agreed, in an exchange of letters, to set the size of the French mission, which arrived in the U.A.R. in October, 1958, at not less than three nor more than five members. Some indication that the host government did not view the group as a diplomatic mission was seen in the fact that they were issued non-diplomatic identity cards, ordinary private plates for their automobiles and were denied diplomatic customs privileges.

On the night of November 23-24, 1961, authorities of the United Arab Republic arrested André Mattéi, Counsellor of Embassy and Chairman of the French Mission; two members of the Mission — Jean-Paul Francois Bellivier, Secretary of Embassy, and Henri Pierre Edouard Mouton, member of the staff of the Service of Private Assets and Interests

---

[56]The most useful report on the U.A.R.-French dispute is by A. D. Watts, "Jurisdictional Immunities of Special Missions: The French Property Commission in Egypt," *International and Comparative Law Quarterly,* XII (October, 1963), 1383–1399.

[57]The facts are taken from the following materials: Watts, *Int. & Comp. L. Q.,* XII, 1383–1399; United Arab Republic, Information Department, *The French Spy-Ring in the UAR: A Conspiracy Confirmed by Confessions* (Cairo, 1962), *passim,* cited hereafter as *French Spy-Ring;* France, Embassy, Press and Information Service, "Document Distributed on December 1, 1961, by the Permanent Mission of France to the United Nations Regarding the Arrest in Cairo of Members of the French Interests in Egypt," *Release No. 896* (New York City, December 1, 1961), cited hereafter as *Release No. 896;* France, Embassy, Press and Information Service, "Decision of the President of the United Arab Republic Promulgating Law No. 216 of 1959 Relative to the Prerogatives and Immunities of the Mission for British Property and of the French Commission of Good Offices in the U.A.R." (taken from the U.A.R. *Journal Officiel,* No. 193 continued, of September 16, 1959), *Release No. 896A;* France, Embassy, Press and Information Service, "Statement by French Foreign Minister Maurice Couve de Murville before the Senate on December 5, 1961; Arrest of French Diplomats in Cairo," *Speeches and Press Conferences No. 170B* (New York City, December 6, 1961), cited hereafter as *Release No. 170B; New York Times,* December 10, 1961, p. 8; April 2, 1962, p. 13; April 8, p. 1; April 9, p. 2.

[58]Agreement of Zurich for the Liquidation of French property in the United Arab Republic. *French Spy-Ring,* p. 2.

Abroad of the French Ministry of Foreign Affairs; André Miquel, Cultural Attaché and Head of the French Cultural Mission; Mlle. Beau, a Mission secretary; and three other Frenchmen who apparently had no connection with the mission or the French Foreign Service: Mme. Cameri, a lawyer, Barthe Dejean and Francois Ferre.[59]

Later Mattéi, Bellivier, Mouton, Miquel and Christian d'Aumale, French Foreign Ministry Counsellor in Paris and former head of the French mission, were accused of conspiring against the security of the state, trying to overthrow the regime of General Gamal Abdel Nasser, and of plotting to kill Nasser (a charge which was not pressed), and went on trial on January 16, 1962, before a special chamber of the State Security Tribunal of the United Arab Republic.[60]

The court first held that members of the French mission were not entitled to immunity but did not give any reasons for its decision. The trial itself on the substantive issues came to a "dramatic ending" on April 7, 1962. The court adjourned *sine die* for "high reasons of State" at the request of the prosecution, which originally had demanded life sentences of hard labor. The four accused were released and returned by air to Paris the next day. The Associated Press in Cairo quoted a "high government source" as saying the four were set free in appreciation of a cease-fire accord signed by France with the Algerian nationals.[61]

The arrest and trial raised the fundamental question whether special missions are entitled, either by international law, by agreement, or by national legislation, to the privileges and immunities enjoyed by diplomatic personnel. A secondary question was whether the treatment of these French officials was incompatible with their status under international law. The temporary nature of the mission was not an issue since the status of a foreign representative, not his length of service, determines the degree to which he is cloaked with immunity. France and the United Arab

---

[59]This discussion deals only with the status of the French Property Mission, also referred to as French Commission of Good Offices in the U. A. R. and Commission for the Liquidation of French Properties in Egypt. The cultural attaché and others involved were not covered by the pertinent agreements, etc.

[60]"The indictment against the French officials contained the following principal charges: (i) participating in a criminal conspiracy aimed at contacting a foreign country with a view to jeopardising the military, political and economic situation of the U.A.R.; (ii) conspiring to stage a *coup d'état* in the U.A.R., one of the means to this end being the assassination of the President of the U.A.R.; (iii) gathering military, political and economic information about the U.A.R. and forwarding it to the French Government; (iv) publishing and distributing anti-U.A.R. leaflets and propaganda; (v) bribing private citizens in order to secure their assistance in collecting political and economic information detrimental to the interests of the U.A.R.; (vi) illegally transferring currency out of the U.A.R." Watts, *Int. & Comp. L. Q.,* XII, 1387. 'd'Aumale was tried in absentia.

[61]*Ibid.,* p. 1398; *New York Times,* April 8, 1962, p. 1.

Republic, although citing the same evidence, reached diametrically opposed conclusions on the matter of diplomatic immunity for the mission members. Pertinent to the arguments of both nations were (a) the Zurich Agreement and (b) United Arab Republic Law No. 216 of September 16, 1959.[62] The Zurich Agreement, under Article 6, provided:

> A Commission composed of a limited number of French experts is to be formed with the mission of extending goodwill efforts towards the Egyptian authorities concerned with sequestration, on behalf of French subjects who may submit applications in respect of their properties or rights.
> This Commission will remain in Egypt only temporarily, and only as is concomitant with the discharge of its mission, and will be accorded during the period of its stay all the facilities requisite for the accomplishment of this mission.[63]

The actual privileges and immunities extended the French Mission were outlined, as A. D. Watts says, "in a rather curious manner." These immunities were based on an Agreement of February 28, 1959, between the United Kingdom and the United Arab Republic (Financial Agreement),[64] a Note of March 23, 1959, from the Swiss Embassy in Cairo to the United Arab Republic Ministry of Foreign Affairs, and a Note of April 23, 1959, which was a reply by the Ministry to the Swiss Embassy (Note of April 23). The texts of the Notes have never been formally published, but they were read at the trial. The brief account which follows is taken from the report by Watts, who was present at the trial.[65]

The general purpose of the Financial Agreement was the same as that of the Zurich Agreement and implied, although not stating so specifically, the appointment of a British Commission to handle the property questions. The Swiss were involved since they were caring for the interests and diplomatic property in Cairo of both the French and British. In its Note of April 23, the U.A.R. agreed to receive a British Commission (limited to five members) who would be granted certain "exceptions and facilities" including "immunities against legal procedures." The Note added that similar immunities and exceptions would be granted the French Commission, although the French apparently did not use the facilities of the Swiss Embassy to reply. Watts concludes that the U.A.R. used the Note of April 23 to provide for treatment of both Commissions on an equal basis.

---

[62]See *French Spy-Ring*, pp. 2–3, and *Release No. 896A*, and Watts, *Int. & Comp. L. Q.*, XII, 1385.

[63]*French Spy-Ring*, p. 2.

[64][British] Treaty Series (1959), No. 35.

[65]Watts, *Int. & Comp. L. Q.*, XII, 1386.

Article 6 was implemented not only by the Note of April 23, 1959, but by the Presidential promulgation of Law No. 216 which provided for inviolability of premises and which outlined the privileges and immunities to be enjoyed by the mission and its members. The essential articles of the law (which covered both British and French missions) are:

ARTICLE 1 — The premises occupied by the Mission for British Property in the Region of Egypt, charged with the implementation of the financial agreement concluded on February 28, 1959, between the Governments of the U.A.R. and of the United Kingdom, as well as its archives and all the documents which it holds or which belong to it, shall benefit, on the condition of reciprocity, from inviolability.

ARTICLE 2 — The following diplomatic immunities and privileges shall be accorded to the Chairman and to the members of the Mission during the performance of their duties:

1) Judicial immunity protecting them from prosecutions directed against them on the occasion of actions performed in an official capacity.

2) Exemption from taxes on the salaries and indemnities which they receive from their Government.

3) Exemption from import and export customs duties and from municipal taxes on all initial expenses for personal property which they shall import, including an automobile for each member (automobile placed under the system of intransferability).

4) Exemption from the formalities stipulated by the regulation on the residence of foreigners. The Ministry of Foreign Affairs shall issue to the Chairman and members of the Mission a "non-diplomatic" identification card.

ARTICLE 3 — The provisions of Articles 1 and 2 shall also apply to the French Commission of Good Offices.[66]

The French government argued that the official mission, accredited by the French government, in agreement with the U.A.R., was appointed to implement an international agreement, the Zurich Accord. The French claimed that "missions of this kind are protected by international law under the same conditions as regular diplomatic missions." Moreover, the French held that, in accordance with provisions of Article 6, the U.A.R. government, through the Foreign Ministry Note of April 23 and Law No. 216, had confirmed these privileges which included the inviolability of premises occupied by the mission and the judicial immunity of its members.

The U.A.R. paraphrase of the law, as provided by the government information office, is essentially the same as the French reproduced copy except for one basic deletion. When the U.A.R. discussed Article 2, it

---

[66]*Release No. 896A.*

referred to "immunities and privileges" instead of "diplomatic immunities and privileges." It further contended "that it is evident" from Law No. 216 "that no diplomatic immunity had been accorded to the members of the Commission."[67] The U. A. R. declared further:

> Thus it clearly appears that neither the terms of the 1958 agreement nor the provisions of the law enacting the privileges and facilities accorded to the members of the Commission imply any allusion to the recognition of this Commission as a diplomatic mission, particularly as its business is absolutely different from the functions of diplomatic missions.
>
> Therefore, this Commission does not enjoy the diplomatic immunity customarily recognized in international practice to members of diplomatic missions.[68]

The two nations disagreed from the start on the nature of the immunities granted the mission: France contended that its representatives were entitled to privileges and immunities deriving from general principles of international law, an explicit international commitment, and domestic legislation;[69] the U.A.R. countered that the Frenchmen, as non-diplomats, were granted judicial immunity of a limited nature and confined to acts executed by them in their official capacity.

In essence, the French based their case on the complete jurisdictional immunities granted under the Note of April 23 (especially the broad grant of immunities against legal procedures) which as a self-executing international agreement should take precedence in case of conflict over Law No. 216, while the U.A.R. argued that the Court could look only at Law No. 216 which granted jurisdictional immunities only for official acts. The core of the dispute appeared to be over whether the Note of April 23 was a valid international agreement or merely a statement of U.A.R. intentions, an expression of courtesy or good will which could be unilaterally withdrawn.[70]

The French claim would be accepted only if the exchange of Notes could legally be placed in the same category as a treaty. It is true that informal instruments such as notes may produce international rights and obligations.[71] Even oral agreements may be binding; however, not all

---

[67]*French Spy-Ring,* p. 3. The version used by Watts does not include the word "diplomatic" but it is taken from the *Journal Officiel de la République Arabe Unie,* No. 198 bis, of September 16, 1959, cited by Watts, *Int. & Comp. L. Q.,* XII, 1387.

[68]*Ibid.*

[69]See statement by Couve de Murville, *Release No 170B.*

[70]The arguments summarized below are based primarily on Watts, *Int. & Comp. L. Q.,* XII, 1393–1395.

[71]C. H. McLaughlin, "The Scope of Treaty Power in the United States," *Minnesota Law Review,* XXXXII (April, 1958), 711.

notes are in this category and the intent of the parties must be clear before such an interpretation can be made.[72] In the present case, the Note of April 23 was in response to a Swiss Embassy Note requesting U.A.R. approval for the establishment of the *British* (not the French) Property Commission. However, it might be argued, as Watts notes, that the U.A.R. undertook a legal obligation through tacit acceptance of its proposal by the French mission. By this reasoning such acceptance would be implicit in the mission operation both prior to and after the U.A.R. issued the Note of April 23. This point and the even more tenuous claim that the U.A.R. obligation stemmed from a unilateral declaration were not raised at the trial.

The U.A.R. not only rejected the contention that the Note of April 23 resulted in an international obligation, but developed other lines of argument. The prosecution invoked the concept of executive determination in pointing out that the U.A.R. Ministry of Foreign Affairs filed with the court a Memorandum denying that the French mission possessed immunity, thus blocking any judicial determination on the point. Also it was claimed that Law No. 216 did not supersede but gave official interpretation to the Note of April 23 and that the failure by the French government to protest the Law in any fashion reflected an acceptance by France of the U.A.R. interpretation.

The French claimed that as a matter of customary international law its mission should enjoy diplomatic immunity. They stressed that the Zurich Agreement gave the mission the diplomatic task of representing and protecting nationals and that the mission should be given diplomatic status recognized by the International Law Commission for special agents. The U.A.R., in turn, viewed the mission strictly as non-diplomatic and assigned, under the Zurich Agreement, with only limited economic, property and cultural functions. Thus the mission fell within Oppenheim's second category as noted above,[73] or in a class with trade representatives who are subject to local jurisdiction and who enjoy no immunities as a matter of *customary* international law.[74]

Another question raised was whether the commission exceeded the

---

[72]E.g. the case between Norway and Denmark concerning the *Legal Status of Eastern Greenland*, Permanent Court of International Justice, Ser. A/B, No. 53 (1933). See also Harvard Research in International Law, "The Law of Treaties," *AJIL*, XXIX (October, 1935), Supp., 730.

[73]*Supra*, fn. 16.

[74]The prosecution referred, according to Watts (*Int. & Comp. L. Q.*, XII, 1398), to *Fenton Textile Association v. Krassin* (1922), 38 T.L.R. 259. See Chapter 11, section on Economic and Commercial Agents, for a discussion of this and similar cases.

limits of its mandate and carried out activities harmful to and against the laws of the host state. The U.A.R. argued that the mission had performed numerous illegal acts: recruitment of Frenchmen and Egyptians who were favorably inclined toward France to collect political, economic and military information; incitement of international public opinion against the regime by distribution of circulars; dissemination of rumors casting doubts on revolutionary actions taken by the U.A.R.; communication through a secret radio station in Marseilles broadcasting unfavorable news and comments beamed at the Middle East; the committing of acts of smuggling on a wide scale (e.g., the illegal export of currency); and plotting not only to upset the regime but to assassinate President Nasser.[75]

The U.A.R. supported its charges by publicizing what is said were confessions by the Frenchmen. The four men on trial, following their release, repudiated the confessions and claimed they had been obtained under duress. French Foreign Minister Couve de Murville termed the U.A.R. charges "a tissue of unbelievable statements" and "utterly ridiculous accusations," "a parody of plotting" and "a parody of justice."[76]

The French charged that the "police machinations" against the representatives of France "appear to be built on an incriminatory exploitation of one aspect of the normal activities of the members of the Commission." Further, it was contended that the reports from the mission to the French government, which the U.A.R. called espionage documents, dealt not with military matters but with political and economic affairs which were part of the mission's normal function. Couve de Murville viewed the dispute in broader terms than a violation of diplomatic immunities:

> Actually, this affair raises a general problem that dominates all international relations in the world today. I am referring to the contrast which is becoming more marked every day, between the principles on which these relations are founded and things as they really are. By principles, I mean the reign of law and an international organization affirmed in theory, whose mission is to see that the law is respected, to settle disputes between states and to oppose violence. This is also the justification of another principle, that of not resorting to force in the settlement of disputes. It is also, in short, the sum of the United Nations Charter.[77]

The French minister sought to place the controversy before either a commission of conciliation or a court of arbitration, or to refer the matter to the International Court of Justice. The French also expressed displeasure over what they viewed as a lack of active support by allied powers against what the Foreign Minister called "a matter in which the law is being

---

[75]*French Spy-Ring,* pp. 3–4.

[76]*New York Times,* April 8, 1962, p. 28.

[77]See *Release No. 896.*

flouted for the purposes of a base undertaking that is directed, in reality, against the entire Western world." [78]

For the U.A.R., at least according to its documentary booklet on the case, the issue was much simpler. The Egyptians claimed that "judiciary immunity does not extend to the pernicious activities exercised by the members of the Commission in exceeding the limits of their mission." The Egyptians said penal actions could be taken against the men since "spying and criminal activities" are beyond the jurisdictional immunities for official acts provided for in Law No. 216.[79]

There is no question but that the U.A.R. had a right to take *some type* of action against the Frenchmen if its executive and judicial branches claimed a violation of the accepted norms of conduct for a foreign mission. A nation does not have to justify, by appearing before an international body, the actions of its authorities in these matters. For example, the United States expelled Russian diplomats in 1950 and 1960 on the basis of executive and judicial action.[80] On the other hand, if members of the mission had diplomatic status, the Egyptians should have declared them *persona non grata,* rather than subjecting them to penal action. Rules of international law would limit the French protest to this single factor.

The U.A.R. seems to have considered the mission in somewhat the same category as a consular establishment. This would be logical since no universally accepted rules governing immunities for consular agents have yet evolved, and such diplomatic privileges and immunities as they do enjoy are granted either by courtesy or in compliance with commercial or consular treaties between the sending and receiving state and by domestic legislation. While consuls may not be liable in civil or perhaps criminal proceedings in respect to official acts, there appears to be no such immunity in respect to acts which do not properly fall within the scope of their consular functions.[81] It should also be noted that Law No. 216 closely

---

[78] *New York Times,* December 10, 1961, p. 8.

[79]*French Spy-Ring,* p. 4.

[80]*United States v. Coplon and Gubitchev,* 84 F. Supp. 472 (1949); 88 F. Supp. 915 (1950); "Departments of State and Justice Recommend Deportation of Soviet Spy," *DSB,* XXII (March 20, 1950), 445; *New York Times,* March 8, 1950, p. 1; March 10, p. 1; *United States v. Melekh,* 190 F. Supp. 67 (1960); excerpted text of opinion in *AJIL,* LX (1961), 734. See also *Princess Zizianoff v. Kahn and Bigelow* (France, 1928), *AD* (1927–1928), Case No. 266.

[81]Oppenheim, I, 841, fn. The *Kasenkina* case is cited as an illustration. For a detailed analysis of this incident, see Lawrence Preuss, "Consular Immunities: The Kasenkina Case (U.S.-U.S.S.R.)," *AJIL,* XLIII (January, 1949), 37–56. Also see *Emmet v. Lomakin,* 84 N.Y.S. 2d 562 *AJIL,* XLIII (1949), 381; "U.S. Rejects Soviet Charges Concerning Refusal of Two Russian Teachers to Return to Soviet Union," *DSB,* XIX (August 29, 1948), 251–262; and "Freedom of Movement Allowed Mrs. Kasenkina and Mr. Samarin," *DSB,* XIX (September 26, 1948), 408–409. For a useful review of consular immunities, see W. E. Beckett, "Consular Immunities," *BYIL,* XXI, (1944), 34–50.

resembles a consular arrangement. It extends inviolability to the premises, restricts jurisdictional immunity, and provides for usual privileges (e.g., exemption from taxes, customs duties, etc.).

A consular agent, covered by such an agreement, would be liable for prosecution if, *outside the scope of his official duties,* he flagrantly violated local laws or regulations. If the charges were fraudulent and ridiculous, as the French claimed, then the Egyptian action would indeed have been a "parody of justice." No judgment can be made, of course, on the basis of available materials. It is not likely that any nation would demean its own judicial procedures; nor would any nation publicly confess to the illegal activities of its agents. However, if the consular line of reasoning is accepted, presumably the mission members would have lost their immunity from local jurisdiction. Since the mission was regulated by treaty and municipal legislation and since it was assigned the narrow task of liquidating French assets, the consular analogy is not without merit.

On the other hand, France considered the mission to be fully diplomatic and entitled to all of the privileges and immunities granted diplomats under international law. For the French, the action taken by U.A.R. authorities "far oversteps the bounds of a simple violation of immunities"[82] and necessitated a "firm reaction by civilized states as a body."[83] The same question was raised earlier when Great Britain sent its sequestration commission to Egypt, and the resolution of this milder conflict with the U.A.R. provides somewhat of a precedent.

The question of the diplomatic status of the British mission also complicated settlement of the desequestration of British property in the U.A.R.[84] Negotiations which started in January, 1959, to provide the settlement were delayed because the Cairo government reportedly was unwilling to grant diplomatic rights that Britain desired for its personnel hired to supervise implementation of the agreement. The British Foreign Office contended that its representatives appointed to watch over the execution of the agreement would need certain rights normally given to diplomats (e.g., access to U.A.R. officials, immunity from interference, and secrecy of communication with London) requirements which Cairo reportedly considered tantamount to a demand for resumption of diplomatic rela-

---

[82]*Release No. 896.*

[83]*Release No. 170B.*

[84]The account of this and the following two paragraphs is taken from the *New York Times,* January 22, 1959, p. 13; January 23, p. 8; January 26, p. 2; March 1, p. 31; March 3, p. 24; December 2, p. 9; October 25, 1960, p. 3; and *The Times* (London), January 26, 1959, p. 7; March 2, p. 7; March 3, p. 10; May 5, p. 10; May 7, p. 10; May 11, p. 10; May 12, p. 8; December 2, p. 12.

tions. The Egyptians apparently wanted a British supervisory mission to have what was called "full facilities," but not to have the rights of diplomatic privileges and immunities. Following additional delays, the Financial Agreement was signed and made public on March 2.

Although the London *Times* contended that in order to carry out the agreement the British would need a representative in Cairo with an "adequate staff" and with "diplomatic immunities and facilities," the financial and trade agreement signed in Cairo did not mention the resumption of diplomatic or consular relations beyond stating that each country would permit freedom of exit and entry for official missions and "accord each other facilities as may be necessary for the implementation of the present agreement." The British government, according to the London *Times* Middle East correspondent, "bowed to the inevitable and accepted the Egyptian terms for the establishment of a mission" in Cairo. The Cairo newspaper *Al Ahram* said that the Mission for British Property would be limited to five senior staff members and a number of assistants, mission members would have only "extremely restricted diplomatic immunities," and that the mission would not enjoy the usual diplomatic right to use a cipher for communication to London. In September, the U.A.R. law relative to the prerogatives and immunities for the British and French missions was promulgated, granting diplomatic privileges and immunities from local jurisdiction for official acts and inviolability to the mission premises and archives.

The problem of facilities also plagued the British mission. Colin Crowe, British Foreign Office representative in Cairo, had been working for three months out of the Canadian Embassy while a skeleton staff of Swiss officials occupied the British Embassy. It was believed that a move by the mission into the embassy might be construed by Egyptians "as conferring too high a diplomatic status on the mission." The British mission of four senior officers and others, who joined Crowe, remained at a Cairo hotel for four months after which time they were permitted by the U.A.R. Ministry of Economy to move into British government villas at Zamalek, a Cairo suburb on the Nile River. The French mission, which for some months had occupied the French Consulate, was also obliged to move, and found new quarters in a rented apartment. The *Times* (London) Middle Eastern correspondent observed that as the Swiss continued to represent British interests until diplomatic and consular relations were resumed, the decision to keep the property commission out of the embassy "is probably diplomatically correct." The British mission moved back into the embassy building following the resumption in December, 1959, of diplomatic relations at the chargé d'affaires level.

The following year, the U.A.R. and Great Britain agreed to exchange ambassadors, and thus brought their diplomatic missions to full embassy level.

While the status of non-diplomatic agents — the French and British mission cases, for example — conducting normal governmental business may be in doubt as far as privileges and immunities are concerned, the position of (a) secret political agents and of (b) "non-functional" agents who conduct what might be called essentially non-governmental business is more easily determined. If a secret agent is admitted by the receiving state, although clandestinely, "his position is essentially the same as that of a public political agent." On the other hand, a secret agent sent abroad for political purposes without formal admission by the state to which he is assigned "has no recognized position whatever according to International Law" and, like any other foreigner, may be tried and punished if he commits a political or ordinary crime.[85]

Privileges and immunities also do not extend to the "non-functional" agent, chiefly local nationals, whose numbers have greatly increased since World War II, especially in the United States. The appearance of this group on the fringes of the regular diplomatic establishment resulted from the largess of the American foreign aid program and the ascendancy of the United States into a position of international dominance. Many nations, ranging from those in highly industrialized Europe to those in underdeveloped Africa and Asia, have for differing reasons felt a need for representation in addition to the personnel attached to their embassies, consulates, and the United Nations missions.

In 1963, there were about 500 "non-functional" agents registered with the Department of Justice in compliance with statutory provisions, compared with 160 in 1944. The specific reasons for this increase are obvious if both the internal and external changes which have influenced the world position of the United States are taken into consideration. First, the number of nations having diplomatic relations with the U.S. increased since World War II from 54 to 108 in early 1963. A majority of these new nations are small and thus need to call upon additional talent, primarily United States nationals, to supplement the work of their diplomatic missions. Second, foreign governments need public relations agents in the U.S. to promote tourism, trade, and investments in their economies. Third, foreign enterprises need to maintain close contacts with economic developments in the U.S. since this nation has emerged as a business and industrial center. And last, while diplomatic establishments are limited by inter-

---

[85]Oppenheim, I, 860.

national law in their involvement in domestic matters, the non-diplomatic agent of the "non-functional" type can exercise influence over the general population, the executive branch, and Congress.[86]

All "non-diplomatic agents" who represent foreign governments in the dissemination of propaganda and for other purposes are required to register.[87] These agents, grouped according to the staff of the Senate Committee on Foreign Relations into four broad categories — (1) government offices and agents (e.g., information) established by the large industrial nations, (2) agents of "controversial" nations (e.g., dictatorships such as Trujillo's Dominican Republic), (3) agents of the newly developing nations, "baffled by the complexities of official Washington," and (4) agents representing parties to international disputes — are subject to prosecutions under United States law. There were thirty-one indictments and twenty-four convictions of these "non-functional" agents from 1938 to 1963.[88]

However, in some ways, this lack of diplomatic status and absence of immunities works to the advantage of the "non-functional" agent as Senator J. William Fulbright, Chairman of the Senate Foreign Relations Committee, discovered when he questioned George W. Ball, Under Secretary of State. The following exchange is revealing:

> FULBRIGHT: In a sense the non-diplomatic agent is much freer to freewheel around the Department than is the diplomat, isn't he? You can declare a diplomat persona non grata, but you can't declare the lobbyist that, can you?

> BALL: So long as he complies with the requirements of the Foreign Agents Act you cannot do so . . . .

---

[86]U.S., Senate, Committee on Foreign Relations, *Hearings, Activities of Nondiplomatic Representatives of Foreign Principals in the United States,* 88th Cong., 1st Sess., 1963, Part 1, p. 10.

[87]For a discussion of the activities of these agents and a history and analysis of the Foreign Agents Registration Act of 1938 and its amendments in 1939 and 1942 (56 Stat. 248–258; 22 U.S.C. 611–621), see U.S., Senate Committee on Foreign Relations, *A Preliminary Staff Study, Nondiplomatic Activities of Representatives of Foreign Governments,* 87th Cong., 2d Sess., 1962, *passim,* and H. Val Visick, "Regulating Nondiplomatic Activities of Representatives of Foreign Governments in the United States," *The George Washington Law Review,* XXXI (June, 1963), 977–996. The constitutionality of the act was sustained in *United States v. Peace Information Center,* 97 F. Supp. 255 (1951). For testimony of officials of the Departments of State and Justice on the operation of the act, see U.S., Senate, Committee on Foreign Relations, *Hearings, Nondiplomatic Representatives,* 1963, Part 1, *passim.* For hearings into the activities of two such agents, John A. O'Donnell, who represented the Philippine Sugar Commission and the National Federation of Sugarcane Planters of the Philippines, and of Richard B. Klemfuss, former Director of the Dominican Republic Information Center, see *ibid.,* Parts 2 and 3, *passim.*

[88]U.S., Senate, Committee on Foreign Relations, *Hearings, Nondiplomatic Representatives,* 1963, Part 1, pp. 64–73.

FULBRIGHT: In most cases he is an American citizen and you couldn't throw him out even if he didn't comply with the act.

BALL: I say under the present circumstances we can't throw him out of the country . . . but, of course, he would be subjected to the criminal penalties of that act.

.   .   .   .

FULBRIGHT: Here you have the rather strange situation, that the acknowledged formal ambassador or representative of a country cannot appear before the committee and can be thrown out of the country if he misbehaves, while the paid agent can appear before the committee, can plead his case anyway he likes and you can't really do much about it.

BALL: I raise the question, Mr. Chairman, as to whether Congress should invite him to appear before committees but . . .

FULBRIGHT: We never have, to my knowledge, invited diplomatic agents except to lunch. We never invited them to testify about a bill or a piece of legislation that I have ever heard of.

BALL: Well, not a diplomatic representative.

FULBRIGHT: That is right. But I am sure whether lobbyists have been invited or not we probably didn't know at the time.

BALL: I think in the case of the committees of the Congress lobbyists have spoken as representing the interests of a particular country.

FULBRIGHT: Sometimes they do. . . .[89]

------

[89]*Ibid.*, pp. 16–17.

CHAPTER 11

Non-Diplomatic Personnel: Part II

THE TRADITIONAL RULES of diplomatic privileges and immunities have been strained since World War II by the remarkable increase of still other types of non-diplomatic personnel in overseas missions. Although the treatment of these agents — economic and commercial, military, and information — is not entirely uniform, states have established many guidelines, especially through treaty arrangements.

Economic and Commercial Agents

States often give foreign assignments to agents representing commercial interests — such as railway and shipping boards, or members of trade delegations. These agents do not have diplomatic status and are not covered by the accepted rules of immunity. They are subject to the jurisdiction of the receiving states, although "no distinct rules have been developed with regard to their positon."[1] However, most states deal with the problem through bilateral agreements such as those which regulated Russian trade delegations in the 1920's and 1930's.

These served as useful precedents for treaties authorizing economic missions, especially by the United States, in various parts of the world since 1945. After the First World War the status of Soviet trade delegates resulted in cases which developed some general rules applying to commercial agents. The experience of the Soviet trade delegation in Great Britain offers an excellent illustration of the practice. Under the Commercial Agreement between Great Britain and the Russian Socialist Federated Soviet Republic of March 16, 1921, each party was authorized to appoint official agents entitled to freedom of movement and communication, exemption from taxes, and immunity from arrest and search.[2] The agreement

---

[1] L. Oppenheim, *International Law,* Vol. I: *Peace,* ed. H. Lauterpacht (8th ed.; London: Longmans, Green and Co., 1955), p. 861. These agents should not be confused with attachés in diplomatic missions who report on commercial and industrial affairs of the receiving state. The latter are part of the official diplomatic staff and are entitled to diplomatic immunities.

[2] Cmd. 1207, cited in *AD* (1919–1922), 296, and by A. D. McN[air], "The Anglo-Soviet Temporary Commercial Agreement, 1934," *BYIL,* XV (1934), 144–145.

was considered by the British Court of Appeals in *Fenton Textile Associa-tion Ltd. v. Krassin,* when Krassin, an official Soviet agent, was sued for the price placed on goods sold and delivered. Krassin claimed immunity as a diplomatic representative. He did not base his claim on the agreement since it contained no express provision covering such civil immunity. The court rejected his plea since he had not been recognized in any capacity other than that of "official agent," a status, according to Lord Justice Bankes, "clearly insufficient to carry with it the immunity accorded to accredited and recognized representatives of foreign States" since his assigned functions were not of a diplomatic character.[3]

Since the U.S.S.R. regarded foreign trade as a state monopoly the British and Soviet governments entered into another agreement in 1934 extending to the U.S.S.R. the right to establish a trade delegation as part of its London embassy with the head of the delegation and his two depu-ties enjoying full diplomatic privileges and immunities.[4] Apparently, in view of the earlier ruling in *Engelke v. Musmann,* British courts would uphold diplomatic immunities for non-diplomatic personnel on the basis of a treaty without legislative enactment, and upon a statement made in court on behalf of the government.[5]

The importance of the agreement, and its limitations, are illustrated by a series of Italian cases. Article 3(c) of the Treaty of March 14, 1924, between the Soviet Union and Italy stipulated that "the Commercial Agent and the members of the Council of the Trade Delegation shall form an integral part of the plenipotentiary mission and shall enjoy personal invio-lability, extra-territoriality for their offices, and all other privileges and immunities accorded to members of diplomatic missions."[6]

In 1933, the Court of Cassation reached the same decision in two

---

[3](1922), 38 T.L.R. 259, 261.

[4]Article 5(2) of the Anglo-Soviet Temporary Commercial Agreement, 1934 (Cmd. 4513), cited by McN[air], *BYIL,* XV, 144, provided: "The head of the Trade Delegation shall be the Trade Representative of the Union of Soviet Socialist Repub-lics in the United Kingdom. . . . He and his two deputies shall be accorded all dip-lomatic privileges and immunities, and immunity shall attach to the offices occupied by the Trade Delegation. . . . No member of the staff of the Trade Delegation, other than the Trade Representative and his two deputies, shall enjoy any privileges or immunities other than those which are, or may be, enjoyed in the United Kingdom by officials of the State-controlled trading organizations of other countries."

[5]McN[air], *BYIL,* XV, 145. McNair reasoned that although the executive determination of immunity in the *Engelke* case applied to a defendant who per-formed some diplomatic functions, the Crown would not be limited to this category in extending immunities as part of its conduct of foreign relations. *Engelke v. Mus-mann,* [1928] A.C. 433.

[6]Cited in *AD* (1933–1934), 180.

cases, *Russian Trade Delegation in Italy v. Kazmann*[7] and *Alexeff v. Trade Delegation of the U.S.S.R.,*[8] in ruling that no distinction could be made between the diplomatic and commercial activities of the delegation.

In the *Kazmann* case, the court held that it had no jurisdiction in an action for wrongful dismissal brought against the Milan branch of the Russian trade group. It reasoned that while jurisdiction over claims of a private character were "incontestable," there could be no jurisdiction in questions of a public law nature. The case fit into the latter category since the Soviet Constitution established a monopolistic regime and the Russian state regarded trading as essentially of a public character.

The editor of the *Annual Digest* noted that "this decision may perhaps be regarded as having overruled" that of the Court of Appeal of Milan in *Slomnitzky v. Trade Delegation of the U.S.S.R.* Here the court, "although adopting the familiar distinction between acts *jure imperii* and those *jure gestionum* and taking note of the diplomatic immunity of the Trade Delegation, held that the employment of an individual was an act falling within the sphere of private law. . . ."[9]

This not uncommon conflict over the extent of immunity applicable to private acts seems to have been resolved in 1934 in *Russian Trade Delegation in Italy v. De Castro,* which followed the *Slomnitzky* rather than the *Kazmann* reasoning. In the De Castro case, the court rejected the view that the treaty of 1924 gave the Trade Delegation complete immunity in respect to commercial transactions:

> It has to be considered that the Russian State must necessarily submit to the private law of a given State in regard to transactions entered into with the citizens of that State within its territory. . . . It must be assumed . . . that the Russian State, in setting up Trade Delegations in various countries, intended to create organs capable of entering into relations similar to those entered into by citizens of different States and that it submitted in each case to the jurisdiction of the courts.[10]

The court cited *Rumanian Government v. Trutta:*

> There it was clearly laid down that a foreign State cannot claim the jurisdictional immunity which it enjoys in respect of all acts done in the exercise of its foreign functions, for acts done within the sphere of private law. For in performing acts of the latter kind the State puts itself in the position of a private person and so submits to the juris-

---

[7] (Italy, 1933), *AD* (1933–1934), Case No. 69.

[8] (Italy, 1933), *AD* (1933–1934), 179, fn.

[9] (Italy, n.d.), *AD* (1931–1932), Case No. 86.

[10] (Italy, 1934), *AD* (1933–1934), Case No. 70, p. 180.

diction in regard to any litigation as to which the courts of another State would be competent if the defendant were an ordinary foreigner.[11]

Courts in France, Norway, and Greece also debated this "private act" controversy with only partially conclusive results. On the one hand, the Court of Oslo in *Kopytoff v. The Commercial Representation of the U.S.S.R.*,[12] and the Conseil de Prud'hommes and the Civil Tribunal of the Seine in *Baitin v. Russian Trade Delegation*,[13] withheld jurisdiction. On the other hand, the Greek Council of State in *Russian Commercial Representation (Greece) Case*,[14] the Greek Court of First Instance of Athens (case unnamed),[15] and the Commercial Tribunal of the Seine in *Chaliadine v. Russian State and Librairie Brenner*[16] claimed jurisdiction over commercial activities of the trade delegations.

In the *Kopytoff* case, the head of the Soviet Commercial Representation successfully pleaded to the jurisdiction of Norwegian courts in a salary dispute with a Soviet citizen who had been a member of a trade group in Oslo. The court based its decision on the Treaty between Norway and the U.S.S.R. of December 15, 1925.[17] In the *Baitin* case, it was held that the Conseil was incompetent to hear a dispute between the head of a section of the Russian Trade Delegation in Paris and the Delegation itself, since the Delegation, as an "emanation of a foreign State," is an administrative organ of the ambassadorial service and its head is a diplomatic agent.

In contrast, according to the Council of State of Greece, a commercial representative appeared not to enjoy immunity in matters other than acts of a public character. The Council ruled that provisions of the Treaty of Commerce and Navigation of June 11, 1929,[18] between Greece

---

[11] *AD* (1925–1926), 179, cited in *AD* (1933–1934), 181. The court also referred to *Russian Trade Delegation in Italy v. Villain and Fassio* (Folo Italiano Repertorio), 1932, sub Competenza Civile, No. s. 38–48.

[12] (Norway, 1932), *AD* (1931–1932), 333.

[13] (France, 1929), *AD* (1929–1930), 312, fn.

[14] (Greece, 1932), *AD* (1931–1932), Case No. 185.

[15] (Greece, 1930), *AD* (1929–1930), 312, fn.

[16] (France, 1930), *AD* (1929–1930), 19, fn.

[17] Article 4(3) stated: "The Commercial Representation shall be under the direction of a person (the Commercial Representative) attached to the Soviet Legation at Oslo. The offices of the Commercial Representation shall enjoy extraterritoriality whether they are situated in the same building as the Legation or elsewhere." Cited in *AD* (1931–1932), 333.

[18] Article 7 provided for diplomatic immunity for the head of the Commercial Representation and for the exterritoriality of its premises. The same article stipulated that commercial transactions of the Representation should be subject to Greek legislation and jurisdiction, but that property of the Representation should not be subject to seizure. As discussed in *AD* (1931–1932), 334.

and the U.S.S.R. did not grant immunity in fiscal matters to the Commercial Representative. The provision in the treaty excluding "commercial transactions" from immunity appears to have been more restrictive than similar provisions in like agreements.[19] The Athens court also held that acts of a private law nature were subject to Greek jurisdiction.[20] And the French Tribunal, according to an editor's note in the *Annual Digest* in the *Chaliadine* case, "pointed out, *obiter* it appears, that the principle of immunity did not apply in cases arising out of purely commercial transactions, in which the Trade Delegation was engaged.[21]

While there appears to be a difference between treaty provisions and interpretation, it is clear that commercial delegations are not entitled to diplomatic immunities without specific agreement. For example, *De Fallois v. Piatakoff et al. and Commercial Delegation of the U.S.S.R. in France* involved a swindle suit against the chief and two assistant chiefs of the Russian Commercial Delegation. The French Court of Cassation stated that personal immunity is restricted to the ambassador, minister or subordinates who are an integral part of the mission and invested with a public character. Under an agreement between France and the U.S.S.R. of January 11, 1934, the head of the trade group and his aides "constitute a part of the embassy and by virtue of this fact enjoy diplomatic privileges and immunities."[22] However, the three persons involved in this case finished their official functions before the treaty was signed; thus they were not immune since, as a general rule, acts of commerce are not vested with immunity in the absence of an agreement. Other decisions support this generalization.[23]

The United States also viewed the activity of the Russian Commercial Delegation as ordinary trade activity, and therefore received Russian commercial agents with diplomatic status only on the basis that they perform only those functions usually devolving upon a commercial attaché (data collection, study of market conditions, etc.) and not engage

---

[19] For example, the French-Soviet Agreement of 1934.

[20] *AD* (1929–1930), 312, fn.

[21] *Ibid.,* p. 19, fn.

[22] (France, 1937), *AJIL,* XXXII (1938), 369, 371. See also J. Mervyn Jones, "Immunities of Servants of Diplomatic Agents and the Statute of Anne 7, c. 12," *Journal of Comparative Legislation and International Law,* XXII (February, 1940), 29.

[23] An Italian court, *In re Serventi,* (Italy, 1921), *AD* (1919-1922), Case No. 211, held that the Russian Commercial Delegation did not have diplomatic status, since its sole purpose in Italy was economic and commercial, and the French Court of Cassation, in *Union of Socialist Soviet Republics v. Association France Export* (France, 1929), *AD* (1929–1930), Case No. 7, ruled that, until decided by agreement, the commercial functions of the Russian Trade Delegation would be regarded as ordinary trade activity and thus the delegation was not immune to suit.

in trade or commercial transactions of any kind or enter into business dealings with American firms. The State Department also ruled that its commercial attachés, authorized by a provision in the Appropriation Act of July 16, 1916, had no authority to enter into any discussion with officials of the Russian government regarding trade or similar matters in that nation.[24]

The Soviet Union, of course, regards the denial of diplomatic immunity to Trade Delegations as an infringement upon rights vested in the missions under international law. The trade representations of the U.S.S.R. are considered part of their diplomatic missions and should,

> . . . enjoy the rights and privileges of diplomatic missions. It is generally recognized that the trade representative of the U.S.S.R. and his deputies enjoy complete diplomatic immunity. They have the right of inviolability of person. They are safeguarded against threats and coercive measures and are exempt from local jurisdiction.[25]

Under the Soviet doctrine, the delegation cannot be sued without consent of the government and even if it voluntarily submits to local jurisdiction, courts cannot execute judgments by force, compel court attendance or take any action which would violate the sovereign rights of the Soviet Union. The U.S.S.R. maintains that by "consistent and resolute policy" the Soviet government defeated such policies as denial of legal immunity to trade groups and that "the rights of the Soviet State in exercising its monopoly of foreign trade are now recognized by the absolute majority of States."[26]

The extensive litigation before World War II does provide valuable criteria for considering developments in the period covered by this study. The rule still prevails that immunities for these agents rest primarily upon treaty arrangements, and host states are still reluctant to classify trade delegates with diplomatic personnel.

For example, the Swiss Federal Tribunal, *In re Vitianu,*[27] refused to grant diplomatic immunity to a Rumanian commercial agent despite a tardy acquisition of diplomatic status. In June, 1948, the Rumanian Legation informed the Federal Political Department of Switzerland that Solvan Vitianu, who had represented various Rumanian commercial undertakings since February, 1947, had been appointed economic coun-

---

[24] 38 Stat. 454, 500. See Green Haywood Hackworth, *Digest of International Law* (Washington: Government Printing Office, 1942), IV, 403, 405.

[25] Y. A. Korovin and Others. *International Law,* trans. Dennis Ogden (Moscow: Foreign Languages Publishing House [1961]), 309.

[26] See *ibid.,* pp. 306-309.

[27] (Switzerland, 1949), *AD* (1949), Case No. 94.

sellor to the legation. On July 11, the Swiss government said the diplomatic appointment was unacceptable and two days later arrested Vitianu and charged him with various acts.[28] The court considered that the appointment, in the absence of an *agrément* by Swiss authorities, had no effect in international law and that Vitianu, as a commercial agent, did not possess immunity.

Since trade delegations are dispatched by nations with monopolistic economic systems, it is understandable why private trading nations, whose citizens are not granted reciprocal immunities, are reluctant to cloak state traders with diplomatic protection. The contemporary Western attitude was expressed by Viscount Swinton who told the British House of Lords that since accepted principles of diplomatic immunity were not accepted by Russia and the satellite states, there was no reason in the absence of reciprocity why trade missions should enjoy immunity in Great Britain.[29] The involvement of commercial representatives in espionage and other illegal activities has not enhanced their position in the post-World War II period. Trade delegates have been imprisoned and expelled for alleged violation of local laws. Josef Popper, an Austrian trade delegate who possessed a diplomatic passport, was arrested in 1952 in Bucharest and sentenced in 1954 to life imprisonment for alleged espionage and failure to turn in gold to the Rumanian regime.[30] Among trade agents expelled were Peter Miroshnikov, a member of the permanent Soviet Trade Delegation, by Sweden, and Jelena Czerova Ivanovna, a member of the permanent Russian Commercial Delegation, by Yugoslavia.[31] Miroshnikov, in Sweden since 1951, was accused of buying information and photographs of radar equipment and plans. Ivanovna was accused of smuggling goods and money to support "hostile activity" toward the Tito regime.

The lines between diplomatic and trade mission personnel were clearly drawn in a 1963 espionage case in the United States. Three members of the Soviet mission to the United Nations were expelled from the U.S. on a charge of belonging to an espionage ring which allegedly had

---

[28]The charges included prohibited acts on behalf of a foreign state, political and economic intelligence activities, blackmail, usury, bribery, and malicious prosecution.

[29]*The Times* (London), March 10, 1949, p. 6.

[30]*New York Times,* April 18, 1954, p. 9; April 19, p. 3.

[31]*Ibid.,* August 22, 1956, p. 59; see also *ibid.,* September 6, p. 5; September 26, p. 13; October 6, p. 43, for trial and conviction of a Swedish citizen in connection with Miroshnikov's activities. For Ivanovna incident see *ibid.,* February 17, 1951, p. 3.

received U.S. defense secrets for transmission to Moscow. However, a fourth Russian — a chauffeur of Amtorg, the Soviet trading agency, in New York City — was denied immunity and held for trial.[32]

Host states have also been reluctant to extend privileged status to other types of commercial agents. A U.S. court, in *Trost v. Tompkins*, refused immunity to the assistant commissioner for Shipping and Immigration of the Royal Yugoslav government. It made no difference that his office was in the Yugoslav Embassy building or that his work was supervised by the ambassador.[33] This refusal to grant immunity to a commercial agent is not inconsistent with other decisions such as those denying exemption from Swedish income tax payments to an official of the United States Shipping Board and refusing immunity to a Belgian tugmaster of a state-owned vessel.[34] Also bearing on this problem was the ruling of an Italian court in *De Semenoff v. Railway Administration of the Norwegian State (RANS)* which stated that the acts of the railway administrators were of a private law nature and thus the court had jurisdiction. The court distinguished between acts which the state performs within the limits of civil or commercial law and "those acts of power which have an essentially political character."[35] The case differed from *Russian Trade Delegation in Italy v. Kazmann* which was based on the treaty of 1924 between Italy and the Soviet Union, and "invested the Delegation with a diplomatic and international status, and gave it diplomatic immunities. . . ."[36]

Consular agents who also perform commercial duties are generally immune only insofar as stipulated by treaty. For example, in 1952, a consul general in Hong Kong who claimed to have carried out duties usually performed by diplomatic officers was denied immunity from local

---

[32]*Ibid.*, October 31, 1963, pp. 1, 5. The driver, Igor A. Ivanov, probably would have been entitled to immunity had he held a similar position with the Soviet Embassy in Washington. For example, see William Barnes, "Diplomatic Immunity from Local Jurisdiction," DSB, XLIII (August 1, 1960), p. 180, where he notes that among persons entitled to immunities are "employees of diplomatic missions in Washington." The usual U.S. policy in espionage cases has been to expel those persons who held a privileged status.

[33]44 A. 2d 226 (1945). The court noted that "the only work on which he is engaged is a matter extrinsic to the diplomatic function of the Ambassador, and does not, in our opinion, entitle him to diplomatic immunity" (at p. 231). Thus the agent was denied immunity as he was merely engaged in representing the interests of his government before the Inter-Allied Shipping Pool and not engaged in its behalf in transactions with the United States government. Also see Virginia S. Mueller, "Notes and Comments," *Cornell Law Quarterly*, XXXVII (June, 1946), 515.

[34]*H.E.W.R. Landahl v. Swedish Government* (Sweden, 1927), *AD* (1927–1928), Case No. 270; *Advokaat v. Schuddinck and the Belgian State* (Holland, 1923), *AD* 1923–1924), Case No. 69.

[35](Italy, 1935), *AD* (1935–1937), Case No. 92, p. 235.

[36]*AD* (1935–1937), 235.

jurisdiction.[37] The court rejected as precedents *Parkinson v. Potter,* since the consul general involved in that case was also an attaché, and *Engelke v. Musmann* since Engelke was an "accredited member of the ambassador's staff." However, higher customs officials sometimes have been recognized as commercial attachés and accorded immunities.[38]

The practice of according treasury (customs) representatives full diplomatic status developed in the 1920's. The United States and France agreed in 1929, following a lengthy dispute over trade arrangements, to assign on a reciprocal basis a ranking United States Treasury official to the American Embassy in Paris as an attaché with diplomatic status. The United States had assigned such agents previously in Canada, South Africa, and Australia although the practice met some objection. It was generally believed that diplomatic status should be reserved for officials dealing with state-to-state relations and not granted to agents whose main function was evaluating goods for export.[39] For example, in the mid-1920's requests by the United States for recognition of "customs attachés" were almost universally refused by foreign governments. By 1935, France was the only nation with whom such arrangements were made. The agents were renamed treasury attachés, as members of United States diplomatic missions.[40] The Franco-American immunities for commercial agents was justified on the grounds that the work was a "matter of concern" to both states, that they were under the general supervision of the diplomatic mission and had a status analogous to commercial attachés, that there was an advantage in avoiding the "unjust pretensions" of some European states which taxed the incomes of foreign agents, including consuls, that the immunity enabled the agent to better carry out his tasks, and that the diplomatic status permitted him to communicate directly with the authorities of the host state's central government.[41]

These treaty-based rules covering economic and commercial personnel have also been applied to the hundreds of economic and technical experts sent abroad by U.S. Agency for International Development and its predecessor agencies.[42]

---

[37]*Juan Ysmael & Company v. S.S. Tasikmalaja* (1952), Hong Kong Law Reports 242, 288; *ILR* (1952), Case No. 94.

[38](1885) 16 Q.B.D. 152 (*Parkinson*) and [1928] A.C. 433 (*Engelke*). See also Oppenheim, I, 861, fn. 1.

[39]Ellery C. Stowell, "Tariff Relations with France," *AJIL,* XXIV (January, 1930), 114–117.

[40]Hackworth, IV, 407–408.

[41]Stowell, *AJIL,* XXIV, 114.

[42]During the preceding post-World War II years the agency was variously known as the Economic Cooperation Administration (ECA), the Mutual Security Agency (MSA), the Foreign Operations Administration (FOA), and the International Cooperation Administration (ICA).

Since the AID mission is non-diplomatic, its employees generally enjoy only those privileges and immunities agreed upon by the United States and the host country. Under these agreements, which differ from country to country, direct hire personnel often receive some of the same privileges and immunities accorded to diplomatic personnel.[43]

U.S. economic aid employees are divided into three categories: direct hire personnel, contract personnel, and third country nationals or local nationals.[44] Normally, directors and deputy directors of U.S. Operations Missions in foreign countries are extended diplomatic privileges and immunities "of the same scope and character as those accorded diplomatic personnel in the country." These officers usually are on the host nation's diplomatic list which determines their eligibility for privileges and immunities. Lower ranking personnel directly hired by the U.S. Operations Mission[45] may also be extended, by agreement, the same privileges and immunities as are granted diplomatic personnel. An illustration is the Economic Cooperation Agreement between the United States and Burma of June 29, 1960,[46] which stipulates that the two governments

> will consider such personnel as part of the Diplomatic Mission of the Government of the United States in the Union of Burma for the purposes of enjoying the privileges and immunities accorded to that Mission and its personnel of comparable rank and grade . . . .

The wording of many other bilateral agreements is almost identical, those with Indonesia and Turkey for example.[47] On the other hand, many of the bilateral treaties "specifically identify certain exemptions such as customs duties, sales taxes, social security taxes, and income taxes, but do not provide for the complete range of privileges and immunities accorded diplomatic personnel," as are provided, for example, under the Burmese and Turkish agreements.

---

[43]Letter to the writer from Mr. Henry T. King, Jr., of December 13, 1960, when the aid agency was known as the International Cooperation Administration (ICA). The writer is indebted to Mr. King for his excellent summary of the position of foreign aid employees. The substance of the analysis of immunities extended these persons which follows is based primarily on Mr. King's communication and on a review of postwar treaties. The quotations in the remainder of this section are from Mr. King's letter.

[44]Hire personnel are employees of the aid agency or other government agencies who are operating under a participating agreement with the aid organization. Contract personnel are either themselves under contract to the aid agency or are employed by firms or institutions under contract to the agency. The third group includes nationals of the country where the aid mission is located and nationals of countries other than the United States or the country in which the mission is located.

[45]This group may include employees of other U.S. government agencies operating aid programs under so-called participating agency agreements.

[46]T.I.A.S. 4601, 11 U.S.T. 2249, which supplements agreement of March 21, 1957, T.I.A.S. 3931, 8 U.S.T. 1862.

[47]See Article IV of the U.S.-Indonesian agreement of October 15, 1960, T.I.A.S. 3624, 7 U.S.T. 2243, and Article VIII of the U.S.-Turkish agreement of July 4, 1948, No. 351, 24 U.N.T.S. 80.

The Economic Assistance Agreement of the United States and Ethiopia of April 25, 1957,[48] is an example of a more restrictive agreement. Here, economic personnel (United States government direct hire and contract, but not nationals) are exempt from income and social security taxes, from taxes for the purchase of personal movable property, and from customs and import and export duties. No reference is made in the agreement to any other diplomatic immunity or privilege. Some of the earlier technical cooperation agreements were even more limited in scope, stipulating only that United States missions carrying out the program would have "sovereign" immunity from suit but without mention of personnel.[49]

In addition to these general bilateral agreements, specific bilateral project agreements or operating level agreements often provide that the host country will arrange to pay any taxes, customs duties, or other levies which are imposted on direct hire and contract personnel.

In summary, direct hire and often (but not always) contract personnel are extended privileges and immunities, either comparable to those granted diplomatic persons of equivalent rank or to some of those granted diplomats specifically designated in a treaty. Nationals appear in general to be excluded from the privileged list.

The United States economic agencies have attempted to work out problems of privileges and immunities by "conforming as closely as" possible with the bilateral agreements. As a result, the aid mission and its related agencies "have had very little litigation with respect to these problems."

Military Agents

Military missions and military assistance groups, like commercial and trade agents, also occupy positions which do not traditionally call for diplomatic immunity. As a result, they too have only such immunity as is granted them by the receiving state "either as a matter of grace or pursuant to the express provisions of an international agreement."[50]

---

[48] T.I.A.S. 3813, 8 U.S.T. 630.

[49] For example, the Technical Cooperation Agreement between the United States and El Salvador of March 21, 1955 (T.I.A.S. 3211, 6 U.S.T. 730), and the Technical Cooperation Agreement between the United States and Peru of December 31, 1954 (T.I.A.S. 3169, 6 U.S.T. 69).

[50] Letter to the writer from Mr. William M. Leffingwell, Deputy Director of Military Assistance, U.S. Department of Defense, June 21, 1960. This study does not deal with the juridical position of military units stationed on foreign soil. The privileges and immunities of these military personnel are frequently determined by so-called "status of forces" agreements, the most important of which is the NATO Status of Forces Agreement of June 19, 1951 (T.I.A.S. 2846, 4 U.S.T. 1792). The United States has similar bilateral agreements with Japan, the Philippines, Libya, and West Germany. Also see Joseph M. Snee and A. Kenneth Pye, *Status of Forces Agreements and Criminal Jurisdiction* (New York: Oceana Publications, 1957).

The fact that a person is serving as a military agent for his government does not entitle him to immunity from local jurisdiction, a rule supported by a 1944 decision of the Supreme Court in Ireland, *Saorstat and Continental Steamship Co., Ltd. v. Rafael de las Morenas.*[51] The defendant, a colonel in the Spanish army, came to Eire as head of a Spanish government commission to purchase horses for use by the Spanish army. He was sued for breach of contract on the charge that he failed to provide the horses at the time stipulated. The colonel claimed immunity on grounds that he entered into the contract as an act of state on behalf of the Spanish government. The Supreme Court held that since the government of Spain was not impleaded, there was no basis for the defendant's claim that pleadings should be set aside. Diplomatic immunity was not claimed and the court reasoned that the colonel had sued in his personal capacity. Justice O'Byrne observed:

> Ambassadors and other diplomatic representatives of foreign states, who are entiled to claim privilege for themselves and their suites, are in a class apart; but I am not aware of any rule of international law under which the mere agents of a foreign State can claim immunity from the jurisdiction of the Courts of the State in which they are carrying out their duties.[52]

The case was similar to *Fenton Textile Association Limited v. Krassin,* discussed above, but with two important differences:

1. The agreements between the Soviet Union and Great Britain provided that agents are free from arrest and search but not immune from service of civil suits. There was no similar Spanish-Irish agreement.

2. Krassin based his appeal on the alleged right of personal immunity, whereas Morenas claimed immunity not on his own behalf but on behalf of his government. The Irish court reasoned that if the colonel was entitled to have the proceedings set aside by indirectly pleading his government, then the same claim might have been put forth by Krassin, but it had not been.

Nevertheless, a duly accredited military mission is, under certain circumstances, immune from prosecution, as indicated by a decision of the United States Court of Appeals for the Allied High Commission for Germany in *Hartje v. Yugoslav Military Mission and Another.*[53] The plaintiff, a German national, brought an action against the acting chief of the mission and the mission, which was accredited to the Allied Control Authority in Berlin, for money allegedly constituting fees for administration and purchase of a building in Berlin owned by the mission. Hartje

---

[51][1945] Irish Reports 291.
[52]*Ibid.,* p. 301.
[53](United States, 1954), *ILR* (1954), 116.

contended, *inter alia,* that since the government of Yugoslavia was represented in Germany by a diplomatic mission accredited to the Federal Republic of Germany, the military mission was entitled to exercise only consular, and not diplomatic functions, in Berlin. Thus neither the acting chief nor the mission itself should be entitled to immunity. The defendants countered that they were a mission of a foreign state, accredited to the Allied Control Authority in Berlin, and were included on the official list of such missions. The name of the acting chief also appeared on the official list and he was entitled, in accordance with a letter from the United States High Commissioner for Germany, to those privileges and immunities which he would enjoy under German law.

The court ruled (1) that the mission was the duly accredited agency of the Yugoslav government and thus entitled to immunity and (2) that the acting chief's name was on the list of persons entitled to diplomatic status and, in any event, he had acted in performance of official duties on behalf of the mission. Also, there was no question that the Yugoslav group was accredited to the control authority as a "diplomatic mission." The fact that Yugoslavia had an embassy accredited to the Federal Republic had no bearing on the "functions and status of its military mission in Berlin which is accredited to another independent governmental authority and territory." Also, as an "agency" of the Yugoslav government, the mission was entitled to sovereign immunity and could not be sued without its express consent. The court found this to be the practice in the United States, Great Britain, and Germany. It rejected the Italian case of *Perrucchetti v. Puig y Cassauro,*[54] upon which the plaintiff relied, as not persuasive since "Italy, unlike other countries," has adopted a "highly rigid application of the restrictive theory of sovereign immunity."[55]

These rulings indicate that military agents, like economic agents, are not, per se, entitled to diplomatic privileges and immunities although a mission with a quasi-diplomatic status (e.g., the Yugoslav Military Mission) might be immune from suit. However, since World War II, most nations appear to rely upon treaties rather than general rules of international law to determine the extent of immunities for military missions. As in the case of commercial agents, the United States, because of its extensive network of military agreements, will be used to illustrate this practice.[56]

---

[54](Italy, 1928), *AD* (1927–1928), Case No. 247.

[55]*ILR* (1954), 119.

[56]No attempt has been made to analyze in detail all of the military agreements signed by the United States with other nations since the end of World War II. However, on the basis of an analysis of a substantial number of the various types of treaties, the following generalizations are believed to be pertinent.

It is not an uncommon practice for military missions to be linked with the United States diplomatic establishment for both operational and jurisdictional purposes. Many treaties stipulate that United States nationals who are members of military groups will operate under the direction and control of the chief of the diplomatic mission and "will have the same privileges and immunities as are accorded to other personnel with corresponding rank in the Embassy of the United States of America."[57] While many of the agreements refer to immunities in these broad terms, some are more specific in reference to civil immunities, exemptions from taxes, etc., for mission members[58] while others provide limited courtesies for contractors on military projects and their employees.[59]

For purposes of determining immunity, personnel are often divided into categories, usually three[60]— although in some instances only the first two categories are specifically listed.[61] The categories include:

First category: Senior military members, senior army, navy, and air force officers and their "immediate" deputies who receive full immuni-

---

[57] Article VII of the Mutual Defense Assistance Agreement between the United States and Japan of April 30, 1954, T.I.A.S. 2957, 5 U.S.T. 661; also in *AJIL,* XLVIII (1954), 138. The same provision is found in numerous other treaties, e.g., the Mutual Defense Agreement between the United States and the United Kingdom of January 27, 1950, T.I.A.S. 2017, 1 U.S.T. 126 (Article IX); also in *AJIL,* XLIV (1950), Supp., 68. Similar agreements were signed the same day with Belgium (T.I.A.S. 2010, 1 U.S.T. 1), Denmark (T.I.A.S. 2011, 1 U.S.T. 19), France (T.I.A.S. 2012, 1 U.S.T. 34), Italy (T.I.A.S. 2013, 1 U.S.T. 50), Luxembourg (T.I.A.S. 2014, 1 U.S.T. 69), The Netherlands (T.I.A.S. 2015, 1 U.S.T. 88), and Norway (T.I.A.S. 2016, 1 U.S.T. 106).

[58] An example is Title IV of the Army Mission Agreement between Argentina and the United States of August 2, 1960, T.I.A.S. 4546, 11 U.S.T. 1964.

Article 13: "Mission members shall be immune from civil jurisdiction of Argentine tribunals for acts or omissions arising out of the performance of their official duties."

Article 15: "Members of the mission and their families shall enjoy the same immuntiy from taxes as members of the diplomatic mission of the United States in the Argentine Republic."

Article 16: (Extends exemptions to mission members and their families from import duties on household effects, baggage and automobiles, and from customs fees, restrictions, and inspections.) "The rights and privileges accorded under this Article shall, in general, be the same as those accorded to diplomatic personnel of the United States Embassy in the Argentine Republic."

[59] Article V of the National Defense Assistance Agreement between the United States and Pakistan of May 28, 1956 (T.I.A.S. 3575, 7 U.S.T. 926) exempts such contractors and employees from income taxes, customs and import duties and sales, property, and similar taxes on household goods and professional effects brought into the country. Local purchases are not included, and goods imported are not ordinarily to be sold in Pakistan.

[60] See treaties, cited *supra,* fn. 57, for examples. Also see Mutual Defense Assistance Agreement between the United States and Cambodia, France, Laos, and Vietnam of December 30, 1950, T.I.A.S. 2447, 3 U.S.T. 2757, 2761.

[61] For example, see Article V of the Military Assistance Agreement between the United States and Libya of June 30, 1957, T.I.A.S. 3857, 8 U.S.T. 960.

ties. (This category would correspond to the official diplomatic personnel of an embassy or legation.)

Second category: Persons who enjoy diplomatic privileges and immunities conferred by "international custom, as recognized by each Government, to certain categories of personnel" of a United States embassy. (The agreements do not make clear just which mission members are included.) These privileges and immunities include: immunities from civil and criminal jurisdiction, immunities of official papers, right of free movement and exemption of custom duties and income taxes. However, privileges and courtesies, such as diplomatic license plates, inclusion on the "diplomatic list," and social courtesies may be waived by the United States government for this category.

Third category: Persons in this group receive the same status as the clerical personnel of the diplomatic mission.

Apparently, the positions of the first category (complete immunity) and second category (jurisdictional immunity and limited privileges) are relatively clear, and decisions in particular cases would be based upon rules of international law and provisions in municipal legislation dealing with corresponding ranks of diplomatic personnel. Families of these mission members are sometimes included. Litigation is limited for these categories and no pertinent cases were found in the course of this study.

However, the Western Provincial Court in Denmark did consider the status of an American who was classified in the third category (i.e., immunities corresponding with those extended to clerks in diplomatic missions), and the decision was more liberal than might be expected. The case, *In re Henderson*,[62] involved an American citizen, one Henderson, employed as a radar engineer by a private American company at the Danish Air Force installation in Aalborg. The lower court in Aalborg (October 1, 1954) found him guilty of driving a motor car while intoxicated and sentenced him to twenty days confinement. During the hearing, Henderson stated that he did not enjoy diplomatic immunity.

The Danish minister of foreign affairs requested that the public prosecutor appeal the decision on the ground that Henderson enjoyed immunity from criminal prosecution. The foreign minister's letter said that Henderson belonged to the group of persons, mentioned in the Mutual Defense Agreement of 1950 between the United States and Denmark, who "will receive the same status as the clerical personnel of the Diplomatic Mission."[63] The lower court's decision was reversed, the provincial tribunal

---

[62] (Denmark, 1955), *ILR* (1955), 550.

[63] T.I.A.S. 2011, 1 U.S.T. 19, Annex B, Section C. One respondent to the Foreign Service Survey claimed that the government of Denmark actually was "loath to grant diplomatic privileges to members of the M.A.A.G. group."

holding that "according to the circumstances in the case the decision of the Court must be based on the declaration of the Foreign Office regarding the status of the accused."

While it is clear that Henderson's status should have been determined by the executive declaration of pertinent treaty provisions, it is not so certain that all states would have extended such immunity since Henderson was not on official duty at the time. Clerical personnel of diplomatic missions might be subject to the jurisdiction of some courts for unofficial acts not connected with the function of the mission.

Some of the military agreements limit immunities to official acts. As noted, the United States-Argentina treaty limits immunity from civil jurisdiction to acts arising from performing official duties, and Belgium limits immunity from civil suit for those who maintain U.S. military cemeteries to duties exercised under the agreement.[64] In some cases, civilian members of U.S. Military Assistance Advisory Groups are subject to local jurisdiction for any violation of local laws and regulations.[65] In other cases the United States military is required to take "disciplinary" action or recall offending persons. For example, under Article 14 of the Army Mission Agreement between the United States and Argentina, mission members and their families are governed by "disciplinary regulations" of the U.S. armed forces. The military agrees to take "appropriate disciplinary action" with regard to all violations and to recall persons at the request of the Argentine government.

Despite the careful treaty language, the assignment of military personnel abroad has led to complications. While the increasing numbers of foreign diplomats often results in strained relations, the position of members of a military advisory group is even more tenuous and perhaps less acceptable to local nationals. It is one thing to extend immunities to new classes of diplomatic personnel; it is quite another to include non-diplomatic persons in the immune classifications.

Libya, for example, considered it an "exceptional measure" to include American personnel of the U.S. Operations Mission in Libya — and only those directly paid by the United States government — in a

---

[64] Article 7 of the Agreement on American Military Cemeteries between the United States and Belgium of November 29, 1959, T.I.A.S. 4383, 10 U.S.T. 2130.

[65] For example, the Mutual Defense Assistance Agreement between the United States and Saudi Arabia of June 27, 1953 (T.I.A.S. 2812, 4 U.S.T. 1485) stipulated:

"Article 7 (A). All United States military members of the [U.S. Military Assistance] Advisory Group, all United States civilians and personnel attached to the Advisory Group and their dependents shall comply with all applicable laws and regulations of the Kingdom of Saudi Arabia.

"(B) Any offense committed by one of the individuals referred to in paragraph (A), excluding military personnel of the United States armed forces, shall be subject to the local jurisdiction of the Kingdom of Saudi Arabia."

(For military personnel, if the act committed is in a training area, the United States assumes jurisdiction.)

category with traditional diplomats even for a limited number of privileges.[66] In some instances, governments have held these non-diplomatic agents to a minimum. Under the United States-Japanese agreement, "the two Governments agree that the number of such personnel accorded diplomatic privileges will be kept as low as possible."[67]

Excessive increases in military staffing by Western nations would give the Communist nations reason to respond in a like manner. An example was the Soviet reaction to a sharp increase in the Norwegian Foreign Ministry's diplomatic list resulting from the granting of diplomatic privileges and immunities to top ranking officers of NATO stationed in Oslo. As these NATO officers were ranked as military attachés, Western military observers greatly outnumbered the Communist military experts with diplomatic standing in the Norwegian capital. As a result, the U.S.S.R. increased its number of military attachés at the Soviet Embassy in Oslo from four to seven, matching the number of United States military attachés in the U.S. Embassy there.[68]

The United States, Great Britain, and the Soviet Union have encountered some opposition to granting a privileged status to their military missions. Such antagonism in Formosa came to a climax in 1957 after a United States court-martial acquitted U.S. Army Master Sergeant Robert R. Reynolds on charges of shooting a Chinese prowler. General Kuo Teh-chuan, co-chairman of the Foreign Affairs Committee of the Legislative Yuan, declared that the special position of the United States forces on Taiwan "obviously rankles Chinese national pride at a time when the self-respect of the beleaguered republic is under assault from many sides.[69]

Although no status of forces agreement was in effect between the United States and Nationalist China, Reynolds would have been exempt from local prosecution as a member of the Military Assistance Advisory Group, which was attached to the United States Embassy with diplomatic status.[70] Formosa's Foreign Minister George Yeh explained that "military assistance personnel enjoy the same immunity from local prosecution as

---

[66] Under terms of a Memorandum of Understanding Relating to Article XVII of the Mutual Defense Agreement between the United States and Libya of September 9, 1954 (T.I.A.S. 3107, 5 U.S.T. 2449) of November 3, 1960. T.I.A.S. 4620, 11 U.S.T. 2382.

[67] Annex F, T.I.A.S. 2957, 5 U.S.T. 668, 678. Similar language is used in the United States-Libyan agreement; Article V, T.I.A.S. 3857, 8 U.S.T. 960.

[68] *New York Times,* March 6, 1955, p. 20.

[69] *Ibid.,* May 30, 1957, p. 3.

[70] Under Article 3 of the Mutual Defense Agreement between the United States and [Nationalist] China of February 9, 1951 (T.I.A.S. 2293, 2 U.S.T. 1499), American personnel who are stationed on Formosa under terms of the agreement, including those on temporary duty, "will in their relations with the Chinese Government, operate as a part of the United States Embassy, under the direction and control of the Chief of the United States Diplomatic Mission."

do foreign diplomatic establishments. Naval and air force men and their dependents, who are here from time to time, are informally considered in the same status." General Kuo claimed that even in embassies all personnel do not have immunity. Legislators, speculating along these lines, suggested that immunity might be restricted to higher ranks, perhaps colonels and up on the military side.[71]

The British encountered similar difficulties in Burma. The presence of their Military Mission, which furnished staff and technical training to the Burmese armed forces, "with diplomatic privileges . . . was widely felt in Burma to be a derogation of her sovereignty as well as compromising her neutrality."[72] The Burmese government gave notice of abrogation of the defense treaty with Britain, which admittedly had been used against the Burmese government by its political opponents and supposedly contributed to a Communist insurrection in 1948.[73]

The Italian Foreign Ministry acted even more drastically in 1953 when it expelled the Soviet military mission sent to Italy in 1945 to supervise repatriation of Soviet citizens stranded there during World War II. The Soviet Embassy in Rome reportedly called the request an "unfriendly act toward the Soviet Union and a violation of international law" but agreed to withdraw the mission.[74]

Information Agents

The stationing of information officers at overseas diplomatic posts usually poses a different problem than the assignment of strictly commercial or military personnel. The information function is often fused with the cultural and educational activities as part of the diplomatic activity although nations are far from agreeing on the privileged status of these persons. In addition, nations operate information services and often hire local nationals as public relations counsellors to issue special newsletters, carry out various projects and undertake liaison with various branches of the information media.[75]

---

[71]*New York Times,* May 28, 1957, p. 4; May 30, p. 3.

[72]*The Times* (London) January 13, 1954, p. 5.

[73]Defense Agreement between Burma and Great Britain of August 29, 1947, No. 904, 70 U.N.T.S. 202. See *New York Times,* January 3, 1954, p. 5; *The Times* (London), January 13, 1954, p. 5.

[74]According to the Italian Foreign Ministry. *New York Times,* January 11, 1953, p. 16.

[75]U.S., Senate, Committee on Foreign Relations, *Preliminary Staff Study, Nondiplomatic Activities of Representatives of Foreign Governments,* 87th Cong., 2d Sess., 1962, p. 1.

Diplomatic privileges and immunities are not extended to these public relations counsellors nor are they accorded to personnel of Western news agencies such as Reuters, the Associated Press, and United Press International although the news services, while having no official link with the foreign ministry of their home nations, probably are useful adjuncts to the foreign policy process in collecting information, etc.

A somewhat anomalous situation arises when these journalists are compared with their counterparts in Communist news agencies which operate as part of the government apparatus. These have enjoyed the protective mantle of state immunity, as illustrated by the British case of *Krajina v. Tass Agency,*[76] discussed in Chapter 2, in which immunity was granted to Russian journalists in Great Britain even though British newsmen covering the Kremlin were denied a similar status. Although Tass Agency's connection with the Soviet government could not be questioned on legal grounds, the extension of diplomatic rights represented an extreme example of state immunity and aroused considerable opposition in Great Britain.[77]

The burden of a foreign office in dealing with these information personnel has become heavier since World War II not only because of the complexity of categories of such agents and the non-diplomatic nature of much of their work, but also because of the vastly increased numbers.[78] This does not mean, however, that the non-diplomat in the information field is peculiar to the recent period. Throughout history, nations have utilized experts in mass persuasion.

Prior to World War II, an article in an American publication accused Hitler of "sheltering his outright propagandists over here under diplomatic immunity."[79] The reference was to the German Library of Information in New York City which circulated three million releases during a period of less than a year. The library at first reportedly disclaimed connection with the German government and was brought into court for failure to register as a business. The German Embassy in Washington then allegedly "hurriedly certified" that the Library staff of more than thirty men were all employes of the Embassy, and "thus immune to American law."[80]

The problem is far more complex today. The status of United States information agents illustrates the problems inherent in this type of non-

---

[76] [1949] 2 All E. R. 274

[77] See *The Times* (London) June 22, 1950, p. 2.

[78] For example, the United States did not have a separate information agency as part of its Foreign Service before the war.

[79] Albert Grzesinski with Charles E. Hewitt, Jr., "Hitler's Branch Offices, U.S.A." *Current History and Forum,* LII (November 26, 1940), p. 12.

[80] *Ibid.,* p. 13.

diplomatic activity even when the functionaries are attached to diplomatic missions. It is U.S. practice, apparently not unique, to incorporate the U.S. Information Agency staff into the diplomatic or consular mission abroad.[81] U.S.I.A. has a limited number of top ranking officers with diplomatic status and considers the attaché or assistant attaché designation as the appropriate diplomatic title for its public affairs, information, cultural affairs, and press officers.[82]

In 1965, the U.S.I.A. employed 1,323 citizens abroad (including thirteen Department of State officers detailed to the U.S.I.A.). Thirty-three were commissioned by the President, 473 held attaché or assistant attaché rank, and 112 enjoyed consul or vice consul status. Nearly 150 of these were secretarial personnel and slightly more than 100 were technicians. The latter, composed chiefly of employees responsible for operating U.S.I.A. radio relay stations and printing facilities, while not necessarily ranking lower than program officers, carry out duties of a type which rarely requires diplomatic or consular titles.[83]

---

[81]In foreign countries, a British information officer, and such assistants as he requires, forms "part of the staff of diplomatic missions." Great Britain, Central Office of Information, Reference Division, *British Government Information Services.* No. R. 5256, December, 1961, p. 5.

[82]Letter to the writer from Mr. Eugene J. Skora, Assistant General Counsel, United States Information Agency, June 21, 1960.

[83]American citizens employed by the U.S.I.A. at posts in foreign countries as of January 31, 1965 (the figures listed parenthetically are the corresponding totals as of December 31, 1959):

Number of officers commissioned by the President

Ministers (Personal rank)	3	(0)
First Secretaries	5	(3)
Information Counsellors	0	(3)
Counsellors for Public Affairs	24	(11)
Counsellors for Cultural Affairs	1	(1)
Totals	33	(18)

Number of officers holding diplomatic title granted by the Secretary of State:

Attachés	424	(220)
Assistant Attachés	49	(22)
Totals	473	(242)

Number of personnel with consular titles

Consuls	75
Vice Consuls	37
Total	112

(Note: The statistics include 2 technical specialists with consular titles and none with diplomatic titles.)

The 1965 figures were provided in a letter to the writer from Mr. Ervin N. Dehn, Assistant Director of Personnel and Training (Planning), United States Information Agency, March 4, 1965. The 1959 figures were provided by Mr. Eugene J. Skora. See U.S. Information Agency, *Manual of Organization and Administration,* Section 540, for details on commissions, title, and rank.

The privileges and immunities granted to agency personnel with diplomatic titles and commissions vary with the country of assignment. However, "in general such officers are attached to the embassy and are accorded privileges and immunities on a par with those accorded diplomatic personnel of the State Department Foreign Service." Personnel of the U.S.I.A. who do not hold diplomatic rank are also attached to the embassy or consulate and are entitled to privileges and immunities at the same level as those extended to Foreign Service personnel of comparable rank. However, not all nations will receive information agents on a par with diplomatic agents. A basic problem

> is the extent to which a foreign government considers information, educational, and cultural activities carried on by the USIS personnel as diplomatic or consular in character. It is the U.S. Government policy, in this regard, to argue that all such activities carried on by USIS personnel are in fact diplomatic or consular in nature and that the officers and employees so employed are entitled to privileges and immunities accorded to all personnel of the embassy of comparable rank.[84]

As might be expected, the United States has encountered the most difficulty regarding information personnel in Eastern Europe. The closing of information centers and arrest of their employees in Hungary, Czechoslovakia, and Rumania were discussed in Chapter 9. The dispute in 1950 between Rumania, on the one hand, and the U.S. and Great Britain, on the other, over the status and activities of information personnel, with its mutual recriminations and retaliatory actions, well illustrates the problem. In 1950 the Rumanian Foreign Office ordered both the United States and Great Britain to suspend information service activities in Bucharest.

Both nations complied, although the United States declared that the "summary character of the Rumanian Government's informal démarche was lacking all elements of customary diplomatic practice and courtesy," and the British called Rumania's action "entirely unjustified."[85] Both nations retaliated. Britain asked Rumania to suspend all information activities in her London legation, including publication of the Rumanian news bulletin; the United States demanded that Rumania close its New York operations known as the Rumanian Commercial Attaché and Office of Packages for Rumania. The State Department said that the office was an "unauthorized extension" of the Rumanian Legation in Washington

---

[84]Letter from Mr. Eugene J. Skora.

[85]"Rumania Requested to Clarify Demands for U.S. to Discontinue Information Activities in Bucharest," *DSB,* XXII (March 20, 1950), 443–444; *New York Times,* March 17, 1950, p. 3.

although Rumanian sources in New York were reportedly puzzled since parcels sent to Rumania had been viewed as part of U.S. propaganda.[86]

The United States demanded a fuller explanation, contending that Rumania's refusal to clarify its views "leaves in doubt the exact nature of the Rumanian Government's demand and its position as regards the informational and cultural activities of diplomatic missions."[87] The State Department pressed particularly for Rumania's position on the maintenance of accredited public affairs, press, and cultural officers. In a Note to the Rumanian Foreign Ministry of March 6, 1950, the United States flatly stated that it considered the activities of these officers directed toward the exchange of information and promotion of cultural relations as clearly falling within established diplomatic practice.[88] In contending that the "free and frank exchange" of information is "essential to international understanding and peace," the State Department elaborated:

> The United States Government is astonished at this action on the part of the Rumanian Government especially in view of the fact that the latter in recent years has maintained on the staff of its diplomatic mission at Washington press and cultural counselors, that its Legation has conducted various informational and cultural activities in the United States and that its Legation is publishing and distributing a weekly news bulletin.[89]

The reasons for the Rumanian action were clarified in a Note of April 14 when the Foreign Ministry declared that "behind the alleged cultural activity," the U.S. Information Office of the United States Legation "served to organize activity hostile to the Rumanian people." Rumania further charged that the informational function covered "espionage activity" and served "as an instrument of war-mongering propoganda" which "tramples underfoot" resolutions adopted by the United Nations General Assembly banning such activity.[90] Rumania also referred to trials of former National Peasant Party leaders which it said showed the role played by Frank R. Shea, head of the Bucharest U.S.I.A. Office, and his staff in "espionage activity of traitors and conspirators sentenced at those trials." Furthermore, Rumania complained about the U.S. refusal to per-

---

[86]"U.S. Requests Rumania Close New York Office," *DSB*, XXII (May 8, 1950), 735; *New York Times*, April 27, 1950, p. 21.

[87]*Ibid.*, March 8, 1950, p. 11.

[88]"Rumania Requested . . .," *DSB*, XXII, 442–443.

[89]*Ibid.*, p. 444.

[90]"Rumania's Charges Against USIS Activities Called Baseless," *DSB*, XXII (May 8, 1950), 733–734.

mit Rumanian scientific and cultural leaders to enter the United States and claimed that the United States had earlier expelled the Rumanian cultural counselor in Washington "without the slightest justification" and then refused to grant a visa for his replacement.[91]

The United States, of course, denied what it called the "ludicrous" charges and reiterated that U.S. activities were within the scope of normal diplomatic functions. The State Department noted that Shea had not been in Rumania since the Communist takeover, caustically blasted the Rumanian inference that United States library cards were membership cards to a subversive organization,[92] and referred to the trial of Rumanian nationals who had been employed by American and British information services.[93]

This type of conflict was not unusual after World War II. For example, when the Polish government ordered the United States in 1951 to close its U.S.I.A. office in Warsaw on charges that the Agency went "far beyond" normal information work and devoted news bulletins to propaganda, the U.S. retaliated by ordering a similar Polish cutback in the United States.[94] The following year, Iran closed U.S.I.A. and British Council centers, two Soviet institutes, and a French center,[95] and Syria banned information bulletins of U.S.I.A., Tass, and similar organs of foreign governments.[96]

Controversies such as the one between Rumania and the United States illustrate not only a basic conflict between Western and Communist approaches to diplomacy but furnish another example of the familiar charges of espionage which have plagued diplomatic as well as information personnel behind the Iron Curtain. The free flow of Western propaganda and the distribution of books and materials no doubt exacerbates the problem of political leaders who are attempting to consolidate a totalitarian regime. In turn, the United States has gone beyond retaliation

---

[91]*New York Times,* April 13, 1950, p. 4. Alexandru Lazareanu, who directed the Rumanian Legation's cultural affairs in Washington, was recalled after having been declared *persona non grata* by the United States. *New York Times,* March 8, 1950, p. 11.

[92]The Department observed that "everyone throughout the world who borrows books from a library will appreciate the absurdity" of the Rumanian inference. "Rumania's Charges . . . ," *DSB,* XXII, 733–734.

[93]See Chapter 9.

[94]*New York Times,* August 10, 1951, p. 1; August 11, p. 4; October 10, p. 2; October 17, p. 19.

[95]*Ibid.,* February 5, 1952, p. 3; February 13, p. 4.

[96]*Ibid.,* April 4, 1952, p. 6.

in requiring registration of information material by other governments, both friend and foe.[97]

Recent regulations in Yugoslavia are even more extreme. That nation's Press Law of 1960 separates information personnel from diplomatic personnel by stipulating that the former should not have diplomatic status, must register with the government, and that information offices and libraries cannot be physically connected in any way with diplomatic and consular buildings.[98] A Yugoslav spokesman explained that the law was reciprocal in nature as a majority of other nations had previously passed similar legislation which governed the activities of Yugoslav information personnel.[99] Although some diplomatic sources viewed the action as aimed principally at the refusal of Soviet and Soviet bloc countries to grant reciprocal privileges,[100] it did affect reading rooms and libraries operated by Great Britain, France, Austria, and the United States as well as by the Soviet Union.[101]

Under the new law, the United States was required to register the physical location of reading rooms in Belgrade, Novi Sad, and Zagreb, as well as personnel, including the director and his staff. However, these operations are only a small part of the U.S.I.A. program in Yugoslavia. The publications, cultural and exchange sections work out of the Embassy and no American member of the U.S.I.A. staff has been placed outside the Embassy. However, the Yugoslav Press Law imposes other restrictions. Authorization is required for all publication activities, although periodicals need only one blanket permit rather than specific authorization for each issue. The U.S.I.A. cannot publish anything which might damage Yugoslav relations with third countries and authorization is required even for the showing of films in U.S.I.A. reading rooms. Strict interpretation of the law could hamper U.S.I.A. activities; however, local

---

[97]Publications issued by foreign governments in the United States bear imprints of this type: "The material is filed with the Department of Justice, where the required Registration statement of [name of agency] under 56 Stat. 248–258 as an agency of the [name of Government] is available for inspection. Registration does not imply approval or disapproval of this material by the United States Government."

[98]The law, published in the Official Gazette of the Federal People's Republic of Yugoslavia, No. 45/60, is reproduced in *Collected Yugoslav Laws,* No. 3: *Law of the Press and Other Forms of Information* (Belgrade: Union of Jurists' Associations of Yugoslavia, 1960), pp. 14–48. See Articles 95, 107, and 108. For a comment on the law, see *New York Times,* October 30, 1960, p. 26.

[99]Bogdan Osolnik, Secretary of the Secretariat of Information of the Federal Executive Council, *Collected Yugoslav Laws,* No. 3, p. 7.

[100]*New York Times,* October 30, 1960, p. 26.

[101]Letter to the writer from Mr. Walter R. Roberts, Public Affairs Officer, United States Foreign Service, of November 7, 1964. The material in this paragraph was supplied by Mr. Roberts who was serving in the American Embassy in Prague when the Press Law was adopted.

officials take into consideration practical problems involved and apparently are quite liberal in their application of the statute.

Conclusions

The extraordinary expansion in the number of foreign agents, both diplomatic and non-diplomatic, has been one of the most significant developments of the postwar period. Purely diplomatic agents are far outnumbered today by quasi-diplomats whose function is primarily non-political — e.g., economic, military, information, and intelligence. The United States is at the center of this "foreign agent explosion" since it has inflated its missions abroad and received vastly increased numbers of agents at home.

This deluge of foreign agents has forced nations consistently to re-interpret the rules of privileges and immunities. Under general rules of international law, treaties, customs, and municipal legislation, these non-diplomatic agents have often been granted some privileges and immunities, but usually — although not always — less than those granted to diplomats.

The "foreign agent explosion" has been greeted with reservations both by host governments and by "old line" diplomats, many of whom complain about the lack of training of the newcomers, their excessive demands for privileges and immunities, and their abuse of the privileged status. Many of these diplomats report a reaction of confusion and annoyance on the part of host governments, coupled with a loss in their own prestige and a tightening of privileges. However, some of their colleagues detect little change in their status.

Nations are more reluctant to grant immunities to non-diplomats than to lower ranking members of diplomatic missions since this extension creates new precedents and could open a Pandora's Box as additional categories of personnel report for overseas duty. The proliferation of foreign agents, especially the military variety, tends to wound national pride.

There is no fully crystallized body of rules regulating and protecting non-diplomats, such as the Vienna Convention which reflects both a codification and progressive development of international law. Nations have taken steps toward creating accepted rules through both bilateral and multilateral treaties covering trade delegations, river and other commissions, economic aid groups, and military missions. This practice was widely followed between World Wars I and II and has been continued since 1945.

A series of treaties and court decisions affecting the Russian Trade

Delegations in the inter-war period provides some precedents. While these decisions were not conclusive, a vague pattern emerges. Immunity was granted in cases involving internal disputes among delegation (or ex-delegation) members, while purely commercial transactions were held to be not privileged.

Another excellent set of treaty precedents is that dealing with various commissions. Before World War I, extension of immunities to members of commissions and to non-diplomatic agents appeared to be an exception to the general rule of international law. However, even during this period immunities were extended through agreements, a practice which was greatly expanded in the 1920's and 1930's. Many commission delegates and ranking secretariat members were granted immunities fully equal to those received by diplomats.

These treaties were not uniform. The trade delegation agreements were both restrictive (immunities limited to official acts) and liberal (full diplomatic immunities for ranking personnel). The economic aid pacts differ from country to country. The military assistance group treaties also vary; some are generous in their terms; others limit immunities to official acts; still others subject personnel to local jurisdiction. In all cases, the basic principle is restated and reinforced: non-diplomatic agents are entitled to diplomatic privileges and immunities, whether for limited numbers or all personnel or whether for official acts alone or official and unofficial acts.

Treaties signed following World War II also incorporate the concept of categorization of personnel to whom differing levels of immunities are extended. This is seen in agreements covering both military assistance and economic aid missions. Informational personnel, in contrast, more often than not are fused to the diplomatic establishment in which case the categorization principle also applies. These agents are granted immunities comparable to those enjoyed by the official and unofficial personnel of diplomatic missions.

A similar divergency in practice is found among other agents of foreign states — members of missions, political agents and nonpolitical agents — although without the treaty point of reference it is more difficult to ascertain general rules.

Public political and similar agents do not enjoy the privileges of diplomatic agents, although they are apparently entitled to a minimum of special protection. Special envoys on temporary missions are usually immune. The International Law Commission has agreed that official missions and itinerant envoys engaged in *ad hoc* diplomacy are entitled to substantially the same rights as diplomats.

Private trading states, whose businessmen enjoy no special privileges, have been reluctant to extend immunities beyond treaties to agents of state trading institutions. Immunity has also been denied to representatives of shipping boards and railway administrations. Military agents *per se* have not been entitled to immunity although this status might be extended to duly accredited missions with a quasi-diplomatic position. In the past, higher customs officials have been recognized as commercial attachés, with attendant privileges and immunities, but nations have been reluctant to take this step. A privileged position has been granted such agents as those executing the Dawes plan and representatives of fallen governments.

Possibly the best example of this basic disagreement on the extension of immunities involved the French and British missions dispatched to the United Arab Republic to help settle the desequestration of property. These missions were entitled to less than full diplomatic status, claimed on the basis of general principles of international law, international agreements, and domestic legislation. Such status was rejected on the grounds that the missions had been granted only specific privileges and immunities to cover official, non-diplomatic functions, similar to those extended consular personnel. Mission members were arrested and subjected to trial, actions which would not have been taken against diplomats under international law. The basic limitations were accepted, possibly because the sending countries had no choice if they desired even limited representation in the receiving state. Even in the face of this host state advantage, it is probably safe to conclude that members of this type of non-diplomatic mission are entitled to less than full diplomatic standing.

Finally, there seems to be no question but that immunities are denied both to secret political agents and to so-called "non-functional agents," those persons, chiefly local nationals, who represent foreign governments in public relations, legal matters, contacts with executive and legislative branches, etc.

A body of rules covering non-diplomats will undoubtedly continue to develop; through international treaties, the fusion of such agents into diplomatic missions, and the efforts of international organizations, as well as through court interpretation, municipal legislation, and evolving custom. While state practice is not uniform, the non-diplomatic agent in many ways occupies a more favorable position today, vis-a-vis diplomatic privileges and immunities, than did his predecessors.

CHAPTER 12

The Changing Nature of
Privileges and Immunities

THE UNDERLYING CURRENTS OF POLITICAL BEHAVIOR have obviously affected the patterns of diplomatic privileges and immunities since World War II. Political pressures are only one among many kinds. Economic, technological, ideological and social forces also influence the norms of international law. These forces more often than not are manifested in political actions which in recent times, perhaps more than in previous periods, have illustrated the intimate relationship between law and politics. This linkage is even more apparent in other areas of international law. For example, in the interests of national security the United States has restricted the traditional freedom of the seas in order to conduct nuclear bomb tests and has distorted the rules of pacific blockade in the case of Cuba.

This same security concept has been used to justify modifications in some of the accepted rules of diplomatic privileges and immunities. The patterns of change in world politics, especially the political and ideological split between Communist and Western nations, have made a deep impression on diplomatic practice. In some instances formalized rules of diplomatic privileges and immunities which are consistently repeated by authorities lag behind international practice. For example, the diplomat is probably not as securely immune from criminal or police jurisdiction as traditional materials may lead one to believe.

Besides these upheavals in international politics, a second major influence on the changing rules of privileges and immunities has been the marked increase in their scope and importance since 1945. In the last twenty years, hundreds of diplomats were directly involved in legal actions and various incidents in which immunities were questioned. Treaty networks were erected to guide states in the treatment of non-diplomatic personnel. The compass of the tasks assigned diplomatic missions was greatly expanded and the categories burgeoned of persons engaged in international work who should be free from local jurisdiction. In 1961, for the first time since 1815, an international convention on diplomatic immunities and diplomacy was signed.[1] While the regulation adopted by the nineteenth-century Congress of Vienna related only to heads of diplomatic missions,[2] the Vienna Convention of 1961 covered the complete body of law and practice on diplomatic privileges and immunities; the 1815 document was signed by only eight European powers, its twentieth-century successor was signed by forty-five states representing many cultures, social systems, traditions, and religions. A fresh approach was taken to the problems of privileges and immunities, not only at Vienna in 1961, but in other state practices after World War II. Transformation and change which marked the vast field of international politics permeated the vital area of immunities.

The rationale for changes in immunities was provided by the theory of functional necessity or of reciprocal functionalism, if one accepts the possible modification of immunities by the exigencies of national security. The functional theory, holding that the diplomat must be free to exercise his public functions, supports the liberal approach in granting immunities for private acts. Many problems raised by the addition of new categories and the expansion of the old were dealt with in the framework of this theoretical concept.

Reciprocity, an old and familiar rule in international law, if anything became more firmly entrenched as a cold-war diplomatic technique. Retaliatory steps were often taken, such as closing libraries, halting mission publications, declaring envoys *persona non grata,* banning travel, and even severing diplomatic relations. The landmark British legislation of 1955 was clearly designed to achieve reciprocity. Customs and import regulations appeared to be even more securely based on reciprocal relations.

The fundamental and universally accepted principles of personal inviolability and immunity from civil and criminal jurisdiction were restated and reinforced through practice, municipal legislation, judicial decisions, and declarations by writers, jurists, and statesmen. Attempts in the United States to pass restrictive legislation in these two areas were repeatedly rebuffed. A restrictive act was adopted in Great Britain in

---

[1] The Vienna Convention on Diplomatic Relations of 1961. See United Nations, Conference on Diplomatic Intercourse and Immunities, 2 March-14 April, 1961, *Official Records.* Vol. II: *Vienna Convention on Diplomatic Relations* (A/CONF.20/14 Add.1) (New York, 1962), pp. 82–88; also in *AJIL,* LV (October, 1961), 1064–1077. A similar convention relating to the rights, duties and privileges of diplomatic officers was signed at the Sixth International Conference of American States held at Havana, Cuba, in 1928. However, only American states were represented.

[2] The regulations were supplemented by the protocol of Aix-la-Chapelle signed by five European powers in 1818.

1955, but it appeared to be designed to bring restrictive states into line with the more liberal British practice than vice versa. No state rejected these principles in theory since they were based on the need to allow free and unhampered operation of the diplomatic mission and the maintenance of diplomatic dignity. But some states deviated at times in practice from adherence to these basic rules of international law.

The diplomat continued to enjoy the right of protection which was usually provided in both normal circumstances and when diplomats were threatened with death or injury. In addition, primarily through their legal codes, most nations provided satisfactory punishment of individuals for offenses committed against diplomats.

While nations agree on certain general principles of diplomatic immunity, albeit with inconsistencies in practice, they also disagree on the rules applying to lower diplomatic personnel, to nationals, and to non-diplomatic persons. Divergencies result from the increase in the numbers of foreign representatives and the assumption of diplomatic-type duties by non-diplomats and subordinate diplomatic personnel. Publicists possibly are more at odds over immunities extended to families than they are to any other category.[3] Beyond these general developments, elements of change are also seen in the extension of privileges and immunities, some of which tend to liberalize, others to restrict, the rules applying to various categories of personnel.[4]

A significant example of liberal change is the more widely accepted practice of extending immunities to unofficial or private acts of diplomatic personnel. While the development is not complete, and exceptions are found, there appears to be greater endorsement of the Anglo-American policy of granting immunity for legal actions arising from private acts. Acceptance of the more liberal approach is indicative of the pragmatic postwar state practice and the spirit of theoretical functionalism.[5]

---

[3] At a minimum, immunity extends to the wife and dependent children of the head of mission and of the official staff. It is doubtful whether other relatives of these diplomats are privileged.

[4] It should be kept in mind that changes noted during any twenty-year period of diplomatic history should be considered within the context of the slow, evolutionary processes operating in this field. The modern rules of diplomatic privileges and immunities have developed over a four-century era with roots for some practices going back even further into history. However, these changes have been accelerated by the modification of venerable rules of international politics since the end of World War II.

[5] The judicial reasoning ran somewhat along these lines: First, historically, diplomats have enjoyed inviolability and immunity from jurisdiction because of the need for freedom of actions. Second, it is difficult to divide the private personality of the diplomat from his public personality or always to distinguish his private from his public acts. Third, the different stages of civilization among nations necessitate full jurisdictional immunities. Finally, international relations will be impaired if action is taken against diplomatic personnel.

Another liberalizing trend is found in those rules pertaining to non-diplomats. While nations were reluctant to extend immunities to trade delegations in the 1920's and 1930's except by treaties which often only provided for limited immunities, the treaty structure erected for American economic aid missions since 1945 often, but not always, provides for full diplomatic immunity. Military missions follow the same pattern, and information personnel, in limited numbers at least, are integrated into the diplomatic establishment.

The retinue of the diplomatic agent is perhaps also in a better position than prior to 1945. States in recent years have placed servants and service personnel in a privileged position at least for official acts, and complete denial of privileges has been less common. This development is reflected in major codification efforts and judicial decisions.

The position of attachés has also been consolidated. States were reluctant to accept various categories of attachés with diplomatic status in the period between the two world wars. Recent executive and judicial practice indicates that the new types of cultural, agricultural and commercial attachés, are in the preferred diplomatic class. In addition, there appears to be a tendency toward greater extension of privileges and immunities to technical and administrative personnel.

Some of the changes since the end of the Second World War redounded to the disadvantage of the diplomat. In some countries, foreign representatives are more hampered by customs inspections, import restrictions, and the levying of fees than in the past. Some restrictions are of a more serious nature — undue delays, withholding of effects for a temporary period, and the stripping and searching of diplomats. Some diplomats believe that most of the restrictions result from a stricter interpretation rather than a revision of existing laws.

Many local nationals employed by diplomatic missions were subjected to more rigid controls, at least before 1960, This, of course, was true in Communist countries but other nations, e.g., Britain and Denmark, passed legislation ending personal immunities for their nationals. A survey of existing legislation also reveals that a number of nations subject their citizens to local jurisdiction. However, most nationals do enjoy immunity at least for their official acts.

In the area of professional, commercial, and private trading activities of diplomats, the movement also appears to have been toward a more restrictive interpretation. The Vienna Convention exempts from civil immunity actions relating to professional or commercial activity by diplomats outside the official function. While practice in many nations is contrary to this rule, change at least is underway.

Beyond these restrictive measures have been major post-war developments of a more serious nature which adversely affected the diplomat. These challenges to traditional practice were far more widespread in East Europe and the Soviet Union than elsewhere. However, in other instances, diplomats, such as Britons in the Middle East, Americans in some newly emerging countries, and Russians in South America, claim that they have been mistreated.

Visiting missions often complained about calculated manipulation by host state authorities in an attempt to frustrate the diplomat in his assigned tasks. The problem involved more than inconvenience, and diplomacy became dangerous for some. At least nine persons attached to foreign missions have been killed and many more injured since 1945.

Diplomats were subjected to attack, assault, insults and other indignities by government representatives and by nationals of the host state. Mob attacks were either directed against the diplomat or were an offshoot of internal violence or rebellion. In some instances, the diplomat became the target of individuals such as snipers or potential assassins. Under this type of cold war diplomacy, charges and countercharges of undiplomatic conduct replaced the more usual apology, restitution, etc.

A consistent pattern of arrests and detention ranging from petty harassment to judicial action and imprisonment of diplomats has evolved since 1945. While the arrest of diplomats is not new, its widespread practice appears to distinguish this modern period from previous eras. In most cases, the diplomats have been detained only while papers were checked and identification verified, but some detentions ranged from two to six weeks. The agents usually were accused of taking pictures in "forbidden zones" or of entering the zone and committing espionage. In some instances, diplomats were subjected to physical mistreatment or threats. Western nations claim that many of the situations were "frameups," but the practice became a part of cold war diplomacy and marked a retrogression insofar as diplomatic privileges and immunities are concerned. In fact, the military attaché is emerging as a full-fledged "diplomatic spy" whose activities are compatible with the new rules of diplomacy.

The harassment and intimidation of local nationals employed by foreign diplomatic missions, especially British and American, marks another significant departure by Communist nations from usual diplomatic practice. The nationals have been driven out of jobs, denied citizenship rights, charged with espionage and other crimes against the state, smuggling, "anti-democratic" activity, attempting to flee the country and plots against the government. They have also been detained, imprisoned, and in some cases, executed.

There are a number of reasons for these restrictive changes in diplomatic practices, all of which are related to the broader developments in international politics since 1945.[6] The first is the cold war diplomacy already discussed, which arose from the restrictive foreign policy procedures employed by Communist and non-Communist protagonists and from techniques of internal control found in totalitarian societies.[7] A second reason stems from the greater emphasis placed on national security in an age of nuclear insecurity. The protective mania, a not illogical reaction to an era of potential wars of total destruction, may account for some of the pressures and harassment of both local nationals and diplomatic and non-diplomatic personnel. The dictum in Canadian decisions that diplomatic immunity may well have to yield to state security in cases of conflict did not appear to be vigorously challenged.

The increasing complexity of international affairs and the attendant expansion of missions both in size and numbers constitute another factor. The tidy pre-World War II arrangement whereby professional diplomats largely conducted the affairs of state ended abruptly with the outbreak of the conflict and disappeared probably forever after the war as the number of independent nations more than doubled and the number of foreign agents rose to astronomical heights. With diplomacy conducted on the economic, military and propaganda, as well as the traditional political front, nations are forced to formulate rules for these new non-diplomatic representatives. At the same time, the size of diplomatic missions is expanding and questions are raised as to the extent of immunities for various categories of personnel.

Little material emerged on practices in the Afro-Asian nations. However, the scanty evidence available indicates that there may be some divergencies in approach to the diplomat in the newly emerging nations who are without strong historical ties to European-oriented rules of international law. While similar immunities are granted to all diplomats in these nations, the attitude toward diplomats in some instances may differ from the approach in older nations.

----

[6] The activities of Western embassy personnel also were curbed through the closing of large areas to travel, delays in processing papers, surveillance both of the embassy and of its members, and similar techniques. As noted in the Preface, this phase of cold-war diplomacy has not been included in this study. But see this writer's *Cold War Diplomacy: The Impact of International Conflicts on Diplomatic Communications and Travel.* The Institute of Government Research: International Studies No. 1 (Tucson: University of Arizona Press, 1966, 67 pp.).

[7] The mistreatment of Soviet and Western diplomats in Communist China in 1967 indicates that the techniques of harassment are still a part of political action in times of inter-nation rivalry.

Finally, some of the restrictions seem to have resulted from abuses of their privileges both by diplomatic and non-diplomatic personnel. Retired United States diplomats and others report a widespread abuse of custom-free import of automobiles and other goods. The record clearly reveals that several diplomats were caught attempting to smuggle drugs, currency, jewels, watches, guns, and ammunition. Some missions have been charged with excessive imports of propaganda. It is not surprising that some states have tightened their regulations. In addition, the U.S.S.R. and East European nations accused both Western diplomats and local nationals employed by Western missions of abusing their privileged status by interference in internal affairs, espionage, etc. While these charges have been persistently denied, it is obvious that the Western powers, like the Communist, finance large intelligence agencies whose activities cannot be completely divorced from the diplomatic mission.

These cold war diplomatic practices may portend some basic alterations in the rules of diplomatic privileges and immunities or they may be aberrations peculiar to a strained period of international relations. However, there has been both a weakening of the sense of community among nations and a fundamental breakdown in some of the *universal* rules of international law. When adverse practices affecting diplomats from Western nations serving in Communist areas are instituted, and vice versa, a substantial portion of the international diplomatic corps finds itself in a less favorable position. Some observers may take hope in the fact that harassment of diplomatic personnel, especially nationals, appears to have declined sharply since about 1955.

Any optimistic speculation that these new diplomatic stringencies may some day disappear rests upon certain assumptions: first, that international tensions will abate, and second, that modifications of present restrictive policies by Communist nations will be matched promptly by positive responses on the part of Western powers.

It is not likely that current international political palliatives will greatly ease tensions in the foreseeable future. The threat of an overwhelmingly destructive war, the spread of thermonuclear capacity, and the disruptive insecurities in established nations continue. Coupled with these facts are the explosive and antagonistic social and political upheavals in underdeveloped areas of the world. Furthermore, it seems forbidding that the United States, under pressure of the military, instituted travel bans for security reasons and not strictly as a measure of reciprocity. Thus, restrictions on diplomatic movement may already have become an accepted practice of nuclear age diplomacy just as the fusion of the diplomatic and espionage functions has emerged as a normal procedure.

In contrast to this trend, the liberalizing practices which have resulted in the extension of some diplomatic privileges and immunities should not be discounted. These may more than offset the restrictive developments. One might also find some hope in the test ban treaty, the Moscow-Washington "hot" line, the agreement not to arm satellites and other forms of recent "creeping cooperation." However, the final answer lies in the future unpredictable course of international politics, since diplomatic privileges and immunities cannot be divorced from the revolutionary impact of this turbulent period of world history.

Selected Bibliography

Public Documents

GREAT BRITAIN, FOREIGN OFFICE. *Diplomatic and Consular Immunities and Privileges* (Memorandum), September, 1957.

NEW YORK CITY, POLICE DEPARTMENT. Office of the Police Commissioner. *Diplomatic Immunity* [N. D.]

UNITED NATIONS. CONFERENCE ON DIPLOMATIC INTERCOURSE AND IMMUNITIES. Official Records, Vol. I: *Summary Records of Plenary Meetings and of Meetings of the Committee of the Whole;* Vol. II: *Annexes, Final Act, Vienna Convention on Diplomatic Relations, Optional Protocols, Resolutions.* Geneva, New York, 1962.

————.INTERNATIONAL LAW COMMISSION. Yearbooks: 1956, Vol. II (A/CN. 4/SER.A/1956/Add.1); 1957, Vol. I (A/CN.4/SER.A/1957); 1957, Vol. II (A/CN.4/SER.A/1957/Add.1); 1958, Vol I(A/CN.4/SER.A/ 1958); 1958, Vol. II (A/CN.4/SER.A/1958/Add.1); 1960, Vol. II (A/CN.4/SER.A/1960/Add.1).

————. SECRETARIAT. United Nations Legislative Series. Vol. VIII: *Laws and Regulations Regarding Diplomatic and Consular Privileges and Immunities* (St/Leg./SER.B/7). New York, 1958.

U.S. DEPARTMENT OF STATE, FOREIGN SERVICE INSTITUTE. *Diplomatic and Consular Immunities,* November, 1960.

————.*United Nations Conference on Diplomatic Intercourse and Immunities: Report of the Delegation of the United States.* Publication 7289, International Organization and Conference Series 24, 1962.

Books

ADAIR, E. R. *The Exterritoriality of Ambassadors in the Sixteenth and Seventeenth Centuries.* London: Longmans, Green & Co., 1929.

ESSEN, JAN LOUIS FREDERICK VAN. *Immunities in International Law.* Leyden: A. W. Sijthoff's Publishing Company, 1955.

HACKWORTH, GREEN HAYWOOD. *Digest of International Law.* Vol. IV. Washington: Government Printing Office, 1942.

HERSHEY, AMOS SHARTLE. *Diplomatic Agents and Immunities.* Washington: Government Printing Office, 1919.

HURST, SIR CECIL. *International Law: Collected Papers.* London: Stevens & Sons Limited, 1950.

HYDE, CHARLES CHENEY. *International Law: Chiefly as Interpreted and Applied by the United States.* Vol. II. 2d ed. revised. Boston: Little, Brown and Company, 1947.

[281]

MOORE, JOHN BASSETT. *A Digest of International Law*. Vol. IV. Washington: Government Printing Office, 1906.

NUMELIN, RAGNAR. *The Beginnings of Diplomacy*. New York: Philosophical Library, 1950.

OGDON, MONTELL. *Juridical Bases of Diplomatic Immunity*. Washington: John Byrne & Co., 1936.

OPPENHEIM, L. *International Law*. Vol. I: *Peace*. Edited by H. Lauterpacht. 8th ed. London: Longmans, Green and Co., 1955.

PARRY, CLIVE (ed.). *A British Digest of International Law*. Part VII, pp. 693-994. London: Stevens and Sons, 1965.

PLISCHKE, ELMER. *Conduct of American Diplomacy*. 2d ed. Princeton, N.J.: D. Van Nostrand Company, Inc., 1961.

REIFF, HENRY. *Diplomatic and Consular Privileges, Immunities, and Practice*. Cairo: Ettemad Press, 1954.

SATOW, SIR ERNEST. *A Guide to Diplomatic Practice*. 4th ed. Edited by Sir Neville Bland. London: Longmans, Green and Co., 1957.

STUART, GRAHAM H. *American Diplomatic and Consular Practice*. 2d ed. New York: Appleton-Century-Crofts, Inc., 1952.

THAYER, CHARLES W. *Diplomat*. New York: Harper & Brothers, 1959.

WATERS, MAURICE. *The Ad Hoc Diplomat: A Study in Municipal and International Law*. The Hague: Martinus Nijhoff, 1963.

Articles

ADAIR, E. R. "The Law of Nations and the Common Law of England," *Journal of Comparative Legislation and International Law*, XIII (1931), 133-137.

BAGINYAN, K. AND LASAREV, M. Review of D. B. Levin, *Diplomatic Immunity* (Moscow, 1949), in *Soviet State and Law*, No. 2 (February, 1951), pp. 91-92, reprinted in *Current Digest of the Soviet Press*, III (May 26, 1951), 3-5.

BARNES, WILLIAM. "Diplomatic Immunity from Local Jurisdiction," *The Department of State Bulletin*, XLIII (August 1, 1960), 173-182.

BINET, HENRI T. P. "Recent Developments Affecting Diplomatic Privileges and Immunities," *Journal of Comparative Legislation and International Law*, XIII (February, 1931), 84-90.

BRANDON, MICHAEL. "Report on Diplomatic Immunity by an Interdepartmental Committee on State Immunities," *International and Comparative Law Quarterly*, I (July, 1952), 358-361.

BROOKFIELD, S. H. "Immunity of the Subordinate Personnel of a Diplomatic Mission," *British Year Book of International Law*, XIX (1938), 151-160.

BROWN, PETER CAMPBELL. "The Defense of Diplomatic Immunity," *Insurance Law Journal*, No. 334 (November, 1950), pp. 812-817.

CARDOZO, MICHAEL H., "Diplomatic Immunities, Protocol and the Public," *Journal of International Affairs*, XVII (No. 1, 1963), 61-69.

COWAN, MARGARET. "Origins of Diplomatic Immunity in England," *The Solicitor Quarterly*, IV (April, 1965), 104-117.

DEAK, FRANCIS. "Classification, Immunities and Privileges of Diplomatic Agents," *Southern California Law Review*, I (March, May, 1928), 209-252, 332-354.

―――. "Immunity, Diplomatic," in *Encyclopedia of the Social Sciences* (15 vols.; New York: The Macmillan Company, 1932), VII, 595-597.

DEENER, DAVID R. "Some Problems of the Law of Diplomatic Immunity," *American Journal of International Law*, L (January, 1956), 115-120.

DINSTEIN, YORAM. "Diplomatic Immunity from Jurisdiction: *Ratione Materiae,*" *International and Comparative Law Quarterly,* XV (January, 1966), 76-89.

"Diplomatic Intercourse and Immunities," *American Journal of International Law,* LIII (January, 1959), 253-291.

"Diplomatic Privileges and Immunities," *External Affairs,* XI (November, 1959), 374-378.

EAGLETON, CLYDE. "The Responsibility of the State for the Protection of Foreign Officials," *American Journal of International Law,* XIX (April, 1925), 293-314.

FELLER, A. H. "A Seventeenth Century Problem in the Application of Prohibition Laws to Foreign Diplomats," *American Journal of International Law,* XXVIII (April, 1934), 349-351.

GORDON, J. C. "Diplomatic Immunity," *Foreign Service Journal,* XXIX (January, 1952,) 23, 46-47.

GREEN, THEODORE F. "Soviet Harassment of Foreign Diplomats," *The Department of State Bulletin,* XXVII (November 17, 1952), 786-789.

GUTTERIDGE, JOYCE A. C. "Immunities of the Subordinate Diplomatic Staff," *British Year Book of International Law,* XXIV (1947), 148-159.

HILL, CHESNEY. "Sanctions Constraining Diplomatic Representatives to Abide by the Local Law," *American Journal of International Law,* XXV (April, 1931), 252-269.

HOLLAND, D. C. "Diplomatic Immunity in English Law," *Current Legal Problems,* IV (1951), 81-106.

HURST, SIR CECIL J. B. "Diplomatic Immunities — Modern Developments," *British Year Book of International Law,* X (1929), 1-13.

HUSSEY, LUTHER N. "The Negligent Diplomat," *Journal of the Bar Association of the District of Columbia,* XIII (April, 1946), 148-153.

JANOUSEK, JOSEPH O. "Some Aspects of the Law of Diplomatic Immunity," *Journal of the Bar Association of the District of Columbia,* VIII (May, 1941), 183-196.

JONES, J. MERVYN. "Immunities of Servants of Diplomatic Agents and the Statute of Anne 7, c. 12," *Journal of Comparative Legislation and International Law,* XXII (February, 1940), 19-31.

KEITH, A. BERRIEDALE. "The Exterritoriality of Ambassadors," *Journal of Comparative Legislation and International Law,* XII (1930), 126-128.

KERLEY, ERNEST L. "Some Aspects of the Vienna Conference on Diplomatic Intercourse and Immunities," *American Journal of International Law,* LVI (January, 1962), 88-129.

LYONS, A. B. "Diplomatic Immunities — Some Minor Points," *British Year Book of International Law,* XXXIV (1958), 368-374.

———."Immunities Other Than Jurisdictional of the Property of Diplomatic Envoys," *British Year Book of International Law,* XXX (1953), 116-151.

———. "Personal Immunities of Diplomatic Agents," *British Year Book of International Law,* XXXI (1954), 299-340.

MONROE, D. C. "Privileges and Immunities," *Journal of Criminal Law and Criminology,* XXXVII (March, 1947), 480-483.

MURRAY, JOHN J. "The Gortz-Gyllenborg Arrest — A Problem in Diplomatic Immunity," *Journal of Modern History,* XXVIII (December, 1956), 325-337.

OGDON, MONTELL. "The Growth of Purpose in the Law of Diplomatic Immunity," *American Journal of International Law,* XXXI (July, 1937), 449-465.

PREUSS, LAWRENCE. "Capacity for Legation and the Theoretical Basis of Diplomatic Immunities," *New York University Law Quarterly Review,* X (December, 1932), 170-187.

————. "Foreign Diplomats and the Prohibition Laws," *Michigan Law Review,* XXX (January, 1932), 333-348.

SCHWARZENBERGER, G. "Diplomatic Immunity," *Modern Law Review,* V (July, 1941), 64-66.

SCHWELB, EGON. "The Diplomatic Privileges (Extension) Act, 1944," *Modern Law Review,* VIII (March, 1945), 50-63.

————. "Restrictions on Diplomatic Privileges," *Modern Law Review,* VII (November, 1944), 223-227.

SIMMONDS, K. R. "The 'Rationale' of Diplomatic Immunity," *International and Comparative Law Quarterly,* XII (October, 1962), 1204-1210.

SMITH, ERNEST H. "Tax Immunities of Diplomats Under Canadian Federal Law," *Canadian Tax Journal,* VIII (September-October, 1960), 318-324.

STIRLING, PATRICK. "The Immunities of Diplomatic Agents," *Law Journal* CVIII (April 18, June 13, 1958), 243-244, 375-376.

STONE, O.M. "Families Personal and Diplomatic," *Modern Law Review,* XXII (March, 1959), 193-194.

STOWELL, ELLERY C. "Diplomatic Privileges and Immunities," *American Journal of International Law,* XX (October, 1926), 735-738.

TAYLOR, J .T. "Diplomatic Immunity," *Criminal Law Review* [n.v.] (April, 1955), pp. 230-234.

THORNELY, P. W. "Extraterritoriality," *British Year Book of International Law,* VII (1926), 121-134.

TUNKIN, G. "Vienna Convention on Diplomatic Relations," *International Affairs* (Moscow), No. 6 (June, 1961), pp. 51-56.

UNITED NATIONS. "Conference on Diplomatic Intercourse and Immunities," *American Journal of International Law,* LV (October, 1961), 1064-1077.

VERDROSS, ALFRED. "The Second Congress of Vienna," *United Nations Review,* VIII (May, 1961), 12-14, 51.

VOLLENHOVEN, C. VAN . "Diplomatic Prerogatives of Non-Diplomats," *American Journal of International Law,* XIX, (July, 1925), 469-474.

WATTS, A. D. "Jurisdictional Immunities of Special Missions: The French Property Commission on Egypt," *International and Comparative Law Quarterly,* XII (October, 1963), 1383-1399.

YOUNG, EILEEN. "The Development of the Law of Diplomatic Relations," *British Year Book of International Law,* XL (1964), 141-182.

YOUNG, RICHARD. "Diplomatic Immunities," *American Bar Association Journal,* XXXIX (September, 1953), 839-840.

Index of Cases

General Index